The Trinity

The Trinity

*Rediscovering the
Central Christian Mystery*

M. John Farrelly,
O.S.B.

A SHEED & WARD BOOK

ROWMAN & LITTLEFIELD PUBLISHERS, INC.
Lanham • Boulder • New York • Toronto • Oxford

A SHEED & WARD BOOK

ROWMAN & LITTLEFIELD PUBLISHERS, INC.

Published in the United States of America
by Rowman & Littlefield Publishers, Inc.
A wholly owned subsidiary of The Rowman & Littlefield Publishing Group, Inc.
4501 Forbes Boulevard, Suite 200, Lanham, Maryland 20706
www.rowmanlittlefield.com

PO Box 317; Oxford; OX2 9RU, UK

Cover photo by Foto Berger, 83209 Prien A. Chiensee, Dr.-Otto-Eyrich-Strolb, Sph
Prien (71150000) 260539.

British Library Cataloguing in Publication Information Available

Library of Congress Cataloging-in-Publication Data

Farrelly, John, 1927-
  The Trinity : rediscovering the central christian mystery / M. John Farrelly.
     p. cm.
  Includes bibliographical references and index.
  ISBN 0-7425-3225-9 (hardcover : alk. paper)—ISBN 0-7425-3226-7 (pbk. : alk.
paper) ISBN 978-0-7425-3226-7
  1. Trinity. I. Title.
  BT111.3.F37 2005
  231'.044—dc22   2004015650

Printed in the United States of America

♾️™ The paper used in this publication meets the minimum requirements of
American National Standard for Information Sciences—Permanence of Paper for
Printed Library Materials, ANSI/NISO Z39.48-1992.

To

Mary Lou and Michael Dellapa,
Patricia and Thomas Hohman,
Mary Sue and Richard Metrey,
Elizabeth and Frank Lostumbo,
Patricia and Frank(+) McCarthy,
Carmelita and Edward Treacy,
in friendship, and a memento of
many years of shared prayer and reflection.

I also thank Carmen Krisai-Chizzola of
Braunau-am-Inn, Austria, for sending me the
photo used on the cover and helping me
get the necessary permissions to use it.
It is a picture of a late fourteenth-century
fresco in a historic church in Urschalling, Bavaria.

Contents

~

Preface

This book is a study of trinitarian theology and spirituality, a study that seeks to be ecumenically aware and sensitive. Christian theologians come from a common historical background of faith in this mystery. The World Council of Churches correctly identifies those churches as Christian which acknowledge belief in God—Father, Son, and Holy Spirit—and belief in the incarnation of the Son of God in Jesus Christ in fidelity to the Council of Nicea and the First Council of Constantinople.

The mystery of the Trinity is the central Christian belief, and on it depends our belief in how God in his love saves us and who we are; it is a mystery revealed to us, as Karl Rahner forcefully asserted, for our salvation; it is a salvific mystery. But belief in this central Christian mystery has seriously eroded in the West in the past few centuries. Even when this mystery is believed by Christians, its centrality for Christian life is frequently not recognized, and so its transformative impact on our ecclesial and individual lives is seriously diminished. Also, it is challenged by believers in God from Judaism, Islam, and other world religions.

Thus our Christian churches and theologians face together a world in which belief in the Trinity has lost its credibility and meaning for many, even for many who are still Christian. With other Christian theologians, we have the task of articulating this mystery in a world radically changed from the classical age. For example, people are now formed largely by modern historical consciousness, by the enormous growth of modern physical and human sciences, by a greater awareness of the equal dignity of men and women, and by more knowledge and respect for world religions in our shrinking world.

Our theological challenge is to inculturate the mystery of the Trinity into this world while being faithful to revelation. Inculturation was brought about in the past, for example in the Greco-Roman culture at the time of Nicea and the First Council of Constantinople. And through that inculturation the trinitarian mystery was transformative for that age. We are called in turn to inculturate it for our age so that it can in our time be a principle of transformation and unity for the Christian people and even for the larger world. It is not enough to repeat earlier theologies of the Trinity; in fact, that would constitute an obstacle to its transformative power in the present age, since such a theology would not have a relation to the presuppositions of our age that it did to the earlier age. And we must not reduce our theology to the presuppositions of our age. It is understandable if Christian theologians from different denominations and within the same denomination differ from each other when faced with this enormous task.

We have knowledge of the Trinity only through God's relationship to us and revelation through Jesus Christ and his Spirit. This very relationship and revelation allow us to say something about the Trinity that is not restricted to God's relationship to us. Classical articulations of the mystery were too associated with a framework they took from Neoplatonism, an overview of creation in relation to God that emphasized the different levels of being but not history. Today we face the future more than a primordial past; and for the mystery of the Trinity to have its proper transformative impact upon us, its relation to creation and history must be shown in this context.

The importance of this area of theology can hardly be overestimated. Postmodernism in much of its theory and practice denies that there is any all-encompassing horizon or story for the human family. There is nothing to unite all of us; in fact, there is not enough unity among human beings to call them a human family. After the terrorist attacks of September 11, 2001, there is a special urgency to show that the Christian proclamation of God's trinitarian action to save us presents a radically different view. This mystery is God's answer to our human search. Our search is not primarily an intellectual search but a search we make as persons, as communities, and indeed as one human community moving through history. The trinitarian mystery is related to our intellectual search and can enrich what we know of our world from modern science; but it has broader implications than that, for it also helps us perceive and respect "what is true and holy" in world religions (Vatican II, *Nostra Aetate*, 2) and celebrate our diversity within that.

It is a mystery, a personal mystery of God's creating and redeeming presence, God's coming to us and calling us beyond our present horizons, not without the cross. This presence is through real symbols such as baptism and the Eucharist, as well as through the communities in which we live and for which we are responsible. What God's loving, saving design for us is, what the Church is, who we are as images of the triune God, the joy he has prepared for us, how God accompanies us on the way, the unity and diversity to which God calls us as Christ's disciples, and much more depend on our deeper understanding of the mystery of the Trinity. The Christian proclamation of the Trinity is God's message that he relates and is present to each of us in our own particularity and circumstances. A theology worthy of its name must help us see this and so reinvigorate our Christian lives and promote our Christian unity.

In the chapters of this book I first seek to identify some contemporary problems with the Christian proclamation of the Trinity in our culture and major differences among theologians of the present time, thus indicating what I propose as the primary issues we should address. As a theological study, this book seeks to show critically the foundations of the Christian belief in the Trinity and its meaning in the sense of what it signifies and what its relevance to us is. In chapter 2 I address the question of the foundations of our trinitarian belief in the witness of Scripture, concentrating here on how the mystery of the Trinity is made known through the salvific and revelatory work of Jesus Christ and the Holy Spirit, and relating this to some current disputes. In chapter 3 I show the early development of the articulation of Christian belief until the First Council of Constantinople, its fidelity to Scripture and its normative character for later Christian belief and theology. Chapter 4 addresses major stages of later development of Christian thought on the Trinity, some major fissures that occurred in the process, and much modern erosion of this Christian belief.

In the following chapters, I seek to articulate the outlines of a trinitarian theology appropriate for today. By this I mean especially appropriate for the countries of the North Atlantic, but also open to the concerns of other parts of our shrinking world. Chapter 5 addresses the question of the relation of the Trinity both to the order of salvation and to that of creation, a much contested issue among contemporary theologians, but also one rich in possibilities of development. Chapters 6 and 7 address respectively the generation of the Son from the Father within the Trinity and the procession of the Holy Spirit from Father and Son. Here I propose that Thomas Aquinas's theology still has validity but has to be integrated into a larger perspective that gives more weight to concerns of Eastern Orthodoxy. This very integration enables our Christian life and theology to breathe through its two lungs, the Western and the Eastern. In chapter 8, I defend the validity of a classical interpretation of the meaning of Father, Son, and Spirit as three *persons* in one God, while, with other theologians, I support the use of a more contemporary interpretation of person as contributing to our understanding of the three as relational persons. In the final chapter, I seek to indicate some implications this theology of the Trinity has for ecclesiology and Christian spirituality in our world of the twenty-first century. One issue here is the relation of our Christian belief in God as triune to world religions.

Since in this book I am making a proposal of a trinitarian theology as a whole, I must give a shorter analysis of some particular parts than a scholarly study of those sections alone would call for. I offer the reader leads to find more thorough studies of these special topics, studies on which I frequently depend.

For what is of value in the pages that follow I owe great debts of gratitude to Scripture scholars, historians of doctrine, and twentieth-century theologians who have studied aspects of the trinitarian mystery. I also owe a debt of gratitude to the Oblates of St. Francis de Sales, particularly Fr. Francis Blood, O.S.F.S., who gave me the hospitality of their Generalate in Rome during a sabbatical year, and to the librarians of the Gregorianum University who kindly gave me the use of their resources. It was there and then that I began this book, though I have taught courses on the Trinity over a forty-year period, and much of my earlier writing informs the present book. Without mentioning here those colleagues and consultants who helped me in this earlier work, I owe much to Pasqualina Young, a former student of mine in theology, who read this entire manuscript and made many suggestions that improved its intelligibility. I thank Alan Truslow who shared his expertise in computers with me.

I profited much from theological suggestions offered by Professor Peter Phan of Georgetown University, past president of the Catholic Theological Society of America, Professor Earl Muller, S.J., of Sacred Heart Seminary in Detroit, and another theologian who prefers to remain annonymous, who generously read and commented on the whole manuscript. I am grateful to two physicists, John Young, Ph.D., and William Stanbro, Ph.D., who read my summary of Paul Davies's *The Cosmic Blueprint*[1] in chapter 5 and gave me their reflections on it. Since I start with the Christian belief in God as revealed through Jesus Christ and the Spirit, I should note that while using much of Paul Davies's articulation of a current cosmogony, I accept his understanding of God's work in creation only in part. Errors and deficiencies that may remain in my work here and elsewhere are my responsibility.

We cannot plumb the depths of God's call and our response unless we see this in its trinitarian context, for it is the Trinity—Father, Son, and Holy Spirit—who share their communion with us. So, even though our words are inadequate, they are necessary and will, we hope, contribute a bit to our deeper understanding of the gift and dignity of God's call and presence.

Note

1. Paul Davies, *The Cosmic Blueprint: New Discoveries in Nature's Creative Ability to Order the Universe* (New York: Simon and Schuster, 1988). This book is soon to be re-released with the same title by the Templeton Foundation Press.

M. John Farrelly, O.S.B.
St. Anselm's Abbey
Washington, D.C.
May 2, 2004
Feast of St. Athanasius

~

Abbreviations

ABD	*The Anchor Bible Dictionary*
AG	Vatican II, *Ad gentes*
ANF	*Ante-Nicene Fathers* (1885 ff)
CG	Thomas Aquinas, *Summa contra gentiles*
DBS	*Dictionnaire de la Bible. Supplément*
DS	Denzinger-Schönmetzer, *Enchiridion symbolorum*, 35th edition
DTC	*Dictionnaire de la théologie catholique*
DV	Vatican II, *Dei verbum*
EEC	*Encyclopedia of Early Christianity*
FZPhTh	*Freiburger Zeitschrift für Philosophie und Theologie*
JAAR	*Journal of the American Academy of Religion*
LG	Vatican II, *Lumen gentium*
NA	Vatican II, *Nostra Aetate*
NCE	*New Catholic Encyclopedia*
NJBC	*New Jerome Biblical Commentary*
NPNF	*Nicene and Post-Nicene Fathers* (1886 ff)
SC	Vatican II, *Sacrosanctum concilium*
ST	Thomas Aquinas, *Summa theologiae*
TDNT	*Theological Dictionary of the New Testament*
TS	*Theological Studies*
UR	Vatican II, *Unitatis redintegratio*

CHAPTER ONE

The Trinity:
The Theological Problematic

The Christian churches proclaim the mystery of the Trinity as constitutive of who they are, what their origin is, what their goal is, and what the legitimacy is of their claims to mediate God's definitive revelation and salvation. They proclaim this mystery as the basis of their faith in the Father's love for us. In Jesus Christ it is the Father's only Son whom he has sent into the world to save us. They proclaim the Trinity's presence to us and offer to us a share in their divine life, because the Father and the Son have sent the Holy Spirit into our hearts to dwell within us and divinize us. The churches call Christians to worship the Trinity. The Trinity is central to the church's liturgy, such as baptism in the name of the Father, the Son, and the Holy Spirit, and the Eucharist, in which the Father is addressed, the Son's paschal mystery is sacramentally represented, and the Holy Spirit is called down ("the *epiclesis*") to transform the bread and wine into the body and blood of Christ and to transform the communicants into Christ. Many churches use the Nicene-Constantinople creed, in which the trinitarian belief is confessed, in their liturgies. The Trinity is also fundamental to who we are as humans and Christians because our identity is to be and to live as an image of the triune God. The relation among the persons of the Trinity is presented to Christians as a model of our relation to God. We are called to relate to the Father as sons and daughters, to be animated by the Holy Spirit, and to relate to one another as brothers and sisters.

The Catholic Church and the Orthodox Church proclaim the trinitarian mystery as the center of their life and worship. And at its Third Assembly in

New Delhi in 1961, the World Council of Churches put belief in the Trinity as the first article of its constitution: "The World Council of Churches is a fellowship of churches which confess the Lord Jesus Christ as God and Saviour according to the Scriptures and therefore seek to fulfill together their common calling for the glory of the one God, Father, Son and Holy Spirit."[1]

And yet, this belief that is so central to Christianity is rejected by much of the world. It is of course rejected by Judaism and Islam as inconsistent with the monotheism that is their belief, but also by other world religions, such as forms of Hinduism and Buddhism, that have differing views of divinity and so of what it means to be human. But this belief was also rejected by some religious factions at the time of the Reformation and more broadly during the Enlightenment. For example, in his *Religion within the Bounds of Reason Alone*, Immanuel Kant acknowledged the value of Jesus as a moral example but expressed the thought that the doctrine of the Trinity was of no practical benefit. Many former Christians of our time in the West continue to be influenced by the presuppositions of the Enlightenment and so hold that the traditional Christian understanding of the Trinity cannot be defended intellectually; it is not coherent or understandable, and should be interpreted symbolically.

There are many Christians who still claim to believe in God as triune, but for whom this belief appears to have little or no effect in their lives. It seems like a museum piece, kept in a place of honor but not having impact upon life. Much reason for this, as we shall see, is the way that the mystery of the Trinity has been taught, or not taught, in the churches. But part of it is also due to the way people's lives are deeply marked by the Western culture we live in, a culture that in practice is largely naturalistic. That is, many people in practice act as though what is of greatest importance in life is what is here and now in history and as though the resources to gain these benefits were restrictedly human and natural. Whether these people are dedicated to life understood simply individualistically or have a genuine concern for social justice, peace, and ecology, the Christian mystery of the Trinity seems very remote from what is central in life.

There is a great paradox here. What Christians historically proclaim as the mystery that God in his great love manifested to us as his friends, many Christians of our time place little value on, even when they do not actively disbelieve it.

Theology has as its function to show the foundations of Christian belief and the meaning and relevance of this belief. And that is what we seek to do in this volume. But before indicating our approach to this reflection as it refers to the Trinity, we should show some representative efforts among theologians in the twentieth century to reflect on this mystery. First of all (I), however, we will present a sketch of the development of the doctrine of the Trinity in the church so that our examination of the contemporary problematic may be more understandable to those who do not have much background in this area. (We will later fill in this sketch in chapters 2 through 4.) Then we will briefly show (II) some Catholic and Protestant theological approaches in the earlier part of the twentieth century, and (III) some more recent approaches. This will help us learn from these efforts and see major current issues. We shall conclude this chapter by indicating our method and giving reasons for it.

I. A Sketch of the Development of the Doctrine of the Trinity

Israel believed in one God, who was to be the focus of their lives: "Hear, O Israel! The Lord is our God, the Lord alone! Therefore, you shall love the Lord, your God, with all your heart, and with all your soul, and with all your strength" (Dt 6:4–5).[2] This belief and injunction had profound implications for the building of the Israelite community: "You shall love your neighbor as yourself. I am the Lord" (Lv 19:18). God had chosen them to be his people, and committed himself to be their God. He had freed them from slavery in Egypt, entered a covenant with them, given them his care, promises, and guidance, and forgiven them their sins. He was transcendent and immanent, and he was present to his people through many mediators in their long history. With time, his revelations and saving actions and creation itself were ascribed in a special way to God's word, spirit, and wisdom.

When Jesus came, his ministry revealed further who God is and what dedication to him is. In fact, there is a kind of threefoldness at the root and as the goal of Jesus' ministry. Jesus spoke of the God that the Jews worshiped as Father. In his parables he showed who the Father was, for example, a father inviting guests to a wedding banquet and the father in the parable of the prodigal son; he affirmed God's care for his sons and daughters and for creation itself; and he showed who God was by his own healings, teachings, and extension of himself in compassion to the poor and sinners.

Jesus also spoke of himself as Son of this God in a unique sense. This is shown too in his actions. For example, he quoted from the law and prophets of the first covenant, but then added, "But I say to you . . ." (e.g., Mt 5:21–21), thus reflecting a relation to God's word far beyond that of any of the prophets. He showed an intimacy with the Father in his prayer and his knowledge of his Father's designs. And he mediated the definitive salvation that God had promised to his people. His people were now to go to the Father through belief in him as God's unique mediator.

There was too a sense of the power that emanated from Jesus for healing and exorcisms that was ascribed at times, perhaps under the influence of the primitive church's experience and fuller belief, to the Holy Spirit. And he called blasphemy the sin of ascribing to Satan what in reality came from the Holy Spirit (Mt 12:31–32).

In the apostolic church, there was a belief in God who was present to his people through his Son and Holy Spirit; and there was such a significant development of this belief that the later church doctrine of the Trinity was not an imposition on Scripture's witness but an explication of it. Paul proclaimed that Jesus was "established as Son of God in power according to the spirit of holiness through resurrection from the dead, Jesus Christ our Lord" (Rom 2:4). And the ecstatic experience that gave rise to Christian conviction and missionary activity was ascribed to the Holy Spirit, sent by the glorified Jesus Christ.

With time, the primitive church in its worship proclaimed "Jesus Christ, who though he was in the form of God, did not regard equality with God something to be grasped at. Rather, he emptied himself, taking the form of a slave" (Phil 2:5–7). Thus, it suggests Christ's divinity as preexistent, while it still speaks of God bestowing "on him the name above every other name . . . Jesus Christ is Lord" (Phil 2:9, 11), because Jesus accepted even death out of obedience to the Father. The earliest church's ascription of divinity in power to Jesus in virtue of his resurrection, however, was found inadequate. For example, Mark ascribes Sonship to Jesus at his baptism by John the Baptist; Matthew and Luke ascribe it to Jesus in virtue of his conception; and John's gospel speaks of a preexistence of the Son or Word: "In the beginning was the Word, and the Word was with God, and the Word was God. . . . And the Word became flesh" (Jn 1:1, 14).

Similarly, agency is ascribed to the Holy Spirit that seems divine. To the Spirit is ascribed the interior transformation of those who believe in Jesus Christ so that they can become holy (Rom 8), and also their knowledge of the deep things of God, for "the Spirit scrutinizes everything, even the depths of God" (1 Cor 2:10). Christians are asked, "Do you not know that your body is a temple of the holy Spirit within you, whom you have from God, and that you are not your own?" (1 Cor 6:19). John's gospel that speaks of the Spirit as the Spirit of Truth and the Paraclete seems to speak of the Spirit as a person or one who will support the followers of Jesus as Jesus had done while he was with them.

Thus there is a kind of threefoldness in the early Christians' consciousness of the mystery of God's saving presence to them. For example, Paul prays for the Corinthians that "The grace of the Lord Jesus Christ and the love of God and the fellowship of the holy Spirit be with all of you" (2 Cor 13:13). This threefoldness is reflected above all in the baptismal formula found at the end of Matthew's gospel. The risen Jesus instructs his apostles to baptize all nations "in the name of the Father, and of the Son, and of the holy Spirit" (Mt 28:19).

The articulation of this trinitarian mystery that we call the doctrine of the Trinity and that Christian churches affirm took several centuries. A question arose as to how one relates this belief to the articulations of pre-Christian beliefs by Jews and the Hellenistic world. There were certain unsuccessful attempts to explicate it by Jewish angelology, but as the early church related more and more to the world of Hellenism, use was made of current philosophical articulations of reality. For example, in the middle of the second century the apologist Justin used a Stoic distinction between a word that remains within a knower and one that is expressed externally to say that the Father already had a word within him or "a certain rational power" before creation, and then begot this word as Son or Logos through whom he creates and directs history.

In Monarchianism there was a reaction against such speculation as endangering monotheism, but there were also in the third century those who furthered Justin's theological reflection. In the West, Tertullian tried to do justice to the threefoldness in God to which Scripture witnesses. He used metaphors in part (e.g., the root, the stem, and the fruit); but, partially with the help of Stoicism, he also used more philosophical terms. He spoke of the unity of Father and Son as a unity of substance, and their distinction as that of persons, terms that became basic for the West's expression of the mystery. Similarly, Origen in the East articulated the mystery with the help of the philosophy of Middle Platonism. He spoke of the Son and the Spirit as eternal emanations from the Father, as light emanates from the sun. The three are one in being (*homoousios*) as light is one in being with the sun, but are three *hypostases* or distinct realities. He tried to do justice to the oneness and the threeness of the Father, Son, and Holy Spirit, but, like Tertullian, did not adequately articulate the equality of the three. The philosophies they used skewed their theologies.

It was in the fourth century that the crisis of trinitarian belief became most acute; in reaction, the church clarified its belief at the Council of Nicea (325) and later at Constantinople I (381). Arius, a priest of Alexandria, expressed the belief that because the Son was 'begotten' there was when he was not. Only the Father is not-begotten, so the Son is not fully divine. In a way, Arius made the categories of Middle Platonism normative; the divine has no origin, everything else does. Counter to Arius, Nicea proclaimed belief in Jesus

Christ, "the only Son of God, eternally begotten of the Father, God from God, light from light, true God from true God, begotten, not made, one in being (*homoousios*) with the Father." There were many divisions in the church in the decades following Nicea, partly for political reasons, but also because some thought that Nicea's articulation did not defend the distinction between the three. Athanasius was Nicea's main defender, and he defended the teaching because the whole of Christian worship and understanding of the effects of God's grace in our lives, namely a kind of divinization, depended on it. But he did not have a word by which to express what there were three of in God.

In the second half of the fourth century, there were articulations of the distinction between the three that were consistent with Nicea's teaching. These came primarily from the Cappadocians (Basil, Gregory Nazianzen, and Gregory of Nyssa). The distinctions were based, as scriptural words like 'Father' and 'Son' indicated, on a distinction of origin and the relations one had to the other, not on a distinction of substance. The East used the words 'substance' or 'being' to indicate what was one in the Trinity, and the word 'hypostases' to indicate that in which they were distinct. During this period too, there was a certain clarification of the divinity of the Holy Spirit. And the Council of Constantinople I (381) clarified the divinity of the Holy Spirit, defining the third person as "the Lord, the giver of life, who proceeds from the Father, with the Father and the Son he is worshiped and glorified."

Most of this development had happened in the East, but in the West it was above all Augustine who was influential for further development, part of which occasioned serious controversies with Eastern Christianity. Partially against lingering effects of Arianism in the West, Augustine emphatically argued the equality of the three persons: They are one in being, while distinct by their mutual relations. He also sought to clarify the Trinity by very imperfect images of it found in creation, particularly in the spiritual dimension of the human being, where there is both a unity and a threefoldness. For example, the self and memory of self in the preconscious gives rise to knowledge or representation of the self, and both of these give rise to love of the self, such love proceeding both from the self and knowledge of the self. The Holy Spirit, like love, proceeds from both the Father and the Son.

Centuries later, this theology of the Holy Spirit as proceeding from the Father *and* the Son was integrated into the Nicene-Constantinople Creed in Visigothic Spain and then in Charlemagne's empire and outposts of Latin Christianity in Palestine. Here it evoked strong opposition from Eastern Christianity as an unauthorized addition to the creed and as faulty theology. Later, patriarchs of Constantinople, Photius in the ninth century and Caerularius in the eleventh century, articulated and used this difference as partial justification for the East being independent from the pope. This difference remains in our time one issue between Latin Christianity and Orthodoxy. The difference represents a difference too of culture and spirituality; it is not simply a matter of words.

In the thirteenth-century West, Thomas Aquinas developed Augustine's theology of the Trinity in a scholastic milieu and a somewhat more metaphysical mode. This has been the most influential trinitarian theology among Catholics in the modern period. The mystery of the Trinity was also influential in late medieval mysticism, for example, that of Jan van Ruusbroec.

In the Reformation period, the mystery of the Trinity was not questioned by Luther, Calvin, or Anglicanism, though Luther reacted strongly against the use of philosophy in scholastic theology. There were more extreme reformers who applied Luther's reaction against tradition to the patristic trinitarian doctrine and rejected the use of words in trinitarian doctrine that were not scriptural. Pushing this further, the Socinians interpreted Scripture by reason and found the trinitarian doctrine opposed to reason since obviously three human persons are not one being. Similar impulses are found in Arminianism and in Latitudinarianism and the Enlightenment period in England and then on the continent. For many cultural leaders in the eighteenth century, the understanding of God was influenced more by Newtonian physics and an effort to find a common denominator among religions than by Christian revelation, which seemed to them an authoritarian imposition and a defense of established religion. Pietism's religious renewal did not stem the erosion of Christian belief in the Trinity, because pietism emphasized devotion and practice and did not foster a vigorous intellectual dimension for Christian life and faith.

In the nineteenth century, there was further erosion of the doctrine of the Trinity for many in the West. Partially, this came from certain attempts to integrate the doctrine of the Trinity as a junior partner to philosophy—as a pictorial expression of reality that philosophy could better express. For example, Hegel interpreted the Christian doctrine of the Trinity as supporting his view of divinity as objectifying itself in the material world and becoming self-conscious in humanity; thus, he integrated the Trinity with creation and history, but in the process lost its transcendence. Left-wing Hegelianism (e.g., Feuerbach, Marx), on the other hand, simply rejected Christianity in favor of an atheistic humanism. The application of the historical-critical method to the gospels seemed to some to undercut the Trinity as a Christian doctrine, since on their premises the earliest gospel, Mark, as closer to the time of Jesus, had more historical value than John's gospel and was less trinitarian than John's gospel.

This context constitutes the problem of a trinitarian theology in our time. So much in modern life seems to erode the centrality of the mystery of the Trinity, and so much of modern thought seems to undercut belief in this mystery. The tension between a Christian belief in the Trinity faithful to Scripture and tradition, on the one hand, and our contemporary world, on the other, poses the problem for those who would construct a trinitarian theology today. We will see in the next sections of this chapter some polarities among theologians in their efforts to resolve this tension. And that will set the stage for our own effort through most of this book.

II. Some Earlier Twentieth-Century Theological Reflections on the Trinity

What we are presenting here is in no way a complete account of a theologian's interpretation of the Trinity, but simply an indication of his or her distinctive starting point and some implications of this. Our point is to see how some major theologians view this mystery in the midst of the tension between the Christian tradition and the present. The rather radically opposed suggestions for addressing this tension that these theologians manifest show us some major issues that a trinitarian theology must address today. I apologize for the difficulty this section may present to the reader or student who comes to this topic for the first time, but I think it is important to see what the current problem is before addressing it. For the most part here we are recalling theologians who have significantly departed from classical theologies of the Trinity; these efforts in particular show us the current issues.

1. Catholic Theological Reflections on the Trinity

Among the most prominent Catholic theologies of the Trinity during this period we must place neoscholasticism, Vatican II, and Karl Rahner.

The dominant Catholic theology of the Trinity during the pre-Vatican II period was that of neoscholasticism or neothomism. While some very fine work was done in the history of the development of the Christian doctrine of the Trinity, systematic theology generally followed Thomas Aquinas's treatise on this mystery. It treated the one God first (his existence and attributes) and then the triune God. Here the central question was how there could be three persons in one God, and for this the Augustinian psychological analogies were used, but as they were put into a more metaphysical mode by Thomas. The procession of the Word from the Father was illuminated by the analogy of how our own conceptual word proceeds from both the thing known and our act of knowledge itself, and the procession of the Spirit was to some extent made intelligible by how our act of love proceeds as a willing of the good does from the good and knowledge of the good. The distinction of persons was explained by the relations each had to the other in view of these processions, not by distinction in being or substance. At the end of the tract there was a study of the missions of the Son and of the Holy Spirit. This was a very sophisticated study; Bernard Lonergan's study of the Trinity during this period was one of the better treatises in this style.

The Second Vatican Council was a pastoral council and so had no systematic presentation of the trinitarian doctrine. Much of its pastoral concern was centered on articulating the mystery and ministry of the church in a way suitable for our time. And it is within this context that it speaks of the Trinity. Thus it speaks of the Trinity not as it is in itself, as theology has traditionally done in the West, but as Father, Son, and Holy Spirit are actively engaged in saving us, or in reference to the economy of salvation. In the very beginning of the *Dogmatic Constitution on the Church (Lumen Gentium)*, the council shows that the origin of the church is trinitarian. The Father planned to save fallen humanity and sent his Son who by his life, death, and resurrection fulfilled the will of the Father and restored all things. When Jesus had risen and ascended, he sent the Holy Spirit "in order that he might continually sanctify the Church, and that, consequently, those who believe might have access through Christ in one Spirit to the Father" (*LG* 4). This shows that the goal as well as the origin of the church is trinitarian, because the whole purpose of the church is to bring human beings into union with God and one another. In fact, it is a sacrament of such salvation, as the council writes: "the Church, in Christ, is in the nature of a sacrament—a sign and instrument, that is, of communion with God and of unity among all men" (*LG* 1). The Trinity is both the source and the model for the unity of saved humanity: "the universal Church is seen to be 'a people brought into unity from the unity of the Father, the Son and the Holy Spirit'" (*LG* 4).[3]

Specifically, Vatican II went far beyond earlier Western teaching to relate the whole of the Christian mystery and life to the Holy Spirit, having in all some 258 references to the Holy Spirit. It brought the Holy Spirit into its definitions of the church and the liturgy, and its renewal of the sacraments. Specifically, it noted that the church is not constructed only by way of institutional means, but also by the great variety of gifts that the Holy Spirit distributes throughout the church (*LG* 12). The Holy Spirit also works in other Christian communions, is the source of the ecumenical movement (*UR* 2), was working in the world before Christ was glorified and "at times visibly anticipates apostolic action, just as in various ways he unceasingly accompanies and directs it" (*AG* 4).[4] The whole missionary activity of the church has its roots and origin in the missions of the Son and the Spirit (see AG 2). Vatican II thus gave a very different thrust to reflection on the Trinity than neoscholastic theology did.

After Vatican II, Karl Rahner critiqued neoscholastic treatises on the Trinity.[5] Rahner critiques the excessively objective, isolated, and intellectualized theology of the Trinity. He thinks that there is an "isolation of Trinitarian doctrine in piety and textbook theology" (10). Christians in their practical lives, he finds, are almost "'mere' monotheists" (10). He suspects that their idea of the Incarnation would have to change but little if there were no Trinity, for they see it as an incarnation of God, not the Logos. And grace is looked upon as a participation in divine nature, leading to a vision of the divine essence—thus not a personal relation to each of the divine persons. When the tract on the Trinity is completed, "its subject is never brought up again" (14), as though the mystery were revealed wholly for its own sake. "The isolation of the treatise on the Trinity *has* to be wrong. There *must* be a connection between Trinity and man. The Trinity is a mystery of *salvation*, otherwise it would never have been revealed. . . . We should show why it is such a mystery" (21). To counteract this isolation, he presents his thesis: "The *basic thesis* which establishes this connection . . . and presents the Trinity *as* a mystery of salvation (in its reality and not merely as a doctrine) might be formulated as follows: *The 'economic' Trinity is the 'immanent' Trinity and the 'immanent' Trinity is the 'economic' Trinity*" (21). By 'immanent' Trinity he means the Trinity in itself, and by 'economic' Trinity he means the Trinity in the order of God's salvific activity in history.

It is the Logos who is incarnate; and in the gift of grace, Rahner, in agreement with many other contemporary Catholic theologians, holds that "each one of the three divine persons communicates himself to man in gratuitous grace in his own personal particularity and diversity" (34–35). Access to the Trinity is offered us only by the missions of the Son and the Spirit, and so theology should follow this order, rather than starting with the Trinity in itself. Moreover, it should bring out the true *mystery* of the Trinity, which is not so much how three persons can be one God but how God communicates himself to us in Christ and the Spirit. Rahner shows that this self-communication of God has two modalities, as truth and as love.

Rahner, like Barth as we shall see, considers that we cannot use the modern understanding of 'person' to say there are three persons in God, because this meaning signifies "several spiritual centers of activity, . . . several subjectivities and liberties. But there are not three of these in God—not only because in God there is only *one* essence, hence *one* absolute self-presence, but also because there is only *one* self-utterance of the Father, the Logos"

(106). Rahner was quite influential in bringing new life to Catholic theologies of the Trinity, but he has met with opposition in reference to his view on 'person' in the Trinity, as we shall see later.

2. Protestant Theological Reflections on the Trinity

While neoscholasticism had overstressed the Trinity in itself, and Rahner reacted against this, liberal Protestant theology of the nineteenth century had overstressed God's presence to us and had relegated the mystery of the Trinity to a secondary status. Karl Barth reacted against this.

Friederich Schleiermacher was very influential in this orientation. In his book, *The Christian Faith*,[6] he established a new methodology for theology, placing it on an *empirical* basis. That is, he held that religion was piety, a feeling of absolute dependence on God. Theology is the explication of the contents of Christian self-consciousness. Thus "all attributes which we ascribe to God are to be taken as denoting not something special in God, but only something special in the manner in which the feeling of absolute dependence is to be related to him" (#50). The doctrine of the Trinity goes beyond this to read distinctions existing eternally in God independent of the union of divinity with human nature. This doctrine then is not "an immediate or even a necessary combination of utterances concerning the Christian self-consciousness" (#170, 3). So it is a secondary doctrine, and Schleiermacher relegates it to an appendix of his study of theology. Nineteenth-century higher criticism of the New Testament tended to support this, because it viewed later New Testament writings, in which statements of the divinity of the Son and Spirit appeared more evident than in earlier writings, as less reliable than earlier writings because they were more influenced by theology.

Karl Barth attacked this liberal Protestantism and restored the traditional place of primacy to the doctrine of the Trinity.[7] He placed his treatment of the Trinity in the prolegomena to his dogmatics. And he found the root of the doctrine of the Trinity to lie in the very reality of God's revelation. By this Barth means the whole existential reality of God's revelation, involving God, the way he reveals, as the New Testament witnesses to revelation, and the person who receives it. The mystery of the Trinity, he holds, is implicitly contained here, as he shows by an analysis of the statement that God reveals. This raises three questions: who reveals, how this happens, and what is the result in the man in whom it happens (see 295–296). The act of revelation involves both a distinction and a unity: "God reveals himself. He reveals himself *through Himself*. He reveals *Himself*. . . . [T]his subject, God, the Revealer, is identical with His act in revelation and also identical with its effect" (296). God reveals himself as the Lord; he reveals himself through the

Word which is the action of revelation; and this revelation is received in faith by the Spirit.

Thus "revelation must be understood as the root or ground of the doctrine of the Trinity. As its root or ground, we say. The doctrine of the Trinity has not yet encountered us directly" (332–333). The development of the concepts in the doctrine, such as one essence and three persons or modes of being, comes later in Christian history. In this doctrine of the Trinity, Barth is speaking not only of the Trinity in the economy of salvation, but about the Trinity in itself. He rejected any other source or roots of the doctrine, and specifically all search for signs or 'vestigia' of the Trinity in creation. We must credit Barth with a great service to theology in reasserting the primacy of the mystery of the Trinity, though we will raise questions concerning the chasm he places between reason and revelation and the way he bases his trinitarian theology more on the analytic study of the notion of revelation than on what Scripture presents as the historical mediation of both revelation and salvation by the Son and the Spirit.

Barth, like Rahner, has a problem with the use of 'persons' in designating the three of the Trinity, because of the modern implications of the word. He writes, "'Person' as used in the Church doctrine of the Trinity bears no direct relation to personality. The meaning of the doctrine is not, then, that there are three personalities in God. . . we are speaking not of three divine I's, but three of the one divine I" (351). He adds, "by preference we do not use the term 'person' but rather 'modes of being' [Seinsweisen] . . . an auxiliary concept which has been used from the very beginning. . ." (359). He sees 'modes of being' as a continuation of the word hypostasis, which the Greek Fathers used to designate the three.

Interestingly, in 1969 N. H. G. Robinson wrote an article titled "Trinitarianism and Post-Barthian Theology,"[8] in which he noted that "in post-Barthian theology there has been an amazingly widespread and quite radical elimination of that kind of metaphysical utterance and outlook of which the trinitarian dogma is an outstanding example" (192), namely, the effort to speak of the very being of God. Robinson offers two examples of this reaction. One is Rudolf Bultmann, who interpreted the New Testament as a doctrine on man and who spoke of God's acts in only a "non-objectifying sense" (193). That is, Bultmann interpreted the New Testament teaching on the preexistence of Christ as meaning that "there exists a divinely authorized proclamation of the prevenient grace and love of God. . . . This is the fact that finds mythological expression in what is said of the preexistence of Christ" (194).[9] And the Spirit is looked upon as "the factual possibility of a new life realized in faith" (194). Robinson's second example comes from English linguistic philosophy. I. T. Ramsey considered religious language to be empirical in the sense that it reflects an experience, and more than this insofar as it evokes a religious situation and commends a commitment. But it does not describe transempirical facts: "In speaking of the eternal generation of the Son, we are not talking about what goes on at all times in some sort of heavenly laboratory, or labour-ward."[10] Robinson's own view is that we need a trinitarianism of God's action to give a basis for the Christian claim, but that we cannot fall into Barth's objective "metaphysical" talk about God's Being.

III. Some Later Theological Reflections on the Trinity

If we seek to describe briefly the landscape of recent studies of the doctrine of the Trinity, we could perhaps more usefully gather diverse works under several themes rather than primarily describe the theologies of individuals. I will indicate some directions in reference to (1) dialogical and dialectical approaches, (2) the question of 'person', and (3) the Holy Spirit. Other questions such as the Trinity and spirituality, the Trinity in relation to world religions, and the Trinity in relation to feminism will be referred to in the course of our illustrations of the issues mentioned above and will be dealt with in the following chapters. I am taking examples primarily from some mutually opposed theologies to show some major polarities in this area of theology, so that the serious problems in this area of theology may be evident.

1. Dialogical and Dialectical Approaches
There are dialectical approaches to the Trinity that have continuity with Barth's in that they start directly from Scripture, particularly its eschatological teaching, and reject philosophy's or metaphysics' competence here as authority. And there are dialogical reflections on the question of the Trinity in the sense that they tend to seek to commend Christian belief in God to reason or as a human value. The first are found particularly in Germany (e.g., E. Jüngel, J. Moltmann, W. Pannenberg) or in some American Lutherans (e.g., R. Jenson). Catholic theologies of the Trinity are dialogical when compared to Barth. The extreme of this latter tendency reduces Christian doctrine to what human beings can accept on the basis of reason or human values without faith. This tendency is found particularly in some theologians of the English-speaking countries. Nicholas Lash writes, "it is especially in the English-speaking world that, with renewed vigour in recent years, the underlying assumptions of eighteenth century theism have dictated the terms of debate concerning the question of God."[11]

a. Dialogical Approaches to the Trinity

There are a number of recent writings, some by prominent theologians, that suggest or more than suggest that the traditional understanding of the Trinity is no longer intellectually and/or morally acceptable. For example, G. W. H. Lampe wrote a book to argue that the message in the New Testament about the Holy Spirit does not support the traditional doctrine of the Spirit as a distinct divine person, but rather signifies God's action and relationship with us humans—an outreach that occurs through Jesus Christ who uniquely realized the relation with God for which human beings were created and who was the means by which others could share this.[12] It is true that Paul and John ambiguously, and then the patristic period more clearly, came to speak of three distinct persons, but, "The roots of their presupposition about the personal subsistence of the Holy Spirit go back, together with their even stronger conviction of the eternal hypostatic existence of the Son, through the Christologies of the New Testament to the quasi-personification of 'Wisdom' and 'Logos' in pre-Christian thought" (223–224). According to Lampe, the Fathers and then theologians were never able to specify adequately the nature of the relations by which they explained how the 'persons' were distinct. Lampe concludes that the problem posed was unreal; the 'Spirit' in Scripture simply designates God in his outreach toward creation.

Similarly, a number of Anglican theologians wrote a collection of essays, *The Myth of God Incarnate*,[13] out of a conviction that the preexistence of Jesus Christ or the Incarnation of God cannot be accepted today, and they tried to commend another interpretation to make Christian faith possible for people in our time, for example, that the doctrine of the Incarnation is a mythological or poetic way of expressing the significance of Jesus Christ to us. If this is the case, we can find new ways of expressing the significance of Jesus without using incarnational language. For example, Frances Young writes that "Jesus is the supreme disclosure which opens my eyes to God in the present" (38), and John Hick holds that Jesus is "one in whose presence we have found ourselves to be at the same time in the presence of God" (184).

In the United States there have been theological movements that also have as a premise that the traditional doctrine of the Trinity is an obstacle to Christian faith in our time. This is true, for example, of process theologians. Their view of God, in dependence on Whitehead's philosophy, is dipolar. God's primordial nature holds out to us the ideals in view of which we can be and are called to be transformed; and God's consequent nature is how he too is contingently transformed by his relation to creation, or, rather, to the universe, since process theologians do not accept a creation out of nothing.

At one point John Cobb and David Griffin wrote that "process theology is not interested in formulating distinctions within God for the sake of conforming with traditional Trinitarian notions."[14] But in other writings, Cobb identifies 'logos' with the primordial nature of God and uses the word 'Christ' for the logos as immanent in the world. He writes of Christ: "He is the not-yet-realized transforming the givenness of the past from a burden into a potentiality for new creation . . . the good in what is now happening is to be completed and fulfilled."[15] Jesus as the Christ is an exemplification of a more universal principle, the logos or primordial nature of God, and this is universally present since creative transformation itself is universally present. But Jesus is unique because he experienced no tension between the initial aim and his subjective aim. Cobb tends to identify the Holy Spirit with the Kingdom of God in the sense of God's consequent nature where all the tendencies in the world toward transformation that are in tension with one another are brought to be compatible.[16]

For Sallie McFague, what we are offered through the traditional trinitarian doctrine concerning Father, Son, and Holy Spirit are metaphors or models of God's relating to us in the sense of being for us. It is this basic relating of God to us that the metaphors of Scripture convey; their more specific meanings during the initial stage of Christianity are subject to critique if they do not now further human development. She adds that "we are created in the image of God (Gen 1:27), so we now, with the model of Jesus, have further support for imagining God in our image, the image of persons. This means that personal, relational images are central for metaphorical theology."[17] McFague makes ontological truth claims that her models and metaphors refer indirectly to the divine, even though she rejects the correspondence theory of truth. She holds that "there is no way to prove one's ontological claim; nonetheless, on the basis of the initial 'wager' or belief—that God is on the side of life and its fulfillment—one asserts that the alternative models are truer to that wager and better for expressing it."[18] She rejects the traditional trinitarian metaphors of Father, Son, and Holy Spirit as representing a patriarchal, hierarchical society and as repressive, particularly for women. And she proposes her own metaphors of Mother, Lover, and Friend, justifying these constructions as ones that will bring about more inclusive, ecologically sensitive, nontriumphalistic, and life-affirming dispositions in people than the traditional metaphors.

We may acknowledge the reality of some problems that McFague deals with but search for ways of responding to them that are faithful to Scripture and the early councils, while not being restricted totally to earlier interpretations of them.

b. Some Dialectical Trinitarian Theologians

There are a number of theologians who claim to be at the other pole in reference to the divide between an approach to the question of the Trinity on
a philosophical and humanistic base and one that is faithful to Scripture. As
Robert Jenson describes a breakup of a marriage between traditional metaphysics and Scripture, there is a group of theologians who, following Barth in
this, explicitly assert that "traditional metaphysical doctrines, as the theology of another religion, have no inherent authority."[19] Within this group
there are those who have rediscovered the gospel's eschatological character.
Contrary to a metaphysical tradition that views God as the power of the beginning to secure time, these theologians view God as the power of the
prophesied End to enliven time. Jenson names Eberhard Jüngel, Jürgen
Moltmann, and Wolfhart Pannenberg with himself as members of this group.
They take "Rahner's Rule" of the identity between the immanent and the
economic Trinity and push it further than Rahner did. The relationality between the Father and the Son is that between the Father and Jesus in history;
thus, eternity incorporates time and the consummation of time in the eschaton: "The 'economic' Trinity is *eschatologically* God 'himself', an 'immanent'
Trinity. And that assertion is no problem, for God *is* himself only *eschatologically*, since he is Spirit."[20] Time, and specifically what happens in the history
of Jesus, is constitutive of who the Trinity is. This is expressed strongly in
Moltmann's *The Crucified God* from the perspective of the cross of Christ. On
the cross the Father in love suffered the deliverance of the Son to death, and
the Son experienced abandonment by the Father. It is in virtue of this rupture that the distinction of Father and Son was retroactively established eternally. And the rupture was overcome by the unifying impact of the love that
is the Holy Spirit. The Trinity is "no self-contained group in heaven, but an
eschatological process open to men on earth, which stems from the cross of
Christ."[21]

In his book, *The Trinity and the Kingdom of God,* Moltmann continues to
view the inner-trinitarian relations, the immanent Trinity, as established
largely by what happens in history or by the Trinity in the economy of salvation; the Trinity in the economy of salvation is the ground for the Trinity
in itself, not vice versa as has been traditionally taught. The immanent Trinity is found above all through the eschatological kingdom; "when the history
and experience of salvation are completed and perfected . . . then the economic Trinity is raised into and transcended in the immanent Trinity."[22] The
immanent Trinity retains a kind of preeminence over the Trinity in the economy of salvation; this preeminence is expressed in doxology. Moltmann does
not want to dissolve the immanent Trinity into the Trinity of the economy

of salvation. He writes that "the divine relationship in the world is primarily determined by that inner relationship [among the persons]."[23] Thus, he seems to draw back somewhat from statements he made in his earlier book. But if the immanent Trinity is the goal of history as largely determined by history, it is hard to see how the transcendence of the Trinity is preserved.

Pannenberg similarly holds that the Trinity in the economy of salvation determines the Trinity in itself. For the latter is based on the event of Jesus' relating to the Father as Lord, as actively differentiating himself from God as Lord though fulfilling his mission in total subordination to the Father, and proclaiming him as Father. This is the ground for Jesus' own status as *homoousion* with God. It follows from this that not only is the Godhood of the Son dependent on that of the Father, but "also, . . . , that the Godhood of the Father is dependent on that of the Son, i.e. on the resurrection of the Crucified One as the basis for the confession of Jesus' divine sonship. . . . Thus, for the Father, the actuality of his own Godhood depends upon the working of the Son and Spirit toward the realization of the kingdom of God in the world."[24] Thus, what happens in history has a retroactive influence on God eternally. God is Lordship, and his Lordship is not fully established until the consummation of history, but it will appear then that this is what God has always been. The influence of the Spirit and Son on history is not through being sent by God from the past, but being sent from this future.[25] Pannenberg, however, wishes also to assert that the "interpretation of the essence of God as eternal also demands the acceptance of the idea of an existence of God preceding the world."[26] We can wonder whether there is an internal coherence between his diverse views. Thus, these dialectical theologians raise for us the question of how we can fully affirm the Trinity's relatedness to history without compromising God's transcendence over all creation. Also, is their view based on Scripture or rather on a philosophy, such as that of Hegel?

2. The Question of Persons in the Trinity
Another serious question discussed in contemporary trinitarian theologies is the meaning of the word 'person' when applied to the Trinity. In the patristic era the unity of God was expressed as a unity of substance or being, and the distinction of Father, Son, and Spirit was expressed as a distinction of *hypostases*, or persons. This distinction was based on the distinct property of each (e. g., the Son being generated and the Spirit proceeding) and because of the *relations* of origin one had to the other, not on the substance or being, which was one. In modern philosophy and common understanding, 'person' has come to mean personality and designate an individual subjectivity, consciousness, and autonomous source of action. It seemed to both Rahner and

Barth that one could not say there were three of these in God without falling into tritheism. And so they preferred an expression such as three 'distinct manners of subsisting' or 'modes of being'. On the other hand, there are now a large number of theologians who apply the modern—or postmodern—sense of person positively to God. And so we have serious disagreement. We shall look at several of these theologians as illustrative of this issue.[27]

Moltmann denies that a traditional substantialist metaphysics has any authority in theology. Also, he thinks that Barth takes his own understanding of person from German idealism that stresses the autonomy of the absolute subject and so makes himself unable to speak of God as three persons. Moltmann finds three actors and subjects in the economy of salvation taking differing relations to one another in the stages of salvation history and, indeed, being oriented to that eschatological moment when salvation will be fully achieved. He concludes that in the Trinity, the unity of the three is a *perichoretic* unity, that is, a union of three persons in their dedication to one another, not in the unity of one substance or one subject.[28] This understanding of the Trinity presents something of a social program for us and a model for our own unity with God and with one another. Moltmann denies that Christianity is a monotheism, in part because he holds that monotheism is the basis of Monarchianism—a patriarchial, hierarchical domination by one ruler. But neither is Christianity a tritheism, because the perichoretic unity of divine community precludes this. Moltmann is not much troubled by the discrepancy between his view and that of Nicea, nor by philosophical questions of how there can be three Gods.

Joseph Bracken, S.J., seeks by his trinitarian theology to support a communitarian theology and polity. He thinks that the individualism of the Western world is largely tied up with a substantialist worldview. He proposes an adaptation of A. L. Whitehead's philosophy as a corrective for this and as helpful for a theological articulation of the trinitarian community. Whitehead took his basic model of reality from psychophysical processes (microscopic and transient actual entities) that are intrinsically related to other such processes and constantly in change toward bringing about the new and the larger community. A human being is a society of such processes that is perduring; it too is intrinsically relational and oriented to a whole of larger and larger communities. Bracken uses this to interpret the Father as a society of actual entities always offering to the Son new possibilities, the Son as such a society always responding positively, and the Holy Spirit as one always inducing the Father to continue to offer such possibilities. If one accepts the fact that the community has a unity that is metaphysically preeminent over that of the individual, one will realize that this interpretation presents an understanding of the three divine persons that is in continuity with the unity that tradition affirms.[29] We think that there remain serious problems with this philosophy both in itself and as an instrument for reflecting theologically on the Trinity. Bracken's effort, however, raises for us the question whether a modification of a classical theology is both possible and can do better justice to the Trinity as a social process.

3. The Holy Spirit

Another major issue in trinitarian theology in our time concerns the Holy Spirit. Pope John XXIII called for a New Pentecost at the beginning of the Second Vatican Council, and there has been a remarkable recovery of the mystery of the Holy Spirit in life and theology in the Western Church. We can reflect on some the following issues associated with this as relevant to our study: the *Filioque* and the churches, the Holy Spirit and feminism, and the Holy Spirit and spirituality.

a. The Filioque *and the Churches*

A central problem for a millennium of differences between Orthodoxy and Catholicism has been the issue of the *filioque*, that is, the Roman Catholic Church's addition to the Nicene-Constantinople creed that the Holy Spirit proceeds "from the Father *and the Son*." This may seem to some Westerners a conflict over words, but for Orthodoxy a trinitarian theology is a spirituality at the center of their life and liturgy.[30] Many Orthodox have accused the West of subordinating the Spirit to the Son, and consequently of subordinating the life of the Christian to law, authority, and institution. They have held that the distinction of the Son and the Spirit within the Trinity is sufficiently guaranteed by the distinct properties of each, as one is generated by the Father and the other proceeds from the Father. Many theologians in the West have accused Orthodoxy of leaving the relation of the Spirit to the Son unspecified by refusing to acknowledge that the Spirit proceeds from the Son as well as from the Father; and they have said that Augustine's theology sufficiently safeguards the primacy of the Father, since it asserts that whatever the Son is (and thus that the Spirit proceeds from the Son as well as from the Father) he is by generation from the Father. In recent decades, happily, there have been major efforts to bring these two positions closer together, and we shall have to consider some of them later.[31]

But we should note that a similar problem affects the Western Church as much as it does the relations between the Western and the Eastern churches. In fact, at the time of the Reformation there was a major dispute concerning the relation between Spirit and the Word as norms or criteria of God's revelation,

sola scriptura

particularly between the Lutherans and Reformed on the one hand and the An-
abaptist movement on the other.[32] And since Vatican II, there has been this dispute within the Catholic Church itself in life and in ecclesiology. Some justify
the legitimacy of their efforts to go beyond the magisterium, and in some instances against it, on the basis that the Spirit is operating in the church as a
whole and not simply in the hierarchy. Thus the issue of the Holy Spirit's relation to the Word or Son is of central significance for the life of the church and
spirituality as well as for theology.

b. The Holy Spirit and Feminism

There have been many women and men in recent decades who have claimed
that women's experience has been overlooked or suppressed in the traditional Christian articulation of who God is. And this is specifically true of
the Christian doctrine of the Trinity—Father, Son, and Holy Spirit. Some
women have claimed that Christianity is so inherently patriarchal that they
have abandoned it for some form of goddess religion. Some women who sym-
pathize strongly with this reaction have still refused to follow this path.
Among these there are those who still call themselves Christian but acknowledge no privileged revelation coming to us from the historical Jesus.[33]

To illustrate this problem we will recall, all too briefly, the position of Elizabeth Johnson, in her book, *She Who Is: The Mystery of God in Feminist Theological Discourse*, but we note that this specific position is not shared by all
feminists.[34] Johnson accepts the validity of God's revelation through Jesus
Christ. But she also cites Vatican II's interpretation of the inerrancy of Scripture as restricted to "that truth which God, for the sake of our salvation,
wished to see confided to the sacred Scriptures" (*Dei Verbum* 11). What
derogates from the dignity and equality of women cannot be for our salvation, but rather represents the bias of the patriarchal culture of Judaism and
the early church. As we critique other views in Scripture, for example, those
on slavery, we must similarly acknowledge the inadequacy of some of its
views about women. There are grounds within Scripture itself for this critique in reference to the patriarchal traditional Christian interpretation of
the Trinity: "the most developed personification of God's presence and activity in the Hebrew's Scriptures" (86–87) is Wisdom or Sophia. Sophia is a
female personification of God's own being in creative and saving involve-
ment with the world; there is a "functional equivalence between the deeds of
Sophia and those of the biblical God" (91).

This continues in the Christian trajectory, where the Spirit is associated
with Sophia. And what Judaism said of Sophia, Christians came to say of Jesus (e.g., in Mt 11:25–27). John's prologue is suffused with the Wisdom tra-

dition. But toward the end of the first century because of the Gnostics and in line with the broader shift in the Christian community toward a patriarchal ecclesial structure, this use of Sophia became problematic for the church, so John used "Word" instead. Counter to this, "it is not unthinkable—it is not even unbiblical—to confess Jesus Christ as the incarnation of God imaged in female symbols"; "Jesus is the human being Sophia became" (99). To correct the tradition, we should "tell the story of Jesus as the story of Wisdom's child, Sophia incarnate" (154). This is in accord with a single nature anthropology, which is against "a notion of human nature polarized on the basis of sex" (155). All three hypostases of the Trinity transcend the categories of male and female, and each hypostasis can be spoken of in female metaphors (see 211). Woman is "imago Dei," and therefore "imago Christi" and "imago Spiritus." God is the unknowable mother of all. And "the mystery of Sophia–Trinity must be confessed as critical prophesy in the midst of patriarchal rule" (225). "She Who Is can be spoken as a robust, appropriate name for God" (243). This interpretation shows God's *care* for all, and it has practical and critical implications.

While we must acknowledge that traditionally in the church God has been spoken of in one-sidedly male metaphors, we can also wonder whether the appropriate correction for this is to speak now of God in one-sidedly female metaphors. As Christians we can be confident that in revelation itself there is a correction for what the church has too often forgotten. In fact, I have examined in Scripture the difference between symbols of the Word of God and those of the Spirit, and presented evidence that the main symbols of the Holy Spirit are feminine.[35]

c. The Holy Spirit and Spirituality

All of the interpretations of the Trinity and, specifically, the Holy Spirit, we have recalled imply a spirituality or a practice; in fact, many of them come from a praxis that they reflect and support. And this is true too of positions that we have not examined, for example, those of the Pentecostals and the Catholic charismatic movement. We have already seen some issues in the area of spirituality that have been raised; we can conclude our survey by recalling several aspects of books on the Spirit by Michael Welker and by J. Moltmann.[36]

Though these books have their differences, there are similarities too. Both see in our current world widespread experiences of the Spirit and much need to reaffirm the Spirit in the larger life of the world today as well as in the church. Moltmann acknowledges that dialectical theology in its biblical approach has not given sufficient attention and weight to human experiences of the Spirit. He clarifies what he means: "By experiences of the Spirit I mean an awareness of God in, with and beneath the experience of life, which gives us assurance of God's fellowship, friendship and love" (M 17). Every experience that happens to us can possess a transcendent element; the recognition of God's Spirit is not limited to the human person's experience of self but can also occur in the experience of the other, of society, and of nature. We must now develop a holistic doctrine of God the Holy Spirit to help human beings embrace the whole community of creation.

Both Welker and Moltmann give rich analyses of historical experiences of the Spirit. Welker dwells on how the Spirit in the Old Testament brought the fragmented and disheartened community of Israel together behind a charismatic leader in the time of the Judges and later. Jesus, animated by the Spirit in his ministry, draws people to the kingdom one by one, for example, by exorcisms and healings; by such actions his reign becomes present. After Jesus' crucifixion and resurrection, through the outpouring of the Spirit at Pentecost a ruptured world begins to grow together. A force field of faith and love is created that leads to a worldwide gathering and renewal. By the Spirit, people are led to a free relation to themselves and to their world.

Both theologians spell out some of the areas where such an outpouring of the Spirit is needed today and where it is already active in part. Both Welker and Moltmannn seek to overcome a dichotomy between creation and redemption that the Lutheran tradition may have fostered. However, both too are very opposed to metaphysics (e.g., see W 155, 221, 223). For example, Welker rejects the notion of God as "Pure Act," and Moltmann calls us to abandon a "pattern of essence and reality, being and act, immanent and economic Trinity" (M 290). Moltmann speaks of the Holy Spirit having "a like nature" to the other divine persons (M 289). A certain dichotomy between nature and life in the Spirit continues in both. Welker writes that it is an error "to conclude that creaturely life should be carried out in accord with nature" (W 109). Moltmann has frequently made a dichotomy between the eschatological future and creation, and has held that to say that human beings have a 'nature' that perdures through time is to deny history.[37] Both wish to foster an 'openness' to the future in Christians and human beings more generally—the future, the transcendence that lies historically in front of us (see W 139). In their view, nature and metaphysics inhibit such openness. Also, they do not seem to hold that the Christian tradition as expressed in the Nicene-Constantinople Creed is normative for present Christian theology and life. For Moltmann, if metaphors "are dogmatized, these experiences become fixed"; "eschatology relativizes them"; a theology of the cross holds that "human and historical concepts never grasp or apprehend God himself" (M 300–301).

It is obvious that we do indeed need a spirituality that opens us to the future, the whole of creation and a changing historical world, but is the view that humans have a nature and the study of this by a critical metaphysics opposed to such a spirituality or a condition for it? Also, it is somewhat surprising that these theologians pay so little attention to the religions of Asia. A spirituality for our time should relate to these non-Christian spiritualities that have been and still are of such central importance for billions of people. They are also important for growing numbers of people in the West.[38] Is there a certain Eurocentrism influencing these theologians?

Conclusion

We have identified some major issues for a trinitarian theology in our time and did so within an ecumenical context. Our study shows that a theology of the Trinity must be recontextualized in our time, because the culture has changed so markedly from what it was during the development of this doctrine. I understand theology's task to be to give critical grounds or foundations for what the church proposes the Christian faith to be, and to explain the meaning of this faith in two senses—what this belief signifies and what its import or relevance is for Christian life. The variety of ways in which theologians have done this in recent times constitutes a problem for a contemporary theology of the Trinity. One central polarity here is between those who start from human reason or human values and seek to make the Christian belief cohere with these so that fewer obstacles are placed in the way of Christian belief, and those who start with Scripture's message of the kingdom of God, at times interpreted eschatologically, and seek to be faithful to this, allowing human reason less right in the area of Christian belief.

The place in the structure of theology where the tract on the Trinity occurs addresses this polarity. It comes after what is called foundational or fundamental theology, and as theology it systematically depends on this. The first part of foundational theology deals with the question of belief in God in our time.[39] Part of this study uses a phenomenology of contemporary experience that seeks to show that God is as central for the meaning and goal of human life in our period of modern historical consciousness as he was for a premodern culture. Another part of an answer to modern disbelief is to show, once more from a contemporary phenomenology, that the human knower does validly reach a knowledge of reality and the self as being. Our present study presupposes a critical religious reading of contemporary human life and knowledge, and will seek to integrate it in some later chapters. This view is counter to some dialectical theologians, who too easily have dismissed their debts to human reason. And it is in dialogue with certain dialogical theologians and philosophers concerning the reading of human existence and knowledge consonant with our time.

The second part of foundational theology deals with faith in God *through Jesus Christ* and seeks to critically evaluate the foundations and meaning of such belief.[40] We critically validate the further revelation God gives us of his way of salvation and himself through Jesus Christ and his Spirit. And so, with dialectical theologians, we cannot accept the limits that some current dialogical theologians put on Christian revelation and, we should add, on salvation. Similarly, with dialectical theologians we acknowledge that Jesus Christ and the primitive church proclaimed the kingdom in an apocalyptic sense and that therefore salvation, like the Holy Spirit, comes to us now from the future where Christ has ascended into his reign as Lord. This interpretation relates God's salvific activity to people with a modern historical consciousness, since it relates the kingdom to us as that hoped-for future of humanity and ourselves, rather than, as too often in the past, to our transcendence of the mutability of time into the permanence of God's eternity. The present book, then, depends on what has been critically validated in this area of foundational theology and seeks to integrate the understanding of salvation and revelation presented there.

The third part of foundational theology treats the norm of Christian faith and the nature of theology. This part critically evaluates the view that God did through Jesus Christ give a message that he intended for the salvation of all, and hence he meant it to be transmitted to all ages in a way that was faithful to his proclamation, that he did see to it that there would be a means by which it was transmitted faithfully through the gift of the Holy Spirit to the church as a whole, through the college of apostles and apostolic succession to proclaim the message in succeeding generations and through the inspired writing of the books of the New Testament. It also critically evaluates in principle the development of doctrine that has occurred, for instance, in reference to the doctrine of the Trinity. What is treated in the third part of foundational theology, abstracting from what is said about the pope's authority, is agreed on by many Christian churches, as seen in convergence statements in ecumenical dialogues of recent decades.[41] The Christian doctrine of the Trinity has been proclaimed by ecumenical councils and has not depended particularly on statements of the popes apart from these councils. This norm of faith does not at all exclude human reason and values that are acknowledged in our time, but shows both a confidence that these are not opposed by Christian revelation and an openness to their integration with Christian belief. A theology of the Trinity depends on this norm of faith, but we will not seek to validate this norm of Christian faith as such in this book.

Our study of the Trinity will exemplify what, in dependence on these norms of Christian faith, we understand theology to be. Thus we have started from current problems with belief in this mystery. With God's help, we seek to critically evaluate the foundations for the church's belief and the meaning of this belief in a way that takes these problems very seriously. Thus, we begin with Scripture (chapter 2), the heart and norm of the Christian faith. We seek to critically evaluate whether indeed this mystery has been witnessed to by Scripture as divinely revealed, how it was so witnessed, and what relevance it had for human life. There is a question of hermeneutics present here, how we can approach an ancient text with current preoccupations and questions; this question was addressed in foundational theology, but it will be recalled here.

Then we will critically evaluate some main strands in the development of this doctrine in the first four centuries (chapter 3) and later periods (chapter 4), an essential task because how we proclaim the Trinity in the churches in our time depends essentially on this development and its validity. This development will also show some bases for present divergences in theologies of the Trinity, such as those between Orthodoxy and the West. In later chapters we shall deal with "constructive" theology, or with how we should in theology articulate the mystery of the Trinity for our time. We cannot antecedently accept the complete adequacy of previous theologies, because they were constructed with the tools of their own time and in view of problems of their age.

Notes

1. W. A. Visser't Hooft, ed., *The New Delhi Report. The Third Assembly of the World Council of Churches, 1961* (London: SCM Press, 1962), 426. Some representatives of member churches voted against this resolution or abstained, for instance, the "International association for Liberal Christianity and religious liberty," the Arminian Church of the Low Countries, the Mennonite Church of the Low Countries, and the Society of Friends in the United States. Also see *Confessing One Faith: An Ecumenical Explication of the Apostolic Faith as It Is Confessed in the Nicene-Constantinopolitan Creed (381)*. Faith and Order Paper No. 153 (Geneva: WCC Publications, 1991).

2. Unless otherwise indicated, my quotations from Scripture are from *The New American Bible*, with the revised New Testament (1987).

3. I use the translation of documents from Vatican II as given in Austin Flannery, *Vatican II: The Conciliar and Post Conciliar Documents* (New York: Costello Publishing, 1975). See Bertrand de la Margerie, *La Trinité Chrétienne dans l'Histoire* (Paris:

Beauchesne, 1975), 303–319. Also see P. Drilling, "The Genesis of the Trinitarian Ecclesiology of Vatican II," *Science et Esprit* 45 (1993): 61–78, where the author shows how, by this trinitarian context of its ecclesiology, the church moved decisively beyond its earlier juridical and christocentric ecclesiology, and how the Orthodox influenced this movement.

4. On Vatican II's teaching on the Holy Spirit, see Y. Congar, *I Believe in the Holy Spirit*, vol. 1, *The Experience of the Spirit* (New York: Seabury, 1983), 167–173.

5. Karl Rahner, *The Trinity* (New York: Herder and Herder, 1970). The numbers in the text at this point indicate pages in Rahner's book.

6. Friederich Schleiermacher, *The Christian Faith* (Edinburgh: T & T Clark, 1989 impression). See Claude Welch, *In This Name: The Doctrine of the Trinity in Contemporary Theology* (New York: Schribner's, 1952), chapter 1. Citations in the text here are to sections of Schleiermacher's book.

7. See Karl Barth, *Church Dogmatics*, vol. 1, *The Doctrine of the Word of God. Part One* (Edinburgh: T & T Clark, 1975 ed.), chapter 2, #8, "God in His Revelation," 295 ff. Citations in text are to this book. See also, Welch, *In This Name*, chapter 6, "The Trinity as the Immediate Implication of Revelation," 161–213.

8. N. H. G. Robinson, "Trinitarianism and Post-Barthian Theology," *Journal of Theological Studies* 20 (1969): 186–201. Page references here in the text are to this article.

9. This quotation, cited by Robinson, is from Rudolph Bultmann, *Theology of the New Testament*, vol. 1 (New York: Scribner's, 1951), 305.

10. I. T. Ramsey, *Religious Language* (London: SCM Press, 1957), 150. See J. Ashley, "Ian Ramsey and the Problem of Religious Knowledge," *Journal of Theological Studies* 35 (1984): 416–440.

11. Nicholas Lash, "Considering the Trinity," *Modern Theology* 2 (1986): 185. This whole issue is on the Trinity. William Hill in *The Three-Personed God: The Trinity as a Mystery of Salvation* (Washington, D.C.: Catholic University of America Press, 1982) gives analyses and evaluations of many twentieth-century theologies of the Trinity from his perspective as a Thomist of our time.

12. G. W. H. Lampe, *God as Spirit* (London: Oxford, 1977). Citations here are to pages in this book. James Mackey's *The Christian Experience of God as Trinity* (London: S.C.M. Press, 1983) similarly contests the inner logic of the traditional Christian dogma of the Trinity. He reinterprets the doctrine in a monotheistic sense he thinks acceptable to Jews and Muslims as well as to the modern world. For critiques of this tendency, see Hugo Meynell, "Two Directions for Pneumatology," *Irish Theological Quarterly* 49 (1982): 172–183; and Ralph Del Colle, *Christ and the Spirit: Spirit Christology in Trinitarian Perspective* (New York: Oxford University Press, 1992).

13. Don Cupitt, et al., *The Myth of God Incarnate* (London: SCM Press, 1977). This is answered by T. V. Morris in *The Logic of God Incarnate* (Ithaca, N.Y.: Cornell University Press, 1986) and R. Sturch in *The Word and Christ* (Oxford: Clarendon Press, 1991). Numbers in the text are to pages in Cuppitt's book.

14. John Cobb Jr. and David Griffin, *Process Theology: An Introductory Exposition* (Philadelphia: Westminster, 1976), 110. Also see Ted Peters, "John Cobb, Theologian in Process," *Dialog* 29 (1990): 207–220, 290–302; and John Cobb Jr., "Response to Ted Peters," *Dialog* 30 (1991): 241f. Joseph Bracken, S.J., uses in several of his writings some elements of process philosophy to articulate the mystery of the Trinity, but seeks to be faithful to the Christian doctrine in its historical sense.

15. John Cobb Jr., *Christ in a Pluralistic Age* (Philadelphia: Westminster, 1975), 59.

16. See Cobb, *Christ*, 261f.

17. Sallie McFague, *Metaphorical Theology* (Phiadelphia: Fortress, 1982), 27. See David Bromell, "Sallie McFague's 'Metaphorical Theology,'" *JAAR* 61 (1993): 485–503; and Terrence Reynolds, "Two McFagues: Meaning, Truth, and Justification in *Models of God*," *Modern Theology* 11 (1995): 289–314.

18. McFague, in her "Response" to reviewers of her *Models of God* (Philadelphia: Fortress, 1987) in *Religion and Intellectual Life* (Spring 1988): 21.

19. Robert Jenson, "The Logic of the Doctrine of the Trinity," *Dialog* 26 (1987): 249. See Ted Peters's description of this direction in "Trinity Talk," *Dialog* 26 (1987): 44–48, 133–138; and W. Pannenberg's in "Problems of a Trinitarian Doctrine of God," *Dialog* 26 (1987): 250–257.

20. R. Jenson, "The Triune God," in Carl Braaten and Robert Jenson, ed., *Christian Dogmatics* (Philadelphia: Fortress, 1984), vol. 1, 155–156.

21. J. Moltmann, *The Crucified God: The Cross of Christ as the Foundation and Criticism of Christian Theology* (New York: Harper and Row, 1974), 249.

22. J. Moltmann, *The Trinity and the Kingdom of God* (London: SCM Press, 1981), 161. See also Roger Olson, "Trinity and Eschatology: The Historical Being of God in Jürgen Moltmann and Wolfhart Pannenberg," *Scottish Journal of Theology* 36 (1983): 213–227.

23. Moltmann, *The Trinity and the Kingdom*, 161.

24. Pannenberg, "Problems," 252.

25. See W. Pannenberg, " Appearance as the Arrival of the Future," in his *Theology and the Kingdom of God* (Philadelphia: Westminster, 1969), 127–143; and "The Trinitarian God," chapter 5 in his *Systematic Theology*, vol. 1 (Edinburgh: T & T Clark, 1991), 259–336. Also see R. Olson, "Wolfhart Pannenberg's Doctrine of the Trinity," *Scottish Journal of Theology* 43 (1990): 175–206.

26. Pannenberg, "Problems," 254.

27. See John Gresham Jr., "The Social Model of the Trinity and Its Critics," *Scottish Journal of Theology* 46 (1993): 325–343; John O'Donnell, "The Trinity as Divine Community," *Gregorianum* 69 (1988): 5–34; Ted Peters, *God as Trinity: Relationality and Temporality in Divine Life* (Louisville, Ky.: Westminster Press, 1993), 34–42; and Christoph Schwöbel and Colin Gunton, eds., *Persons, Divine and Human* (Edinburgh: T & T Clark, 1991).

28. Moltmann, *The Trinity and the Kingdom*, 150. In his *Trinity and Society* (New York: Orbis, 1988) Leonardo Boff has a similar position both in basing the unity of

the Trinity on the perichoretic community of three persons and in taking this community as a social program for human beings.

29. See Joseph Bracken, "Process Perspectives and Trinitarian Theology," *Word and Spirit* 8 (1986): 51–64; and Bracken, *The Triune Symbol: Persons, Process, and Community* (Lanham, Md.: University of America Press, 1985).

30. See George Khodr, "L'Esprit Saint dans la Tradition Orientale," in *Credo in Spiritum Sanctum. Atti del Congresso Theologico Internationale di Pneumatologia (1982)*. 2 vols. (Vatican: Libreria Editrice Vaticana, 1983), vol. 1, 377–408.

31. See Lukas Vischer, ed., *Spirit of God, Spirit of Christ: Ecumenical Reflections on the Filioque Controversy.* Faith and Order Document #103 (London: S.P.C.K., 1981); Y. Congar, *I Believe in the Holy Spirit*, vol. 3, *The River of Life Flows in the East and in the West* (New York: Seabury, 1983); "Contributions to an Agreement," 174–214; and Theodor Stylianopoulos, "An Ecumenical Solution to the Filioque Question?" *Journal of Ecumenical Studies* 28 (1991): 260–280.

32. See Hans Küng and Jürgen Moltmann, eds., *Conflicts about the Holy Spirit. Concilium*, vol. 128 (New York: Seabury, 1979).

33. For an example of one who now rejects Christianity because of the harm it does to women, see Daphne Hampson, *Theology and Feminism* (Oxford: Blackwell, 1990). In a review article on this book in *Scottish Journal of Theology* 43 (1990): 390–400, Rosemary R. Ruether does not accept Scripture as a reflection of a revelation as Vatican II does. She dichotomizes the future and "past events," and holds that "It is this redemptive future, not past events, which is ultimately normative" (399). Also on this question see the survey by Anne Carr, *Transforming Grace: Christian Tradition and Women's Experience* (San Francisco: Harper & Row, 1988), chapter 7, "Feminist Reflection on God"; Ted Peters, "The Battle over Trinitarian Language," *Dialog* 30 (1991): 44–49; and Donald Hook and Alvin Kimel, "The Pronouns of Deity: A Theolinguistic Critique of Feminist Proposals," *Scottish Journal of Theology* 46 (1993): 297–323.

34. Elizabeth Johnson, *She Who Is: The Mystery of God in Feminist Theological Discourse* (New York: Crossroad, 1992). Citations in the text here are to pages of this book.

35. See J. Farrelly, *God's Work in a Changing World* (Lanham, Md.: University Press of America, 1985; now distributed by the Council for Research in Values and Philosophy, Washington, D.C.) chapter 3, "Feminine Symbols and the Holy Spirit," 49–76.

36. Michael Welker, *God the Spirit* (Minneapolis: Fortress, 1994); Jürgen Moltmann, *The Spirit of Life: A Universal Affirmation* (Minneapolis: Fortress, 1993). Page citations in the text here are to these two books: W (Welker) or M (Moltmann).

37. See Douglas Schuurman, *Creation, Eschaton, and Ethics* (New York: Peter Lang, 1991), 125; Jürgen Moltmann, *Hope and Planning* (London: SCM Press, 1971), 117–118. I have argued against this dichotomy between nature and eschaton in *Faith in God through Jesus Christ. Foundational Theology II* (Collegeville, Minn.: Liturgical Press, 1997), 263–264, 269–274. In reference to Moltmann's and Welker's rejection of metaphysics, see *Modern Theology* 11 (1995): 1–161 for articles that show in postcritical modern theology new recognitions of a need for metaphysics.

38. See Angelo Amato, ed., *Trinità in Contesto* (Rome: Libreria Ateneo Salesiano, 1994) on Buddhism (213–224), Hinduism (171–190, 199–212), and Islam (223–272), and my *Belief in God in Our Time. Foundational Theology I* (Collegeville, Minn.: Liturgical Press, 1992), 277–299.

39. I have sought to develop this section of foundational theology in *Belief in God in Our Time*.

40. I have treated this in *Faith in God through Jesus Christ*.

41. See the Anglican–Roman Catholic and Lutheran–Catholic dialogue statement on authority in the church. The Orthodox accept ecumenical councils through the first eight centuries.

CHAPTER TWO

~

Scripture and the Roots of Christian Belief in the Trinity

In our theological study of the grounds and meaning of the Christian belief in the Trinity, we first turn to Scripture, the *norma normans non normata* of Christian belief. We turn to Scripture with questions we have from the present belief of the church, major difficulties with this belief, and diverse theological interpretations of it current in our time. We look for the roots of the Christian doctrine of the Trinity in Scripture. The formulation of the doctrine took centuries, though the church asserts that what its formulation expresses is what God revealed through Jesus Christ and his Spirit.

We look for grounds of our belief in the Trinity in Scripture in accord with the way that it mediates God's revelation. Did God reveal the mystery of the Trinity, and what did it mean, that is, what did it signify and what is its relevance to our lives? God's revelation was a dialogue with his people through many generations, coming to a definitive stage only with the ministry, death, and resurrection of Jesus and his sending the Holy Spirit. This revelation took place in the course of God's saving activity with his people, and it was mediated by such saving activity and the words that accompanied it. In fact, God's great actions, such as the liberation of Israel from slavery in Egypt and entrance into a covenant with them by the mediation of Moses' actions and words, were in reality symbols of God's dispositions toward his people—of who God is and who God's people were called to be.[1] The revelation of who God is occurred through his activity of saving his people. A deeper understanding of who God is was conveyed as in the course of history deeper dimensions of their need for salvation became apparent to God's people and

31

the inadequacy of earlier conceptions of this salvation became evident. The people's acceptance of Yahweh as their God, the tensions they experienced in this acceptance, and their resistance to belief in Yahweh shaped their identity.

It is only in the New Testament that the mystery of the Trinity was revealed. But there was a preparation for this in the earlier covenant with God's people. We shall then in this chapter treat (I) the preparation in the Old Testament for the revelation of the Trinity, recalling here also something of the Hellenistic world and intertestamental Judaism; (II) the ministry of Jesus and mystery of the Trinity; and (III) the early church's developing trinitarian belief in the apostolic age. And we will recur to some of these scriptural themes in later chapters. Here we seek only to show that the grounds and meaning of our belief in the Trinity are conveyed by revelation witnessed to by Scripture; a full treatment of any one of these themes would take us too far afield. Our call and identity as Christians depends upon our interaction with God who has revealed himself to be Father, Son, and Holy Spirit.

I. The Old Testament and Preparation for the Trinitarian Mystery

It is important to reflect on God's preparation to reveal the mystery of the Trinity. This mystery is the profoundest revelation of God, and it is characteristic of a personal interaction for one to reveal himself or herself to another more deeply only after lesser revelations, as the relationship itself becomes deeper. When we look back to this earlier special relationship between God and this particular people from the perspective of Christian belief in the Trinity, we can see stepping stones that lead toward this further revelation, without however reaching it. God was preparing and, indeed, cumulatively preparing his people for the further revelation he would give through Jesus Christ and his Spirit. Even the words used in the New Testament to express the mystery, such as 'Father', 'Word', 'Spirit', and 'Wisdom' are used in ways that are not totally new or discontinuous with God's earlier revelation. Rather, the earlier revelation providentially prepared for their later trinitarian use, while not detracting from the genuinely *new* character of Christian revelation.

We are not, we should add, saying that there is no divine preparation for peoples outside of Israel for the revelation of this mystery, though we hold that the preparation of Israel was special and more immediate than that of other peoples. In fact, we shall see that Wisdom literature and intertestamental Hellenistic Judaism used and adapted certain Hellenistic themes to write of God's Wisdom, Word, and Spirit. In the next chapter, when we treat the development of the doctrine of the Trinity in the patristic period, we shall see how the Fathers exploited some Hellenistic themes in articulating the mystery of the Trinity. In the ninth chapter we shall raise the question of how we, with our belief in God as triune, relate to world religions.

It is indeed important to reflect on this preparation. Part of the reason many Christians sense that the Trinity is not related to their lives comes from their similar feeling in reference to God, or at least to God understood in continuity with the Christian tradition. If the whole question of God is not sensed as vital to one's life, the question of the Trinity cannot be sensed as vital. Similarly, if people do not sense their need for a knowledge superior to their own, a power for salvation superior to their own, a forgiveness they cannot give themselves, a need for a wholeness for themselves and for the community of men and women that human beings cannot achieve, they will not be open to the mystery of the Trinity. The revelation of this mystery is only for those who have some deeper understanding and acceptance of themselves than that which much of our society fosters. We shall examine the Old Testament preparation through recalling something of the Old Testament message about God, and specifically about God as Father, God's Word, Spirit, and Wisdom.

Who the Israelites were and who the individuals were within this community depended on their belief that *God* had acted toward them to make them his people and who they believed God to be.[2] Their future was dependent upon the covenant God had made with them and their fidelity to God. Initially, Israelites generally were not monotheists; they committed themselves to worship Yahweh as their God but believed there were many gods. Monotheism has its clearest expression in II Isaiah centuries after the covenant (Is 45:14–25), and it had been a real struggle through the intervening generations for Israel to be faithful to God (or observe the Shema, Dt 6:4–6) rather than turn to other gods for their perceived needs, a struggle in which they frequently failed. The one and all-holy God was finally understood to be transcendent to all that is other than he, the creator of all (Is 40:21–22, 28), and to be the One whose glory is shown by his creation, saving deeds, and manifestations (Nm 14:21; Ex 14:18; 33:18). This God was also present to his people, whom he had chosen; it is he who had saved them from many oppressions from which there was no human escape; he was accessible, as the prayers of the Psalmist showed; the temple was a sign of his dwelling or presence among his people (1 Kgs 7:16–21). In fact, they called on images of a mother to express God's tenderness toward them: "Can a mother forget her infant, be without tenderness for the child of her womb? Even should she forget, I will never forget you" (Is 49:15).

This mysterious God, beyond any human measure and of whom Israel was forbidden to make images (Ex 20:4–6), was also spoken of as *Father*. Initially, he was spoken of only rarely as father, perhaps because many surrounding peoples considered their gods as their fathers by natural generation, as though they had been born of these gods. It was particularly in the postexilic period that God was called father. This relationship of paternity depended on his free and loving choice of Israel as his people, who were thereby his adopted children (Is 63:15–16; 64:7). God was the father in a special way of the king and of the Anointed One or Messiah who was to come (2 Sm 3:14; Ps 2), but also of the poor and weak for whom he cared (Ps 68:6). Still later he is considered father of the just one (Ws 2:1–23; 5:5) and father of all (Ws 14:3), because he created all. Correlatively, his people were his sons and daughters, and the king was his son by a special title. The major images of God in the Old Testament are masculine (king, warrior, father), but Israel found that these images did not do justice to God's relation to them and so to God. God is therefore spoken of also in motherly imagery (e.g., Hos 11:3–4, 8; Is 49:15). We shall also see the use of feminine metaphors below in the symbols of Spirit and Wisdom.   and Word and Spirit

There were mediators of God such as kings, prophets, and priests; and there would be future mediators of salvation, such as the Messiah, the suffering servant, and the Son of Man. But here we are interested in those mediating extensions or powers of God that were, toward the end of the Old Testament period, to different degrees personalized and used later to express the new mystery of God revealed in the New Testament. In the postexilic period, reverence for God and his name was so stressed among the Jews that they would not even pronounce the divine name. But at the same time the mediations of God were given greater emphasis as extensions of God's presence among his people.

One of these was the *Word* of God.[3] The most important Hebrew term for "word," *dabar*, signifies a content or what a thing was, as in Adam naming the animals. *Dabar* also signifies an active force, as when Isaac blessed his son Jacob. Words were ascribed to God as the word *of* God when it is said that God speaks or the prophet speaks the word of God. This is a metaphor; it is like a human word and yet not like it because God's word can be conveyed in different ways, such as through dreams or through events. God's word that came to Moses promised to liberate his people from Egypt and effected this (Ex 3:4ff). So the word of God is an intentional act; it conveys the will of God. We can see this, for example, in the commandments of the covenant that are called the words of God (Ex 20:1ff; 34:28). These words bring light and understanding (Ps 119:130); their purpose is life-giving. We can see

God's word in the prophetic word that comes to the prophets who convey it to the people for very specific historical circumstances (e.g., Jer 1:11; Ez 2:8f); the prophet becomes the mouth of God (Jer 15:19). We can see it in the creative word of God by which chaos was shaped and formed. God spoke and the universe was formed (Gn 1); "By the word of the Lord the heavens were made" (Ps 33:6). There is a certain personification of the word of God at times: "he sent forth his word to heal them and to snatch them from destruction" (Ps 107:20; see also Ps 119:81, 114, 147; 130:5; Ws 16:12; 18:15).

The *spirit* also mediates God's presence.[4] The word for spirit *(ruah)* initially meant wind or breath. The wind brought water from the Mediterranean in the form of rain to nourish fields and flocks, or a sirocco from the desert. And the Israelites thought that the seat of life was in the breath; God breathed into Adam the breath of life (Gn 2:7). This wind or breath was used also as a symbol to designate the divine dynamism or force operative in humans to make them capable of exceptional deeds for the liberation of the people and to bring the community to coalesce around such leaders, and so it was called the "spirit of the Lord." For example, the spirit of the Lord came upon Samson and he rose up as a defender of Israel (Jgs 13:25; 15:14–15). And the ecstatic state of the bands of prophets and of Saul when he joined them was ascribed to the spirit of God (1 Sm 10:10). Later, Saul was tormented by "an evil spirit sent by the Lord" (1 Sm 16:14). When Samuel anointed David, "the spirit of the Lord rushed upon David" (1 Sm 16:13).

Gradually, a more interior empowerment of the person and community in reference to God was ascribed to the spirit of God. Isaiah predicted that the spirit of the Lord would not only come to but would also "rest upon" the Anointed One who was to come to save his people, and by this he would receive "a spirit of wisdom and understanding, a spirit of counsel and of strength, a spirit of knowledge and of fear of the Lord" (Is 11:2). At the time of the exile, Ezekiel recognized that the renewal of Israel to be a faithful people would depend upon God's giving them a new heart and a new spirit (Ez 36:25–27). This recalls the Psalmist's prayer for "a steadfast spirit . . . your presence and your holy spirit . . . and a willing spirit" (Ps 51:12–14). Joel promised in an apocalyptic vein that on the day of the Lord God would pour out his spirit generously on humankind, on men and women, servants and handmaids (Jl 3:1–2). At times the "spirit of the Lord" was spoken of almost as a person, as in Isaiah: "they . . . grieved his holy spirit. . . . Where is he who put his holy spirit in their midst. . ." (Is 63:10, 11). The Book of Wisdom asserts that "the holy spirit of discipline flees deceit" (1:5) and asks "who ever knew your counsel, except you had given Wisdom and sent your holy spirit from on high?" (9:17).

We should note that the word of God and the spirit of God are interrelated at times in reference to God's creative and saving activity. In the first
chapter of Genesis, God speaks his word and different parts of creation are
formed; but before he spoke "the spirit of God was moving over the face of
the waters" (Gn 1:2 RSV; see also Ps 33:6). The word for this "moving"
(mrhpt) is also found in Deuteronomy 32:11 to describe God's encouraging
presence to his people in the desert after the Exodus: "As an eagle incites its
nestlings forth by *hovering* over its brood, so he spread his wings to receive
them and bore them up on his pinions." This image of an eagle symbioti-
cally inciting its young to fly by hovering over them is found also in the creation story. Creation and salvation are ascribed to God through his word
and his spirit. The word primarily defines, forms, shapes, or guides; the spirit
does not define or form so much as enliven. This, we propose, suggests mediations of God that are expressed in the one case by predominantly masculine and in the other case by predominantly feminine symbols, a theme
we will return to later.

Wisdom is still another mediation of God in the Old Testament important
for the New Testament articulation of the mystery of the Trinity. The word for
wisdom (*hokma, sophia*) indicated a practical knowledge, how to act in practical circumstances of all sorts, secular and religious, though primarily religious.
As Roland Murphy writes: "biblical wisdom is basically religious, not secular.
. . . That is to say, the sages held that there was a fundamental order in the
world, discernible by experience, and the teachings were designed to bring
about conformity with this order that had been determined by God."[5] The
psalms hold salvation and wisdom together, because they are focused on the
present life, both rehearsing God's saving deeds in Israel's history and presenting to God the distresses and needs of the individual. "The God of immediate
experience, i.e. the wisdom experience, is the creator who is also the *goel* or redeemer of Israel. He is 'the personal god' of patriarchal religion" (924). Behind
the wisdom literature is the wisdom experience: "The sayings, or the 'wisdom
teaching', are the encoding of a lived experience, and only facets of this encounter with reality can be captured in words. It is the encounter which generated the insights into the world and human beings" (925). It is only if a person has reverence for God that he will discern aright the implications of
experience of the world and of human life; that is why again and again wisdom
writers call for fear of the Lord as the beginning of wisdom (e.g., Prv 9:10; Jb
28:28). Wisdom is personified as Lady Wisdom (Jb 28; Prv 1, 8, 9; Bar 3:9–4:4;
Sir 24; Ws 7:1–9:18). She invites the simple, addresses the simple, gives an account of all the benefits she will give those who walk her ways. Wisdom literature identifies the righteous with the wise person (e.g., Prv 10-15). Since God

is the source of creation, what is taught by creation is taught by God, and so "Is Wisdom not the Lord, who turns toward creatures and summons them through creation, through wisdom experience?" (927).

At times Wisdom is identified with the book of the Law (e.g., Sir 24:23). But its mode of invitation is more feminine than the establishment of the Law, and the responsiveness it looks for is a kind of character formation (partly out of self-interest) and an openness to how God is speaking to one through experience, one's own and that of Israel's tradition. It seems that what was previously ascribed to the word of God on the one hand and to the spirit of God on the other are fused in Wisdom. For example, creation was ascribed to the word of God in Genesis 1, and Wisdom is later spoken of as acting in God's process of creation (Prv 8:27–30; Ws 7:22). Also Wisdom is called a spirit: "Wisdom is a kindly spirit" (Ws 1:6), and "the spirit of the Lord fills the world, is all-embracing, and knows what men say" (Ws 1:7); "in her is a spirit" (Ws 7:22). Perhaps, as we shall see in a New Testament text, Wisdom in the sense of *what* God teaches is more closely associated with the word, while Wisdom in the sense of the experiential access to this is more closely associated with spirit. On the whole, Wisdom is a feminine symbol of God more because of its association with spirit than with word. This theology of Wisdom appeals to a basic human openness to truth and goodness and promises great benefits coming from God to such as listen to her. Wisdom is presented as a gift of God that is an answer to prayer (Ws 9). It comes from God's word—mediated by creation and human experience—and spirit, and it evokes an open spirit and a listening to this word.

Some authors see an influence of Stoicism on the Book of Wisdom, and they note that while in earlier Greek thought *logos* and spirit (*pneuma*) were clearly distinct in their influence, in Stoicism they coalesced.[6] However, while in Stoicism the spirit that gave wisdom was not differentiated from the material order, in the Book of Wisdom and in the New Testament, it always comes from above. In Stoicism the immanent *logos* that structured the world was dynamic, and spirit pervading the world to shape it and give it life was identified with this. In the New Testament wisdom is associated both with the Holy Spirit and with the Son, but the dominant words for these trinitarian persons were not Wisdom, but rather Spirit on the one hand and Word or Son on the other.

God addresssed as father, and the personifications of Word, Spirit, and especially Wisdom indicate the divine guidance and empowerment that God shares with us and that we can gain by turning to him. Also these personifications suggest, perhaps, a fullness of divine being and even a plurality in the Godhead. There are other expressions that seemed in the past to suggest plurality in God. For example, in Genesis 1:26 "God said, 'Let us make man in our image, after our likeness'" (see also Gn 3:22; 11:7). God seems to appear in the form of three men to Abraham (Gn 18:1–15); and Isaiah hears the seraphim call out, "Holy, holy, holy is the Lord of hosts!" (Is 6:3). These are suggestive, but not indicative that the authors had any insight into the mystery of the Trinity.

It is helpful to recall briefly some elements of both the *Hellenistic world* and of the *intertestamental* period for Judaism in preparation for our study of the New Testament revelation of the mystery of the Trinity. This will show both the newness of this revelation and yet a kind of preparation for it that Irenaeus and others called providential. Here we shall first take a look at the Hellenistic world surrounding Palestine and the primitive church and then at the intertestamental period for Judaism. The latter's engagement in dialogue with Hellenism was itself a preparation of both cultures for further revelation and further engagement.

In the Hellenistic world at the time of the birth of Jesus Christ and of the Christian church, there were many religious tendencies, some of which made the acceptance of Christianity seem totally alien to many people and some of which made such acceptance seem feasible and indeed even a fulfillment of what people already believed. Specifically, in reference to the mystery of the Trinity, we recall the popular religions that were largely polytheistic, mythological, and naturalistic in the sense of a deification of natural forces, but we also recall that much of this had been subject to a philosophical critique for a long time.[7] Earlier classical philosophies had given way to some philosophies, such as Stoicism and Middle Platonism, that were more religious in their orientation and more engaged in directing individuals in their lives. Middle Platonism, prominent in the first two centuries of the Christian era, fostered belief in a God transcendent to our world of matter and mutability, and it integrated into the divine mind what had earlier been in Plato the "world of ideas," so that God was thought of as having within himself the *logos* by which he shaped the cosmos. Stoicism was a philosophy that showed wonder at the rational order that courses through the physical world and sought to bring human beings into accord with this order. It tended then to consider deity as immanent within the world and to meld the principle of order (*logos*) and movement (*pneuma* or spirit) that had earlier been distinguished, for example by Aristotle. Of the Greek concept of *pneuma* Hermann Kleinknecht writes that it is never spiritual in the strict sense but a vital natural force.[8] Also, there is a poetic and mythico-religious sense in Greek manticism that considers *pneuma* as an origin of knowledge (*epinoia*). In the

Pythia of Delphi the prophetess was considered to be endowed with a special and momentary ecstatic knowledge by the spirit arising from a cleft in the mountain or a well. Her enigmatic sayings were translated then by the Delphic priests or prophets.

Though monistic, there is a religious sense in some Stoics that we can see in Seneca, who writes: "A holy spirit dwells in us, the discerner of good and evil. . . . No man is good without God. . . . A divine power descends toward us, but the greater part is there from which it descends" (Epistle 41: 2). And: "Do you marvel that man goes to God? God comes to men; indeed he comes to what is deepest in men; no mind is good without God" (73:16).

In reference to intertestamental Judaism, we can make the following points. In Palestinian Judaism there are many indications that there was a widespread expectation that a new age was near and a profound longing for this. Sometimes God's coming intervention was imagined as without a mediator. Frequently, the hope was expressed for a messianic figure, whom God would send to renew his people. In one passage this expectation was spoken of in terms of the king who would be the "Lord Messiah" (*christos kyrios*) (Psalms of Solomon 17:32).[9] In part, this longed-for renewal was envisioned as a throwing off of oppressors, but even more as an interior renewal of the people of God. This hope also took the form at times of apocalyptic expectations. The rabbis considered the present an age without the Spirit, because of the lack of prophets since the age of Aggeus, Zacharia, and Malachi. The coming of the Spirit was hoped for in the last days. Qumran, on the other hand, shows a kind of dualism between the spirit of truth and the lying spirit; it held that the Spirit was present in their own community.

As an example of Hellenistic Judaism we may recall Philo of Alexandria who lived c. 50 B.C. to c. 50 A.D.[10] He wished to give a philosophical interpretation of the Old Testament, and used allegory largely to get to its deeper meaning. In this interpretation he used much Greek philosophy, particularly Stoicism and Platonism. He did not wish to compromise his Jewish beliefs, but to commend them to the larger culture and to Jews drawn by this culture. With Platonism he stressed that God formed the world from his ideas, considered as his own thoughts. With Stoicism, he understood *logos* as a divine principle operative throughout the world and active as a divine power. To preserve God's transcendence he identified intermediaries between God and the world, the highest of which was *logos*. The *logos* is the answer to the problem of how God enters into relation with this world, how the infinite relates to the finite. Philo describes *logos* in different ways—as the instrument in the creation of the world, the firstborn son of God, the angel of Yahweh, the ideal high priest vested with the world, and so forth, and above all as "second God."

But he avoids ascribing divinity to him in any unreserved sense. Some texts seem to indicate the *logos* is a person, but others do not. We will return to Philo when we consider the prologue to John's gospel.

II. The Ministry of Jesus and the Mystery of the Trinity

The mystery of the Trinity was revealed, Christians hold, through the life, ministry, death, resurrection, and exaltation of Jesus and through the sending of the Holy Spirit by Jesus and the Father, though it is not articulated as such in the New Testament.[11] It is only through the ministry, death, and resurrection of Jesus and the sending of the Spirit that Jesus is clearly declared Lord and Christ (Acts 2:36) and that one can say "Jesus is Lord" (1 Cor 12:3). It is only through the historical and free missions of Jesus Christ and the Spirit—the Trinity in the economy of salvation—that the Trinity is communicated and revealed to us; the Trinity is presented as a soteriological mystery. It is not enough to start from what is clearest in reference to this mystery in the New Testament. If we would start, for example, from John's prologue, we would start from the term of a long period of reflection in the primitive church and lose the experience that led to this profound insight. There would be a danger that we would divorce the Christ of faith from the Jesus of history. The mystery of the Trinity might consequently be presented as an appendix or superfluous addition to the center of Christ's saving action, rather than as a deep penetration of Jesus' salvific work, necessary for its understanding. We must start with the ministry of Jesus as reflected in the Synoptics, even though we recognize that the evangelists wrote these texts in the light of Jesus' resurrection, the coming of the Holy Spirit, and the developing understanding of the early church. The post-Easter faith of the church was not divorced from the ministry of Jesus but rather allowed the apostles and evangelists to understand more deeply what Jesus actually said and did in his public ministry (Jn 14:26; 15:26).

Our question here then is whether the Trinity is implicitly witnessed to in the ministry of Jesus. To understand the ministry of Jesus do we need to see it in trinitarian terms? Is the mystery of the Trinity implicitly revealed in what Jesus offered those who believed and in the very way that Jesus proclaimed and mediated the kingdom of God or salvation? We depend here on a theme developed in foundational theology, namely, that the gospels were substantially faithful to the words and deeds of Jesus and that the evangelists presented these in such a way that their readers could see what God was doing and revealing through this ministry. These writings, like the early Christian community, were based on the belief that God was intervening and expressing his revelation for the salvation of his people through Jesus. It was primarily God's creative imagination that was behind the symbolic activity and words by which Jesus himself proclaimed the kingdom of God and behind the creative imagination of the evangelists in constructing their gospels. What was central to Jesus' ministry was the proclamation and mediation of God's offer of salvation or the kingdom of God. Through Jesus God offered this salvation and revealed it. Building on this, we now ask whether and how through his mediation of the kingdom there is an implicit revelation of the Trinity in the ministry of Jesus.

The evangelists summarized the ministry of Jesus by recounting his words: "This is the time of fulfillment. The kingdom of God is at hand. Repent, and believe the gospel" (Mk 1:15, par.). Jesus proclaimed that God was offering his people the definitive salvation that was the fulfillment of all the earlier promises. His offer of salvation would be received by those who repented and believed. He proclaimed this through words and deeds; and his ministry, deeds, word, and person were a symbolic presence of God's offer of this salvation to his people. Does this mediation of the kingdom offer us the roots of the revelation of the mystery of the Trinity, of God as Father, of Jesus as Son, and of the Holy Spirit? Is such a revelation implicit in Jesus' ministry, as the early church came to believe?

Jesus was proclaiming not himself but what God was doing. Jesus proclaimed the God of the Old Testament. He is moreover the creator of the world and provides for his creatures; before him one should have reverence (Mt 5:34–35). All are called to love God with their whole heart, and love others as themselves (Mt 22:37–40). We should note that the word 'God' in the New Testament almost always refers to the Father.[12] Jesus spoke of him as Father in his care for men and women (Mt 6:25–34), and one whom the people should address confidently as "our Father" (Mt 6:9–15). Jesus' actions were a symbol of what God was doing, and his words and deeds were God's revelation. Like the Father in the parable of the prodigal son (Lk 15:11–32), God was taking loving initiative in reconciling his son to himself and seeking to reconcile his sons with one another. And like a woman who has found a lost coin, God rejoices at the sinner who repents (Lk 15:8–10). This God was through the mediation of Jesus offering salvation to his people and proclaiming this offer. He was forgiving sins (Mk 2:5–11), for who but God can forgive sins. He was exorcising demons (Mt 12:24–32, par.), because such exorcisms can only happen by the "finger of God" (Lk 11:20). These actions were a sign that the kingdom of God had come among the people. God's saving power came through this man to those who believed and it healed them, another sign of God's saving presence promised of old (Lk 7:2; Is 35:5–6;

61:1). We will return in a later chapter (chapter 6) to a consideration of God as Father and contemporary difficulties raised against this.

Behind the titles explicitly conferred upon Jesus during his lifetime and those used by himself—many of which are controverted by exegetes—there is an implicit Christology in his actions and words that entails a relation to God that is unique and breaks through the limits of all categories for mediators in the Old Testament (see Lk 11:31–32; 20:41–44, par.).

This uniqueness of Jesus' relation to God is shown by his referring to God as 'Abba' and his consciousness of himself as *Son*. This word 'Son' had a broader reference at the time of Jesus than it had in later Christian reference to Jesus, for it could refer to Israel, the angels, the king, and the righteous in their relation to God. The gospels indicate that this term was used by Jesus of himself:

> Jesus speaks of God as his father (Mark 3 times . . . Matthew's special material 31, John over 100).
>
> There is sufficient indication that the process that permitted Christians to call Jesus Son of God had already begun with Jesus himself. The basic data is Jesus' habit, as it appears to have been, of addressing God as "Father" in prayer . . . the Aramaic *abba* (so Mark 14:36) . . . a family word, expressive of intimate family relationship. So the deduction lies close to hand that Jesus used it because he understood (we may even say experienced) his relationship to God in prayer in such intimate terms.[13]

Jesus taught his disciples to pray to God as "Our Father" (Mt 6:9), but he did not identify their relationship with the Father with his own, and the early church understood that the disciples of Jesus are God's sons and daughters because through faith they were given a share in Jesus' relation to the Father. Their greatest and only fulfillment comes from entering into the relationship with the Father that Jesus himself has. It became more and more apparent to Christians that the measure of the Father's love for them was shown above all in his sending Jesus, his Son, to save them (see the parable of unjust tenants, Mt 21:33–46; and later statements of Paul [Rom 8:32] and John [3:16–17]). Finally, this leads to the conviction that "God is love" (1 Jn 4:15).

Jesus' relation to the Father is also seen in his proclamation of the kingdom as a divine revelation. He mediated God's word in a way that totally transcended the way that the prophets of old had done. He felt free to quote the Law that had come from God and yet modify it, getting to its source, purpose, and deeper meaning, saying "But I say to you" (Mt 5:22, 28, 32, 34, 39, 44). He does not say, as the prophets did, "The word of God came to me," but pronounces on the Law on his own authority as unique mediator and

Son. He presents his words as superseding the Law, not abolishing it but fulfilling it (Mt 5:17). He shows a knowledge of the Father's intentions that is wholly confident and has a basis in a relationship with the Father that is marked by a mutuality; each is identified through relation to the other. He praises the Father for having revealed his mysteries to the little ones: "Yes, Father, such has been your gracious will. All things have been handed over to me by my Father. No one knows the Son except the Father, and no one knows the Father except the Son and anyone to whom the Son wishes to reveal him" (Mt 11:26-27).[14] In its context Jesus' claim refers, in a way more limited than John's comparable statements, to a knowledge that is connected with Jesus' and his disciples' proclamation of the kingdom, and within this to a mutuality between Father and Son. Similarly, Jesus speaks in words that recall Lady Wisdom's invitation to the simple in Sirach and suggests almost an identification between himself as Son and Wisdom (Mt 11:28–29; see Sir 51:23, 26), though this passage may in part have been due to Matthew's editing of Jesus' words. We see in his ministry a form of mediating and revealing the saving Lordship of God among his people that implies a claim that is at the root of the later development of Christology.

Such claims may well be, as all the evangelists indicate, what led to the growing opposition toward him by the leaders of the Jews and his condemnation and death. At the trial of Jesus before the Sanhedrin, Mark recounts the high priest's question and Jesus' response: "'Are you the Messiah, the son of the Blessed One?' Then Jesus answered, 'I am; and you will see the Son of Man seated at the right hand of the Power and coming with the clouds of heaven'" (Mk 14:61–62).

While Jesus says very little directly about the Holy Spirit during his ministry, there is the frequent theme of *dynamis* or power coming from him in his healings (Mk 5:30; par.) and his exorcisms (Mt 12:22–32, par). Luke speaks of the power by which Jesus exorcised as "the finger of God" (11:20; Q [the collection of "sayings of Jesus" that many exegetes infer from the way that Matthew and Luke cite these at times with identical words]), but Matthew perhaps retouched this in terms of how the early church understood this power when in his parallel passage Jesus asserts that he exorcises by "the Spirit of God" (Mt 12:28). John the Baptist had prophesied that the one who came after him "will baptize you with the holy Spirit and fire" (Mt 3:11; par.); and, according to the evangelist John, he was told, "On whomever you see the Spirit come down and remain, he is the one who will baptize with the holy Spirit" (Jn 1:33). When John baptized Jesus, there was a theophany, probably for both Jesus and John, in which the Spirit was seen to descend like a dove and the Father's voice was heard: "This is my beloved Son, with whom

I am well pleased" (Mt 3:16–17). Jesus was understood to be a charismatic, and Luke recounts that he opened his ministry in Nazareth by choosing a reading in the synagogue: "The Spirit of the Lord is upon me, because he has anointed me to bring glad tidings to the poor" (Lk 4:18; see Is 61:1–2). The Spirit seems to take initiative in empowering Jesus for ministry, as the Spirit was earlier acting in the conception itself of Jesus—a theme important for a contemporary Spirit Christology. The three Synoptics recount Jesus' warnings against those who blaspheme against the Holy Spirit (Mk 3:29, par.). This warning fits in so well with the situation in which the opponents of Jesus seek to give another interpretation to his exorcisms, that it most probably reflects the words of Jesus.

There is then sufficient material in the Synoptics that reflects the ministry of Jesus to show that there is implicit here a threefold activity in his mediation of God's saving presence, that of the Father, of the Son, and of the Holy Spirit. This implication was not clear enough for the closest disciples of Jesus to understand, but it shows that the early church's developing proclamation of the Trinity was not discontinuous with but rather grounded in and essential for understanding the meaning of Jesus' ministry.

III. The Developing Trinitarian Belief of the Apostolic Age

During the apostolic age, as reflected in the books of the New Testament, we see a development of Christian belief in God as Father, Son, and Holy Spirit who are divine, personal, and distinct from one another, although the words and concepts in which the later church expressed its trinitarian belief are not yet present. During this period the development has its origin in the experience of the resurrected Jesus and the ecstatic experience ascribed to the Holy Spirit. As James Dunn writes:

> After Jesus' death the earliest Christian community sprang directly from a sequence of epochal experiences of two distinct sorts—experiences in which Jesus appeared to individuals and groups to be recognized as the one who had already experienced the eschatological resurrection from the dead, and experiences of religious ecstasy and enthusiasm recognized as the manifestation of the eschatological Spirit.[15]

We will not treat here the historical question of the resurrection of Jesus and its meaning. We will treat the gradual emergence, starting from these experiences, of the primitive Christian belief in Jesus as divine, the Holy Spirit as divine and personal, and of the early tripartite expressions of belief in God, Father, Son, and Holy Spirit, though these themes necessarily overlap. It is by this development that the understanding of the definitive salvation and revelation mediated by Jesus Christ was deepened, and it was by this greater penetration into the meaning of this salvation and revelation that the mystery of God as Father, Son, and Holy Spirit was conveyed and expressed. This early emergence of belief shows that the Trinity in the economy of salvation is the Trinity in itself, though the expression of the latter was not conceptually developed. At the end of this chapter we will compare what we find here to some varied contemporary theological interpretations of the Trinity.

1. The Apostolic Age and Belief in the Divinity of Jesus

An important present contrast on this issue is between exegetes like James Dunn who doubt that Paul taught the personal preexistence of one who became Christ, and those like Brendan Byrne who contests Dunn's view. Dunn accepts John's teaching that the Word became flesh and that this is normative for Christians, but one issue is whether earlier New Testament writings taught a personal divine preexistence for the Son or Christ.[16] Another important contrast is between those (again like James Dunn) who think that Paul blurred the distinction between the exalted Christ and the Spirit, and those who hold just the opposite.[17]

What is essential to recall is that the experiences of the resurrected Jesus and of the Spirit were interpreted within an apocalyptic tradition.[18] In Daniel (12:1–3) the resurrection from the dead was prophesied for the last days, and in Joel (3:1–5) the generous outpouring of the Spirit was similarly prophesied for the last days. If the first fruits of the harvest are already in hand, the rest will follow shortly; similarly, Jesus' resurrection constitutes such first fruits, and the general resurrection would come soon, preceded by Jesus' return (e.g., 1 Thes 1:10; 4:14–18; 1 Cor 15:20). It seems that the first ascription of divinity to Jesus was in reference to the divine powers of judgment and salvation that he would exercise when he came again in glory. The primitive Christian prayer, *Marana tha*, "O Lord, come!" (1 Cor 16:22, see Rv 22:20) reflects this, for it associates Jesus' Lordship with his coming that was yearned for. At his coming, he will save those who believe in him, and he will judge all. These are divine prerogatives. Salvation was initially considered, in accord with the apocalyptic tradition, a future reality, one that would be given when Jesus came again (see, e.g., 1 Cor 5:5; Rom 5:9; Heb 9:28). Thus the kingdom was expected: "Thy kingdom come" (Lk 11:2). Through his death and resurrection, Jesus won this for us; and he won the position of being the agent of this salvation, as Philippians 2:9–11 asserts. For the Jewish mind, one's identity is shown by one's functions and relationships, and the first Christians are here ascribing divinity to the parousiac Jesus in virtue of his expected exercise of divine powers. There is then a real sense in which Jesus becomes Lord as this concerns the exercise of a divine function.

It was soon realized that rather than becoming Lord in the sense of exercising the divine prerogatives of saving and judging only when he came again, Jesus was already Lord through the resurrection and glorification. Thus, Paul proclaims "the gospel about his Son, descended from David according to the flesh, but established as Son of God *in power* according to the spirit of holiness through the resurrection from the dead, Jesus Christ our Lord" (Rom 1:3). Through his death and resurrection and glorification or ascension to the right hand of the Father, Jesus has already become "a life giving Spirit" (1 Cor 15:45) and "Lord to the glory of God the Father" (Phil 2:11). What was expected to happen when Jesus comes again is *already* in part happening now; that future salvation is already being mediated to us in part from Jesus' exercise in the age to come of that power of the age to come, the gift of the Spirit (Acts 2:33). The first Christians sought an understanding of what happened in texts of the Old Testament, and one that they used was Psalm 110:1: "The Lord said to my Lord, 'Sit at my right hand until I make your enemies your footstool.'" Through his death and resurrection and exaltation or ascension, Jesus sat at God's right hand and was 'Lord'. As the expected future coming or 'adventus' of Jesus is from the age to come, so too the salvation that comes to us now is an 'adventus' from the age to come and a gift of the power of the age to come. Traditional soteriology has emphasized that salvation came to us from the past, because it concentrated on how Jesus won this for us, namely, through his death and resurrection. But it lost the early church's sense that what he won for us comes to us now from the future or the age to come and meets us in a way that is similar to and an anticipation of the way that Jesus will meet us at the *parousia*.

This relationship of the exalted Christ to the Spirit has led some exegetes to hold that for Paul these were not distinct. However, counter to this interpretation, we can show with exegetes like Gordon Fee that the blurring of the distinction is based on misinterpretations of certain passages of Paul, and with exegetes like Max Turner that Paul's assertion that the exalted Christ bestows the Spirit presupposes both the distinction and the divinity of Christ and the Spirit. This is counter to some forms of 'Spirit Christology' current today.

One passage used to blur the distinction is Paul's statement that "the Lord is the Spirit" in 2 Corinthians 3:17. But here Paul is using for his purposes a free adaptation of Exodus 34:34 where it is said, "Whenever Moses entered the presence of the LORD to converse with him, he removed the veil until he came out again." For his present argument—that if the Jews turn to the

Spirit, the veil of unbelief will be removed—Paul uses a literary device (*midrash pesher*), and says the Lord of Exodus is the Spirit. He is here identifying the Spirit neither with the God (Father) nor with Christ; in fact, he goes on to speak of the Spirit as the Spirit of the Lord (here taking "Lord" in the meaning of the Exodus passage as it was written) in "Where the Spirit of the Lord is, there is freedom." And in the following verse (2 Cor 3:18), he speaks of Christ as the "glory of the Lord" into whose image we are to be transformed by "the Lord who is the Spirit." Similarly, when Paul plays on the comparison and contrast between Adam and the exalted Christ in 1 Corinthians 15:45, saying that while Adam was "a living being" and thus gave life, Christ is for him "a life-giving spirit," not *the* life-giving Spirit. Neither this nor similar passages (e.g., Rom 1:4; 8:9–11) can support a blurring of the distinction between Christ and the Spirit.

Fee makes the point that we should begin methodically where Paul begins, not with several obscure passages. Paul was a monotheist who met Jesus on the way to Damascus and subsequently encountered the Holy Spirit. This changed his understanding of the one God and thus too our human existence. God is saving us through the redemptive work of Christ and our appropriation of this by the Holy Spirit. By this Paul's "understanding of God had become functionally trinitarian and . . . the distinctions between Father, Son and Spirit were presuppositional for him" (Fee, 327). This is shown by his trinitarian texts, for example, 2 Corinthians 13:13: "The grace of the Lord Jesus Christ and the love of God and the fellowship of the holy Spirit be with all of you." Here Paul does not "*assert* the deity of Christ and the Spirit. But what he does is to *equate the activity of the three divine persons* (to use the language of a later time) *in concert and in one prayer*, with the clause about God the Father standing in second place" (Fee, 328).

With similar effect, Max Turner argues from texts such as Acts 2:33 and others that "the exalted Jesus is regarded as standing in that sort of relationship to the Spirit of God that in Judaism and early Christianity normally characterizes God's own relationship to the Spirit; that is, the Spirit mediates the person and actions of the exalted Lord . . . and the Spirit of God has thus become the 'Spirit of Christ' too" (Turner, 413). Jesus, for example, becomes the author of the charismata that are the gifts and operations of the Spirit. For Jesus to pour out the Spirit is beyond anything the Old Testament ascribes to any creature, for the Spirit of God there is so identified with God. Thus, Turner argues that

> if Jesus' "lordship" of the Spirit in the sphere of salvation promotes the conclusion that Jesus must somehow be fully one with God, that same experience

of lordship would also press in the direction of a trinitarian understanding of the Spirit (for it otherwise led to the blasphemous assertion of the Son's "lordship" over the Father, or to demotion of the Spirit to a nondivine mediating power—neither of which pertains). (Turner, 423–424)

For Paul, the Spirit is said to be the Spirit of God much more frequently than the Spirit of Christ. We will return later to point out distinctions between the salvific actions of Christ and those of the Spirit.

While it may be, as some exegetes hold, that John's incarnation Christology is the final development of the Christology of the apostolic age, the initial Christian view of Jesus *becoming* Lord was consistent with a belief in the preexistence of the one who is Jesus Christ, and a preexistence that involves personal choice. And it may be, as some exegetes hold, that Paul asserted the preexistence of a personal divine being who became human in Jesus. The interpretation of Jesus as Son in terms of the Old Testament teaching on Wisdom probably helped the early church to understand the Sonship of Jesus as compatible with Jewish monotheism earlier than some exegetes think this happened. For example, the hymn in Philippians speaks of Christ: "Who, though he was in the form of God, did not regard equality with God something to be grasped. Rather he emptied himself . . ." (Phil 2:6–7). Dunn interprets this in the line of Jesus as the second Adam. The first Adam, made in the image and likeness of God, did grasp at equality with God, but Jesus did not. However, according to Byrne and others, Paul seems to be ascribing here a *free choice* to the preexistent one who was in the form of God and yet emptied himself and became a slave for us, and so Paul supposes a preexistence that is personal.[19]

This Philippians passage is a pre-Pauline Christian hymn, so it may be that in the context of worship the community burst forth to an expression of faith that leaps beyond that of many other Christians at the time. Paul may be ascribing the same kind of preexistence to the Son in writing about God sending his Son (Rom 8:3; Gal 4:4) and, "He who did not spare his own Son but handed him over for us all, how will he not also give us everything else along with him?" (Rom 8:32). Also, in reminding Corinthians that "for your sake he [our Lord Jesus Christ] became poor although he was rich" (2 Cor 8:9), Paul seems to suppose a personal preexistence of Christ.

In proclaiming to the Corinthians "Christ the power of God and the wisdom of God" (1 Cor 1:24), Paul is adapting his message to the broader Hellenistic world and using the wisdom tradition of the Old Testament for this purpose. Some exegetes hold that he implies only the preexistence the Old Testament ascribes to God's wisdom and not a personal preexistence, but the question is whether Paul's teaching on the Son should be reduced to this Old Testament wisdom teaching or whether the Old Testament preexistent wisdom teaching helps Paul to recognize as consistent with monotheism the preexistent Son as a personal, divine reality who freely and generously became human in Jesus Christ. The latter seems more consistent with some of Paul's statements that we recalled above.

While Jesus had been declared by Paul to be "Son of God in power" by the resurrection (Rom 1:4), by the time the gospels were written it was thought he must already have had in his ministry the anointing that made him Messiah and Son of God. The synoptic authors saw christological implications in the baptism of Jesus and, later, in his very conception. Thus, the earliest of the gospels, Mark, shows that in his baptism Jesus was declared to be Son of God. On coming up out of the water after his baptism by John, "a voice came from the heavens, 'You are my beloved Son; with you I am well pleased'" (Mk 1:11). Son of God was a very significant title for Mark (see 15:39).

In Luke and Matthew, the christological moment is ascribed particularly to Jesus' very conception. Luke recounts the words of the angel to Mary at the annunciation about the son she would bear: "He will be great and will be called Son of the Most High, and the Lord God will give him the throne of David his father . . . the child to be born will be called the Son of God" (1:32, 35). Paul had distinguished the time of Jesus' being established as Son of God in power from that of his being Son of David (Rom 1:3–4), but Luke ascribes both of these to his very conception. Similarly, Matthew recounts that it is through the Holy Spirit that Mary conceived her son in fulfillment of the prophecy: "'Behold, the virgin shall be with child and bear a son, and they shall name him Emmanuel,' which means 'God with us'" (1:23), and uses the title 'Son of God' of Jesus over twenty times. The title 'Son of God' could have varied meanings at the time of Jesus, such as the "just one" or the Messiah, but for Matthew it had a still greater meaning, for it pointed to divinity. In this he is expressing an understanding of Jesus beyond that of Jesus' closest disciples during Jesus' ministry, and he is doing so from the greater insight of the early church. But this insight had grounds in what Jesus said and did in his ministry. Neither Luke nor Matthew explicitly ascribe preexistence to this Son of God. Jesus was given the mission and dignity of Messiah and Son of God by baptism or conception, but this is not counter to the earliest Christian view that he came to his definitive exercise of the power to save and judge through his death, resurrection, and exaltation, or was then "established as Son of God in power" (Rom 1:4).

In Colossians, written probably by a disciple of Paul, the author uses the wisdom tradition of Israel and Hellenistic Judaism to explicitly ascribe a kind

of preexistence to Christ. One problem this community may have been facing was the sense, prevalent among many people of their time and place, that
their lives were threatened by cosmic forces. And some Christians, perhaps
under the influence of Jewish apocalypticism, had taught Christians that
they must seek wisdom not only in Jesus Christ but also in "thrones or dom-
inations or principalities or powers" (1:16).[20] Counter to this, the author
turns to the Jewish wisdom literature to ascribe all wisdom to Jesus: "He is
the image of the invisible God, the firstborn of all creation. For in him were
created all things in heaven and on earth. . . . He is before all things, and in
him all things hold together" (1:15–16, 17; see Prv 8:21–31; Ws 7:22–8:1; Sir
1:4). In him "are hidden all the treasures of wisdom and knowledge" (2:3).
But is this a personal preexistence? James Dunn cast doubt upon this,[21] but
with Byrne and others, we suggest that the Old Testament wisdom tradition
allowed Christians to see early that ascribing divine Sonship to the one who
became Jesus Christ was not counter to Jewish monotheism. They ascribed
Wisdom's attributes to one who was God's or the Father's "beloved Son" (Col
1:13) and thus seemingly to one who had a *personal* preexistence and not
only to one identified with the divine design or agency. Thus, the Colossians
should put their whole trust in Jesus Christ who is the fullness of divine wisdom and who will save them from all alien forces. We will see that such
phrases were later used by Arius to argue that though the Son was the first-
born of all creation, there was a time when he was not.

It was in the Johannine writings that the preexistence and divinity of Jesus as Son of God was expressed most forcefully. The community from which
these writings came, toward the end of the first century and beginning of the
second, has been studied in reference to its Christology quite thoroughly in
recent decades.[22] Readers can find elsewhere a study of the development of
this community and its Christology. Here we will concentrate on the prologue and then much more briefly on the body of the gospel of John and the
Johannine epistles.

It is widely agreed that the prologue of John's gospel (John 1:1–18) includes and adapts an earlier hymn.[23] There is not full agreement on what this
preceding hymn was, but there is substantial agreement, based largely on the
unified structure and rhythm of this hymn. Dunn holds that in this pre-
Christian hymn: "prior to v. 14 nothing has been said which would be strange
to a Hellenistic Jew familiar with the Wisdom tradition or the sort of mystical philosophizing that we find in Philo" (Dunn, 241). This pre-Christian
hymn is not gnostic; it is probably a fragment of an ancient myth of Wisdom
adapted to 'Word' in a Judaeo-Hellenistic milieu, reflecting the medium by

which the transcendent God made contact with the created world. This part of the hymn is thought by some exegetes to come from the same milieu as Philo's efforts came from.   *John 1:14*

In integrating this pre-Christian hymn within his gospel, the author, and perhaps also an earlier Christian community, adds the key verse 14 and identifies the Word with the Son of God, the term by which he designates Jesus throughout the gospel. By doing this he gives a specifically Christian meaning to the whole of the poem, asserting a personal preexistence of the Word as divine in the proper sense; it is this personal preexistent Word who became flesh in Jesus Christ. The reason for the insertion of this prologue into John's gospel is that "only the demonstration of the divine origin of the revealer can throw proper light on his unique significance for salvation, as it is later displayed in the words and work of the earthly Jesus" (Schnackenburg, 224). Or, as Moloney writes: *but John the BD?*

> The positioning of the prologue at the very beginning of the narrative is part of the real author's strategy. The reader comes to the prose narrative section of the Gospel (1:19–20:31) armed with the information provided in the poetic narrative of the prologue. . . . Things will not happen as the reader of the prologue might expect. This is so because the prose narrative is a story of God's self-revelation within the context of "the wayward paths of human freedom." (Moloney, 25)

The structure of the hymn as incorporated in the prologue may be seen as three sections: verses 1–5 on the preexistent being of the *Logos*; 6–13 on the coming of the Logos to the world of men, with the Incarnation hinted at; and 14–16 or 18 on the event of the Incarnation and its meaning for believers.

In verse 1, "In the beginning was the Word (*o Logos*), and the Word was with God (*pros ton Theon*), and the Word was God (*Theos*)," the threefold "was" indicates first that the Word exists outside time, then that he has personal communion with God (*o Theos*, with the article), and then that he is divine (*Theos*, without the article) or "what God was, the Word also was" (Moloney, 28). The Word here does not just designate God's function of communicating; it is different from the metaphors of Wisdom (Ws 7:25f). Rather, the Word is a personal preexisting divine being. "It is only the fullness of divine being . . . which guarantees his [Jesus'] absolute power as revealer and redeemer (cf 3:35)" (Schnackenburg, 234). The prologue begins as the book of Genesis begins, "In the beginning," because what Jesus initiates is a new creation. In Genesis, we hear that God made the world *by* his word (Gn 1; also Ps 33:6, 9; 147:15–18); so in verse 3, all things are said to be made by the Word. It is also asserted in verses 4–5 that this Logos has a relation to the human world, as giving light and life: "Whether and how long since the work of creation this task of Logos, to give light to men, was actually performed is not specifically considered here" (Schnackenburg, 242). The light shone in the darkness, but the darkness did not comprehend it, that is, embrace it with mind and will, or overcome it. In fact, in the original hymn verse 11, "He came to what was his own, but his own people did not accept him," may have referred to Wisdom's historical comings to God's own people (Wis 7:7), but in the present prologue it refers to the Incarnate Word. The addition to the pre-Johannine hymn of verses 6–8 refers to John the Baptist's witness to the light that all might believe. Verses 12–13 show the hand of the evangelist.

A climax is reached in verse 14: "And the Word became flesh and made his dwelling among us, and we saw his glory, the glory of the Father's only Son, full of grace and truth." This may have been part of a pre-Johannine Christian hymn, because John's gospel itself does not use the title 'Word' of Jesus. This coming of the Word in the Incarnation is distinct from earlier spiritual comings of the Logos. It is a turning point in the history of salvation. The Word comes to such an extent that he became flesh—indicating the createdness and vulnerability of the human condition. This is very different from gnostic views or from mythologies, and indeed "all other religions of redemption in Hellenism and Gnosticism" (Schnackenburg, 267). In verse 18, "The only-begotten Son, who is in the bosom of the Father, he has brought good tidings" (Schnackenburg's translation, 277–278); this verse shows that "the revealer can speak with authority, because he is the only-begotten, and remains most intimately united to his Father, even in his earthly life, at one with him in nature and action" (Schnackenburg, 280).

We should make a few further comments on the origin and meaning of Logos or Word in the prologue. The closest parallel to John's use of Word here is Jewish wisdom theology, but John's Logos "is on another plane, by reason of the personal character of the Logos, his real personal pre-existence and above all his incarnation" (Schnackenburg, 481). This Logos is different from Greek philosophical use of this concept, because the latter is a cosmic principle, not a person. There is precedence in the Old Testament for the use of the 'word', as that by which God creates, reveals, and saves; but this is not its main source. Word and wisdom are closely related in the Old Testament (e.g., Wis 9:1f). As we said above, Logos occurs frequently in Philo. But John's Word is personal and becomes incarnate in a historical figure; this is radically different from Philo's conception. "The personal character of the Logos in the hymn is dictated by Christian belief in the historical coming of Jesus as Christ-Logos . . . this faith was the only possible source of the per-

sonal character being asserted so definitely" (Schnackenburg, 493). The prologue shows also the inadequacy of a Spirit Christology that ascribes divinity
to Jesus only in the sense that the Spirit came upon him. Such a Spirit Christology would be completely at odds with the message of John who sees the
Word as a person, as we now would call him, distinct from the Spirit, who
was "another Paraclete" (14:15).

Judaism had a notion of preexistence of certain goods, such as the Torah,
that were very important for human beings (see also Mt 25:34). In addition
to the preexistence of Wisdom we mentioned above, this 'preexistence'
meant that these goods were present in the thoughts and plans of God; God
had prepared them beforehand. In Gnosticism there is a sense of the preexistence of the *pneuma* dwelling in the deepest part of a person; here cosmogony was used as a way of understanding the real nature of human beings.
But in the prologue, the Logos existed in the beginning, had a personal communion with "the God," and was divine; this is a personal preexistence of the
Word who later becomes incarnate. The positive source of this belief is the
Christology of the primitive church before John.

We can ask why, if a major source of the theology of the Word was Jewish
wisdom speculation, John did not use the word 'Wisdom' or 'Sophia' in the
prologue rather than 'Word'. Surely, the importance of 'Logos' for the Hellenistic world and earlier Hellenistic Judaism's use of this term to engage that
world was important. Furthermore, in Jewish wisdom theology 'word' was
God in his self-revelation, not something other than God. The 'word' was in
the beginning (Gn 1:1–2) as God's power put forth for creation and revelation. The other reason why John used 'Logos' rather than 'Wisdom' was that
Jesus was male, and 'Sophia' was characterized as feminine in wisdom speculation. The dominant category of John's Christology, as seen in the gospel,
was "Son of God."[24] To see John's reason for the use of 'Word' rather than
'Sophia' as due to an early Christian patriarchalism is an imposition on the
text. We will return to this question in chapter 6.

In the body of John's gospel, disputes current between Christians and Jews
and among diverse groups of Christians toward the end of the first century
are evident. These disputes center on who Jesus is. The great discourses of Jesus in John are quite different from those in the Synoptics, but there is, as we
saw, a basis for them in the Christology implied, and perhaps in part expressed, in the historical Jesus of the Synoptics. In both the Synoptics and
John, Jesus definitively reveals God's way and God. In John's high Christology the legitimacy of this is traced back to Jesus as the only Son of God, as
shown in the great discourses (e.g., Jn 5:19–46; 7:16–24) and the "I am" passages, for example, "Amen, amen, I say to you, before Abraham came to be,

I AM" (8:58). As Son of God, Jesus is unique *(monogenes)*; the Father and he are one (10:30), and to see him is to see the Father (14:9). These christological pronouncements come to a climax in Thomas's profession of faith after the resurrection of Jesus: "My Lord and my God" (20:29).[25] His Sonship shows the continuity between the Father and the Son, and so too the authority of the Son's witness. It shows also the highest possible love the Father has for us: "God so loved the world that he gave his only Son, so that everyone who believes in him might not perish but might have eternal life" (3:16).

In the epistles of John we see a reflection of a church in crisis, because through them we can see that some of the Johannine community so stressed the divinity of the Word that they began to cast doubts on his really becoming flesh. Thus the test now is: "This is how you can know the Spirit of God: every spirit that acknowledges Jesus Christ come in the flesh belongs to God, and every spirit that does not acknowledge Jesus does not belong to God" (1 Jn 4:3). This group that split off from the community on this issue is on the path toward docetism, Gnosticism, and Montanism.[26] We will return to John's theology of the Spirit below.

2. Experience and Theology of the Holy Spirit in the Apostolic Age

At the beginning of the church's existence there was an experience that was ascribed to the Spirit. This experience is expressed most dramatically in Luke's account of Pentecost. When the believers in Jesus were gathered with the apostles in one place, "Suddenly there came from the sky a noise like a strong driving wind, and it filled the entire house in which they were. Then there appeared to them tongues as of fire, which parted and came to rest on each one of them. And they were all filled with the holy Spirit and began to speak in different tongues, as the Spirit enabled them to proclaim" (Acts 2:2–4).[27] In priestly circles and Qumran, in the first century B.C., the feast of Pentecost recalled the covenant and Law given to Israel through Moses. At that event the people had experienced cosmic phenomena such as thunder and lightening, a trumpet blast and smoke surrounding the mountain (Ex 20:18) that mediated a theophany. Luke emphasizes this parallel. What was basic was an experience of a living faith and empowerment that resulted, in Luke's account, in those so gifted going out and proclaiming boldly what God had done. First there was an experience, and then it was ascribed to the 'Spirit' or 'Holy Spirit'. The word by which they designated the source of this experience is not a proper name, like that of Jesus. It is a *symbol* taken from the experience of natural phenomenon such as wind and breath, and from its use in Jewish tradition and by Jesus himself. Initially, as we saw in the Old Testament, it designated symbolically the empowerment itself. In the New

Testament it is difficult at times to know whether it designates such dynamic influence on the community's or individual's life or a divine person who is the source of this gift or both. What was central in the earliest church was this transforming influence and its acceptance in the Christians' lives; a theology that analyzes it was secondary. It is *praxis* more than *theoria*.

Also, we should note that this gift was understood as an *eschatological* and even *apocalyptic* gift, as predicted by the prophet Joel (3:1–5). It was, like the resurrection, an event of the last days. It was the power of the age to come sent from that age to come by the glorified Jesus Christ who had gone into the future kingdom. Paul speaks of the gift of the Spirit as a kind of "first installment" and pledge of the glory to come (2 Cor 1:22). John does not put the gift of the Spirit on the Feast of Pentecost but on Easter itself for the forgiveness of sins (Jn 20:21–23), foreshadowed or anticipated by Jesus, who on dying on the cross "handed over the spirit" (Jn 19:30). But for John too, the Spirit is the gift of the glorified Jesus (7:38–39). For Luke and John, the Spirit is given to Christians through their faith and baptism (Acts 2:38, Jn 3:5; 19:34).

We will return to John, but first we shall show briefly some major elements of this gift in Paul and Acts. And we will conclude this section on the Spirit by suggesting that the major symbols of the Spirit in the New Testament, when compared to those of the Son, are feminine. This has importance, because it has been so neglected in the tradition. We are not giving a full scriptural pneumatology but rather recalling some grounds and meaning that are a basis for the later church's development of its trinitarian belief. We will return to this theme from the perspective of a trinitarian spirituality in our final chapter.

We can ask what Paul ascribes to the Spirit, and how he relates the Spirit to Christ and to God. First, the Spirit is a gift that comes from God's love for us: "the love of God has been poured out into our hearts through the holy Spirit that has been given to us" (Rom 5:5). The Holy Spirit within us enables us to respond to God; such response is not our initiative, but God's gift. The eighth chapter of Romans is almost a paean celebrating what believers in Christ receive through the Spirit, as had been predicted in the Old Testament (Ez 36:26; Jer 31). What the law, as external, could not do, God has done through the gift of the Spirit (8:2). This gift enables us "to live not according to the flesh but according to the spirit" (8:4).[28] Division, however, remains in the one who has been converted and believes in Jesus. For Paul, the authentic believer recognizes "that he is a *divided man*, a man of split loyalties. He lives in the overlap of the ages and belongs to both of them *at the same time*."[29] This view differs both from the Jews who still expected the

Spirit in the last days and from early Gnostics who thought of themselves as already fully freed by the Spirit.

Through the Spirit too we have some genuine sense of God's love for us and adoption of us as his children (Rom 8:5). And so in the Spirit we cry out "Abba, Father!" (8:15) and pray beyond what words can express (8:26). We have the freedom of children of the household (2 Cor 3:17). Through the gift of the Spirit we also have insights into the wisdom of God, as through the human spirit a human person understands somewhat what is within (see 1 Cor 2:7, 11–12, 16). Also, each of the "spiritual gifts" or charisms is a "manifestation (*phanerosis*) of the Spirit" (1 Cor 12:4, 7), that is, a sort of "brilliant epiphany, like the sparkling reflection of a crystal ball as it rotates in the light."[30] These gifts, ministries, or services that are meant to build up the church have the Spirit as their subject who acts through the Christian endowed with the Spirit. Also, the Spirit not only gives us initial life in Christ but brings us to grow in that life and the image of Jesus or sanctification: "All of us, gazing with unveiled faces on the glory of the Lord, are being transformed into the same image from glory to glory, as from the Lord who is the Spirit" (2 Cor 3:18).[31]

Paul frequently speaks of the Spirit as the Spirit of God and several times as the Spirit of Christ or of God's Son (e.g., Rom 8:9; Phil 1:19; Gal 4:6). For Paul there is no autonomous pneumatology, since the Spirit is closely related to Christ, and the criteria for whether one is speaking or acting in the Spirit or not is found in this relationship (1 Cor 12:3). Paul ascribes the effects of the Christian life to both Christ and the Spirit (e.g., to be in Christ and the Spirit, to be justified, joy, peace), but not with an exact equivalence between the expressions, as our earlier references to the action of the Spirit within the Christian show (also compare 1 Cor 1:30 and Rom 8:9; Gal 2:17 and 1 Cor 6:11; 2 Cor 5:21 and Rom 14:17). For example, it was through his personal work in history that Christ won salvation for us, and through his intercession for us in heaven and his sending of the Spirit that he effects our salvation. It is through presence within us as the gift of God and of the exalted Christ that the Spirit saves us.

Finally, we can note that while many of the passages we have referred to above suggest the divinity of the Spirit (e.g., the Spirit enables us to understand the mysteries of God), this is brought out in a particular way by Paul's words to the Corinthians: "Do you not know that your body is a temple of the holy Spirit within you, whom you have from God, and that you are not your own?" (1 Cor 6:19). A temple is a building for God to dwell in. The Spirit's divinity and distinction from Father and Son is also suggested by some triadic formulas in Paul, for instance, "The grace of the Lord Jesus

Christ and the love of God and the fellowship of the holy Spirit be with all
of you" (2 Cor 13:13; see also 1 Cor 12:4–6; and 2 Cor 1:21–22).

We have seen that Luke in Acts ascribes the beginning of the church to
the Spirit given to the initial Christian community gathered together at Pentecost and the repetitions of the gift of the Spirit (e.g., 8:14–17, 10:44). Luke
emphasizes the Spirit as at the origin of the church's impulse to proclaim the
good news, as shown by the Pentecost event itself, and at the origin of other
initiatives (see 7:55; 8:29, 39; 13:2). The Spirit is active in the reflections of
the church at the Council of Jerusalem, where the decision of the council
was prefaced by: "It is the decision of the holy Spirit and of us not to place
on you any burden beyond these necessities . . ." (15:28), an ascription of personal and divine agency to the Spirit. Luke ascribes so many acts of the early
church, particularly at crucial times, to the Spirit that this book has at times
been called "the gospel of the Holy Spirit," for it recounts the acts of the
Holy Spirit as the four gospels recount the actions and word of Jesus Christ.

In the last discourse in John's gospel, there is a new title or name given to
the Spirit not found in the Bible outside Johannine literature: the Paraclete
or Advocate who is also the Spirit of truth. We recall that the context in
which this gospel was written was the late first century, when the church was
being attacked both by Jews and Romans, when it was threatened from
within by early Gnosticism in which a number of people claimed the Spirit's
authority for views counter to the teaching of Jesus, and when John's church
was losing or had lost the presence among them of an eyewitness to the
events of Jesus.

Among the consoling messages Jesus offers his disciples in preparation for
his departure is his promise: "I will ask the Father, and he will give you another Advocate to be with you always, the Spirit of truth, which the world
cannot accept, because it neither sees nor knows it. But you know it, because
it remains with you, and will be in you" (14:16–17). This Advocate or Paraclete will take away from them their orphaned state, and with the Spirit's
coming Jesus and the Father will also come and make their dwelling in the
disciples (14:23). This Spirit gives a kind of knowledge of its presence. John
calls the Spirit "another Paraclete" or Advocate. The word *parakletos* signifies one who is called to one's side. It most probably refers to one who in the
Greek court assists defendants to plead their cause, not by arguing their case
for them but by suggesting to them how to plead their case. More broadly, Jesus was a defender, assistant at the side of his disciples while he was among
them; after his departure when he is no more visibly among them, the Spirit
will be "another" Paraclete or Advocate: "The distinction between the physical Jesus, who is departing, and the 'other Paraclete', who will be given (see

v. 16), must be maintained. They are two different characters in the narra-
tive, however closely their roles may be linked."[32]

John notes one function of this Advocate. The church of John's time still
had to struggle for self-definition and do so in the midst of conflicts not explicitly addressed in earlier times. Thus, there is still a need for them to understand more deeply the message of Jesus. When the Spirit comes, "he will
guide you to all truth. He will not speak on his own, but he will speak what
he hears. . . . He will glorify me, because he will take from what is mine and
declare it to you" (16:13–14; see 14:26). As Jesus' message had been that of
the Father, so too the Spirit's message will be that of Jesus. Another function
of this Paraclete is to aid the disciples in the cosmic trial that they will face,
as Jesus had faced it. They will be attacked by the world. But by their lives
faithful to Christ, the Paraclete acting in them will "testify" to Jesus and
"convict the world in regard to sin and righteousness and condemnation"
(16:8) because they did not know Jesus.

The Spirit's identity is, in biblical terms, its mission and relations. The
Spirit's divinity is shown, I suggest, because as Jesus says, "it is better for you
that I go. For if I do not go, the Advocate will not come to you" (16:7). It is
a good exchange for the disciples to have the invisible presence of the Spirit
over the visible presence of the Son. And the Spirit has the dignity of being
another Paraclete, one who will do what Jesus had done for his disciples. This
implies the Spirit's personal character as well as equality with the Son.

Jesus will send "the Spirit of truth that proceeds (*ekporeuetai*) from the Father" (15:26). In the gospel this word "proceed" is used of the Spirit in reference to the Father, not the Son (but see Rev 22:1). This word here refers not
to the internal and eternal relations among the Father, Son, and Holy Spirit,
but to the mission of the Spirit in the economy of salvation. And it is to be
understood in the context of John's spatial symbolism.[33] Here below is a
realm of darkness and lies, while light and truth come from above. Thus the
Spirit like the Son comes from above, from the Father. John 15:26 was a key
text in the conflict between the Eastern and the Western Church on the
question of the *Filioque*, that is, on whether the Holy Spirit eternally proceeds from the Father *and* the Son. The Son *sends* the Spirit (15:26), and, as
breath is referential or is someone's breath, the Spirit is the 'breath' of the
Messiah (Jn 19:30; 20:22). The Spirit is also the "Spirit of truth" and so has
an intimate relation with the Son as well as with the Father. This in no way
detracts from the primacy John gives to the Father. We will return to that
question in a later chapter. We conclude that John's gospel seems to be the
clearest witness in the New Testament to both the divinity and the personal
character of the Holy Spirit, distinct from both the Father and the Son.

To redress an imbalance in our Christian understanding of the triune God, it is important to reexamine some symbols of the Holy Spirit used in the New Testament. A number of exegetes and theologians in recent decades have recognized that the major symbols of the Spirit in the New Testament are feminine.[34] Space allows only a brief treatment of this theme here. We will note symbols of the Spirit found in the accounts of the baptism of Jesus, in 1 Corinthians 12:1–3 and in Revelation 22:1–2.

In the synoptic accounts of the baptism of Jesus there is a theophany. Matthew expresses the symbol of the Spirit here as follows: "Suddenly the sky opened and he saw the Spirit of God descend like a dove and hover over him" (Mt 6:16; see Mk 1:10). It is the movement of the dove that is emphasized, and particularly the *hovering* of the dove over Jesus. This movement recalls the hovering of the Spirit at creation (Gn 1:2; see too Dt 32:11); the baptism of Jesus is like the beginning of a new creation. Rabbinic commentaries compare this hovering at Genesis to the brooding of a dove over her nest, which points to the feminine character of this symbol—the action of the dove as life-giving.[35]

However, when Luke gives his account of the baptism of Jesus, he changes the symbolism a bit, for he writes: "The Holy Spirit descended on him in visible form like a dove" (Lk 3:22). He emphasizes not the movement but the form of the dove. Luke, who was probably from Syrian Antioch, was in his gospel addressing Christians from a primarily Gentile background. He was aware that the dove was a symbol associated with goddesses of the Near East, such as Atargatis, Astarte, Istar, Venus, and Athene.[36] It is reasonable to suppose that one reason why he shifted the tradition he had inherited was that by emphasizing the form of the dove he would make contact with the religious symbolism of the larger Hellenistic world and thus would emphasize the feminine character of this symbol in a way his readers could more easily understand. This offers some insight into Luke's theology of the mission and person of the Spirit. We should note that in Luke's account of the annunciation to Mary, the Holy Spirit *overshadows* her (Lk 1:35). This overshadowing shows that the manner of begetting of Jesus was creative rather than sexual; the Spirit is not presented as supplying the male element in the conception of Jesus.[37]

In Paul, we could recall how Jesus and the Spirit mediate God's salvation differently—the one from his earthly ministry and evoking faith from his disciples' proclamation to the point where he becomes the form of the Christian life, the other from action within the person to change dispositions and relationships that are then expressed externally in love. And we could suggest that this difference of mediation is correlated with a difference between men and women's usual ways of relating and caring for others, such as their children. But we will restrict ourselves to one passage here. When Paul speaks to the Corinthians about spiritual gifts, he prefaces his remarks by recalling to them that: "You know that when you were pagans you were constantly attracted and led away to mute idols" (1 Cor 12:2). The point he is making is that they can confuse what comes from the Spirit of God with the spirits that impelled them in their pagan past. There are certain criteria for discernment of spirits. When he refers to their pagan cultic past, he makes "a reference to the unbridled religious enthusiasm and emotionalism so highly esteemed by pagans, such as the prophetic trance of the Pythia of Delphi and of the priestesses of Dodono, and the orgiastic frenzies of the devotees of Dionysos."[38] It is interesting that when Paul cites pagan experiences that may still have their influences on Christians and that they could falsely interpret as experiences coming from the Spirit, he cites cults that were associated with goddesses or feminine oracles. This is evidence that the experiences Christians ascribed to the Spirit were symbols that were more feminine than masculine.

Finally, we can recall that in Revelation 22:1–2, the seer has a vision: "Then the angel showed me the river of life-giving water, sparkling like crystal, flowing from the throne of God and of the Lamb down the middle of its street. On either side of the river grew the tree of life that produces fruit twelve times a year, once each month." This vision is of the consummation of God's salvific activity, and it recalls to us the original scene of paradise. The river of life-giving water is a symbol of the Holy Spirit (see Jn 7:37–39) whom the glorified Christ sends from the Father. This river of life-giving water is a symbol of fertility, and goddesses rather than gods were the principles of fertility. It is also a symbol of immanence; and earth gods tended to be feminine, while sky gods tended to be masculine.[39] So this symbol of the Holy Spirit is feminine. In accord with this symbol, I ask the reader to allow me to use henceforth the feminine personal pronoun when, not quoting from another, I refer to the Holy Spirit.

In our reflections on the grounds and meaning of the revelation of the Trinity in Scripture, we should mention the baptismal formula of Matthew and a trinitarian spirituality found here and elsewhere in the New Testament, themes we will return to in our final chapter. Matthew's account of the risen Christ's appearance to the eleven disciples in Galilee includes his commission to preach the good news to all nations, and to baptize them "in the name of the Father, and of the Son, and of the holy Spirit" (Mt 28:19).[40] The earliest baptism was in the name of Jesus Christ (Acts 2:38), so the risen Jesus would not have expressed himself exactly as Matthew puts it. This baptismal formula probably reflects the practice in Matthew's church at the time the gospel was written. And it does have antecedents. Paul seems to give a trinitarian interpretation of baptism when he tells the Corinthians that "you have had yourselves washed, you were sanctified, you were justified in the name of the Lord Jesus Christ and in the Spirit of our God" (1 Cor 6:11). "The name" was a Jewish reverential alternative for Yahweh, and it is used in the singular in the baptismal formula, while in place of the name Yahweh, there are the personal names or titles 'Father', 'Son', and 'Holy Spirit', distinct from one another and parallel to one another. By baptism people were forgiven their sins, justified and sanctified by the Father, Son, and Spirit, and were consecrated to them. We can note that in Paul's passages concerning the three, the order among the names of Father, Son, and Spirit is not always the same (see 1 Cor 6:10–11; 2 Cor 13:13; Rom 8:14–17). The relationship of Christians to God is a relationship to Father, to Jesus Christ his Son, and to the Holy Spirit, or to the Father, through the Son, in the Holy Spirit.

We can say that the disciples of Christ are given a share in the relation to the Father that Jesus himself has (Jn 17:21), so they too can address God as Father; through the Father's free gift they are made sons and daughters in the Son. And they are empowered by the Spirit, as by a river of life-giving water, through sharing that dynamism or love of the Father breathed forth upon them by the Son.

This self-gift of the Father through the Son and the Spirit to those who believe and are baptized implies too a relationship of love and unity among the sons and daughters of God that will be a witness to the world that the Father had sent Jesus. This gift represents a partially realized eschatology, that is, an anticipation and participation even now of that communion with God and one another that the disciples of Jesus will inherit when Jesus, who went to prepare a place for his disciples in his Father's house, comes back and takes them to himself, so that they may be where he is (14:2–3). The scriptural message we have analyzed shows us that there is a real sense in which the Trinity in the economy of salvation is the Trinity in itself. Salvation is a communication of the Father, Son, and Holy Spirit; and Christian revelation is through the Word or Only Son become Incarnate.

Conclusion

In conclusion, we may note some implications of this scriptural witness for several tensions among Christian theologians in the diverse trinitarian theologies we recalled in the first chapter. We only note this here; we will also return to these themes later. There are some dialectical theologians who have taught that the Trinity comes to be through the ministry, life, death, and resurrection of Jesus Christ. This is quite different from the traditional view of the Trinity as eternal. We have seen that there is a sense in which Jesus became Lord in that he became the one through whom God will save and judge the world when the Son of Man appears in his glory. And there is a sense that in this redemptive order God *comes to us from the future* in that the Son sends the Holy Spirit from the world to come into which he entered through his resurrection and glorification. The Holy Spirit is the power of the age to come already present in this age. We will see later that, in part through the influence of Neoplatonism, the scriptural eschatological perspective was for centuries largely lost in Christianity. But the recovery of this scriptural perspective today does not take away from the eternity of the Trinity and its independence from the fact of creation and the Incarnation. Jesus as Lord is *Alpha* as well as *Omega* (Rev 1:8; 22:13). Nor can one say that because in the order of redemption God's salvific gift comes from the future, God creates as the power of the future. One cannot transpose the time relation found in one order to the other.[41] And it is likewise very important to realize that God did give his definitive revelation of himself at one time in the past through his Son become Incarnate. This is a revelation, however, that is still to be completed when Christ comes again and which, in a true sense, Christ is now communicating to the church from that future world into which he has gone.

Finally there is a tension between some currrent Spirit Christologies and more traditional Christologies. We have seen that the Spirit takes initiative in the ministry of Jesus and that Jesus also gives the Spirit, so that there is a certain mutuality of precedence between Jesus and the Spirit in the economy of salvation. Acknowledgment of this is important for theology, spirituality, and ecclesiology in our time. But it does not justify those forms of Spirit Christology that would reduce Jesus' divinity to mean no more than God extending his salvific activity to the world through him, or that would deny that he is a divine person distinct from the Father and the Holy Spirit.

Notes

1. See J. Farrelly, *Belief in God in Our Time* (Collegeville, Minn.: Liturgical Press, 1992), 73–99, "Scripture and Our Belief in God. I. The Old Testament." On how God's revelation is mediated by words and deeds witnessed to by Scripture, see J. Farrelly, *Faith in God through Jesus Christ* (Collegeville, Minn.: Liturgical Press, 1997), chapter 3, "The Revelation Jesus Offered and the Faith He Called For," 121–161. Scriptural quotations are from *The New American Bible* with its revised New Testament.

2. On the whole subject of the Old Testament preparation for the revelation of the Trinity, see Raphael Schulte, "La préparation de la révélation Trinitaire," in *Mysterium Salutis*, vol. 5, *Dieu et la révélation de la Trinité* (Paris: Cerf, 1970), 71–117. Also, see John Scullion, "God in the OT," *ABD* 2:1041–1048.

3. See Terrence Fretheim, "Word of God," *ABD* 6:961–968; and James Dunn, *Christology in the Making: A New Testament Inquiry into the Origins of the Doctrine of the Incarnation*, 2nd ed. (Grand Rapids: Wm. Eerdmans, 1996), 217–220. Concerning 'word', 'spirit', and 'wisdom' in the Old Testament Dunn notes that "all three expressions are simply alternative ways of speaking about the effective power of God in his active relationship with his world and its inhabitants" (219).

4. See F. W. Horn, "Holy Spirit," *ABD* 3:260–280; F. Baumgärtel, et al., "*pneuma*," *TDNT* 6 (1968): 359–451; E. Kamlah, et al., "Spirit, Holy Spirit," in Colin Brown, ed., *The New International Dictionary of New Testament Theology*, vol. 3 (Exeter: Paternoster Press, 1978), 689–709; George Montague, *The Holy Spirit: Growth of a Biblical Tradition* (New York: Paulist, 1976); M. J. Farrelly, "Feminine Symbols and the Holy Spirit," in *God's Work in a Changing World* (Washington, D.C.: University Press of America, 1985), 49–76; and Michael Welker, *God the Spirit* (Minneapolis: Fortress Press, 1994).

5. Roland Murphy, "Wisdom in the OT (hokma; sophia)," *ABD* 6:920–931, here 922. Also see Elizabeth Johnson, "Jesus, the Wisdom of God: A Biblical Basis for a Non-Androcentric Christology," *Ephem. Theol. Lovan.* 6 (1985): 261–294; Bernard Lee, *Jesus and the Metaphors of God* (New York: Paulist, 1993); Martin Scott, *Sophia and the Johannine Jesus* (Sheffield: Sheffield Academic Press, 1993); and Leo Lefebure, "The Wisdom of God: Sophia and Christian Theology" and "The Wisdom of God: Dialogue and Natural Theology," *Christian Century* (Oct. 19 and 26, 1994), 951–956, 984–988. Citations in the text here are to pages of Murphy's article.

6. See Horn, "Holy Spirit," 262.

7. See Eric Osborn, *The Beginnings of Christian Philosophy* (London: Cambridge University Press, 1981); and Robert Grant, *Gods and the One God* (Philadelphia: Westminster, 1986).

8. See Hermann Kleinknecht, "*pneuma*," *TDNT* 6:357–358.

9. See James Charlesworth, ed., *The Old Testament Pseudepigrapha* (New York: Doubleday, 1985), 665–669. Also for different expressions of Judaism at the time, see J. Andrew Overman and William S. Green, "Judaism in the Greco-Roman Period," *ABD* 3:1037–1054.

10. See S. Lila, "Judaeo-Hellenism," in *EEC* 1:455–456. Also see Alan F. Segal, "'Two Powers in Heaven' and Early Christian Trinitarian Thinking," in Stephen Davis, Daviel Kendall, Gerald O'Collins, eds., *The Trinity*, 73–95, esp. 81–84. Segal also shows that the rabbis spoke against those who say "there are two powers in heaven"—probably a reference to early Christian teaching concerning the Father and the Son, but perhaps also to some Hellenistic Jews.

11. See, for example, Dunn, *Christology*; F. S. Schierse, "La Révélation de la Trinité dans le Nouveau Testament," in *Dieu et la Révélation de la Trinité*, 121–183;

Marinus de Jonge, *The Servant Messiah* (New Haven: Yale University Press, 1991); Martinus De Boer, ed., *From Jesus to John: Essays on Jesus and New Testament Christology in Honour of Marinus de Jonge* (Sheffield: JSOT, 1993); Francesco Lambiasi, *Lo Spirito Santo: mistero e presenza* (Bologna: Edizioni Dehoniane, 1987), 48–89; Joel Green and Max Turner, eds., *Jesus of Nazareth: Lord and Christ: Essays on the Historical Jesus and New Testament Christology* (Grand Rapids: Eerdmans, 1994); Gerald O'Collins, "The Scriptural Roots," in his *The Tripersonal God. Understanding and Interpreting the Trinity* (New York: Paulist, 1999), 11–82; and Craig Evans, "Jesus' Self-Designation 'The Son of Man' and the Recognition of His Divinity," in Davis, *Trinity*, 29–47.

12. See Karl Rahner in "*Theos* in the New Testament," in *Theological Investigations*, vol. 1 (Baltimore: Helicon, 1963), 70–148. See too, Denis Farkasfalvy, "Jesus Reveals the Father: The Center of New Testament Theology," *Communio* 36 (1999): 235–257; and Rock Kereszty, "God the Father," *Communio* 36 (1999): 258–277.

13. James Dunn, "Christology (NT)," *ABD* 1:981. The simple invocation of God as Father was not totally unknown in Judaism of the time. Kessler (324) points to Sirach 51:10 and Aramaic paraphrases of Psalm 89:27 and Malachi 2:10. It is the frequency, immediacy, and confidence with which Jesus used this term in prayer that is so striking.

14. See S. Légasse, "Le logion sur le Fils révélateur," in J. Coppens, ed., *La notion biblique de Dieu* (Gembloux: Duculot, 1976), 245–274; and Donald Hagner, *Matthew 1–13. Word Biblical Commentary*, vol. 33a (Dallas: Word Books, 1993), 315–325. Hagner notes the difference of views about this passage in its relation to the historical Jesus. He concludes that the more restricted its meaning the more likely it is that these are substantively the words of Jesus. The sense of his unique Sonship was part of his messianic consciousness; "it is certain, however, that the early Church soon drew more dramatic christological conclusions from this logion (e.g., Jesus' pre-existence and deity)." (317). Also see Farkasfalvy, "Jesus Reveals the Father," 240–245, who relates the passage both to the themes of Wisdom and divine Sonship.

15. James Dunn, *Jesus and the Spirit* (London: SPCK Press, 1975), 357.

16. Brendan Byrne, "Christ's Pre-Existence in Pauline Soteriology," *TS* 58 (1997): 308–330; and see Dunn, *Christology*, 2nd ed., "Foreword to Second Edition," xi–xxxix. On the development of New Testament Christology also see Raymond Brown, "Christology," in *NJBC*, 1357–1359. In his article Byrne discusses much of the recent literature on this question.

17. See Gordon Fee, "Christology and Pneumatology in Romans 8:9–11—and Elsewhere: Some Reflections on Paul as a Trinitarian," in Green and Turner, *Jesus of Nazareth*, 312–331; Max Turner, "The Spirit of Christ and 'Divine' Christology," in Green and Turner, *Jesus of Nazareth*, 414–436; and Gordon Fee, "Paul and the Trinity: The Experience of Christ and the Spirit for Paul's Understanding of God," in Davis, *Trinity*, 49–72. For Dunn, see *Jesus and the Spirit*, 319–321. Dunn writes, for example, "The Spirit of God can [for Paul] be more precisely defined as the Spirit of Jesus' own relationship with the Father and as the Spirit which both brings

about the same relationship for believers and makes it existentially real" (320). In the text, quotations from Fee and Turner's articles in *Jesus of Nazareth* are indicated by their name.

18. In *Faith in God through Jesus Christ*, 186–199, I present more fully than here the evidence for the initial apocalyptic interpretation of the resurrected Jesus and gift of the Spirit and the emerging sense that what Christ will do when he comes again he is now doing in part.

19. See Byrne, "Christ's Pre-Existence." He is arguing against Dunn, who in his first edition of *Christology* interpreted this passage only as a contrast with Adam, and in the second edition defends the view still: "the Philippians hymn is an attempt to read the life and work of Christ through the grid of Adam theology; . . . it still seems to me an open question as to whether the hymn contains any thought of pre-existence, *other than the pre-existence involved in the paradigm*—that is, the metahistorical character of the Adam myth" (2d ed., xix). Byrne points out that the comparison and contrast of Christ with Adam was still most probably a part— but not the whole—of Paul's thought here. Byrne's critique of Dunn applies also to others who have similar views, for instance, Josef Kuschel, *Born before All Time? The Dispute over Christ's Origins* (New York: Crossroad, 1992).

20. See Thomas Sappington, *Revelation and Redemption at Colossae* (Sheffield: Sheffield Academic Press, 1991).

21. See Dunn, *Christology*, 2d ed., xx. Dunn is here responding to critics of his position in the earlier edition of this work. The 'functional' divinity ascribed here to Christ is different from the apocalyptic functional agency initially ascribed to him, because this latter refers to the divine works of salvation and judgment, while the first part of the Colossian hymn refers to the divine work of creation. Byrne (and others) differ from Dunn and those who share his view that it is only John who ascribed a personal preexistence to Christ as divine, but Byrne does not treat the Colossian passage. On the errors the author of Colossians was opposing, see Sappington, *Revelation*.

22. See particularly Raymond Brown, *The Community of the Beloved Disciple: The Lives, Loves, and Hates of an Individual Church in New Testament Times* (New York: Doubleday, 1979).

23. See Thomas Tobin, "Logos," *ABD* 4:348–356; Gérard Rochais, "La formation du Prologue (Jn 1:1–18)," *Science et Esprit* 38 (1985): 5–44; 161–187; R. Schnackenburg, *The Gospel According to St. John*, vol. 1, trans. Kevin Smith (New York: Herder and Herder, 1968), 221–281, 481–505; Dunn, *Christology*, 239–250; Rudolf Schnackenburg, *Jesus in the Gospels: A Biblical Christology* (Louisville, Ky.: Westminster John Knox Press, 1995), 283–394; and Francis Moloney, *Belief in the Word: Reading John 1–4* (Minneapolis: Fortress Press, 1993). Dunn differs from Schnackenburg on some issues (see 349), such as the personal character of the Word before John 1:14; but this difference refers more to the pre-Johannine poem than to it within John's use of it (244). Numerical references in the text here are to pages in the work of Schnackenburg (*The Gospel According to St. John*), Dunn, or Moloney, as indicated.

We note that our interpretation of this passage and how it relates to other New Testament Christologies differs from that of Roger Haight, *Jesus Symbol of God* (Maryknoll, N.Y.: Orbis, 1999) chapter 6, "The Pluralism of New Testament Soteriologies and Christologies," 152–184. He sees each New Testament Christology as one expression of a soteriology, or one expression of how Jesus is experienced as savior, and each as orthodox. He does not see these Christologies as legitimately or coherently interrelated, with John's as most developed. With the exegetes I cite, I differ from Haight's position.

24. See Dunn, "Christology (NT)," 988.

25. See Francis Moloney, *Glory Not Dishonor: Reading John 13–21* (Minneapolis: Fortress, 1998), 177.

26. See Brown, *Community of Beloved Disciple*, 146f.

27. On the Spirit in the early church, see references in notes 4 and 11 and also Max-Alain Chevallier, *Souffle de Dieu. Le Saint-Esprit dans le Nouveau Testament*, vol. 2, *L'Apôtre Paul—Les récits johannique—L'héritage paulinien—Réflexions finales* (Paris: Beauchesne, 1990); and Farrelly, "Holy Spirit," in Michael Downey, ed., *The New Dictionary of Catholic Spirituality* (Collegeville, Minn.: Liturgical Press, 1993), 492–503.

28. See 1 Thessalonians 5:23 for Paul's distinction in the human person of 'spirit' (*pneuma*), 'soul' (*psyche*), and 'body' (*soma*). Also see J. C. O'Neill, "The Holy Spirit and the Human Spirit in Galatians," *Eph. Théol. Lov.* 71 (1995): 107–120.

29. Dunn, *Jesus and the Spirit*, 312.

30. George Montague, *The Holy Spirit: Growth of a Biblical Tradition* (New York: Paulist, 1975), 148.

31. On 2 Corinthians 3:17, see, in addition to our earlier citations, Emily Wong, "The Lord is the Spirit (2 Cor 3,17a)," *Ephem. Théol. Lovan.* 61 (1985): 48–72. Also see Lambiasi, *Lo Spirito Santo*, 73–74, where, depending on M. McNamara, *I Targum e il Nuovo Testamento* (Bologna, 1978), 131–133, he writes, "It is not possible therefore on the basis of 2 Cor 3:17 to confuse Christ with the Spirit." See Chevallier (299–300) who interprets this passage more on the lines of 1 Corinthians15:45, but draws a similar conclusion with reference to the question of the identity of Christ and the Spirit. He notes in relation to such passages as "The Lord is the Spirit" that "Unhappily, we often read this type of description with a sensibility culturally oriented toward the nature of beings, toward their essence. The historical and, if one wishes, dramatic perspective of biblical writings is falsified by a metaphysical interest that is alien to them."

32. Moloney, *Reading John 13–21*, 43–44. See Moloney on the interpretations of "Paraclete" and on the whole discourse.

33. See M. A. Chevallier, "L'Evangile de Jean et le 'Filioque,'" in his *Souffle de Dieu*, vol. 3 (Paris: Beauchesne, 1991), 73–91.

34. See my article, "Feminine Symbols and the Holy Spirit." Also see S. Schroer, "Der Geist, die Weisheit und die Taube. Feministisch-kritische Exegese eines neutestamentlichen Symbols auf dem Hintergrund seiner altorientalischen und hellenistisch-frühjüdischen Tradition," *FZPhTh* 33 (1986): 197–225; and H. Schungel-Straumann,

"Ruah (Geist-, Lebenskraft) im Alten Testament," in M. Kassel, ed., *Feministische Theologie. Perspektiven zur Orientierung* (Stuttgart, 1988), 59–73.

35. See Leander Keck, "The Spirit and the Dove," *New Testament Studies* 17 (1970–1971): 63.

36. See E. Goldsmith, *Ancient Pagan Symbols* (New York: Putnam, 1929; reprinted 1973), 114–115; John Ferguson, *The Religions of the Roman Empire* (Ithaca, N.Y.: Cornell University Press, 1970), 19, 22; P. Gerlitz, *Ausserchristliche Einflusse auf die Entwicklung des Christlichen Trinitäsdogmas* (Leiden: Brill, 1963), 135; and C. K. Barrett, *The Holy Spirit and the Gospel Tradition* (London: S.P.C.K., 1966), 35.

37. See Raymond Brown, *The Birth of the Messiah* (New York: Doubleday, 1977), 124.

38. Richard Kugleman in *Jerome Biblical Commentary* (Englewood Cliffs, N.J.: Prentice-Hall, 1968), vol. 2, 271. Dionysus was originally an earth god rather than a sky god, and was a consort of Atargatis, subordinate to her.

39. See Ferguson, *Religions of the Roman Empire*, 13f., 32f.

40. See Chevallier, *Souffle de Dieu*, vol. 1, 157–159.

41. See Farrelly, *Faith in God*, 272–274, where I treat this question.

CHAPTER THREE

~

Soundings in the History of Christian Reflection on the Trinity: To Constantinople I (381)

To give a critical grounding for the Christian church's present belief in the Trinity, our study of the mystery must include not only the Trinity as witnessed in Scripture but also how the Christian church reflected on it through the ages. The way the churches (in the sense of "many Christian communions" and "different Churches," as used by Vatican II, *Decree on Ecumenism*, 1, 4) now express this belief, for example that the Son is 'one in being' with the Father, or that the Father, Son, and Holy Spirit are three 'persons' in one God, is not found in Scripture. We can distinguish the Christian faith in the Trinity from the way the church officially expresses this, namely its doctrine; the latter depends on the development of the Christian understanding of the mystery. We must then see how this took place through the ages. Why and how did it develop? How can we answer those who claim that this development was not faithful to what Scripture witnessed? What was the meaning and relevance of belief in the Trinity for Christians? Our study of these questions is critical for our Christian *identity* as a community and as individuals, because what the church is and who we are depends on who we are in relation to God and who God is in the light of God's self-revelation. This study is essential if we are to understand more deeply what it means that God is revealed definitively and saves us definitively through Jesus Christ and the Spirit.

This study depends on what is critically evaluated in foundational theology concerning God's intention that what he revealed for the salvation of all would be passed on to all ages intact, the means he chose to assure this, as through the apostolic proclamation, the whole Christian community's holding onto the faith and proclaiming it, and the apostolic succession of bishops who were to continue the apostles' proclamation—all under the influence of the Holy Spirit (Jn 16:13). The fact of the development of doctrine and the nature and authority of Christian tradition under the Holy Spirit are such that Christians do not gain their full *certainty* of what they believe from Scripture alone. Our study is in accord with the teaching of Vatican II on these issues in *Dei Verbum* (*The Constitution on Divine Revelation*, chapter 2) and *Lumen Gentium* (*The Dogmatic Constitution of the Church*, 22).

This issue of the development of doctrine is of great ecumenical importance, and it has been recognized as such in recent decades. The Fourth World Conference of Faith and Order in Montreal in 1963 acknowledged the central importance and validity of Christian tradition in handing on the Christian faith intact and encouraged joint studies of this tradition among Christian scholars. The Seventh Assembly of the World Council of Churches at Canberra in 1991 recognized explicitly the importance of Christian unity expressed in its creeds:

> Canberra makes explicit references to the uniting value of the creeds. The unity of the Church to which we are called is a *koinonia* given and expressed in the *common confession of apostolic faith*: a common sacramental life entered by the one baptism and celebrated together in one eucharistic fellowship; a common life in which members and ministries are mutually recognized and reconciled; and a common mission witnessing to all people to the Gospel of God's grace and serving the whole of creation.[1]

The Faith and Order Commission of the World Council of Churches sought to promote the recognition, explanation, and confession of the apostolic faith by a series of works. To help in this effort it produced from an ecumenical perspective a commentary on the Nicene-Constantinopolitan Creed entitled *Confessing One Faith: Towards a Common Confession of the Apostolic Faith as Expressed in the Nicene-Constantinopolitan Creed (381).*[2] The Fifth World Conference of Faith and Order at Santiago de Compostela, held in 1993, recognized that the common confession of the apostolic faith, and specifically belief in the trinitarian God, is fundamental for Christian identity and an essential condition and expression of Christian unity.

There are historians of Christian doctrine who have thought that the developed trinitarian doctrine as articulated in the Nicene-Constantinople Creed was a betrayal of the original Christian belief. Some thought it was a Hellenization of the earlier belief (e.g., Adolf Harnack), and others ascribed it to the influence of some Jewish reflections on preeminent angels as almost equal to God (e.g., G. Werner). There are Christian theologians of our own time, as we saw in the first chapter, who hold that this creed was a mistake or that it is not normative or meaningful for us in our time.

We will show that this creed was a terminal point of a long theological development, during which educated Christians of the Greco-Roman world sought to understand and articulate this mystery in dialogue with both non-Christian opponents and alternate Christian explanations. These Christians lived in two worlds, the Christian and their Hellenistic culture. The tools by which they could understand the Christian message were largely those of their culture, yet they could not reduce the mystery to this culture. Their efforts through many generations to articulate this mystery was a communal enterprise and, in a way, one of trial and error. Many thought that God had revealed himself *in part* through elements of Greek philosophy, and so found it helpful to use this to seek understanding of what they believed as Christians. As I wrote elsewhere,

> If we accept, as I think we must, a structuralist dimension to the development of Christian doctrine . . . , we must say that the articulation of Christian doctrine does not depend exclusively on the intrinsic significance of the Christian mystery but also on the resources of a particular culture such as its concerns and understanding of humanity and the cosmos.
>
> For example, Nicea's statement that the Son was *homoousios* (the same substance) with the Father depended in part on the philosophical concerns and concepts of Hellenism. This is not relativism, because there is something valid transculturally concerning what it means to be human, what being is, and who God is; and each culture from its perspective has something to contribute to . . . our understanding of the inexhaustible Christian mystery. We do not, of course, say that the perspective of a particular culture should be simply affirmed rather than critiqued.[3]

While we evaluate this creed critically as faithful to the belief witnessed to by Scripture, we can still acknowledge that the faith's expression can develop beyond it. We now recognize that creeds of the past were historically conditioned by the conceptuality available to their authors and the errors they were addressing.[4]

In our first chapter we gave a sketch of the development of the trinitarian doctrine; a reader may wish to look at that lest in what follows he or she lose the forest for the trees. In our survey here of this development, we depend largely on patristic scholars and historians of Christian doctrine. In this chapter we will treat the development of trinitarian doctrine to Constantinople I (381), and in the next chapter the development from Augustine through the Middle Ages and some reflections during the modern period. In the present chapter, we will discuss first the development before the fourth century and then the crisis of trinitarian faith in the fourth century.

I. Theological Development before the Fourth Century

What was basic to the belief in the earliest stages was shown in the development of primitive creeds associated with baptism and a rule of faith. One can see in these creeds how central a trinitarian belief was to Christian life, liturgy, and identity. The creeds developed before an analytic theology of the Trinity did, but they stimulated the development of a theology: The symbol gave rise to thought. A very early "theological" articulation of the "Trinity" is found in Judaeo-Christianity in terms of its angelology, though this was sporadic and marginal to the great current of reflection at the beginning of trinitarian reflection. We will say a word about these trends before beginning a recall of theologies contributory to the development of the doctrine of the Trinity.[5]

Judaeo-Christianity, which existed both in Jerusalem and in some areas of the Jewish diaspora, was itself a mixture of disparate groups, some of which were orthodox and some heterodox. The latter showed their heterodoxy particularly through an interpretation of Jesus' Sonship as one of adoption. Judaeo-Christianity was apocalyptic, as we recalled in our second chapter, and inherited from late Judaism a developed angelology. This angelology gave particular prominence to Michael and Gabriel, to such an extent that at some point rabbis had to caution Jews not to make them equal with God. In some Christian apocryphal writings of Judaeo-Christianity (Ascension of Isaiah, Gospel of the Hebrews), there is an interpretation of Jesus and the Spirit by these Jewish categories as angels. This is found also in the Shepherd of Hermas who speaks of the Son as a preeminent angel: "This angel is given the name of Michael, and the conclusion is difficult to escape that Hermas saw in him the Son of God and equated him with the archangel Michael."[6] At this stage such a view is not so much heterodox as a searching for an understanding within the categories that were at hand for this body of believers. Judaeo-Christianity also influenced the theology of the apostolic Fathers, such as Ignatius of Antioch. He spoke of the Trinity in the context of the economy of salvation. He addressed Christians as "stones of the temple of the Father, prepared for the building of God the Father, and drawn up on high by the instrument of Jesus Christ, which is the Cross, making use of the Holy Spirit as a rope" (Eph. ix, 1; ANF 1:53).

The great current of reflection on the Trinity developed from the early creeds and was influenced (as we saw in the prologue of John's gospel) by Hellenistic Judaism. There are brief confessions of faith in the New Testament, such as "Jesus is Lord" (1 Cor 12:3); and there are two forms of baptism reflected in the New Testament, one in the name of Jesus (Acts 2:38; 19:5), and one in the name of Father, Son, and Holy Spirit (Mt 28:19). In the early church two situations called for brief creedal expressions, one as a rule of faith (regula fidei) and the other associated with baptism. A community needed to have a short synthesis of its faith to express its identity, both for the community and for the individual (e.g., in catechesis). In both these situations there was a continuity of both the christological formula and the triadic formula. In the mid–third century Pope Stephen claimed to know of a form of baptism in the name of Jesus alone and to consider it valid (Cyprian, Ep. 73, 4,1; 16,1,2).

In the mid–second century, in speaking of baptism Justin says, "in the name of God, the Father and Lord of the universe, and of our Savior Jesus Christ, and of the Holy Spirit, they then receive the washing with water" (1 Apol., 61; ANF 1:183). He also shows this triadic formula as present in the eucharistic anaphora, for he writes that when the presider at the assembly receives the gifts of bread and wine with water, he "gives praise and glory to the Father of the universe, through the name of the Son and of the Holy Spirit, and offers thanks. . ." (1 Apol., 65; ANF 1:185). In the early third century Hippolytus attests to a form of baptism in Rome in which the one to be baptized was asked successively whether he or she believed in God, the Father almighty, in Jesus Christ, the Son of God, and in the Holy Spirit, and after each response was immersed in water.[7] In this baptismal creed, an extended christological formula is integrated into the trinitarian formula.

The doctrinal formulas as rules of faith were implicit in the baptismal formulas. In fact, it seems that the old Roman creed that later gave rise in the West to what we know as the Apostles' Creed was a direct descendent from the baptismal interrogative formula we have just recalled from Hippolytus. The interrogation was simply put into declarative form. The creeds were differently expressed in different churches, reflecting as generalized summaries of the Christian faith what was taught in each place, but everywhere containing the same essential doctrine. Exegesis of Scripture was to be in accord with the regula fidei, but the church also developed these creeds as rules of faith to express what Scripture witnessed to. By the second generation of the third century, a newly elected bishop would send the creed of his church to other churches to invite their communion with him. The creed of Nicea was a modification of such a preexisting creed, probably of Syria or Phoenicia.

Theological development of the doctrine of the Trinity took its rise from the belief of the church expressed in these creeds, its liturgy, and its life. Trinitarian theology was in service to and secondary to the living relationship reflected in baptism, the Eucharist, and the Christian life. Initially, this trinitarian relationship was viewed within the context of the economy of salvation interpreted apocalyptically; that is, Christians looked forward to the *parousia* of Jesus Christ, who was even now sending his Spirit from the future kingdom. We will give examples of second- and third-century developments before treating the Arian crisis and its aftermath in the fourth century.

In the second century, we can look at *Justin Martyr* as an example of an apologist and Irenaeus as an example of a writer against heresies.[8] The apologists faced objections to Christianity from both Jewish monotheism and the Gentile accusation of atheism, because Christians did not worship the gods of Rome. They used Middle Platonism to argue that there was only one God who was transcendent and immutable. And with this they integrated specifically Christian views of God taken from revelation. Justin admits that all men are given some participation in the Logos or Word, and because of this the philosophers knew the truth partially "on account of the seed of reason [the Logos] implanted in every race of men" (2 Apol. 8:1). Christians, however, possess the Word entirely (2 Apol. 10:3), and so the full truth comes only through the prophets and the apostles.

The use of "Word" (Logos) puts emphasis on the preexistence of the Son. Justin used this name to be in dialogue with the philosophers, but he also used it in his dialogue with the Jew Trypho, who accused Christians of believing in "another God." Justin writes:

> God begat before all creatures a Beginning, a certain rational power from himself, who is called by the Holy Spirit, now the glory of the Lord, now the Son, again Wisdom, again an Angel, then God, and the Lord and Logos. . . . When we give out some word, we beget the word; yet not by abscission, so as to lessen the word in us, when we give it out." (Dialogue with Trypho 61)

And in defense of his position, he refers to Old Testament passages concerning Wisdom (Prv 8:21–36), for example, Proverbs 8:22: "The Lord established me in the beginning of his ways in view of his works." Justin has a sense that the begetting of the Son was in reference to creation, as it is through the Son or Logos that God creates and directs history. Thus, this begetting comes from God's will and is related to time. In dependence on Stoicism he distinguished the word that remains within, our rational thought, from that which is spoken or brought forth. Justin argued that it was this Son or Word who was present in the theophanies of the Old Testament. He accepted much of Middle Platonism and Stoicism and applied some of their terms and concepts to Christ, thus seeking a kind of inculturation of the Christian belief. Justin's trinitarian theology is centered on the economies of creation and salvation and thus does involve some subordinationism.

It was the apologist Theophilus of Antioch (died c. 183) who first used the word "Trinity" (*trias*) (To Autolycus 2:15) for the three, "God, his Word, his Wisdom." We note here that Theophilus, like Irenaeus after him, identified Wisdom with the Spirit; most others identified Wisdom with the Word.

Irenaeus, bishop of Lyons (died c. 187), developed his teaching on the Trinity within his conflict with the Gnostics. He insisted on keeping faithful to the rule of faith that is known by the tradition of the apostolic churches. As the Gnostics proclaimed a way to salvation, Irenaeus's theology of the Trinity was wholly oriented toward the economy of creation and salvation. Counter to Mani who distinguished the demiurge or creator from another and superior God, Irenaeus held that the creator was the one God and Father of the Son. This Word or Son was generated by the Father eternally. But Irenaeus refused to speculate on how this generation occurred, and he held that the analogy of coming to be of the human intellectual word was inadequate. There were Gnostics who spoke of some intermediate gods as one in being (*homoousios*) with the one from whom they emanated. Irenaeus showed the inner contradiction of their view, and he did not use this word of the Son in relation to the Father. However, other expressions show his view that the Son is equal to the Father: "The Father is Lord, and the Son is Lord. The Father is God and the Son is God, because the one who is born of God is God. Thus if we consider his being and his power, we ought to confess one God alone" (Dem., 47).[9]

In his economy the Father creates and reveals through the Son and sanctifies through the Spirit, thus bringing creation and humanity toward its fulfillment through the Son and the Spirit as his executors or 'two hands' (*Adv. Haer.* V,1,3; V,5,1; V,28,1). God recapitulates all in Jesus Christ, the New Adam, who is the mediator between God and flesh. Of Irenaeus's theology A. Orbe writes:

> Only . . . when He [Jesus] is . . . glorified with the glory that he had before the creation of the world, does the same *caro gloriosa* . . . become the origin—through the outpouring of his Spirit—of man's divinization, . . . as one who receives "*secundum carnem*," from the Father, the Spirit which He then infuses

into that of men, his brothers, disposing them toward the divine heights of his own life. (414)

Irenaeus holds that the Word and the Spirit were acting in the world from the beginning, but this does not detract from the uniqueness of the mediation that occurs through the Incarnation and the glorified Son's sending of the Spirit from the Father. Irenaeus's teaching that it is the glorified Son who sends the Spirit shows us his fidelity to the apocalyptic context we found in the New Testament and a mediation of salvation from the future.

Toward the end of the second century there was a certain reaction against Logos theology out of fear that it was a danger to the divine unity. This movement, called Monarchianism by Tertullian, occurred particularly in the West and took two forms. For Theodotus, Jesus was a mere man who was adopted as a Son of God and endowed with divine power (dynamic Monarchianism). Another form was modalist Monarchianism, and this had more popular support than the former. Praxeas was one who held this, but Sabellius was the more famous. He held that there was one divine being who manifested himself or appeared under different modes and names, as Father, Son, and Holy Spirit. Popes Zephyrinus (198–217) and Callistus (217–222) seemed initially to tend to Sabellius's position but later shied away from it. Callistus excommunicated Sabellius.

In the third century, there was a movement of reflection from the Trinity in the economy of salvation to the relations of the Father, Son, and Spirit within the Trinity. We see this particularly in Tertullian and Origen. It was Tertullian who helped the West get beyond Monarchianism and contributed the basic Western terminology on the Trinity.[10] He was the first to use the Latin word "Trinitas," and he distinguished between person and substance, holding that there are three persons but one substance in God. His main work on the Trinity is *Adversus Praxeas* (213). In it he moves from the economy of creation and salvation, from the missions of the Son and the Spirit, to a distinction in the Godhead that is antecedent to the economy. He also seeks to answer the difficulties of reason that inclined many toward Monarchianism for fear of worshiping two gods. He held that the *oikonomia* or God's salvific design realized by the missions of the Son and the Spirit manifests a disposition within the unique divine substance.

Justin had spoken of God's bringing forth the word in relation to creation, but Tertullian goes further. He writes "Before all things God was alone. . . . He was alone because there was nothing outside of him. However he was not even then alone, for he had with himself what he had in himself, his reason"

(*Adv. Pr.* 10). God was planning silently within himself what he would do and say (*Adv. Pr.* 5, 4). We do not speak without having thought first, and our word is an expression of what we think. So too God possessed an interior word which was in relation to him a second. He argues this from Scripture's statements that God had Wisdom with him before he created the world (e.g., Prv 8:22). As we bring forth a word that we have thought interiorly, God brings forth or generates this Word in relation to his creation of the world, and as such the Word is called Son (*Adv. Pr.* 7).

What Tertullian says of the Son he extends to the Spirit. From Stoicism he thought that everything that exists is bodily in some way, no matter how refined: "God puts forth his Word, as the root the stem, and the source the river, and the sun the ray." The Spirit is third, "as the fruit derived from the shoot is third from the root" (*Adv. Pr.* 4). All three are God, "of one substance and one status and one power, because one God, of which the successions (*gradus*) and forms and appearances are indicated in the name of the Father and the Son and the Holy Spirit" (*Adv. Pr.* 2). The Father is the first person of God. "The second person is the Word of the same and the third is the Spirit in the Word" (*Adv. Pr.* 12). The Father and the Son are not *unus* but *unum*, because there is among them unity of substance and not of number. Father, Son, and Holy Spirit are three persons, but one substance (*tres personae, una substantia*). These formulations of Tertullian contributed greatly to the church's understanding, though the words he used did not have all the content they later came to have. We have to acknowledge, however, that there is a degree of subordinationism that remains in Tertullian, as in all the writers before Nicea.

Origen (died 254) accepted the rule of faith and wanted to teach only in accord with this rule.[11] He sought to promote a genuine *gnosis*, particularly on those subjects that had been left open by the apostles for further research. He approached this reflection from a background in Middle Platonism that so emphasized the transcendence of God that there was a need for intermediaries between him and lower creation and that held an eternal creation of spiritual beings. Thus Origen held the preexistence of souls; in turning from God souls fell and became cold in their love of God. The Son by his descent and emptying of himself (*kenosis*) even to the point of death gives us the ability to be conformed to him and come to God by the resurrection of faith and then a general resurrection.

God is of a spiritual nature. God too is perfect unity, perfect goodness, and power; he eternally had a world of created spirits on which to exercise this goodness and power. To mediate between his perfect unity and their diversity he had his Son—the image of himself. There never was when the Son was not; he was eternally generated, a generation that Origen describes as an effluence known by Middle Platonism:

> What else are we to suppose the eternal light is but God the Father, who never so was that, while He was the light, His splendor (Heb 1:3) was not present with Him? . . . Thus Wisdom, too, since it proceeds from God is generated out of the divine substance itself . . . 'a sort of clean and pure outflow of omnipotent glory' (Wis 7:25). Both these similies manifestly show the community of substance between Son and Father. For an outflow seems *homoousios*, that is, of one substance with that body of which it is the outflow or exhalation (*In Hebr.*, quoted in Quasten, 78).

The Son was generated as an image of the Father (see Col 1:15), as the will proceeding from the mind. The Father eternally wills the Son and makes him know his own will; eternally the Son acquiesces in his Father's will which he never ceases to contemplate. And God engenders us in the Savior if we have the spirit of adoption. God is the good in itself, and the Son is an image of the goodness of God, but not the good in itself, as the ray is like the sun from which it emanates but only an image of the sun, and thus somewhat less. Thus, though in one way Origen says the Son is consubstantial with the Father, he also distinguishes them. In fact in one place he expresses this distinction by a distinction of *hypostaseis*: "As to us, who are persuaded that there are three hypostases (*treis hypostaseis*), the Father, the Son and the Holy Spirit . . ." (Com in John, II, 10). The word *hypostasis* at this time was not really distinct in meaning from 'substance' or *ousia*; they both meant concrete reality. By his view Origen refuted modalism, but he also shows some subordinationism.

Of the Holy Spirit he holds, largely because of the baptismal formula, that he is associated in honor and dignity with the Father and the Son; he is the Spirit both of the Father and the Son. When speaking of the mode of procession of the Holy Spirit, he writes: "In this it is not clearly seen whether he was born or not born" (De Prin., Preface, 4; this is Rufinus's Latin translation; Jerome translates this as "created or not created," though this is less probably Origen's query). In accord with John 1:3, Origen holds that the Spirit came to be through the Son, though he is superior to all else that came to be through the Son. He is especially interested in the Spirit's distributing graces and actualizing gifts within human beings, dependent on our cooperation, by which we are progressively assimilated to Christ. Origen's trinitarian theology was in service of a Christian *gnosis* and mysticism. But his overdependence on Platonic philosophy resulted in his loss of the apocalyptic context of the primitive church's understanding of God's present influence on us from the future and our return to God through going to this future kingdom. Origen interiorizes and individualizes the kingdom, understanding it as God's action within the soul that obeys.[12]

II. The Arian Crisis and Its Aftermath (315–381)

The Christian consensus on the question of the Son's relation to the Father and the divinity of the Holy Spirit, a consensus that is still central to Christian identity, resulted from the crisis that was provoked by Arius, was answered by Nicea, and yet was unresolved or not received by the church as a whole for the next two generations. We will briefly treat the central issues here in three sections: (1) the initial conflict, Nicea, and the aftermath until the death of Constantine (337); (2) the conflicting positions under Constantius until the Second Council of Sirmium (357); and (3) toward a resolution in the First Council of Constantinople (381).

1. The Initial Conflict, Nicea, and the Aftermath until the Death of Constantine (337)

In about 318, Arius, a priest of Alexandria, began to teach a doctrine about the Son of God that provoked hostile reaction because it reduced the Son's divinity in a way not consistent with the rule of faith.[13] The patriarch of Alexandria, Alexander, invited Arius to debate the issue publicly before his clergy twice, and then he called upon him to renounce his opinion. Arius turned to friends of his, such as Bishop Eusebius of Nicomedia, for support. Alexander called a synod of the bishops of Egypt and Lybia in 320, and they excommunicated Arius. When Emperor Constantine defeated Licinius in the East, he supported Christianity and found the conflict provoked by Arius's teachings posed a threat to the unity of Christianity and so too of the political order. Perhaps at the suggestion of his ecclesiastical adviser, Bishop Ossius of Cordoba, he called a council of bishops to meet in Nicea in 325 to discuss the issue.

From the fragmentary remains of Arius's writings, we can know that he taught that God is ingenerate (does not have an origin) and eternal; since the Son is generated he is not eternal, but created by the will of the Father, as Proverbs 8:22 indicates of Wisdom: "The Lord begot me, the first-born of his ways." The Son can be called "begotten" and thus is God in only a metaphorical sense. Scripture shows that the Son is inferior to the Father (e.g., Jn 14:28), that there is only one true God (Jn 17:3), and that Jesus suffers (Mk 13:12), as God cannot because God is impassible.

Origen has been accused of being the source of the teachings of Arius. But while Origen's trinitarian theology had the ambiguity of underdevelopment,

Arius's clear categorizing of the Son among creatures was not faithful to Origen. Many have ascribed his views to the influence of Middle Platonism. For example, this philosophy proposed there was a pretemporal time; Arius used this to teach that the Son was produced before all ages, and yet there was a time when he was not (H 86). Also this philosophy taught that God was first a Monad and that the 'Idea' or perfection in itself (e.g., Truth, Righteousness, Word, Wisdom) was one thing and what participated in it was less. Thus, Arius contrasts what God is 'of himself' and what the Son is by participation and contingently (H 87). But Arius may have derived his view that the Son is created out of nothing from Scripture's view of a creation from nothing.

Counter to an earlier prevailing view, Robert Gregg and Dennis Groh argue that Arius's view was more soteriological than cosmological and that it depended on Stoicism.[14] Gregg and Groh "believe that the Son as represented by Arius, whether pre-existent or incarnate, was envisaged as an example of certain virtues prominent in the teaching of later Stoicism, especially in view of the Arian doctrine that the Son, being mutable (treptos), was capable of showing moral progress (prokope)" (H 89). According to Gregg and Groh: "Arians are arguing not for the stratification of the universe but for the dynamics of redemption whereby creatures, in emulation of the creature of perfect discipline, may be themselves begotten as equals to the Son" (Gregg and Groh, 113; quoted in H 91). Hanson concurs with this interpretation that Arius's doctrine was soteriological, but he also accepts R. D. Williams's view that there was a metaphysics here.[15] According to Williams, Alexander of Alexandria had taught that the Son was "proper (idios) to the ousia of the Father," and Arius found this to be Sabellian. Counter to Alexander, Arius denied that the Son is a "'consubstantial part' (meros homoousion) of the Father" (H 92), because this would make God a composite, and there cannot be two ingenerate principles.

Hanson basically agrees that Arianism involved a soteriology. Gregg and Groh interpret this soteriology as accepting Christ as vulnerable and passible, and as the example given by God the Father to us that we can, like him, achieve moral progress (procope) that will enable us to become divine as he is (see H 96). Hanson adds that Arius thought it necessary for our salvation that God suffer in Christ, and that this suffering could not be done by the High God, but only by a reduced God. So to hold that the Son was a reduced God could make it possible to hold that he was capable of suffering, and by suffering redeem man (H 121). The supporters of Nicea, such as Athanasius, understood God to be impassible; and they did not do justice to the sufferings of Christ as sufferings of God. Many patristic scholars now admit that Arius had a soteriology, though there is not agreement on what this is.

At the Council of Nicea (325), Ossius presided as the representative of Constantine, and Victor and Vincentius, the two representatives of the Bishop of Rome, enjoyed a precedence. There were between 250 and 300 bishops present, almost all from the East. Arius and his sympathizers were allowed to present their case, and his position was condemned. A baptismal creed was modified in its second section to make clear the rule of faith on the matter of dispute, stating that we believe in Jesus Christ "the Son of God, begotten as only-begotten of the Father, that is of the substance (ousia) of the Father, God from God, Light from Light, true God from true God, begotten not made, consubstantial (homoousios) with the Father, through whom all things came into existence." This was a startling statement. The word homoousios was used because it would unequivocally distinguish the true faith from Arius's position, since Arius read in his own sense the statements of Scripture itself. We will examine its meaning below. The council also condemned those who say "there was a time when he did not exist," or that he came from another hypostasis or ousia than the Father (see H 188, 201–202).[16] Almost all the bishops present signed the decrees of Nicea, even some who did not hold its theology (e.g., Eusebius of Caesarea). Arius was exiled, and three months later Eusebius of Nicomedia too was banished.

While Constantine was alive, there was a degree of peace with Nicea. But around 328 Eusebius of Nicomedia, who had been reinstated, reconciled the emperor to a formula less developed than that of Nicea. In 328 Athanasius became patriarch of Alexandria. In 335 Arius was readmitted to communion by Constantine upon his signing a creed less clear than Nicea's. And in 335 Athanasius was deposed at the Council of Tyre, partly because of his high-handed activities as patriarch but primarily because of the influence of Eusebius of Nicomedia and the fact that Athanasius would not readmit Arius. He was exiled to Trier. In 336 Arius died, and in 337 Constantine died.

2. The Conflicting Positions under Constantius until the Second Council of Sirmium (357)

Constantine's empire was divided between Constans in the West and Constantius in the East. Under the latter, Eusebius of Nicomedia received the see of Constantinople and influenced the emperor to substitute more flexible formulas for that of Nicea. There was a series of such formulas accepted by councils in the East; but while Constans lived, the bishops in the West were free to accept the Roman faith. When Constans died (350), Constantius extended his policy of a broader rule of faith for the sake of political unity to the West, forcing bishops there to sign such formulas or face exile.

Under Constantius there was a period of great confusion. The basis for this confusion was not simply political. In the view of some, Nicea had rejected Arius's teaching at the expense of not clearly distinguishing the Son from the Father. The word *homoousios* had been used earlier by Sabellians to express their view that the Father and the Son designate one subject who manifests himself in different guises. Thus the use of the word at Nicea was thought by some to run the danger of identifying the Father and the Son. In the East the words *ousios* and *hypostasis*, both meaning the concretely real, were not clearly distinguished at this time, as they would be later. Thus Athanasius generally spoke of the Father and the Son as one *hypostasis*; though he clearly distinguished the Father and the Son, he did not have a word to indicate what there were three of in the Trinity.

There were also differences between the West and the East. The West had the advantage of Tertullian's clear distinction between *substantia* and *personae*, but etymologically the Greek *hypostasis* was the same as the Latin *substantia* (what stands under the appearances), and was translated into Latin as three *substantiae* in God. To hear Greeks speaking of three *hypostaseis* in God then sounded heretical to Latins. On the other hand, an earlier pre-Christian use of the Latin *persona* was similar to that of the Greek *prosopon*. Both referred to the mask worn by an actor in drama that indicated which part the actor was playing. So when the Greeks heard the Latins say there were three *personae* in God, they would be suspicious of Sabellianism, for this view had held that God adopted three *prosopa*, that is, three roles or manifestations. Also in the East, the words *genetos* (having come into existence) and *gennetos* (generated) had been used interchangeably by Origen. The opposite of the latter (*agennetos*— not generated) was thought by Arians to be distinctive of God, and thus the Son could not be God in the proper sense, and there could not be two ungenerated beings. Did generation mean that the Son came into existence, and so there was a time when he was not; or was he both *agenetos* (i.e., not having come into existence) and *gennetos* (i.e., generated)?

The basic theological conflicts after Nicea were between those who wished to hold for the equality of the Son with the Father and those who wished to clearly distinguish the Son from the Father. There were a few who supported Nicea (Eustathius of Antioch and Marcellus of Ancyra) who, with some plausible basis, were accused of Sabellian leanings; neither accepted that there were three *hypostaseis* in God. Both were deposed by the influence of Eusebius of Nicomedia (who also had a hand in the deposition of a number of bishops of Nicean sympathies), but Marcellus continued to be supported by Athanasius and Rome (341). One cannot call all those who had reservations with Nicea Arians or Arian sympathizers or semi-Arians; it is difficult to find one

word that designates all who had reservations with Nicea. The Council of
Nicea was the first ecumenical council, and though the Fathers of the council had a sense of the authority of their decrees, there was not yet a sense in
Christianity of the special authority of an ecumenical council that would draw
all to accept it. The situation was likened by Basil of Caesarea to ships fight-
ing at close quarters in the dark, not knowing whether they were engaged with
friends or enemies. To indicate some of the confusion, we will note some
councils called during this period (337–357) and then the teaching of
Athanasius (d. 373), who was the most prominent defender of Nicea.

In 341 there was a council in Antioch, whose leading spirit was Eusebius
of Nicomedia, probably called to react against a statement of Pope Julius at
the Council of Rome (341). What is called the Second Creed of Antioch or
the "Dedication" Creed was Antioch's most important act. Of this, Hanson
writes:

> Its chief *bête noire* is Sabellianism, . . . and the most obvious recent example of
> a formula which appeared to make this mistake was N [Nicea]. . . . It is inter-
> esting to note . . . what significant terms in N this Dedication Creed does not
> reproduce: *ek tes ousias tou patros* ('from the *ousia* of the Father') 'begotten, not
> made', *homoousion* . . . [though it said] the Son is 'the exact image of the God-
> head.' (H 287–288)

This creed of Antioch was not compatible with that of Nicea. The council's
fourth creed was even further removed from Nicea's.

In 344 there was a council in Sardica (the modern Sophia); both Eastern
bishops (about eighty) and Western (about ninety-eight) were present. The
Eastern bishops presented as a substitute for Nicea the fourth creed of Antioch, but the Western bishops condemned the view that the hypostases of the
Father and the Son are distinct. The Western bishops' document distinguishes for the first time in the controversy between *gennetos* and *genetos*, but
they "have no conception of the distinction between hypostasis and *ousia*"
(H 303). The council ended in an impasse and with a mutual condemnation
between the Eastern and the Western bishops.

When Constans died and Constantius became emperor in the West as
well as in the East, he sought to bring unity in the empire as a whole on the
issue. In the years from 351 to 357, "he favored one solution to the problem
of the Christian doctrine of God, that which is best called Homoian, and
. . . he rejected others, the Homoousian and the Anhomoian" (H 324); that
is, he favored saying the Son was like the Father, but was against saying he
was of the same substance or that he was unlike. He followed this policy at
councils of Sirmium (351), Arles (353), and Milan (355). He called the West

to reject Athanasius and demanded acceptance of a formula that stepped back strongly from Nicea. Hilary of Poitier and Pope Liberius were exiled; the pope later signed a compromising formula. Athanasius was exiled for the third time in 356.

In 357 there was the Second Council of Sirmium that produced a recognizably Arian creed in the sense that it declared the Son to be inferior to the Father. Sirmium prohibited the preaching of *ousia* in reference to the Son's relation to the Father, whether *homoousion* or *homoiousion* ("of a like substance," the first use of this word in the controversy) and declared that the Father is clearly greater than the Son (H 344–345). The creed of the Second Council of Sirmium was "the first clear declaration of Homoian Arianism" (H 567), that is, that the Son is like the Father, while rejecting the view that he is like in substance. Hanson writes: "The Second Creed of Sirmium of 357 constituted a landmark. It . . . attacks N [Nicea], no longer covertly, but directly and openly. . . . It enabled everybody to see where they stood" (347).

This is a good place to recall Athanasius's teaching on the issue. He wrote his *Treatises against the Arians* between 338 and 350. He approached the problem of the relation between the Father and the Son from a soteriological and not from a cosmological point of view. God did not need a mediator to create the world. Athanasius placed the mediating role of the Son primarily in reference not to creation but in the Incarnation. "This was a new, indeed revolutionary, theological idea, and one entirely consonant with Scripture" (H 424). The Son can reveal the Father only if he is ontologically one with the Father. The Son is begotten by the Father, not created; he is a Son by nature. From Scripture Athanasius attacked the three major arguments of the Arians against the eternity, generation, and immutability of the Son based on their confusion between becoming and generation. He taught that the Father is not eternally Father unless he eternally generates the Son. A central argument of Athanasius is that the Son cannot make us participate in his filiation unless he is Son by nature.

Athanasius makes one reference to *homoousios* around 336, but then not again until his *De Decretis* (356–357). At this time, he begins to defend it, probably in opposition to Constantius who was forcing bishops to accept creeds that did not fully support the unity of the Father and the Son, and against the Second Council of Sirmium that explicitly denied that it was proper to speak of *ousia* in the relation of the Father and the Son (H 438). But even at this time, Athanasius treated *ousia* and *hypostasis* as synonyms. Athanasius is clearly not Sabellian, though he did not have a word to indicate what there were three of in the Trinity. His teaching on the Incarnation was more defective, in that at least until 362, while he taught that the Logos took flesh to himself, he did not see the need of maintaining that Jesus had a human soul or mind, and he was very resistant to saying that as God Jesus suffered. We shall return to his teaching about the Holy Spirit below.

3. Toward the Resolution at the Council of Constantinople (381), and Conflicts Concerning the Holy Spirit

Leaving aside other participants in the dispute at this point (among whom Hilary of Poitier and Didymus the Blind are important), we should note that the Second Council of Sirmium sparked a reaction in Basil of Ancyra and his associates. In 358, they condemned the view of Eudoxius of Antioch that the Son is *anhomoios*, or unlike the Father, as well as the view that the Son is *homoousios* in the sense of identical in substance (*tautousion*) with the Father. And they called the Son *homoiousios*, or of a like substance with the Father; this word had been used for the first time in the dispute only in 357, thirty-two years after Nicea. Basil of Ancyra's party came to speak of three *hypostaseis* to express "the subsisting and existing proprieties of the Persons" (H 367), noting that this position was not against the oneness of God. This shows the background for the Cappadocians' later theology, though Basil of Ancyra and his associates are still implicit believers in the subordination of the Son to the Father. For a time Constantius allied himself with Basil against Eudoxius, but Constantius died in 361 and Julian became emperor. Julian was a pagan and allowed bishops who had been exiled to return to their dioceses.

Athanasius called a council in Alexandria in 362, and the participants addressed themselves to the church at Antioch, giving conditions to a faction there for the restoration of communion. This 362 council said "that *ousia* and *hypostaseis* could be used in different senses, that it was possible to speak of *three hypostaseis* in an orthodox sense" (H 644), that is, if those who spoke thus accepted that the Son was *homoousion* with the Father. This statement was a concession and was a diplomatic step toward agreement in orthodoxy with the party of Basil of Ancyra. We should add that at this council too, it was said that the Son in becoming flesh also accepted a human soul.

During the second half of the fourth century a "second-generation" of pro-Arians developed, whom Hanson calls "Neo-Arian" and others call Anhomoians (unlike in substance) or Eunomians (from Eunomius of Cyzicus). The leader of the group was Aetius, and his watchword for the Son was *heterousios*, of another substance. He claimed to know God with such clarity that he did not know himself better than he knew God (H 603). He sought by logical analysis to show that the Son could not possibly be like the Father in substance. For example, if God had a Son, God would be subject to time. Eunomius taught that the Son was like the Father according to Scripture, but not like him in substance, because this would subject the High God to the experience of passions; begetting means process. The Son received his existence by the will of the Father. Eunomius made a distinction of "God's power or activity (*energia*) and his essence . . . a distinction which the Cappadocian fathers warmly embraced and which was to become an integral part of Eastern Orthodox theology" (H 626–627). Eunomius held that we can know God's substance; it is ingenerateness. This whole group used Aristotelian logic to support their all-prevailing rationalism.

The teaching of the Cappadocian theologians—Basil of Caesarea (died 379), Gregory of Nazianzus (died c. 389), and Basil's brother Gregory of Nyssa (died c. 396)—was of enormous importance in bringing about the resolution of the conflict and contributing to the church's doctrine on the Trinity. They came from the party of Basil of Ancyra, and behind that from the tradition of Gregory Theodorus (Thaumaturgus) and Origen, in that they emphasized the distinction among the Father, Son, and Holy Spirit; were initially cautious with the term *homoousios*; and spoke of the three as three *hypostaseis*, while they defended the equality among them. They came from a Platonist background and were aware of some writings of Plotinus; they may have been helped by Plotinus's use of the term *hypostasis* for the ultimate realities, but they rejected his view that there were three ultimate realities, holding that the Father alone is the ultimate source (H 677–678) and the Son and Spirit are equal with him. They certainly learned much from Athanasius (H 679) but faced a new generation of opponents and used more philosophy than Athanasius. We will first recall their trinitarian teaching here and then their specific treatment of the Holy Spirit.

Basil held that we could know the activities (*energeias*) of God and his works, but, against Eunomius, that only the Son can know his *ousia*. His main contribution to the trinitarian doctrine was perhaps to insist on the use of *hypostasis* for the three, as identifying the peculiarity of the three. He did come to the acceptance of *homoousios* and became a defender of Nicea, though moving beyond and against Nicea's almost identifying *ousia* and *hypostasis*. Concerning *ousia* and *hypostasis* he writes:

> The distinction between *ousia* and *hypostasis* is the same as that between the general and the particular. Wherefore, in the case of the Godhead, we confess one essence (*ousia*) so as not to give a variant definition of existence, but we confess a particular *hypostasis* in order that our conception of the Father, Son and Holy Spirit may be without confusion and clear. (Ep. 236,6)[17]

Thus at times he compares *ousia* to *hypostasis* as the general to the particular within a 'species', but Hanson notes: "in the *DSS [On the Holy Spirit]* he dismisses the idea that the distinction between the Godhead and the Persons is that between an abstract essence, such as humanity, and its concrete manifestations, such as man, so that the Holy Spirit could be regarded as a subclass within the Godhead" (H 698). That Basil was not wholly consistent is not surprising; "he was in a sense a pioneer in theology . . . [his teaching] was well designed to bring about theological consensus" (699). He uses *prosopon* (person) at times as an alternative to *hypostasis*, and also uses *hyparxis* (subsistence) or *tropos hyparxeos* (mode of subsistence) to indicate the three. The three are distinguished by their properties or peculiarities, not by their *ousia*. He insists that there is an order that exists among the persons, the Father being the sole origin or source or root, the Son being second, and the Holy Spirit third. It is important to note that the rationale for his theological work on the Trinity was Scripture and the tradition, the church's liturgy (particularly baptism), and his extensive teaching on spirituality.[18]

Gregory of Nazianzus taught as his friend Basil did, but in more lucid and lapidary phrases at times. He distinguishes between *ousia* and *hypostasis*, and permits the use of *prosopon* in an anti-Sabellian sense. The three hypostases or persons are equal and equally adorable; there is diversity in number but not in substance. He identifies the characteristic property of each, as ungenerated, being generated (not by material generation but by a generation somewhat like that of light coming from the sun), and proceeding *(ekporeusis)*. "'Father' designates neither the substance nor the activity but the relationship *(skesis)*, the manner of being, which holds good between the Father and the Son" (Oration 29:16; see 31:7,9).[19] He writes: "The three are a single whole in their Godhead and the single whole is three in its individual distinctions" (Oration 31:9, in Norris). We will return to the Cappadocians' teaching on the distinction of persons in chapter 8.

Similarly, Gregory of Nyssa wrote against Eunomius. Gregory taught the distinction between *ousia* and *hypostasis*, using the analogy of the distinction between a universal essence and distinctions within this, but insisting that other analogies too are necessary. He shows different analogies for the generation of the Son, but insists that for the understanding of this no analogy from corporeal generation is adequate; similarly, any suggestion of a time difference between Father and Son is false. There is no difference of rank among the three, but just one of order. The distinction of persons is due to their origin. The Father is the cause *(aition)*, and the other two are caused; the Father is unbegotten, the Son begotten or the only begotten, and the Spirit proceeds.

The Cappadocians both insisted against Sabellianism on the distinction of the three as three hypostases and accepted Nicea. They held to the unity of the persons. Gregory of Nazianzus writes that, "Each of the three Persons is as entirely one with those with whom he is connected as he is with himself, because of the identity of the essence and of the power" (Oration 31:16; quoted in H 736). "While none of the three held a doctrine of identity of substance as strict as that of Athanasius, none of them believed in a thinly disguised form of the *homoiousios*" (H 736). They did not deal with the Incarnation as much as Athanasius, but held against Apollinaris that the Logos had a human mind. Gregory of Nazianzus wrote, "What was not assumed was not healed" (Ep 101). And they attributed all Jesus' sufferings to his humanity; his divinity was unaffected.

We must realize that the passion of this whole controversy was not over words but because of the connection of the interpretation of the trinitarian mystery with the Christian life. Only if Jesus Christ was Son of God by nature could he know God and thus reveal him; only if he was Son by nature could he make us genuine sons or children by adoption, restore in us the image and likeness of God by his redemption, or give us a participation in his own Sonship and thus divinize us.[20]

The theme of the Holy Spirit was not particularly treated in the creeds and confessions between 325 and 360. But then during the second half of the fourth century there were also attacks on the divinity of the Holy Spirit. These insistent denials of the Spirit's divinity drew important responses from Athanasius and the Cappadocians, not that they were the only ones to defend the Spirit's divinity. Hanson notes Cyril of Jerusalem, George of Laodicea, Hilary, Gregory of Elvira, and Marius Victorinus as among the defenders of the Spirit's divinity. We will recall Athanasius's teaching and then that of the Cappadocians.[21]

Athanasius was the initiator here through his *Letters to Serapion* who had brought to Athanasius's attention attacks on the divinity of the Spirit. Athanasius argues to the Spirit's divinity from Scripture. He notes the prerogatives and activities Scripture ascribes to the Spirit; the Spirit sanctifies, vivifies, and makes us participants in the divine nature: "He who unites the creature to the Word cannot himself be numbered among creatures; he who confers sonship by adoption cannot be a stranger to the Son" (*Let. to Serap.* 1:25). The Father creates through both the Son and the Spirit (Ps 33:6), and he acts through both (1 Cor 12:4–6); he sends both, and they dwell together in us. So we should adore God in Spirit and Truth, that is in the Spirit and the Son (Jn 4:23–24). If the Spirit is a creature, this is the ruin of our baptismal faith, and there is no Triad but a Dyad. The Spirit is not created or generated, but "proceeds" (Jn 15:26), though this refers to the Spirit in the economy of salvation. Athanasius interprets the activity of the Holy Spirit without using the apocalyptic context of the New Testament. As Hanson writes, "Athanasius, like all Christian writers from the third century onwards at least, had lost the eschatological note which the NT witness to the Spirit contains" (H 752).

Some who attacked the divinity of the Holy Spirit at this time were called Macedonians after the bishop of Constantinople who is said to have accepted the divinity of the Son but refused to ascribe this to the Spirit. Eustathius of Sebaste was later the leader of this group. Others were called Pneumatomachians—those who fought against the Spirit. Their arguments were largely rationalistic. For example, they held that the Spirit is either generated or created; he is not generated, because the Son is the only begotten, and so he is created.

Basil had a custom of using two forms of the doxology, the traditional form, giving glory to the Father *through* the Son and *in* the Holy Spirit, but also a newer form, giving glory to the Father *with* the Son and *with* the Holy Spirit. And he was attacked for adding the latter to the traditional doxology. He argued on linguistic grounds that Scripture ascribed equality of adoration to the Spirit with the Father and Son. And he argued from the names and activities Scripture ascribes to the Spirit. He says that the Spirit "proceeds from the Father . . . as the breath of his mouth" (H 774; *On the Holy Spirit* 16:38). And he supported his position from the baptismal liturgy. In fact, he said that some mysteries of the faith not clearly in Scripture were preserved by the practices of the church. Out of prudence and a desire to promote consensus rather than division, he refrained publicly from directly saying that the Holy Spirit is God, but he indirectly said this in terms later incorporated in the Nicene-Constantinople Creed.

Gregory of Nazianzus refuted those who held that the Spirit was a creature by showing that there is a "mean" between being ungenerated (Father) and generated (Son), namely, that the Holy Spirit "proceeds" from the Father. Thus, he understood "proceeding" to refer not simply to the mission of the Spirit but to the Spirit's origin within the Trinity: "In so far as he proceeds from the Father, he is no creature; in as much as he is not begotten, he is not Son; and to the extent that procession is the mean between ingeneracy and generacy, he is God" (Oration 31:8, in Norris). He gives images for this 'proceeding' such as the "source, spring, river" and "sun, beam, light," but he acknowledges he does not know what 'proceeding' means within God. And he concludes from the way Eve came from Adam that it is possible to be of the same nature with another who is "ungenerate" (as Adam in a sense was) without being generated (as Seth was). He supports the divinity of the Spirit from the effects ascribed to him in Scripture. From these effects he finds that the Spirit is not simply an activity of God: "He says things, he decrees, he is grieved, he is vexed [1 Cor 12:11; Acts 13:2; Eph 4:30; Is 63:10]—all of which belong to a being "*with* motion, not to the process of motion" (Oration 31:6, in Norris). So he explicitly says that the Spirit is God and that he is consubstantial with the Father and the Son (Oration 31:10). He noted that there was an 'economy' or gradualness in God's revelation. The Savior had truths that, as he said at the time, could not be borne by the disciples. Gregory of Nyssa similarly concluded to the divinity of the Spirit from the functions and effects (*energeia*) of the Spirit witnessed to in Scripture. These Fathers teach very differently from some theologians in our time who reduce the Spirit to an outreach or activity of God, and they base their views on Scripture's authentic witness and authentic Christian tradition.

On becoming emperor, Theodosius declared Nicea to be the official doctrine of the Roman Empire. A council was convened in 381 in Constantinople that proclaimed a creed that did not survive. But in 451 at the Council of Chalcedon, an authority was ascribed to what came to be known as the First Council of Constantinople, and it was stated that this council had confirmed the faith of Nicea. The creed we know as Nicene-Constantinople comes from Chalcedon; it may not be the exact statement in all details of the earlier council but, perhaps, an existing creed that had integrated the 381 council's additions to Nicea. The additions primarily concern the Holy Spirit: "We believe in the Holy Spirit, the Lord and Giver of Life, who proceeds from the Father, who together with the Father and the Son is worshipped and glorified, and who spoke through the prophets." These additions are based on Scripture and reflect Basil of Caesarea's way of stating the divinity of the Holy Spirit; they imply that the Spirit is consubstantial with the Father and Son and a distinct *hypostasis* from them. The anathemas of Nicea were omitted, because now there was a clearer distinction between *ousia* and *hypostasis*. Theodosius confirmed the council. After this council there was a general acceptance of the Christian doctrine of the Trinity. The main reason it found such wide acceptance is that there was a consensus worked out in the two generations that separated Nicea from the First Council of Constantinople. Elements of consensus were in place before Theodosius, but unfortunately the suspicions Pope Damasus had toward Basil and Basil's use of three hypostases in speaking of the Trinity prevented them bearing fruit before Theodosius. The group that did not accept the council were the Goths who had been evangelized with an Arian belief by Bishop Ufilas; this would later have repercussions in the West.

Conclusion

In the period that separated the first Christian generation from the First Council of Constantinople there was a real development of the church's expression of its trinitarian belief or of doctrine. The ecumenical implications of this fact are widely recognized in our time. This is not the place to articulate these adequately; such a study belongs, it seems to me, particularly in that part of foundational theology that treats the norm of faith and the nature of theology.[22] Here we note only the following.

The history of the development of the trinitarian doctrine shows in practice how Scripture, tradition, a particular culture, and a realistic metaphysics are all operative and essential. We examined Scripture's witness to God's saving and revealing action through Jesus Christ and the Spirit he sent. And the baptismal practice of the early church showed a lived, if not articulated, faith in God as Father, Son, and Holy Spirit. The problem of proclaiming this faith to a culture other than that of Judaism had already become apparent in the apostolic age, and initial efforts in that direction had been made, in part in continuity with earlier and analogous efforts of Hellenistic Judaism. This proclamation was a problem of inculturation and hermeneutics. How were people with a different language and understanding or conceptuality of themselves in the universe to understand the message that was addressed to them, and integrate it into their lives in a way that was both faithful and transformative? A whole succession of Christian theologians, most of whom had a good education in Hellenistic culture, sought by a trial-and-error process to articulate this mystery and its implications for their lives. The successive interpreters used the tools of their culture, and later interpreters frequently learned from the gains and limitations of earlier interpreters. It was a real process of discovery. In fact, we can see more than simply human agency at work in this development; the Holy Spirit was present to guide the church "to all truth" (Jn 16:13). The passion shown in these disputes, discoveries, and controversies showed that it was not only words that were at issue. The passion was due to the participants' realization that views expressed on these issues had an enormous bearing of what it meant to be human and Christian, since this identity depended above all on God's relation to us and our relation to God.

Interpretations of this development as a Hellenization of an initially simple Christian faith, or as process of free speculation not rooted in Scripture's witness and authentic Christian tradition, or as a defense of an initial 'orthodoxy' are all distortions of what happened and are not supported by the evidence. The mystery witnessed to by Scripture was and is so profound and transcendent to simple human resources, whether individual or cultural, that it took generations for it to be sounded to the depth that it was toward the end of the fourth century. Any reflection on the Trinity today must be faithful to such roots if it wishes to be authentically Christian.

Notes

1. Official report of the Canberra Conference, 2.1, as quoted in Michael Driscoll, "From Faith through Creed to Unity? From Montreal to Santiago," in *Unum Omnes in Christo in unitatis servitio. Miscellanea Gerardo J. Békés O.S.B. Octogenario dedicata* (Pannonhalma, Hungary: Bencés Fóapátság, 1995), 229–230.

2. Faith and Order Paper 153 (Geneva: WCC, revised edition, 1991).

3. J. Farrelly, *Faith in God through Jesus Christ. Foundational Theology II* (Collegeville, Minn.: Liturgical Press, 1997), 261–262.

4. See Pope Paul VI, *Mysterium ecclesiae*, 24 June 1973, in Austin Flannery, ed., *Vatican Council II: More Post Conciliar Documents* (Northport, N.Y.: Costello Publishing, 1982), 433–434.

5. On both of these, see Adalbert Hamman, "La Trinité dans la liturgie et la vie Chrétienne," *Mysterium Salutis*, vol. 5, *Dieu et la révélation de la Trinité* (Paris: Cerf, 1970), 185–204; and Leo Scheffczyk, "L'élaboration du dogme dans le Christianisme primitif," *Mysterium Salutis*, vol. 5, *Dieu et la révélation*, 211–227; R. P. C. Hanson, "Creeds and Confessions of Faith," *EEC*, 1:206–208; Bernard Sesboué and Joseph Wolinski, *Le Dieu de Salut*, vol. 1, *Histoire des Dogmes* (Tournai: Desclée, 1994), 1–92. Unless otherwise noted, my translations of pre–fourth century writers are from the French of Sesboué and Wolinski.

6. J. N. D. Kelly, *Early Christian Doctrines*, 2nd ed. (New York: Harper and Row, 1960), 95. Kelly also points out that for Hermas "as pre-existent the Son of God is identified with the Holy Spirit, so that before the incarnation there would seem to have been but two divine persons, the Father and the Spirit" (94).

7. See J. Neuner and J. Dupuis, ed., *The Christian Faith in the Doctrinal Documents of the Catholic Church*, 5th ed. (London: Harper Collins, 1992), 3.

8. See in Sesboué and Wolinski, *Dieu de Salut*, 135–176; W. Rordorf, "La Trinité dans les écrits de Justin Martyr," *Augustinianum* 20 (1980): 285–297; and Alan Segal, "'Two Powers in Heaven'" and Early Christian Trinitarian Thinking," in Stephen Davis, Daniel Kendall, and Gerald O'Collins, eds., *The Trinity: An Interdisciplinary Symposium on the Trinity* (Oxford: Oxford University Press, 1999), esp. 84–88. He relates Justin's teaching to the "Two Powers in Heaven" Hellenistic Jewish tradition.

9. On Irenaeus, see Wolinski, *Dieu de Salut*, 159–176; F. Vernet, "Irénée (Saint)," *DTC* 7: 2442–2451; and A. Orbe, "Irenaeus," *EEC* 2:413–416.

10. On Tertullian, see Basil Studer, *Trinity and Incarnation: The Faith of the Early Church* (Collegeville, Minn.: Liturgical Press, 1993), 65–75.

11. See Wolinski, *Dieu de Salut*, 203–233. On the question whether there is to some degree a subordinationism in Origen's trinitarian theology, there is a dispute. See Johannes Quasten, *Patrology*, vol. 2 (Westminster: Newman, 1953), 76–79, 94–100; Joseph W. Trigg, *Origen: The Bible and Philosophy in the Third-century Church* (Atlanta: John Knox Press, 1983), 95–99; H. Crouzel, *Origen: The Life and Thought of the First Great Theologian* (San Francisco: Harper & Row, 1985), 186–192.

12. See Everett Ferguson, "The Kingdom of God in Early Patristic Literature," in Wendell Willis, ed., *The Kingdom of God in Twentieth-Century Interpretation* (Peabody, Mass.: Hendrickson, 1987), 191–208.

13. In this section I depend particularly on R. P. C. Hanson, *The Search for the Christian Doctrine of God: The Arian Controversy 318–381* (Edinburgh: T & T Clark, 1988), now widely recognized as the standard work on the subject, and one that summarizes interpretations of the controversy over the last 100 years. Page references in the text to H are to this book. See Rowan Williams's review article on this book in *Scottish Journal of Theology* 45 (1992): 101–111. Also see Sesboué, *Dieu de Salut*, 235–279.

14. Robert Gregg and Dennis Groh, *Early Arianism: A View of Salvation* (Philadelphia: Fortress Press, 1981).

15. See R. D. Williams, "The Logic of Arianism," *Journal of Theological Studies* 34 (1983): 56–81.

16. Here, Hanson relies on the work of Christopher Stead, *Divine Substance* (Oxford: Clarendon Press, 1977), though Hanson himself (H 167–168) thinks this anathema was ambiguous.

17. This text is cited by Catherine LaCugna, *God for Us: The Trinity and Christian Life* (San Francisco: Harper, 1991), 79, note 84. Hanson (690) cites to the same effect Ep. 38,3, but this letter is now widely ascribed to Gregory of Nyssa. See LaCugna, *God for Us*, 66–68 and notes for a discussion of the dispute among patristic scholars on the Cappadocians' views of this issue. Also see Joseph Lienhard, "*Ousia* and *Hypostasis*: The Cappadocian Settlement and the Theology of 'One *Hypostasis*'," in Davis, *Trinity*, 99–121. Lienhard describes "the current that resisted the confession of three *hypostases*, and suggest[s] that it was much stronger, and much more widespread, than is normally assumed" (102).

18. See, for example, G. Bardy, "Basil," *Dictionnaire de Spiritualité* 1 (1937): 1272–1283.

19. This translation is from Frederick Norris, ed., *Faith Gives Fullness to Reasoning: The Five Theological Orations of St. Gregory of Nazianzen*, trans. Lionel Wickham and Frederick Williams (Leiden: E. J. Brill, 1991).

20. See, for example, Jean Kirchmeyer, "Grecque (Eglise)," *Dictionnaire de Spiritualité* 6 (1967): 807–872. Kirchmeyer shows the influence of Genesis 1:26 (God made man in his own image and likeness) and the Platonic notion of forms in the spirituality of the Greeks: "The authors who do not distinguish the image from the likeness,

and this includes above all Athansiaus of Alexandria, Didymus, the Cappadocians, Evagrius, Pseudo-Macarius and Cyril of Alexandria, exploit at the same time the dynamism of the hellenistic notion of image (nostalgia for the archetype) and the perfective character of this image in the soul of the redeemed sinner. With certain Fathers the image seems to give everything in the beginning and to coincide with an original perfection that the creature has to conserve, of which there only remain vestiges and which grace permits one gradually and laboriously to recover. This is the optic of, among others, an Origen or an Athanasius. The idea of spiritual progress takes on then the appearance of a march backwards, of a return to paradise, of a restoration (apokatastasis) of what fundamentally constitutes one's nature . . . , but it still has to do with an authentic growth" (820). Also see A. O. Erhueh, Vatican II: Image of God in Man (Rome: Ubaniana University Press, 1987), chapter 1, "Classical Imago Dei Doctrine: History and Development."

21. See Sesboué, Dieu de Salut, 262–271; Hanson, Search, chapter 22, "The Doctrine of the Holy Spirit," 738–790.

22. See, for example, John Henry Newman, An Essay on the Development of Christian Doctrine (Garden City, N.Y.: Doubleday, 1960); Bernard Lonergan, The Way to Nicea: The Dialectical Development of Trinitarian Theology (Philadelphia: Westminster, 1976); J. C. Murray, "The Theological Problem: The Understanding of God," in The Problem of God (New Haven: Yale University Press, 1964), 31–76; William Reiser, What Are They Saying About Dogma? (New York: Paulist, 1978); Alister McGrath, The Genesis of Doctrine: A Study in the Foundations of Doctrinal Criticism (Oxford: Blackwell, 1990); Harding Meyer, "Scripture, Tradition, and the Church: The Ecumenical Nexus in American Lutheran Ecumenical Dialogue," Journal of Ecumenical Studies 28 (1991): 401–411; Hanson, Search, 869–875; Christopher Seitz, ed., Nicene Christianity: The Future for a New Ecumenism (Grand Rapids, Mich.: Brazos, 2001). On different degrees of authority ascribed to ecumenical councils by Christian churches, see Frans Bouwen, "Ecumenical Councils," in Nicholas Lossky, et al., eds., Dictionary of the Ecumenical Movement (Grand Rapids, Mich.: William B. Eerdmans, 1991), 336–339.

∼

CHAPTER FOUR

Later Soundings: The Fifth to the Nineteenth Century

In the preceding chapter we examined the development of the doctrine of the Trinity to the point of the Nicene-Constantinople Creed. We should now examine further developments that in part opened up fissures among different Christian bodies and still later led to a rejection of the Christian belief in the Trinity by erstwhile Christians. In this chapter we shall recall some significant reflections on the Trinity from (I) Augustine through the Council of Florence (1439), and then (II) from the Protestant Reformation to the nineteenth century. Adequate studies of these themes can be found elsewhere. These soundings in the history of reflection on the Trinity are important if we are to be adequately aware of the crises facing Christian belief in the Trinity in our time and place.

I. Major Reflections on the Trinity from Augustine through the Council of Florence (1439)

During this period we will recall reflections on the Trinity found in (1) Augustine and his early influence, (2) the question of the Spirit in Eastern Christianity and disputes with the West until the eleventh century, (3) the Trinity in scholasticism and medieval spirituality, and (4) Orthodoxy and efforts to resolve trinitarian differences from the thirteenth to the fifteenth century.

1. Augustine and His Early Influence

Augustine's teaching on the Trinity has been of enormous influence in Western Christianity and basic for its differences on trinitarian issues from Eastern Christianity. But this teaching and its influence have been variously interpreted.[1] We will look at his basic defense of Christian belief in the Trinity against the Arians and other adversaries, his use of analogies from the human mind to understand the Trinity, and his teaching specifically on the Holy Spirit.

Augustine shows his intent in writing his *De Trinitate* when he writes that he will defend "the rightness of saying, believing, understanding that the Father and the Son and the Holy Spirit are of one and the same substance or essence" (Bk I, 4). Part of his overriding emphasis on the *unity* of essence of the Father, Son, and Holy Spirit is due no doubt to the persistence of the Arian problem, particularly in the West where the Goths who were Arian were now widely settled. The polemical context of his theology of the Trinity has not always been recognized. Perhaps this emphasis on unity was due also to the influence of Neoplatonism on Augustine, with its emphasis on the One as the ultimate principle, from which the Nous and World Soul emanate.[2] Initially, it does seem that Augustine thought that he found the doctrine of the Trinity in the Neoplatonists' triad, though later he reacted to the diminished reality of the second and third of this triad when compared to the first.

Augustine starts from the faith of the church in his time, and to justify it, he states that "we must establish by the authority of holy scriptures whether the faith is in fact like that" (Bk I, 4). He turns to this in books I through IV. He argues for this by the theophanies of the Old Testament and the *missions* of the Son and the Holy Spirit in the New Testament which manifest their eternal *processions* from the Father and the Father and Son respectively. The Son and the Spirit are equal to the Father, though what is in the form of man in Jesus Christ is not equal.

In books V through VII Augustine shows and rebuts the arguments from reason that the Arians put forward to defend their view that the Father and the Son cannot be of the same nature or essence. The Arians, using Aristotelian categories, say that God is simple, so the distinction between Father and Son must be one of substance; the essence of God is to be unbegotten and of the Son is to be begotten. Augustine counters that the distinction between the persons is not in nature but in *relationship* (Bk V, 6f.). The words 'Father' and 'Son' are relational words, indicating the reference of the Father to the Son and vice versa. Similarly, the Holy Spirit is the *gift* of the Father and the Son, and the Father and the Son are the *giver* of the Spirit (Bk V, 12f.). They are one in being; thus, all absolute terms are said in the singular—one God, one Wisdom, one omnipotence, and so forth, though some perfections are *appropriated* to one person rather than another because of their fittingness to the relationship that constitutes that person. Augustine discusses the difference of vocabulary between the Greeks and the Latins. He acknowledges difficulties with the word 'person'. Perhaps his difficulty here comes from his interpreting the word 'person' as said absolutely and not in reference to another. Thus he writes: "[The Father] is called person with reference to himself, not with reference to the Son or Holy Spirit" (Bk VII, 11). He suggests that the reason we "say three persons while we never say three Gods or three beings, is that we want to keep at least one word for signifying what we mean by trinity, so that we are not simply reduced to silence when we are asked three what" (Bk VII, 11).

In reflection on this first part of the *De Trinitate* we can see that for Augustine what was prominent in his consciousness was the Trinity in itself as an examplar of the human self and its return to God, a theme we shall explore more below. He does of course treat the Trinity in the economy of salvation, or the missions of the Son and the Spirit, in many contexts and specifically as the means by which we can know something of the relationship among the persons within the Trinity. Through his focus on the Trinity in itself he had an influence on directing later Western theology to this theme to the point of marginalizing the Trinity in relation to the economy of salvation.

It seems that Augustine derived his notion of 'relations' from Gregory Nazianzen, but he used it differently. The Greeks tended to speak of the Father as God and to defend the equality of Son and Spirit with the Father from the fact that the Father generates one like to himself in nature in the Son and 'breathes' forth the Holy Spirit. For them, relation was secondary to generation, and the distinction of persons was primarily due to property of each—unbegotten, begotten, and 'proceeding'. Augustine tended to show equality by emphasizing first of all the unity of essence of the three; relations were a way of showing that there could be distinctions among the three who were one in essence.

In the second part of his *De Trinitate* Augustine searches for *images* of the Trinity in the human being, particularly in the mind of man—in fact, in the male of the species, because the male is particularly associated with the higher function of the mind (contemplation) and woman with the lower (practical affairs) (Bk XII, ch. 1–3). Man, that is Adam, was made in the image of God (Gn 1:26), and God is triune. This search for images serves an anagogic purpose, because it presents us with a way to return to God, somewhat as Plotinus directed human beings to return to the One by way of turning within and then from within toward union with the One.

Augustine finds a number of images of the Trinity in the human being, but he particularly stresses the mind of man, because it is our spiritual activities of knowledge and love that make us most similar to God. He understands the mind more on the Platonic than the Aristotelian model. For Augustine, "the soul, or the mind as he calls it in that particular context, is primarily a center of self-awareness, of reflexive presence. It knows itself, and . . . it loves itself, simply by being itself."[3]

Our mind involves memory, knowledge, and love. Memory expresses the reality that, "when [the mind] is not thinking about itself . . . it still knows itself by being somehow its own memory of itself" (Bk XIV, 8):

> That is why we were constantly presenting a trinity in this way, placing in the memory that from which the gaze of thought is formed, treating the actual conformation as the image that is printed off from it, and finding the thing that joins both together to be love or will. So when the mind views itself by thought, it understands and recognizes itself; thus it begets this understanding and self-recognition. . . . These two, begetter and begotten, are coupled together by love as the third, and this is nothing but the will seeking or holding something to be enjoyed. (Bk XIV, 8)

This is an image of the Trinity. The mind's knowledge of the self is found in memory. Memory in turn allows the mind to form the *verbum mentis*, or interior word. Thus we have an image of the Father begetting the Son or Word (see Bk XV, 19–20). And one not only knows oneself; one loves oneself; in fact, it is love that keeps the mind's attention directed to the self. This is an image of the Holy Spirit. A still better image is the mind's memory of God (rather than self), understanding of God, and love of God (see Bk XIV, 12, 15). There is one mind, and yet there are distinctions within it that depend on an opposition of relations, and the three are within each other. It is a very imperfect image, however, since in God the three are not actions modifying one substance but three who are one substance.

Augustine is not seeking by these images to prove that God is triune, but to get some deeper understanding of what he believes based on God's revelation, as well as to show the implications of this faith for our own return to God. An unfortunate result of this approach, as rich and valid as it is, is that it tends to induce a spirituality that is excessively interior and individualistic. Also, it does not sufficiently reflect the way God comes to us now in the order of redemption through the Son and the Spirit from the future of the kingdom, as we have shown from Scripture. Moreover, Augustine contributed significantly to Western patriarchy by the way he considered the image of God to be found in the man more than in the woman.

Thirdly, Augustine sees from Scripture that the Holy Spirit is the Spirit of the Father (Mt 10:28; Jn 15:26) and the Spirit of the Son (Gal 4:6; Jn 14:26) and has a name common to both, since Father and Son too are holy and spirit. If he is the Spirit of both, he proceeds from both. He is said in Scripture to proceed from the Father (Jn 15:26) because he principally proceeds from the Father (see Bk XV, 17, 29), and everything that the Son has he has from the Father. Augustine noticed that in Scripture the Spirit is spoken of as the *gift* (Acts 8:20; Rom 5:5; Jn 4:7). He concludes that while the Spirit is the gift of the Father and Son, the Father and Son are the giver of the Spirit, a relationship that is found not simply in the economy of salvation but in the interrelationship among the three within the Trinity. While the Father is love and the Son is love, being constituted as a person by love itself is ascribed to the Spirit because in the economy of salvation we receive the gift of love from the Spirit. Moreover, "if the charity by which the Father loves the Son and the Son loves the Father inexpressibly shows forth the communion of them both, what more suitable than he who is the common Spirit of them both should be distinctively called charity?" (Bk XV, 37) Augustine was not the first in the West to teach that the Holy Spirit proceeds from the Father *and* the Son *(Filioque)*, but he developed this view in a way more thorough and more influential for the West than his predecessors. We will see below how his view of the Spirit was contested by the Greeks.

Augustine's influence in trinitarian doctrine was more and more accepted in the West in the following several centuries, as we can see from the "Athanasian Creed," Fulgentius of Ruspe, and the Spanish Church. We recall that the Goths and Vandals were Arian and that they became overlords in the south of Gaul, North Africa, and Spain where the expressions of faith we will mention below were formulated. Thus, an overriding concern of these churches was to combat the Arian heresy, and so they emphasized with Augustine the Trinity within itself almost to the exclusion of the Trinity in the economy of salvation.[4]

The creed *Quicumque vult* (Whoever wishes), ascribed to Athanasius for many centuries, probably came from Augustinian circles in the south of Gaul in the second half of the fifth century. This creed affirms unity and equality in the divinity and in every absolute attribute of the three persons who are one in substance; it also affirms the distinction among the Father who comes from no one, the Son who is generated, and the Spirit who "proceeds from the Father and the Son" (DS 75).

Fulgentius of Ruspe (died c. 533), from North Africa but in exile in Sardinia, was the preeminent Western theologian of the sixth century. Against a Western anti-Nicene, Fabian, who considered the Son and Spirit to be of lower status than the Father, he used the argument that since the Spirit was sent by Father and Son, he proceeds from the Father and the Son (*a patre filioque procedit*). The later disputed *Filioque* had an anti-Arian root.[5]

The Visigoths in Spain upheld an Arian position until Recared became king and embraced Catholicism (587). In 589 he inaugurated the conversion of his Visigothic kingdom to Catholicism at the Third Council of Toledo, at which an anti-Arian creed was promulgated, declaring the unity in substance and the distinction of persons in the Trinity. Recared also incorporated the creed *iuxta orientalium partium morem*, the Nicene-Constantinopolitan creed, into the Mass.[6] Later, while Isidore was the metropolitan of Toledo, the Fourth Council of Toledo (633) once more promulgated a creed, now with the addition affirming the Spirit as "proceeding from the Father and the Son" (DS 485). This was repeated in the Sixth Council of the Toledo (DS 490) in 638 and the Eleventh in 675. The last named used much Augustinian terminology. For example, it professed that, "In the relation of persons number is seen: but in the substance of divinity what is numbered is not included" (DS 530). This council's sense of the analogical or paradoxical character of its language is shown in its statement that the Son was born "from the womb of the Father (*de Patris utero*)" (DS 526). The Nicene-Constantinopolitan Creed was used in the Mass in both Spain and Gaul, and at some point, perhaps the last decade of the sixth century, the *Filioque* was added, no doubt in good faith.

2. The Holy Spirit in Eastern Christianity, and Disputes between East and West until the Eleventh Century

Eastern theology is a reflection of a spirituality in which the Holy Spirit has a central part. We shall comment on this spirituality in a later section of this chapter, because it was very much influenced by Gregory Palamas in the fourteenth century. First, we will briefly recall something of the Spirit in Eastern Christianity's theology until the eighth century, and then the disputes between West and East from the late eighth until the eleventh century. Here, suffice it to recall Gregory Nazianzen's assertion that, "It is the Spirit in whom we worship and in whom we pray," and his question that if the Spirit is not to be worshiped, how can he deify me at Baptism? ("The Fifth Theological Oration," 12, see 28).

The image of the Holy Spirit in Eastern Christianity is somewhat different from that of Augustine. Basil had written about the Spirit before Augustine: "He [the Spirit] is moreover said to be 'of God' . . . in the sense of proceeding out of God, not by generation, like the Son, but as Breath of his

mouth" (*On the Holy Spirit*, ch. 18, para. 46). And, citin
this same image to speak of the Spirit's operation in crea
the resurrection of the dead: "By the word of the Lord were i
and all the host of them by the breath of his mouth" (Letter &
ing from Ps 33:6).[7] This image of the Spirit is not that of int
ceeding from the good and knowledge of the good, so much as ___ breath
that comes from the mouth as it speaks the word. This image emphasizes the
Spirit's 'proceeding' from the same source as that of the generation of the
word, the simultaneity of its origin with that of the word, a certain mutuality of influence between word and breath and the difference in manner of
origin. It is to be noted that in this image the coming of the Spirit from the
Word or Son is not asserted.

Congar recalls three Eastern Fathers of the church from the fourth to the
eighth centuries who asserted in one way or another a certain origin in being of the Spirit from the Son within the Trinity: Cyril of Alexandria, Maximus the Confessor, and John Damascene. Cyril sought to show against
Nestorius that the Spirit belonged to the Incarnate Word, but he based this
on the relations between the Spirit and the Word within the Trinity. He has
formulae "relating to the Spirit as proper to the Son (*idion*), coming from
him (*ek*), the Spirit as proceeding from the Son (*proïenai* or *procheitai*) and
proceeding from the two (*ex amphoin*), that is, from the Father and the Son
or from the Father through the Son."[8]

In the seventh century, Maximus the Confessor taught that the Spirit proceeded from the Father "by means of the Son" (*dia mesou tou Logou*). And he
defended Pope Martin I who had written in a letter that the Spirit "has his
ekporeusis [proceeding] from the Son." Writing to the Cypriot priest Marinus
in 655, he defends the Romans, because:

> [they] have produced the unanimous evidence of the Latin Fathers, and also of
> Cyril of Alexandria. . . they have shown that they have not made the Son the
> cause (*aitian*) of the Spirit—they know in fact that the Father is the only cause
> of the Son and the Spirit, the one by begetting and the other by *ekporeusis*
> (procession)—but that they have manifested the procession through him (*to
> dia autou proïenai*) and have thus shown the unity and identity of the essence.[9]

For the Greeks 'cause' (*aitia*) meant the first source, and this first source of
the Spirit is the Father. Maximus acknowledged that the Latins, because of
their language, did not express themselves as precisely as the Greeks. This
letter shows that there was a difference of expression between the Latins and
the Greeks on this issue even at that time, but that this did not disturb their
ecclesial unity.

In the eighth century, John Damascene wrote his synthesis of the faith of the church, *De fide Orthodoxa*, depending, in his section on the Trinity, on the work of an unknown author called "pseudo-Cyril." John speaks of the mutual indwelling of the three persons in one another (*perichoresis*), the generation of the Son, and the procession of the Holy Spirit. John professes ignorance of the difference between generation and procession. He writes, "[the Spirit] is the Spirit of the Son, not because he comes from him (*ouch hos ex auton*), but because he comes through him (*all' hos di' autou*), since the Father is the only cause (*monos aitios ho Pater*)," and, "Through the Word, the Father produces the Spirit, who manifests him . . . proceeding through him from the Father."[10] The relation of breath to word is present here, as J. Grégoire interprets John:

> His [the Spirit's] hypostatic property, the procession, is only accessible and understandable—insofar as it can be made intelligible—by reference to the Son, just as the breath can only be accessible by reference to the word. . . .
> If the Spirit comes from the Father by procession and remains in him, unlike our breath which disappears into the air, this must be by 'penetrating' the Son until he remains and dwells in him at the same time as he does in the Father. The procession must therefore be *dia Huiou* (as John Damascene claims) or else the Spirit must rest *in* the Son (as Pseudo-Cyril says).[11]

What we have written above shows that aside from any polemical context there was a difference in understanding the Spirit between the East and the West. This difference became an important and divisive ecclesial problem in the centuries that followed.[12] Charlemagne reacted against the confession of faith proffered by the patriarch Tarasius to the Second Council of Nicea (787), because Tarasius said that the Spirit proceeded from the Father *through* the Son, rather than from the Father *and* the Son. Pope Hadrian I affirmed the orthodoxy of Tarasius's belief. But Charlemagne gathered bishops at a council at Frankfurt in 794 that affirmed the *Filioque*, and a later synod that justified the addition of the *Filioque* to the creed.

Some years later, in Palestine, an Orthodox monk became aware that Frankish monks of a monastery at the Mount of Olives were using the *Filioque* in the creed at Mass, and he denounced this as heresy. On their appeal to the West, the Western monks were defended by a Frankish council (809). Pope Leo III agreed with the doctrine of the *Filioque*, but he rejected its addition to the creed. He signalized this rejection by having the creed without the *Filioque* engraved in Greek and Latin in two tablets and hung on the two sides of the main altar at St. Peter's. The creed with the *Filioque* was not used at Rome until 1014, and then at the insistence of Emperor Henry II.

At this time the churches of the West and East were in communion, though the cultural and political differences between them were becoming more evident. We will not elaborate on the causes that brought this tension between Rome and Constantinople to a head in the ninth century. We simply recall that it was Patriarch Photius of Constantinople who raised the *Filioque* question into a reason justifying the Eastern Church's rejection of the authority of Rome. Photius wrote an encyclical in 867, which he sent to the Eastern patriarchs and in which he accused the West of heresy because of the *Filioque*. Twenty years later, after several changes in fortune, Photius in exile composed his book *The Mystagogy of the Holy Spirit* that contained his theology of the Holy Spirit—a theology later used by generations of Orthodox.

In his theology, Photius held that the Holy Spirit proceeds from the Father alone (*ek monou tou Patros*). The monarchy of the Father means that he and he alone is the 'cause' of the Son through generation and of the Spirit through procession. Photius interpreted Scripture's statement that the Spirit proceeds from the Father (Jn 15:26) as meaning that the Spirit proceeds from the Father alone. He interpreted Scripture's words that the Spirit is the Spirit of the Son as indicating the Spirit's consubstantiality with the Son; and Christ's words that the Spirit "will take from what is mine" (Jn 16:14) as being applicable only to the economy of salvation. He tried to support his views by the Fathers of the church, but omitted statements of the Fathers that differed from his view or bent them to his own position. He held that the persons of the Trinity are distinguished adequately by their personal properties—unoriginate, generated, and proceeding. And he held that an action is either due to one divine person alone or to their common nature. Thus the Holy Spirit could not proceed from both the Father and the Son or from the Father through the Son.

Political and cultural differences between the papacy and Constantinople were once more acute in the mid–eleventh century. And the patriarch Michael Caerularius (1043–1058) developed a campaign against the papacy based on ritual differences such as the use of unleavened bread in the Latin rite and the practice of fasting on Saturdays. He added the issue of the *Filioque*. Western legates sent to Constantinople by Pope Leo IX exacerbated things severely by their highhandedness. They excommunicated the patriarch and his accomplices on July 16, 1054, accusing them of a number of heresies. Later that month the emperor convoked a synod that turned back the excommunication on the legates and their supporters. This is usually considered the beginning of the Caerularian Schism, though the legates had not attacked the Eastern Church as such, and Caerularius had not excommunicated the pope, who, in any case, was dead by the time his legates acted in Constantinople.

3. The Trinity in Scholasticism and Medieval Spirituality

In what follows we are only taking some "soundings" or probes in the incredible flowering of spirituality and scholasticism in the West.[13] We are interested in illustrating three issues: first, the focus on the Trinity in itself more than on the Trinity in the economy of salvation; second, the continuing dominance of the Neoplatonic *exitus–reditus* context for trinitarian theology and spirituality, though this dominance was questioned by the historical and apocalyptic approach of Joachim of Fiore; and third, the difference of interpretation of the Trinity in Richard of St. Victor and Thomas Aquinas.

An indication of a doxological approach to the Trinity as it is in itself rather than as it is in the economy of salvation is offered by the preface for the Feast of the Trinity, the use of which on Sundays is attested in the twelfth century and more widely in the thirteenth. The Feast of the Holy Trinity was approved by Rome for use throughout the church shortly thereafter:

> It is truly proper and just, right and saving, that we should at all times and in all places give thanks to you holy Lord, Father almighty, eternal God, who with your only begotten Son and the Holy Spirit are one God, one Lord, not in the unity of a single person, but in the Trinity of one substance. For what we believe, through your revelation, of your glory this we believe of your Son and of the Holy Spirit, without difference or separation. So in confessing your true and eternal Deity we adore distinction in persons, oneness in being and equality in majesty.[14]

We can add that interventions of the magisterium concerning trinitarian issues in the late eleventh to the early thirteenth century were directed to the unity and distinctions within the Trinity. Thus the tritheism associated with Roscelin's nominalism was condemned by the Synod of Soissons (1092). The Council of Rheims in 1148 (DS 745) rejected a distinction between the persons and the divine essence and the view that there is some distinction between that by which God is God (*divinitas*) and God himself that some accused Gilbert de la Porrée of holding.[15] The Fourth Council of the Lateran (1215) (DS 803-805) condemned the view of Joachim of Fiore that the divine essence and three persons constituted a quaternity.[16]

The influence of Augustine's notion of the human person as image of God and its implications for our spiritual growth was evident in Richard of St. Victor (d. 1173). Richard has profound analyses of stages of spiritual growth and contemplation in his books *The Twelve Patriarchs* and *The Mystical Ark*. But what is immediately relevant to our theme here is the way that Richard reflects on human experience to illuminate the mystery of the Trinity. What he takes from this human experience is not what Augustine primarily takes, but rather our experience of the centrality of interpersonal love as a supreme value. In the third book of his book, *The Trinity*, he argues that since God is the supreme good, "true and supreme charity cannot be lacking [in God]. For nothing is better than charity; nothing is more perfect than charity. However, no one is properly said to have charity on the basis of his own private love of himself. And so it is necessary for love to be directed toward another for it to be charity. Therefore, where a plurality of persons is lacking charity cannot exist."[17] Thus, in God there must be not only one person but another divine person who can properly be loved and respond with a supreme charity. This need could not be fulfilled by creatures, since creatures' perfection is not commensurate with such a supreme love. These persons could not be equal unless they were of one substance.

But further, in the human experience of the greatest charity, those two who enjoy mutual love wish to share this greatest of goods with yet another so that this other is loved equally with the good that one has. Thus, the perfection of charity requires a Trinity of persons. Richard presents this illumination by reasoning based on faith and Scripture. It is associated with the spirituality of the Victorine canons regular, but more universally with common Christian experience that reflects human beings as images of God.

We should note that much of the late medieval mysticism was based on an Augustinian image tradition that incorporated Pseudo-Dionysius's apophatic Neoplatonism. This is particularly true of Meister Eckhart (c. 1260–1328) and, in varying degrees, those whom he influenced. Here the *exitus–reditus* context for understanding spirituality is emphasized. For example, in Eckhart human beings are more what they are in God by exemplarity and by their birth in God in the birth of his Son before they actually exist than they are in their earthly existence. In life they are called to return to what they were before they were in concrete existence.[18]

Joachim of Fiore (c. 1135–1202) broke with the Western tradition concerning the Trinity in the sense that what was central for him was not the Trinity in itself but the Trinity in the economy of salvation, and his model for understanding this Trinity was not the human person as an image of God but a hermeneutics of Scripture that interpreted successive and overlapping stages of history as associated by way of appropriation with persons of the Trinity.[19] The first stage was that of the Father; it included the dispensation before the Law and under the Law, and was the stage of married people. The second stage was that of Christ; it began with Ozias, bore fruit from the time of Zachary, the father of John the Baptist, and was having its consummation in Joachim's time. It was characterized by the clerical order and preaching. The third stage is that of the Spirit, which began with St. Benedict, was bearing fruit from the twenty-second generation after him and will be consummated at the end of the world. This stage is characterized by contemplatives, primarily monks, and a spiritual understanding of Scripture. The married and clerical orders do not end with the third stage; members of these orders can be true contemplatives. Joachim shifts the focus of the church toward the stage of the Spirit, but this does not replace that of Jesus Christ, because in people of the third stage Christ will reign more powerfully. This vision placed the focus of church reform in the future rather than in the past. Though critiqued for good and bad reasons (e.g., because of the excessive influence in these critiques of the *exitus–reditus* model), this model does catch something of the early apocalyptic Christian focus on the future. According to that, the present influence of the Son and Spirit on the Christian should be interpreted primarily as a coming from the future and leading us to transcendence and God through our orientation to the future kingdom.

We will have many occasions later in this book to recall Thomas Aquinas's teaching on the Trinity and so shall restrict ourselves here simply to noting the following. He basically followed Augustine's use of the human mind's acts of knowledge and love to illuminate our understanding in faith of the Trinity in itself. Both Augustine and Thomas were metaphysicians, but while Augustine spoke more on the level of experience Thomas wrote more on the level of metaphysical analysis. Thomas's study of the Trinity (especially in *Summa theologiae*, I, QQ 27-43) systematically investigates the Trinity in itself first and only then (in Q 43) the Trinity in the economy of salvation, though we must remember that his students had already studied Scripture. His lack of an understanding of the New Testament's apocalyptic message and his adoption of the *exitus–reditus* context for theology, a theme we will return to in the next chapter, contributed to his curt rejection of Joachim of Fiore's interpretation (see ST, I–II, 106, 4).

4. Orthodoxy and Efforts to Resolve Trinitarian Differences at the Council of Florence (1438)

We will reflect briefly on this theme by recalling Orthodox spirituality and institutions in relation to the Trinity, the foundations for Hesychasm given by Gregory Palamas, and some efforts to resolve trinitarian issues at the Second Council of Lyons but particularly at the Council of Florence.

Orthodox trinitarian theology is more a spirituality than a theology in, at least, the scholastic sense. It has been more closely related to life than Western trinitarian theology in the modern era.

A study of Othodox spirituality can be found elsewhere, but here we restrict ourselves to noting that what is central to it is the mystery that is communicated to us by God through Jesus Christ and the Spirit and that is celebrated by the liturgy and lived by the Christian community.[20] It is the contemplation of this mystery that is central to Eastern spirituality from early times. Irenaeus writes: "When we are born again in baptism, given us in the name of the three Persons, we are endowed in this second birth with good things which are in God the Father, by means of his Son and the Holy Spirit . . . knowledge (gnosis) of the Father is the Son, and knowledge of God's Son is obtained through the Holy Spirit."[21] It is the glorified Christ who sends us the Spirit so that we may be introduced to this mystery through faith and baptism and may be transformed into the image and likeness of the Trinity or be deified. And it is in the church that the mystery is revealed.[22] Central to this whole process is the liturgy. Contemplation is fostered particularly by the symbolic character of the liturgy. It is a kind of knowledge that is in the Spirit or one that engages the whole human person; it is dependent upon purification and is transformative or leads toward communion with God and deification. It is more a knowledge of presence by divine illumination than a directly intellectual knowledge.

The mystery of deification "reflects the trinitarian 'economy of salvation,' and particularly the economy of the Spirit."[23] The Holy Spirit introduces in souls the divine energy by which they have the capacity to know God and love him.[24] Or, as Dimitru Staniloae writes, Christ "is seen as he who acts now in us by the uncreated energies of the Holy Spirit leading us toward his resurrected state, while in the West the disregard of the uncreated energies which come within us tend to mean that the Christ is rather viewed in function of remembrance, filled with thanksgiving, of his passion accomplished in history."[25]

This leads us to consider Gregory Palamas (1296–1359) who is the classical theological defender of the Eastern form of prayer called Hesychastic.[26] This prayer form united a kind of 'mantra' such as the constantly repeated Jesus prayer ("Lord Jesus Christ, Son of God, have mercy on me") with the breathing process. The practitioners, primarily but not exclusively monks, claimed that it could lead to a vision of God or of the glory and light of God, calling upon Scripture's account of the Transfiguration (e.g., Mt 17:1–8) and John 17:24: "Father . . . that they may see my glory that you gave me before the foundation of the world." A Calabrian monk, Barlaam, attacked this form of prayer, its interpretation of the light at the Transfiguration as the uncreated glory of God, and the claim that the creature could see God in this life. Gregory defended the prayer and theology of Hesychasm, a defense that was later vindicated by the Eastern Church.

To defend the validity of this prayer in a way that was consistent with the transcendence of God, Gregory Palamas, partially depending on Gregory the Cypriot, the patriarch of Constantinople (d. 1290), made a distinction between the essence of God and the uncreated energies (*energeiai*) of God. He held with the Cappadocians (in their battle against Eunomius) that the essence of God is unknowable, but claimed that by the grace of God human beings can know and participate in the uncreated divine energies. For example, he writes: "[N]either the uncreated goodness, nor the eternal glory, nor the divine life nor things akin to these *are* simply the superessential essence of God, for God transcends them all as Cause. . . . He Who is beyond every name is not identical with what He is named, for the essence and energy of God are not identical."[27] These uncreated energies are ontologically distinct from the divine essence and are 'enhypostatic' in the three divine persons, or are within the hypostases of the divine persons.[28] Among the energies is the divine glory, which, through the gift of grace, can be seen by human beings and can be participated in by human beings. Thus, a genuine deification is possible; it is not, however, possible for the human being to be so united with the essence of God, because then such a being would be God.

As to his *hypostasis*, Gregory agrees with Photius that the Holy Spirit proceeds from the Father alone, but according to his energies he proceeds through or from the Son.[29] It seems that the uncreated energies, light or glory and life that are given to human beings and seen by some of them are in Gregory's mind particularly associated with or mediated by the Holy Spirit, though in complete union with the economy of Christ.[30]

As a reflection on Gregory Palamas, it is good to recall his intention, as Meyendorff writes: "The only concern of Palamas was to affirm simultaneously the transcendence of God and His immanence in the free gift of communion in the Body of Christ. This concern could not be fully expressed in philosophical or conceptual terms."[31] Western theologians have frequently attacked Palamas's assertion of a real distinction between the divine essence and the uncreated energies of God.[32] This distinction seems incompatible with Thomas's view of the simplicity of the divine being. But medieval Western theologians' interpretation of grace as a predominantly created gift may itself be inadequate to account for a genuine 'deification' given us through grace. In the twentieth century, a number of Western theologians have emphasized the uncreated gift of grace, namely, the gift that the divine persons make of themselves to human persons.[33]

Concurring with other recent theologians, we will suggest in our final chapter an approach that, we hope, may do justice to the Orthodox experience and theology of the Spirit and also contribute to the Western understanding of the Spirit. The issues of our participation through grace of the 'energies' particularly associated with the Holy Spirit and of the Spirit's 'proceeding' from the Father as 'breath' are mutually connected, and perhaps the dominant Western theology has not done justice to Orthodox experience.

There were efforts to resolve the "Caerularian Schism," for example at the Second Council of Lyons (1274) and particularly at the Council of Ferrara-Florence (1438–1439). At the Second Council of Lyons there was so little discussion of the issue of the Holy Spirit at the council that the emperor's agreement that the Holy Spirit proceeds from the Father and the Son as one principle (see DS 850–853) seemed like a Western imposition and was repudiated by his successor in Constantinople when the political reasons for its acceptance diminished.

The discussion at the Council of Ferrara-Florence on the question of the procession of the Holy Spirit lasted some months in the first part of 1439 at Florence, where the council had been transferred, before an agreement was signed by the Catholics and almost all the Orthodox representatives. The letter of Maximus the Confessor that we quoted above, the citations by Western representatives of many Greek Fathers asserting that the Spirit proceeds through the Son, and the teaching of many Western Fathers led the Greeks to acknowledge that there was an influence of the Son on the procession of the Spirit and that this was asserted in similar ways by the Greeks and the Latins. Thus virtually all the Greeks subscribed to the following statement of the council:

> We define that . . . the Holy Spirit is eternally from the Father and the Son; . . . he proceeds from each eternally as from one principle and by a single spiration. . . . [W]hen the holy Doctors and Fathers say that the Holy Spirit proceeds from the Father through the Son, this has the meaning that the Son is, as the Greeks say, the cause, and as the Latins say, the principle of the subsistence of the Holy Spirit, as the Father is. And since the Father gives by generation to the only begotten Son everything that belongs to the Father, except being Father, the Son has eternally from the Father that the Holy Spirit proceeds from the Son. . . . We define also that the explanatory words 'Filioque' were licitly and reasonably added to the Creed for the sake of declaring the truth and because of imminent necessity. (DS 1300–1302)

Unfortunately, the reunion based on this agreement and several others was disowned by some prominent clergy in the East and by the people who remembered causes for resentment, for example, the sack of Constantinople by the crusaders and the imposition on them of a Western kingdom. The council's statement still today offers some hope for further discussions, though as Congar writes, we must acknowledge that it may seem to subordinate the Eastern theology of the Trinity to that of the West by using the word 'cause' to indicate the influence of the Son on the being of the Spirit, and the word 'procession' to express this influence. Both of these words had been reserved by the Greeks to the relation of the Father to the Spirit.[34]

II. Some Reflections on the Trinity from the Protestant Reformation to the Nineteenth Century

During this period there have been radically different views on the Trinity in the West proposed by those who call themselves Christians, as well as a widespread erosion of belief in God as triune. We shall first (1) note some views from the sixteenth to the eighteenth centuries, and then (2) in the nineteenth century.

1. The Protestant Reformation to the Eighteenth Century

Luther and Calvin held to the Christian doctrine of the Trinity as articulated by the Nicene-Constantinople creed. Perhaps one can say that they proclaimed the Trinity more as it was operative in the economy of salvation than as it was in itself. For example, Luther proclaims that it is only the Holy Spirit who "by the Gospel has called me, with his gifts has enlightened me, through genuine faith has sanctified and sustained me, just as he calls, gathers together, enlightens, sanctifies and sustains, by Jesus Christ, in true and proper faith, all Christendom."[35] Luther did not deny the Trinity, but it was secondary to the question of justifying faith. Luther's revolt was initially and largely a reaction to scholasticism and what he interpreted as its speculative and objective study of the Christian mysteries out of a spirit of curiosity.[36]

Perhaps we can say that much late medieval scholastic theology merited some of Luther's criticisms but that his and others' attempts to present the mysteries of the faith as relevant to us were built on bases that gave too much weight to religious experience and detracted from doxology. Calvin was so faithful to the Christian trinitarian belief that he approved of the execution of Servetus (1553) as a heretic because he denied the Trinity. The Lutheran and Reformed official confessions and the Anglican liturgical books included the Nicene-Constantinople Creed.

Luther and Calvin's belief in the Trinity was contested in varied ways by the radical reformers or Anabaptists. Generally, Luther and Calvin held that the Spirit was bound to the word of Scripture, so that an interpretation of

Scripture contrary to the word could not come from the Spirit. Some radical reformers had more confidence in the illumination that came from the Spirit:

> It was, above all, the radical Anabaptist Hans Denck who pushed the antithesis of Spirit versus structure to the point of setting the Spirit into antithesis also with the "false literal understanding of Scripture." Anyone who did not have the Spirit but sought to understand Scripture, he insisted, would find darkness rather than light, . . . conversely, "anyone who genuinely has the truth can take account of it without any Scripture."[37]

The Anabaptists were united in applying the principle of *sola scriptura* to resist church tradition on infant baptism and to accept the baptism of believers only, as seemed to them to have been practiced in the apostolic church. This same principle of resistance to church tradition could be used to undermine the Nicene-Constantinople articulation of the Christian trinitarian belief. Some Anabaptists refused to draw this conclusion (e.g., Menno Simons, Balthasar Hubmaier), but Hans Denck was silent about the Trinity when he wrote a doctrinal statement on the Christian understanding of God.[38]

An energetic antitrinitarianism was promoted particularly by Faustus Socinus (d. 1604), one of a group of Italian religious dissidents who took up residence in Poland and the one who was very influential with an antitrinitarian group there. Socinus accepted *sola Scriptura*, and he held that we should not accept later unscriptural terms such as *homoousios* that are not conformable with Scripture but should rather interpret Scripture by reason. One can see here the influence of the Renaissance humanism. Jesus' salvific function was to proclaim the mercy of God, and thus he did not have to be the 'Son of God' in the ontological traditional sense, but just one who was adopted as God's Son.[39] The Holy Spirit is a kind of power or efficacy of God, as is indicated by the word 'spirit' that in Hebrew meant 'breath'. His followers' *Racovian Catechism* (1605) supported this by holding that the divine essence is only one and thus cannot be three persons, since a person is an intelligent, indivisible essence. This doctrine influenced much of Arminianism in Holland, in that the Arminians sought to dispense with doctrinal terms that went beyond Scripture.

The need of defending the confessions of the various Christian churches led to a period of renewed scholasticism in which Lutherans as well as Catholics systematized their beliefs. The basis of Christian belief in the Trinity in Scripture and tradition was studied. For example, the Catholic Petavius, or Denis Petau (1583–1652), studied the bases for belief in the Trinity in Scripture and tradition in his *Dogmata theologica* (4 vols., 1644–1650).

Two responses to the interdenominational differences and the wars and polemics that came in their wake were pietism and an increasing dominance of reason over Christian revelation, both of which seriously affected the Christian belief in the mystery of the Trinity.

Philipp Jakob Spener (1635–1705), the most prominent founder of the pietist movement, called for a renewal of personal religion. Without denying Lutheran doctrine, he promoted Christianity as a matter of the heart more than of the mind and sought to form a clergy whose heart was right with God even more than one whose doctrine was orthodox. Later, Count von Zinzendorf (d. 1760) fostered the pietistic movement by his writings, which insisted on a devotion of the heart as central to Christianity, and by his support of the Moravian Brethren at Herrnhut. The importance of personal experience and of community were both emphasized. The pietistic movement revitalized the Lutheran Church in Germany and engaged in a remarkable missionary endeavor, but: "Emotion played so large a part in the religious life that the role of reason was seriously disparaged. . . . 'He who wishes to comprehend God with his mind becomes an atheist,' wrote Zinzendorf. Pietism failed to keep spiritual vitality and intellectual vigour in proper balance, and this was its most serious defect."[40]

This emphasis on the subjective is found in another way in nonconformist movements in England, and in an extreme fashion in George Fox (1624–1691), the founder of the Religious Society of Friends. Fox came to have such confidence in the inner divine light that illumines all who come into the world (see Jn 1:9), that this light became an all-sufficient religious principle, making what one believed secondary. Many of Fox's disciples retained a trinitarian belief, but with time many did not, such as William Penn, the leader of the Pennsylvania colony. We noted in our first chapter that the Arminian and Mennonite Churches of the Lowlands and the U.S. Society of Friends were among the members of the World Council of Churches who did not accept the council's affirmation of belief in the Trinity as constitutive of what it means to be Christian.

A reaction to tradition, doctrine, and organized Christian religion that was more extreme and, eventually, more influential in the later Western world was found in the increasing dominance given to 'reason' over tradition and Christian revelation. It is this movement that is, particularly in its eighteenth-century shape, called the "Enlightenment."[41] This movement was based on both modern knowledge, for example, on mathematics and Newtonian physics, and on practical concerns, such as in the general desire for greater autonomy in human affairs. The latter led to the critique of ecclesiastical institutions and doctrines as constraining and inhibiting this autonomy. Also, the movement was supported by the new knowledge Europeans had of non-Christians, many of whom were morally good, that came from the Americas and China. Once this dominance of 'reason' over Christian revelation is established, it eliminates all distinctively Christian doctrines, both in the foundations for their belief and in their practical relevance to human life. For example, John Locke, in his book *The Reasonableness of Christianity* (1695), accepted Jesus as Messiah, miracles, and resurrection, but rejected such doctrines as predestination and the Trinity. Newtonian physics came to have more influence on many in their understanding of God than traditional Christian belief. Deism came to full bloom in Matthew Tindal's *Christianity as Old as Creation* (1730), which reduced what is acceptable in Christianity to what reason can prove. And David Hume's empiricism and religious skepticism fostered such deism.

In the United States it was largely under such influences that a number of churches withdrew from the Calvinist Congregationalist Churches of New England to become Unitarians. A prominent exponent of this position, Ralph Waldo Emerson, placed the basis of religion in human subjectivity: "Jesus Christ belonged to the true race of prophets. . . . Alone in all history he estimated the greatness of man. One man was true to what is in you and me. He saw that God incarnates himself in man, and evermore goes forth anew to take possession of his world. He said in the jubilee of this sublime emotion, 'I am divine.'"[42] Eventually Emerson left even this position and embraced a vaguely pantheistic religious view.

The English resistance to Christian revelation became very influential on the continent during the eighteenth century through such philosophers and publicists as Voltaire, the Encyclopedists, and Rousseau. The rationalist tradition influenced Gotthold Lessing (1729–1781) who, while agreeing that positive religions were necessary, particularly in the childhood of the human race, held that the present and future ages were the stage of 'reason', the "new eternal Gospel" (*The Education of Mankind*, 1780). Thus, Lessing used the development of historical consciousness to challenge the traditional doctrine of the Trinity. The beginning of the application of the historical critical method to the gospels was not for all under the influence of naturalistic assumptions (e.g., R. Simon); but for some it was, for instance, in the works of Reimarus published by Lessing, and thus it too contributed to a broader erosion of trinitarian belief. Finally, Immanuel Kant (1724–1804) defended a natural faith in the human sense of moral obligation, for by this experience we are justified in postulating a supreme lawgiver, human freedom, and immortality. Such a faith, however, does not justify belief in God as triune, save as a representation of a practical idea. If we were to take this faith as describing "what God is in Himself, it would be a mystery transcending all human concepts, and hence a mystery of revelation, unsuited to man's powers of comprehension; in this account, therefore, we can declare it to be such."[43]

2. Some Reflections on the Trinity in the Nineteenth Century

In this period we shall restrict ourselves to notes on Hegel, Schleiermacher, and varied late-nineteenth-century estimates of the value of the development of the doctrine of the Trinity in the patristic age, and also on several Catholic theologians. We recognize that there were both Protestant and Catholic theologians who continued earlier orthodoxies. But we agree that a theology of the Trinity in our time must accept the challenges posed by historical consciousness (e.g., in Hegel) and subjectivity (in both Schleiermacher and Hegel), so that repetitions of earlier orthodoxies are not adequate. The application of the historical-critical method to the New Testament in the nineteenth century also undercut Christian belief in the Trinity, because it credited the gospel of Mark as being both historically and theologically closer to the life of Jesus and tended to discredit the gospel of John where the more explicit trinitarian passages are found. We do not follow this trend here, because we have addressed it in our earlier chapter on Scripture.

Georg W. F. Hegel (1770–1831) sought to integrate the Christian doctrine of the Trinity with modern historical consciousness and self-consciousness in a way that has influenced not only later humanistic atheisms but also some Christian interpretations of the Trinity. He attempted to address the dichotomy between the Enlightenment and Christian orthodoxy as a Christian philosopher.[44] Without showing how he defends his view in his *Phenomenology of Spirit*, his *Logic*, and his history of religion, we note that he seeks to give a central place to the doctrine of the Trinity. The Ultimate is not substance but Spirit or Subject—specifically Spirit that expresses itself dialectically. Religion, and in particular the absolute religion, Christianity, expresses the dialectic of Spirit in the mode of representation (*Vorstellung*) or pictorially; and philosophy depends on its content. But the deeper meaning of religion is achieved when philosophy renders its content as concept (*Begriff*). Even in the 'immanent' Trinity, the Father is understood to express himself in the Other, the Son, and there is a return to the Father in the Spirit. But without creation, this emergence is a kind of play or not real:

> Creation, to put it with deliberate ambiguity, is that same going forth which is essential to the nature of Spirit. . . . What the Idea is intrinsically cannot be so separated from its manifestation of itself. The Other is the external world . . .

[we should not] imply the false idea that the eternal Son of the Father is simply identical with the world. Yet it is of course also true that for Hegel God has his self-consciousness in man's consciousness of him, that Spirit thus comes to self-consciousness.[45]

We will not analyze how for Hegel the Spirit expresses itself in the varied religions and finally in the 'God-man' Jesus who dies and rises; we only note that Jesus' community becomes the community of the Spirit:

The name 'Holy Spirit' refers to the unifying and liberating power of divine love arising from infinite anguish—the same love that was objectively represented on the cross of Christ but that now works inwardly, subjectively, building up a new human community. . . . The Kingdom of God is the Spirit, or more precisely, 'the Kingdom of the Spirit', which is the name for the third sphere of the Consummate Religion.[46]

Hegel's view is not a pantheistic monism, but rather a kind of panentheism: "God is dependent or 'consequent' upon the world to become God in the true and actual sense. God is God-in-process. 'Without the world God is not God' (L.P.R. [Lectures on the Philosophy of Religion] I: 114–115, 200)."[47] The basis for our acceptance of this interpretation is in part the external origin of this view in history (i.e., the Christian symbols), but this external attestation to it is a matter of indifference: "if it is to be valid, this validity can only build itself up upon the foundation of all truth, in the witness of the Spirit."[48] By this, Hegel means that this interpretation must make a difference to me that is desirable; in this sense, it is founded on the "witness of the Spirit."

We can see that Hegel somewhat integrates the Trinity with the historical process and with its fulfillment in human self-consciousness. We also see that the source of this knowledge for Hegel is not revelation in its full Christian meaning as a free communication through the historical Jesus Christ from a personal God distinct from and transcendent to human beings.

Friedrich Schleiermacher (1768–1834) was, like Hegel, influenced by romanticism in his theology. He came from a pietist background, and he identified religion, not with doctrine or with practice, but with feeling, specifically a feeling of absolute dependence. What we primarily mean by God is the source and 'object' (or the whence and whither) of this feeling.[49] Thus, religion is not subject to the critique of philosophy, because it is 'sui generis'. Christian religion, as an historical positive religion—and the highest—is that consciousness of union with God found in Jesus and those who accept his mediation. What is central in Christian religion is redemption—the overcoming of a sense of division from God by a sense of union with God—through the mediation of Christ. Theology is the explication of the contents of Christian self-consciousness.

For Schleiermacher there is no essential difference between the God-consciousness of Jesus and that of the church. Moreover, he held that the doctrine of the Trinity goes beyond the data of Christian self-consciousness to read distinctions existing eternally in God and independent of the union of divinity with human nature. Trinitarian doctrine is not "an immediate utterance concerning the Christian self-consciousness but only a combination of several such utterances."[50] His view here is in accord with his teaching that "all attributes which we ascribe to God are to be taken as denoting not something special in God, but only something special in the manner in which the feeling of absolute dependence is to be related to Him."[51] Schleiermacher held that the true Christian understanding of our fellowship with God does not demand the traditional doctrine of the Trinity.

In all this Schleiermacher thought that his notion of theology, as dependent upon and an analysis of his Christian self-consciousness or religious experience, was in continuity with Luther's. For us, his view does not accord with either Scripture or tradition. True, theology should be dependent upon the believer's relation to God; but this relation itself is dependent upon God's relation to the believer, as witnessed by the revelation of Jesus Christ and the Spirit. For Schleiermacher, religious experience has precedence as the criterion of revelation over God's relation to us as witnessed by Scripture. He does not make room for the Otherness of God.

Toward the end of the century diverse values were ascribed to the development of the doctrine in the early church. For example, the Anglican Aubrey Moore accepted the legitimacy of this development, citing John Henry Newman's work on the Fathers as support. Moore found in the Christian belief in God as triune an answer not simply to the moral concern of his time but to the concern to integrate reason or philosophy with genuine religious faith.[52] On the other hand, A. von Harnack, a disciple of the Protestant liberal theologian Albrecht Ritschl, held that the center of Jesus' teaching was the kingdom of God and its coming, the fatherhood of God and the infinite value of the human soul, the higher righteousness and the commandment of love. He interpreted the development of the trinitarian dogma, starting with the preexistence of the Logos, as a distortion of the historical Jesus and a Hellenization of Christianity.[53]

Among Catholic reflections on the mystery of the Trinity in the nineteenth century, we can first note that Johann Adam Möhler (1796–1838) of the Tübingen school of Catholic theologians wrote on the unity of the church soon after Schleiermacher's writing on that theme, and he gave to the genuine Christian doctrine of the Trinity a centrality in the interpretation of the church that Schleiermacher did not.[54] We will limit ourselves here to presenting an example of a trinitarian theology that used post-Kantian idealist philosophy and then describing the renewal of Thomistic theology that contributed to Vatican I.

Anton Günther (1783–1863) took the problem of harmonizing faith and reason as the central task of the theologian. This meant for him the problem of harmonizing the historical Christian revelation and the demands of necessary scientific knowledge. Positive revelation had to be transformed into a necessary and systematic knowledge. In this process he opposed the Hegelian notion of an impersonal Absolute that is necessarily objectified in nature and comes to consciousness in human beings. He used Descartes' *cogito* to start his philosophical anthropology from a self-awareness that gives us access to knowledge of noumenal reality. By thematization of this knowledge and opposition to the non-ego we realize that we are spirit or subject. Thus the human spirit

> must achieve its actual self-consciousness through a dynamic process. In the first moment of that process the spirit is simply a 'substance'. . . . In order to become a 'subject', the 'substance' must determine itself to the state of being a knower and lover. . . . The human spirit is thus enabled to define itself as an Ego, a knowing subject, over against the Non-Egos presented to it in its act of knowledge.[55]

God also is a self-conscious spirit. And so God must have determined himself to be such a spirit through a timeless triadic process:

> The Father knows himself and, in knowing himself, emanates [*sic*] the Son as his objectivated image. . . . They are related to each other through the opposition of thesis and antithesis . . . [an opposition that must be overcome] by a subsequent act of knowledge in which the being of the Father and the being of the Son is seen to be identical. . . . This subsequent act of knowledge is the Holy Spirit. . . . Through the procession of the Holy Spirit God becomes aware of himself. . . . Therefore a self-conscious God must be triune.[56]

This theology, though opposed to Hegelianism, claims that after the passive reception of divine revelation, the theologian can prove at least the positive possibility of the trinitarian mystery. And Günther also implies an interpretation of 'personality' in the Trinity associated with a processive achievement of conscious self-identity. Günther's view was rejected by Rome as a semi-rationalism in 1857, and he humbly accepted this.

er's opponents in Rome was Joseph Kleutgen, S.J., perhaps
nd of the Jesuit neothomists, who in the second half of the
.ntury were realigning Catholic theology with Thomas
: of the implications of this realignment was the recognition
.rine of the Trinity was the linchpin of theology. Thomas had or-
gani.. ᵒology on the *exitus=reditus* model, seeing all reality flowing from
the triune God and, by redemption, returning to God through Jesus Christ
and the Spirit, grace and the theological virtues, the church and the sacraments.[57] This view did not relate the Trinity in the economy of salvation to
the apocalyptic character of the kingdom of God or to modern historical
consciousness. But the renewed use of Thomas helped the church in Vatican
I to clarify the relation of faith and reason and to reassert that mysteries of
faith such as that of the Trinity are strictly supernatural and cannot be
known unless they are revealed by God (see DS 3005).

Conclusion

From this account of reflections on the mystery of the Trinity in Christian or
post-Christian countries of the West, it seems that the major problem for
Christian theologians today in this area of theology is to join forces to present an articulation of our belief that is both faithful to Scripture and early
tradition and relates it to aspects of modern culture that have contributed to
the erosion of trinitarian belief. The loss of the centrality of trinitarian belief
for many Christians is a more serious problem than opposition to one or another Christian theology. But in addressing the problem, we should also seek
to do justice to the insights of varied contemporary theologies. We cannot
address the most important issue of trinitarian theology in a vacuum.

Notes

1. We will use Augustine, *The Trinity*, with introduction, translation, and notes by
Edmund Hill, O.P. (Brooklyn: New City Press, 1991). Our quotations are from that
book. For some recent interpretations of Augustine's teaching on the Trinity and ref-
erences to earlier differences of interpretation, see William Hill, *The Three-Personed
God: The Trinity as a Mystery of Salvation* (Washington, D.C.: Catholic University of
America Press, 1982); Yves Congar, *I Believe in the Holy Spirit*, vol. 3, *The River of Life
Flows in the East and the West* (New York: Seabury Press, 1983), 80–95; Catherine
Mowry LaCugna, *God for Us: The Trinity and Christian Life* (San Francisco: Harper,
1991), 81–109; Colin Gunton, "The Trinity and the Theological Crisis of the West,"
Scottish Journal of Theology 43 (1990): 33–58; Basil Studer, *Trinity and Incarnation:
The Faith of the Early Church* (Collegeville, Minn.: Liturgical Press, 1993), 170–185;

Gaetano Lettieri, "Agostino," chapter 11 of Enrico del Covolo, ed., *Storia della teologia*, vol. 1, *Delle origine a Bernardo di Chiaravalle* (Rome: Edizioni Dehoniane, 1995), 353–421; Michael Barnes, "Augustine in Contemporary Trinitarian Theology," *Theological Studies* 56 (1995): 237–250; Sara H. Lancaster, "Three-Personed Substance: The Relational Essence of the Triune God in Augustine's *De Trinitate*," *Thomist* 60 (1996): 123–140.

2. This is held by O. du Roy, *L'Intelligence de la foi en la Trinité selon S. Augustin. Genèse de sa théologie trinitaire jusqu'en 391* (Paris: Etudes Augustiniennes, 1966), 458, cited in Congar, *I Believe*, vol. 3, 83. Barnes, "Augustine," 244–245, contests this.

3. Hill, *Three-Personed God*, 259.

4. On this period, see Congar, *I Believe*, vol. 3, 49–53; Edmund Fortman, *The Triune God: A Historical Study of the Doctrine of the Trinity* (Philadelphia: Westminster, 1972), 154–165; Hubert Jedin, ed., *History of the Church*, vol. 2 (New York: Crossroad, 1980), chapters by Karl Baus (129–136), Eugene Ewig (558–573), and Hermann Vogt (707–722).

5. See Vogt, 716–718.

6. See Ewig, 570.

7. Th. Spidlík, "Orthodox spiritualité," *Dict. de Spiritualité* 11 (1982): 997, states that the Orthodox compare the presence of the Holy Spirit to our hearts to the presence of air to our breathing.

8. Congar, *I Believe*, vol. 3, 35. References are given by Congar. We shall limit ourselves to the following quotation from Cyril (*Thes.*, PG 75, 608A-B), cited by Congar: "Since when Christ renews us and makes us enter a new life, it is the Spirit who is said to renew us, as the psalmist says: 'Send forth thy Spirit and they will be created and thou wilt renew the face of the earth' (Ps 104:30), we are bound to confess that the Spirit is of the *ousia* of the Son. It is by having his being from him according to nature and by having been sent from him to the creature that he brings about the renewal, being the fullness of the holy Triad." Cyril was attacked by Theodoret of Cyrrhus for saying that the "the Spirit has his existence either from the Son or through the Son" (Congar, 35), but he continued to use formulae to this effect.

9. Maximus, letter to Marinus, PG 91, 136, cited by Congar, *I Believe*, vol. 3, 52–53.

10. *De fide orthodoxa*, I, 12 (PG 94, 849), cited by Congar, *I Believe*, vol. 3, 38–39.

11. J. Grégoire, "La rélation éternel de l'Esprit au Fils d'apres les écrits de Jean de Damas," *Revue d'histoire ecclésiastique* 64 (1969): 750–751, 753.

12. On what follows, see Congar, *I Believe*, vol. 3, 53–60; H. Jedin, ed., *History of the Church*, vol. 3, in chapters by Eugene Ewig (82–83, 97), and Hans-Georg Beck (174–193, 404–425); Francis Dvornik, *The Photian Schism: History and Legend* (Cambridge: Cambridge University Press, 1948); Fortman, *Triune God*, 93–95.

13. On this period in the West and East, see Bernard McGinn, John Meyendorff, and Jean Leclercq, eds., *Christian Spirituality: Origins to the Twelfth Century* (New York: Crossroad, 1985); and Jill Raitt with B. McGinn and J. Meyendorff, eds., *Christian Spirituality: High Middle Ages and Reformation* (New York: Crossroad, 1988).

14. Roman Missal, for Feast of Holy Trinity. For a history of the development of Christian liturgical prayer from the earlier way of addressing the Father *through* the Son and *in* the Holy Spirit to the later doxology, and so forth, to the Father *with* the Son and *with* the Holy Spirit, see Catherine LaCugna, *God for Us*, chapter 4, 111–142. For the emergence of the Feast of the Holy Trinity, see P. Mulhern, "Trinity, Holy, Devotion to," *NCE* 14:306–307. For medieval prayer to the Holy Spirit and hymns *(Veni Creator, Veni, Sancte Spiritus)*, and charitable institutions under the patronage of the Holy Spirit, see Congar, *I Believe*, vol. 1, 104–114.

15. See Fortman, *Triune God*, 181–185; Étienne Gilson, *History of Christian Philosophy in the Middle Ages* (New York: Random House, 1954), 140–144.

16. See Fortman, *Triune God*, 197–201.

17. *The Trinity*, book 3, chapter 2, in Richard of St. Victor, *The Twelve Patriarchs. The Mystical Ark. Book Three of the Trinity*, trans. and intro. by Grover Zinn (New York: Paulist, 1979), 374. See the more traditional treatment of the Trinity in St. Hildegard of Bingen (1098–1179), *Scivias*, trans. Mother Columba Hart and Jane Bishop (New York: Paulist, 1990), book 2, chapter 2, and book 3, chapter 7. We should note too that Hildegard, like some other medieval spiritual writers, speaks of "God's maternal love, which has nourished us unto life and is our help in perils, and is the deepest and sweetest charity and prepares us for penitence" (162).

18. See Alois Maria Haas, "Schools of Late Medieval Mysticism," in Raitt, *Christian Spirituality: High Middle Ages*, 148f.; Paul Rorem, "The Uplifting Spirituality of Pseudo-Dionysius," in McGinn, *Christian Spirituality: Origins*, 132–151; and "Meister Eckhart," in Louis Dupré and James Wiseman, O.S.B., eds., *Light from Light: An Anthology of Christian Mysticism* (New York: Paulist, 1988), 152–172.

19. See Bernard McGinn, *The Calabrian Abbot: Joachim of Fiore in the History of Western Thought* (New York: Macmillan, 1985); and my *Faith in God through Jesus Christ* (Collegeville, Minn.: Liturgical Press, 1997), 224–229, where I also evaluate Thomas Aquinas's critique of Joachim.

20. See M. J. Le Guillou, *The Spirit of Eastern Orthodoxy* (New York: Paulist Press, 1964); Sergius Bulgakov, *The Orthodox Church*, revised trans. (New York: St. Vladimir's Seminary Press, 1988); articles on Orthodox spirituality in McGinn, *Christian Spirituality: Origins* and Raitt, *Christian Spirituality: High Middle Ages*; Georges Khodr, "L'Esprit Saint dans la tradition Orientale," *Credo in Spiritum Sanctum. Atti del Congresso Theologico Internationale di Pneumatologia (1982)* (Vatican: Vatican Libreria Editrice, 1983), vol. 1, 377–408.

21. *Adversus haereses*, 4:7, as cited in Le Guillou, *Spirit*, 17.

22. See Le Guillou, *Spirit*, 19. This relation of the church to mystery is relevant to the growing estrangement between the Eastern and Western Churches after the Gregorian reform, the Crusades, the "imperial" papacy, and the rise of scholasticism and universities. John Meyendorff writes in "Two Visions of the Church: East and West on the Eve of Modern Times," in Raitt, *Christian Spirituality: High Middle Ages*, 446: "The East, meanwhile, remained quite allergic to the institutional developments of the West, particularly to the centralized papacy, whereas the monastic the-

ology triumphant in Byzantium in the fourteenth century emphasized the experiential, mystical, and eschatological elements of the Christian faith rather than the legal and the rational principles that dominated the ecclesial institutions and the schools of the West."

23. John Meyendorff, "Christ as Savior in the East," in McGinn, *Christian Spirituality: Origins*, 241.

24. See Khodr, "L'Esprit Saint," 380.

25. Dimitru Staniloae, "Le Saint Esprit dans la théologie Byzantine et dans la réflexion Orthodoxe contemporaine," *Credo in Spiritum Sanctum*, vol. 1, 669.

26. See, for example, Gregory Palamas, *The Triads*, ed. with an intro. by John Meyendorff, trans. Nicholas Gendle (New York: Paulist, 1983); Congar, *I Believe*, vol. 3, 61–71; LaCugna, *God for Us*, chapter 6, "The Teaching of Gregory Palamas on God," 181–205; Markos Orphanos, "La procession du Saint Esprit selon certains Pères grecs postérieurs au VIIIe siècle," in Lukas Vischer, ed., *La Théologie du Saint-Esprit dans la dialogue entre l'Orient and l'Occident. Document Foi et Constitution*, #103 (Paris: Le Centurion, 1981), 29–53, especially 38–53; Jacques Lison, "L'Énergie des trois hypostases divine selon Grégoire Palamas," *Science et Esprit* 44 (1992): 67–77; J. Lison, *L'Esprit répandu, La pneumatologie de Grégoire Palamas* (Paris: 1994); and Stavros Yangazoglou's review of Lison's book in *The Greek Orthodox Theological Review* 42 (1997): 160–166. The bibliography on Gregory Palamas is noted by Congar and LaCugna and is immense.

27. Palamas, *Triads*, III, ii, 10, p. 97.

28. Lison, "L'Énergie," 74, writes, "The divine energy (will and action of God) come from the unique tri-hypostatic essence to produce a single work of the three hypostases. But each hypostasis produces this movement of the one energy according to its order: the Father is the primordial cause of it, it unfolds through the Son and it manifests itself finally in the economy of the Spirit."

29. See Orphanos, "Procession," 40.

30. See Palamas, *Triads*, III, l, 9, p. 71. Meyendorff comments on this "deifying gift" as follows (137, fn. 2): "The point here is that the divine energies (or light) *are* the very life of God (the 'divinity') in which the saints are called to share; yet God ineffably transcends this life or divinity in His essential nature." While referring to this passage in Palamas, LaCugna writes (202, fn. 24): "This has led some to claim that Gregory's theology of divine light is really a pneumatology. It is the Spirit who deifies."

31. Meyendorff, introduction to *Triads*, 22.

32. It is not only Western theologians who attacked Palamas and Hesychasm. See Hans-Georg Beck, "The Byzantine Church: The Age of Palamism," in Hubert Jedin, ed., *History of the Church*, vol. 4, *From the High Middle Ages to the Eve of the Reformation*, 488–520.

33. See, for example, Karl Rahner, "Grace," *Sacramentum Mundi* (New York: Herder and Herder, 1968), vol. 2, 412–427. Lison suggests that there is reason to hope for a mutual understanding between Orthodoxy and the West on the Filioque, but

that "In what concerns pneumatology, the chasm is without doubt deeper between the western conception of created grace and the eastern of uncreated grace" (75).

34. See Congar, 184–191. Also see Joseph Gill, S.J., *The Council of Florence* (Cambridge: Cambridge University Press, 1959).

35. Luther, *Short Catechism*, quoted by Alasdair Heron, *The Holy Spirit* (Philadelphia: Westminster Press, 1983), 100.

36. See Jaroslav Pelikan, *Reformation of Church and Dogma (1300–1700)*, vol. 4 of *The Christian Tradition*, (Chicago: University of Chicago Press, 1984), 156. On the whole modern period also see Robert Franks, *The Doctrine of the Trinity* (London: Gerald Duckworth, 1953), 136–177; A. Michel, "Trinité. III. La Crise Protestante et ses Répercussions dans la Théologie Catholique," *DTC* XV, 2 (1950): 1766–1796.

37. Pelikan, *Christian Tradition*, vol. 4, 320. See also Hans Küng and Jürgen Moltmann, eds., *Conflicts about the Holy Spirit*, Concilium, vol. 128 (New York: Seabury, 1979). While some radical reformers claimed the Spirit as the source of truth, many claimed the Spirit more to justify the congregational principle, that is, the Spirit as illuminating the local Christian community, and as a principle of appropriation of the truth.

38. Pelikan, *Reformation*, 321.

39. See Pelikan, *Reformation*, 326.

40. G. R. Cragg, *The Church and the Age of Reason, 1648–1789* (Baltimore: Penguin, 1966), 104.

41. See James Livingston, *Modern Christian Thought: From the Enlightenment to Vatican II* (New York: Macmillan, 1971), chapters 1–3.

42. Emerson's address to graduates of Harvard Divinity School in 1838, cited in John Hardon, S.J., *The Protestant Churches of America* (Westmister: Newman Press, 1956), 243. Emerson's viewpoint continues to be prominent in the United States. Harold Bloom writes in *The American Religion: The Emergence of the Post-Christian Nation* (New York: Simon & Schuster, 1992), 259: "The God of the American Religion is an experiential God, so radically *within* our own being as to become a virtual identity with what is most authentic (oldest and best) in the self. Much of early Emerson hovers near this vision of God: 'It is by yourself without ambassador that God speaks to you. . . . It is God in you that responds to God without, or affirms his own words trembling on the lips of another.'"

43. Kant, *Religion Within the Limits of Reason Alone*, cited in Kimball Kehoe, *Theology of God: Sources* (New York: Bruce, 1971), 256.

44. On Hegel see Peter Hodgson, "Georg Wilhelm Friedrich Hegel," in Ninian Smart, et al., eds., *Nineteenth Century Religious Thought in the West*, vol. 1 (Cambridge: Cambridge University Press, 1985), 81–121; Claude Welch, *Protestant Thought in the Nineteenth Century*, vol. 1, *1799–1870* (New Haven: Yale University Press, 1972), 86–107.

45. Welch, *Protestant Thought*, 101–102. See Hodgson, "Hegel," 91: "Concrete existence belongs necessarily to the concept of the Absolute because in order to be itself it has to become something other than itself, positing an actual world into which

it directs itself and from which it returns to itself, enriched, spiritualized, 'existentialized.'"

46. Hodgson, "Hegel," 106.

47. Hodgson, "Hegel," 101.

48. Hegel, *Lectures on the Philosophy of Religion*, vol. 1, trans. E. B. Speirs and J. Sanderson (New York: Humanities Press, 1962), 43.

49. See Welch, *Protestant Thought*, 59–85; B. A. Gerrish, "Friedrich Schleiermacher," in N. Smart, *Nineteenth Century Religious Thought*, vol. 1, 123–156. Also, see C. Welch, *In This Name: The Doctrine of the Trinity in Contemporary Theology* (New York: Scribner's, 1952), chapter 1, "The Doctrine of the Trinity in the Nineteenth Century," 3–41; and James Livingston, "Friedrich Schleiermacher," 96–112.

50. Schleiermacher, *The Christian Faith* (Edinburgh: T & T Clark, 1928), #170, l.

51. Schleiermacher, *Christian Faith*, #50.

52. See Aubrey Moore, "The Christian Doctrine of God," in Charles Gore, ed., *Lux Mundi: A Series of Studies in the Religion of the Incarnation* (London: John Murray, 1890), 55–109.

53. See A. von Harnack, *What Is Christianity?* (New York: Harper and Row, 1957), 51, and *History of Dogma*, trans. from 3rd German edition (New York: Dover, 1961), vol. 1, 41–48, 328–331.

54. See Dennis Doyle, "Möhler, Schleiermacher, and the Roots of Comunion Ecclesiology," *TS* 57 (1996): 467–480.

55. Gerald McCool, *Catholic Theology in the Nineteenth Century* (New York: Crossroad, 1977), "Anton Günther's Dualism," 102.

56. McCool, *Catholic Theology*, 103.

57. See McCool, *Catholic Theology*, "Kleutgen's Theological Synthesis: II. Practical and Speculative Theology," 197.

CHAPTER FIVE

~

The Trinity's Relation to the Orders of Salvation and Creation

We have studied some major current issues in the theological interpretation of the Christian mystery of the Trinity, and then Scripture and tradition on this mystery. Remaining faithful to Scripture and tradition we now seek to articulate aspects of the mystery in a way appropriate to our own culture. Some theologians call this section of theology "constructive" theology because we articulate, partially in our own voice, the theology of the Christian mystery to communicate with our time and place. This section deserves this title in a special way. However, what we have done so far in this volume also deserves it since we approached the interpretation of Scripture and tradition from the perspective of our current problems and resources, and not only from the perspective of the times of their writing.

We are responsible for presenting the mystery in a way that it and its implications for human existence may be authentically understood in our time as it has been for previous cultures in Christian history. Theologians of previous ages explained the mystery by relating it to their understanding of the humanity–cosmos–God relationship as they were able to know this in their time and place. And so we are following in their footsteps by seeking to do that in our time and place. Our understanding of this relationship has changed significantly in recent centuries because of the development of science, historical consciousness, and human experience more broadly. We have to take this into consideration in our theology of the Trinity. As Vatican I said, "When reason illumined by faith seeks it with care, piety and sobriety, it gains by God's help some understanding, and that most fruitful, of the mysteries from analogy with things naturally known, and from their relation among themselves and with the goal of humankind."[1] Also, the understanding of Scripture has developed so that we understand the place of apocalyptic in early Christian theology; this affects the way one relates the mysteries to one another. To be satisfied with any previous theology as wholly adequate for today is to create obstacles to the understanding of the Christian mystery in our time.

In our first chapter we identified three central theological problems concerning the Trinity in recent times: (1) the relation of the Trinity to the orders of salvation and creation, (2) the understanding of the Holy Spirit, and (3) the meaning of persons in the Trinity. In this section we begin with the first of these problems (chapter 5); second, we treat the processions within the Trinity of the Son from the Father (chapter 6) and of the Spirit from the Father and the Son (chapter 7); and third, we examine the meaning of the Father, Son, and Holy Spirit as three persons in one God (chapter 8). We will conclude with a study of a trinitarian spirituality (chapter 9). In the present chapter, we shall begin with a recall of the problem and then reflect on the relation of the Trinity to human beings and the world (I) in the order of salvation and (II) in the order of creation.

In traditional modern Catholic theology the mystery of the Trinity was presented in a way that its implications for human life were perhaps obscured. Traditionally, the central theological focus in treatises on the Trinity was on how there could be three persons in one God. Perhaps this focus resulted from the church's need to counteract the heresy of Arius, but it had the consequence that for many Christians the mystery of the Trinity was believed but was thought not to have much relevance to their lives. The recent recognition of this problem has resulted in many disparate answers, answers that are mutually opposed and, in some cases, opposed to what we have found to be revealed in Scripture. So we begin this section of our study of the Trinity by seeking some answer to this question.

We consider this a more central question than even what divides the Western and the Orthodox Churches in reference to the Trinity, because all Christians need to proclaim the mystery to people in our rapidly changing culture dominated by science and pragmatism where faith is seriously questioned. This common problem may help us put our theological differences in perspective and, indeed, give us a context in which to address these differences that is more conducive to a happy outcome than the context of the past. Our treatment here of the present issue will be complemented by our study of a trinitarian spirituality in our final chapter.

The current problem in this area, we suggest, is shown starkly by the contrast between an interpretation of the relation of the Trinity to salvation and creation that comes from a premodern experience of the world and time and one that comes from an acceptance of modern historical consciousness, in part in dependence on Hegel. We will begin our treatment here by briefly recalling and comparing Thomas Aquinas's way of relating the Trinity to the orders of salvation and creation with that of some dialectical theologians of our time.

Thomas's theology of Trinity is based on the Christian revelation of the relations among the Father, Son, and Holy Spirit; but he places it within the exitus-reditus framework he received from Augustine and through him from Plotinus.[2] Thus, in his *Summa theologiae* he systematically treats the one and triune God first and then successively creation, the return of humanity to God through the moral life and grace, and the way God has given us to return to him through Jesus Christ and his church. His treatise on the Trinity (ST I, QQ 27–43) deals primarily with the Trinity in itself, and at the end (Q 43) it has a question on the missions of the Son and the Holy Spirit. Here he analyses the visible missions of the Son (in the Incarnation) and the Holy Spirit (e.g., at the baptism of Jesus and Pentecost) and the invisible missions through the graces of faith and love by which we return to God and have the privilege of the indwelling of the Trinity. Of course, he recognizes that our only knowledge of the Trinity comes through the missions of the Son and the Spirit, though, in accord with the *exitus–reditus* framework, he puts the missions systematically at the end of his treatise. And he interprets the *reditus* that these missions make possible in a way that accentuates the vertical character of this return to God rather than integrates the future of history, as the early church's theology did.

Once we have the mystery of the Trinity revealed to us, we can see the relation of the Trinity to the order of creation as well as to that of salvation. This theme is found particularly in Thomas's commentary on the first part of Peter the Lombard's *Sentences* and has been studied recently by Gilles Emery.[3] While Thomas held with the scholastics generally that it is God as one who is the efficient cause of creation, he held also (with Albert and Bonaventure) that "the procession of persons, which is perfect, is the reason and the cause of the procession of creatures" (I *Sent.*, d.10, q.un., a.1, sol.). The more perfect is the origin of the less perfect. Thus, the eternal procession of persons is the exemplary cause of the procession of creatures in their diversity. As Emery comments, "Thomas does not recur here to the method of appropriation, but in proper discourse he attaches the procession of creatures directly to the procession of persons."[4] Thomas relates the procession of creation differently to the procession of the Word and to that of the Spirit. The Word as generated naturally by God in the intellectual order is the exemplary cause of creatures. The procession of the Holy Spirit as in the order of will or love is the reason for the procession of creatures from the divine love and generosity. Thus, the doctrine of the Trinity clarifies creation, since the procession of persons is the origin and cause of the procession of creatures; and what we know rationally about creatures helps us in our understanding of the Trinity.

In his later writings on this theme, Thomas perhaps recurs more to the method of appropriation, but he does relate creation to the procession of the Word and the Spirit. He teaches that the Father expresses himself and all he knows in the Word. But as God's knowledge is creative as well as expressive of creation, so "the Word of God . . . is expressive and causative (*operativum*) of creatures; and for this reason it is said in Ps. 32 'He spoke and they were made,' since a causative reason (*ratio factiva*) of those things God made is found in the Word" (ST I, 34, 3). And of the Spirit he writes:

> As the Father says himself and all creatures in the Word, . . . so he loves himself and all creatures in the Holy Spirit insofar as the Holy Spirit proceeds as love of the first good, according to which the Father loves himself and every creature. And thus it is clear that a secondary reference to creatures is found both in the proceeding word and love insofar as divine goodness and truth are the principles of understanding and loving all creatures. (ST I, 37, 2, ad 3)

Since the world and God are so intimately related, the understanding of the cosmos and man's place in it current in the medieval world affected the theological understanding of how the triune God interacted with human beings. With the medieval world generally, Thomas understood the universe to be geocentric, surrounded by the seven planets that influence material things on earth, and then further surrounded by several spheres in the lowest of which are the fixed stars. He thought that there were four elements and that the matter of the heavens was different from that on earth.[5]

In the Incarnation, the Son was imagined as descending from the 'empyrean' to restore order. The hierarchical view of the cosmos influenced the view of the church as a hierarchical order.[6] And it influenced the way Thomas understood the triune presence to human beings, because this picture of the world is part of the *exitus–reditus* framework by which he interpreted the missions of the Son and the Holy Spirit and the way they lead us back to the Father. They have an impact on human beings, but since they are immutable, they are not themselves changed by this relationship. The relationship is real from the part of creatures, but not from the part of God. This theology does not reflect a philosophy of history so much as a philosophy of being—one very closely related to medieval cosmology, though not restrictively dependent on that cosmology.[7]

What we found in some contemporary dialectical theologians in our first chapter is quite counter to this interpretation of the relation of the Trinity to the orders of salvation and creation.[8] Depending in part both on their interpretation of the apocalyptic in the New Testament and on Hegel, they seek to relate the Trinity to modern historical consciousness, and in some of their writings they make the constitution of the Trinity depend on what happens in history, understood apocalyptically.

There is a richness in the analyses by these theologians that we do not even touch here, and we can and should integrate some of this into a theology of the Trinity for our time. But the polar opposition between some statements by the dialectical theologians on the one hand and Thomas on the other call for some treatment. My thesis is that the apocalyptic nature of the kingdom of God as found in the New Testament is indeed essential for our understanding of how the Trinity is related to us in the order of salvation, though this does not show that what happens in history is constitutive of the Trinity. Also one cannot transpose to the order of creation the same time framework that is found in the order of salvation to conclude that God creates from the future. Here Thomas is, I suggest, closer to the truth. One must, of course, correct Thomas's cosmology to show for our time the relation of the Trinity to creation, but in this process Thomas's philosophy has something to contribute. Part of the justification of the following study will be found in later chapters, for instance, on the processions of the Word and Spirit.

I. The Relation of the Trinity to the Order of Salvation

We only know God is triune through the missions of the Son and the Spirit in history. And it is only after knowing these missions that we can interpret lower creation and human beings as vestiges and images of the Trinity, though there is something in these realities antecedent to the revelation of the Trinity that had already led people of the past to interpret them as manifesting God's word and spirit. In this chapter we are reflecting primarily on the relation of the Trinity to the orders of salvation and creation, while in our final chapter we shall primarily reflect on the practical relation of us to the Trinity in a trinitarian spirituality. Here we shall first recall briefly what we saw in chapter 2 on the New Testament revelation of the Trinity and then apply that to current disputes.

In the ministry of Jesus we found that the revelation of the Trinity is *implicit*.[9] With time, the early church began to realize that it needed to interpret Jesus' ministry in a trinitarian context to be able to understand its meaning, source, effect, and uniqueness. The mystery of the Trinity is no superfluous appendix to Jesus' ministry, but this ministry in its depth. We cannot understand the source of the proclamation he offers us or the salvation he offers us except through a full trinitarian interpretation.

In the apostolic age, we have shown that the first ascription of divinity to Jesus was in all probability in reference to the divine prerogatives of saving and judging he would exercise when he comes again at the *parousia*.[10] Very soon it was realized that what Jesus would do when he came again he was already doing *in part* from that future kingdom and position at the right hand of the Father that he had entered through his resurrection and glorification. Reflection on the Holy Spirit in the early Christian church was secondary to the *experience* of the dynamism or empowerment that came to the church. This dynamic influence and empowerment comes to the Christians from Jesus Christ as he has gone into the future kingdom (see Acts 2:33). It comes to us from this future, as a first installment on that salvation he will give us when he comes again; this gift represents a partially realized eschatology, and it orients us to God through the kingdom to come.

It came to be realized that there is another sense in which Jesus was the "Son of God" during his ministry from the time of his baptism, and indeed from his conception. In fact, preexistence was ascribed to the Son: "In the beginning was the Word and the Word was with God and the Word was God . . . and the Word became flesh" (Jn 1:1, 14). This preexistence is an ontological dimension of the Son, and it does not imply that Jesus, Son though he was, was eschatological savior and judge without going through obedience even to death and resurrection. True, he revealed definitively in that past period when he walked the earth and he merited salvation for us, but what this salvation is is shown by what he will do at the *parousia*, and it is that salvation that he offers us in part even now from that future. As it was realized that Jesus was Son during his ministry, his ministry and death were understood all the more as a sign of the Father's love for us (Rom 8:32; Jn 3:16).

Thus, the Father acts on us to save us now through his "two hands" (as Irenaeus put it), the glorified Christ and the Holy Spirit. He acts upon us from the future, for both Christ and the Spirit now come to us from this future of the kingdom. But this is not to detract from the eternal existence of either the Son or the Spirit, because we must speak of the Spirit as John did of the Son. As the baptismal formula (Mt 28:19) unites Father, Son, and Holy Spirit in the one Name, so we must affirm the ontological unity of the three in the one divinity.

What then does this mean for the current dispute between the dialectical theologians and a classical position such as that of Thomas Aquinas? It is true, as Rahner has written that, "*the 'economic' Trinity is the 'immanent' Trinity and the 'immanent' Trinity is the 'economic' Trinity.*"[11] The Trinity in the order of salvation is the Trinity in itself; and the Trinity in itself is the Trinity in the economy of salvation, though the Trinity in itself is not wholly known or comprehended by its presence in the redemptive order. It is indeed the very Word of God who became flesh; it is indeed the very Spirit of the Father and the Son who came upon the disciples of Christ at Pentecost; it is indeed the Father himself who indwells the faithful. What is given us in the economy of salvation is indeed the Trinity in itself, God's self-gift, rather than simply a created participation in God's nature through grace.

This does not mean that Jesus first came to be the Son of God through the crucifixion or through the resurrection and that God is eternally triune in virtue of what happened in history, or that eternity and the eschatological fulfillment of history are the same so that the relations among the triune persons are established through the economy of salvation. This is not the sense of Rahner's thesis, but it is what is meant by the extension of his thesis that was adopted by some dialectical theologians. Such a theological interpretation is not supported by Scripture. Whether God created or not, God would be triune. And in some later writings of the dialectical theologians, this seems to be recognized. Perhaps when they wrote of the triune persons coming to be they were influenced by Hegel and the modern sense of history—by our experience of our own human persons. Indeed, we do come to be through time; our personalities in the sense of our mature relationships and self-consciousness come to be through historical relationships. But neither Scripture nor philosophy gives us a basis to ascribe this to God. Nor do the early councils of the church, as we showed earlier in this book.

Given what we have written above, the question remains whether there is a history to the trinitarian relations. And this involves two questions: Do the missions of the Son and Spirit show us that relations of the Father, Son, and Holy Spirit with human beings change? And do these missions show us that the relations among the divine persons change? The question of divine suffering comes into these questions.

Weinandy

1. The Trinity's Relation to Human Beings and Change

In the first question, we are not addressing once more whether the Father, Son, and Holy Spirit have a history in the sense of an impact upon us human beings so that *we* are changed by their self-gift. The implications for humanity follow from everything that Christianity is and proclaims. We are asking whether the triune persons are changed by their missions to us. Does the Word of God's becoming flesh change the Word, and the Spirit's indwelling of the new people of God and individuals within it affect the Spirit, and the Father's sending of the Word and Spirit change the Father? Are they affected or changed in relation to us through this history of salvation and revelation?

I have treated this question before, as have many others,[12] and am constrained here by space appropriate to an introduction to a theology of the Trinity. What I propose here, in part in agreement with other disciples of Thomas, I do so tentatively. What we can first of all assert is that many disciples of Thomas Aquinas of our time have difficulties with his denial of real relations to God in God's relation to human beings and with God's apparent lack of receptivity in his teaching. They question whether Thomas's language here is adequate to the mystery of God as revealed to us by Scripture and Christian experience. For example, Thomas's denial that the Son of God has a real relation to Mary as his mother (*ST* III 35,5) seems inadequate.[13] Similarly, the view that it is inconsistent with God's perfection to receive from another does not seem to adequately express Christian belief about the Trinity.[14] And Thomas's view that God has mercy in the sense that he relieves another's suffering, but not in the sense that God is at all saddened by another's suffering,[15] seems rather thin compared with Scripture's statements, even recognizing that these are largely metaphorical.

There is not full agreement on how to answer these problems among those who recognize them and yet claim to be disciples of Thomas. There is partial agreement. For example, Thomas's understanding of relations is that they are either transcendental, that is, part of the nature of something, or predicamental, that is, an accidental modification of something and so an increase or decrease of perfection: "God does not make creatures because his nature compels him to do so, but by mind and will, . . . [t]hat is why in God there is no real relation to creatures" (*ST* I, 28, 1, ad 3). It seems that it is a technical meaning of real relation that Thomas is denying here. We can agree with this, and also that God's relation to creatures does not increase or diminish his perfection, and yet think that there can be a *real* divine relation to creatures that entails neither of these consequences.

What seems to me to be central in this question is that our primary analogue for God should not be being but *personal* being, and personal being who

*Note—Furrelly [?] denyer
[the] immutability of God* [handwritten marginal note]

is totally actual in knowledge and love. And what is under discussion is not whether God grows in perfection, but whether God has *real* relations with human beings and is affected by such relationships, so that we make a difference to God. Relationship does not directly say perfection, for it ascribes to a being a reference to another rather than a perfection. From God's free and loving decision to create and redeem it seems to follow that we must ascribe *relationships* to him, personal relationships to human beings. In his intentional consciousness God has relationships he would not otherwise have had, since he freely, contingently, and with love has human beings as objects of his knowledge and love. And these are personal relations. Because of the fullness of love from which God creates, sustains, and interacts with creatures, it follows that these relationships make a difference to God. These relationships affect God so that God is in a way distinct from who he would have been if he had not created them and interacted with creatures. That is, God changes as these relationships change. There is a kind of mutuality between God and the creatures who are the result of his love.

Philosophical problems that classically were raised against this scriptural teaching came, I suggest, from identifying God too directly with total actuality (*ipsum esse*) rather than with totally actual *personal* being. The relationship or a change in such a relationship we suggest does not seem to be inconsistent with the divine perfection since, as the traditional trinitarian doctrine shows in another way, ascribing a relationship to one divine person is not an ascription of a *perfection* to that person that the others do not have. Nor does this view ascribe potentiality to God, since Thomas recognized that there is a kind of process that does not involve potentiality, for example, the process by which a concept or intellectual word proceeds from the intellect in its knowing an object (See *De Pot.* 8,1), since knowledge is an *actus perfecti*, very different from, for example, our moving of a physical object. In our intellectual act, the more fully we know, the more fully does a concept flow—or proceed—from our knowledge. Similarly, there is a process in the will when united with its object, the good, namely the process of love or desire—also an *actus perfecti*. The trinitarian processions should make us aware of how dynamic God's life is and that there is a sense that process is consistent with such life. We will return to these issues in the following chapters.

Further, this view does not seem to be opposed to divine simplicity. If we consider the divine actuality not on the model of being but on the analogy of our personal intentional activity (knowledge and love), though infinitely transcendent to this, the inclusion of finite selves in the range of God's love and knowledge shows not additional parts in God but the infinite range of

God's relationality. Ascribing multiple real relations to the Trinity is not contrary to divine simplicity but shows the richness of this simplicity.

So when we say that the Son became man and that he changes, we are saying that he is changing in his humanity and that what we ascribe to one nature we can ascribe to the whole person (e.g., the Son of Man can forgive sins, or men crucified the author of life [see Acts 3:15]; this is classically called *communicatio idiomatum*). We are also saying that the Son changes by assuming flesh and being present in a way he was not present before. Rahner writes cautiously about this:

> God who is unchangeable in himself can change in another (can in fact become man). But this "changing in another" must neither be taken as denying the immutability of God in himself nor simply be reduced to a changement (sic) of the other . . . he, though unchangeable "in himself," can become something "in another." The immutability of God is a dialectical truth like the unity of God.[16]

It seems to a number of us that we must go further than Rahner and assert that the Son has a new and real relationship to his individual humanity and to the whole of the created order. This comes from his love. And it comes from the Father's love (Jn 3:16). To ascribe anything less to the Son or the Father is to diminish their self-gift to us and thus not to adequately express at all their love for us. The *Son* has a *real* and *new* relationship with us, and the *Father* takes a real and new initiative and relationship with us; they are involved with us in a new way.[17]

2. The Son's *Kenosis* and Trinitarian Relationships

Paul encourages Christians to imitate: "Christ Jesus, who, though he was in the form of God, did not regard equality with God something to be grasped. Rather, he emptied (*ekenosen*) himself, taking the form of a slave, coming in human likeness; and found human in appearance, he humbled himself becoming obedient . . ." (Phil 2:5–8a). This action of the Son shows us something of the Trinity. Or, as Hans Urs von Balthasar puts it, there is in the Trinity a precondition for the possibility of such a self-giving: "in serving, in washing the feet of his creatures, God reveals himself even in that which is most intimately divine in him, and manifests his supreme glory."[18] He continues:

> if one wishes to understand [this] . . . in the framework of Christology and so eventually of Trinitarian theology, then one must allow an 'event' into the God who is beyond the world and beyond change. This event, described in the

words 'emptying' and 'humiliation' consists in abandoning equality with God
. . . in what touches the precious possession of 'glory'.[19]

The antecedent condition of possibility for such a *kenosis* is not only God as
personal but the trinitarian God, the antecedent relation of Father and Son.
The incarnation and whole life of Jesus show us something of this relationship. The incarnation is a supreme gift from the Father and a self-gift of the
Son in obedience to the Father. This shows us that in his very being as Father, the Father is loving self-gift. Balthasar calls this a kind of 'emptying' of
himself to give his divinity to the Son. (There are other theologians who do
not think this term appropriate to express the Father's self-gift to the Son
within the Trinity, and I agree, because 'emptying' signifies a kind of humi-
lation or loss, and the Father's eternal generation of the Son does not imply
this.) This 'event' of the Father's loving self-gift to the Son is something that
not only happened at some point in eternity, but is a constant happening, a
constant process that identifies the Father as Father.[20]

Similarly, the Son's self-gift in the Incarnation is out of obedience to the Father and a loving humiliation in his solidarity with sinful humanity. This and
the whole course of his life is a reflection of his relation to the Father—a relationship that John frequently elaborates (see Jn 8:28, 29, 38, 49). His Incarnation and life is his expression of his eternal relation to the Father, his communion with the Father, his obedience to the Father. There is some eternal
'event' that is the antecedent of this—namely his reception of all that he is
from the Father's love and his imaging in love the Father wholly by his being.

Although we are considering the Son's self-emptying here, we should at
least recall another aspect in which the earthly mission of the Son has its antecedent in the eternal relation of the Son to the Father, namely the fact that
he *revealed* the Father in a unique and definitive manner. The antecedent for
his revelation of the Father is expressed by John when he asserts that Jesus
was the "Word made flesh," that Word that was in the beginning with God
and was divine. The condition of possibility for his earthly ministry of being
the definitive revealer of God in the whole of history was his eternal relation
to God as God's Word—an eternal expression in and by his very being of
who the Father was and is. And similarly the antecedent of the Son's revealing the Father is that the Father speaks this Word eternally or, what comes
to the same, generates this Son, this perfect image of himself. In that sense
the Son is the *locum tenens* (holds the place), as Barth teaches, of the definitive revealer of the Father.

The meaning of the *kenosis* of the Son in his Incarnation is beyond the
scope of our treatment here. That mystery is treated more fully in Christology.

But, holding to the early councils of the church, and particularly Chalcedon (451), it is clear that it does not mean that the Son become flesh is no longer God or that his divinity is diminished. Neither does it mean that the humanity of Jesus loses what is distinctive of it and its limits. I suggest that developmental psychology and its implications for philosophy may have something to tell us about one aspect of Christ's *kenosis*, namely the gradual character of the emergence of Jesus' human consciousness and agency. In reference to the question of the development of the person, I previously wrote about the help Erik Erikson and others could give us:

> we use the word 'I' for the person or subject in the metaphysical sense of the one who is and acts. We can use the word 'self' for this same person considered as an indirect or direct object of consciousness and speech, though of course the self is not fully known. But the 'I' acts through a whole series of structured dynamisms that evolve in the course of the child's, adolescent's, and adult's development, as analysed by Erikson and others. Since we are indirectly and directly aware of the self only through our agency in these structured dynamism, it is usually limited dimensions of the self of which we are conscious. Much of the self usually escapes us, since we are acting through limited dimensions of it.[21]

Since Jesus was fully human, like us in all things but sin, what we write here was presumably analogically true of him also. Does the fact that he was the Word or Son of God mean that he was always humanly aware of this? We human beings are not even aware of all the potentialities of our human being, and so it would seem that Jesus' human agency need not have been initially operating out of a full awareness of who he was.

This *kenosis* even reaches to the point where the Son and the Father accept the *suffering* of the crucifixion for us. This is asserted by Scripture. For example, Paul writes of the Father as "He who did not spare his own Son but handed him over for us all" (Rom 8:32). And in the process the Father and Son reveal their love and selves in a unique way. As Balthasar writes: "in the uttermost form of a slave, on the Cross, the Son's glory breaks through, inasmuch as it is there that he goes to the (divine) extreme in his loving, and in the revelation of that love. . . . [I]n the Incarnation [on the cross] the triune God has not simply helped the world, but has disclosed himself in what is most deeply his own."[22]

We need not hold that the Father "delivered" his Son over to death in the sense of taking the initiative to sacrifice him, as Abraham is said to have done to his son Isaac. He simply sent him into a sinful world that could easily resist his loving presence and message to the extent of trying to get rid of him by killing him (see Mt 21:13–43). Thus the Son and the Father accepted initially a vulnerability and later the reality of the suffering on the cross. It was not necessary for our salvation that Jesus Christ be crucified; what was necessary was that people believe in him. Scripture does not seem to support the view that it was a foregone conclusion that he would be rejected by his own people. So we cannot say that the Incarnation happened *so that* Jesus would die on the cross. We can say that God used human beings' rejection of his Son to show us even more graphically his love for us and who the Son and the Father are.

The crucifixion is indeed a revelation of the Trinity itself. With a growing number of theologians, we propose that what we said above of change is true of suffering. Is it sufficiently faithful to Scripture to ascribe suffering to the Son only in his humanity and by virtue of this to the person of the Son only by a *communicatio idiomatum*, or must we not rather say that the Son suffers in an analogical sense also in his divinity? Is it not diminishing the Son's love for us to say that he did not suffer at all in his divinity for us, or that the Father did not suffer at all when he allowed human beings to put his Son to death? What vulnerability is there in the Father if he experienced nothing of the Son's suffering by a genuine compassion? Why is the cross of Christ the greatest and indeed unique sign of the Father's love for us, one that should assure us to trust him in all possible circumstances of life, if it did not cost the Father at all?[23]

It would seem that philosophical principles do not demand this denial of any suffering to God. If God's total perfection is understood on the analogy of the human person's fullest intellectual and loving activity, God has a relation of love for all human beings whom he has freely and lovingly created for communion with himself and one another. If self-destructively some human beings reject God's love for them, in God's knowledge of this can he not experience a certain emptiness, an emptiness for them because of his great love for them and not out of egoism? Knowledge of human sin is not opposed to God's perfection, so need a certain, in a way, painful experience of the harm people do to themselves and others by this be incompatible with God's perfection? Or, rather, if God is profoundly involved with his creatures in love, would it not be imperfection for him not to be affected by this? Our human experience is that we can paradoxically be both happy and involved with others to the extent of feeling their pain. Can less be said of God?

Traditional Christian worship was closer to the mark than scholastic theology in sensing a deeper reality in God's love shown on the cross. We are not here ascribing suffering to the Son and Father in a univocal sense with what that means for us. As Abraham Heschel wrote of God, paraphrasing

Isaiah 55:8–9: "My pathos is not your pathos. . . . For as the heavens are higher than the earth, so are My ways higher than your ways, and My pathos than your pathos."[24]

Among the Fathers of the church this was expressed most directly, and perhaps surprisingly, by Origen. As J. Galot summarizes:

> Origen begins by declaring that "the Savior came to earth out of compassion for the human race, and he shared our sufferings before enduring the cross and deigning to assume our human flesh." . . . [H]ere it is a suffering anterior to his earthly life that is affirmed. "If he had not had compassion he would not have come to share our human life. First he had compassion, and then he descended and became visible." . . . [I]t is compassionate love that is at the origin of the coming of the Savior.
>
> Then Origen asks himself "Does the Father himself, God of the universe, patient and of great mercy (Ps 103,8), compassionate,—does he not also suffer in a certain manner?" The response seems evident to him. "Do you not know that since he wants good for human beings, he shares human suffering? . . . The Father himself is not impassible. When one invokes him, he takes pity and is compassionate, suffers in his love, and engages himself in a reality where he could not be according to the greatness of his nature; for us he endures our human sufferings."[25]

The antecedent or condition of possibility for this compassion is not only the personal God, but the Father and Son's relation in the Trinity—that they are a process of mutual self-giving love to such an extent that they can and do freely engage human beings to such a depth. As they can receive from one another, they can, because of the depth of their loving choice, receive from human beings. Gerry O'Hanlon expresses Balthasar's view to this effect:

> In God suffering is supratemporal and free, it is a perfection entirely compatible with joy and happiness, and with the divine victory over the negativity of human suffering. This is very different from our experience of suffering, although there are indeed some positive similarities, as evidenced, for example, by the co-presence of joy and pain in the human situation.[26]

This view is radically different from the position of Moltmann because he held that the Trinity was constituted by what happened on the cross. We hold that what happened on the cross was the result of God's free love.

We have defended the view that there is a kind of history of the trinitarian relations with human beings, showing that through the example of the Son and the Father. We could as well have shown it by the mission of the Holy Spirit (see, e.g., Eph 4:30: "do not grieve the holy Spirit of God").

We have also defended the view that there is a kind of history in the relationships among the persons of the Trinity themselves. Due to their freely accepted real relations to human beings through creation and redemption, it seems we should acknowledge that there is something to their innertrinitarian relationships that is not independent of this relation to human beings. For us to say that the Father has compassion for the sufferings of his Son on the cross (without this implying 'Patripassianism', that is, the view that the Father, as not really distinct from the Son, suffered on the cross) indicates that there is some change in the relation of the Father to the Son and the Son to the Father.

II. The Relation of the Trinity to Creation

What relation can we discern in physical creation to the Trinity? In this whole question there seems to be a *dichotomy* between modern consciousness and the consciousness reflected in Scripture and classical theology, such as that of Thomas. We saw earlier that in Scripture physical creation and history are ascribed to the initiative, creativity, and activity of God.[27] Creation and history are preeminently the work of God through his "two hands," the Word and the Spirit.

This view is found too in classical theology. Earlier in this chapter we saw how Thomas Aquinas used his philosophy of knowledge and love to reflect on the revealed message that God created through his Word and his Spirit.[28] God created the world out of nothing in the sense that there was no preexistent material on which he worked. We know by divine revelation that this creation was in time, or better, that time began with the creation of the material universe, but we could not know by reason alone that creation was not everlasting since this is demanded neither by the nature of creation nor by the free will of God that is its source.[29] Creation itself means primarily the total dependence of finite being on God who alone is essentially being (*ipsum esse*), and secondarily its derivation by God's causal act at some time in our past. Thomas's theological reflection was closely associated with the physical science of his time.

Much modern consciousness formed by science and a naturalistic sense of history seem very opposed to this perspective. The human being did not come from creation but rather through evolution from higher anthropoids, which in turn came from other mammals, from earlier aquatic animals, and even from some pre-organic soup from which life initially emerged, and behind this from the big bang that started it all, perhaps some fifteen billion years ago. This development is considered by many scientists to be due to chance and natural selection; there is no need to recur to divine agency. Human history similarly comes from human decisions and the natural resources humans have in many different physical environments and cultures.[30] When an evolutionary or historical view has been related to Christian belief, it has led not infrequently to a subordination of Christian belief to this consciousness.

Part of the dichotomy between the Christian scheme of things and modern consciousness has come from the association of classical theology with premodern science and a culture that was not as historically conscious as the modern world is. This is true of the theology of Thomas Aquinas as of other earlier theologies. And so the dichotomy cannot be answered or overcome simply by a reinterpretation of Scripture with the help of modern science; there must be a philosophical dimension to the answer. Thomas's metaphysics of being was not essentially related to his scientific view of the physical world; rather, his metaphysics found its application in the then-current physical view of the world and was imaginatively associated with it in his mind and that of his age. Thomas's metaphysics, like that of Aristotle before him, was derived primarily from a first-order knowledge, for example, from the reality of change and permanence in the same physical thing, and the implication this had for the understanding of the physical thing as composed of potency and act. These principles found an instantiation throughout the whole of creation because creatures are not *essentially* being; rather, they participate in being. Thus their essence and existence are distinct. Questions that arise from our experience of the evolutionary world today raise some of the same questions that Thomas had to face in a nonevolutionary world. His philosophy, it seems to me and many others, has a potential to help elucidate these questions, interrelate with the physical and human sciences of our time, and be developed and corrected by this relationship.[31] I will recall one example to illustrate such a fruitful relationship and then reflect briefly on how the evolutionary world as we know it may reflect the action of the Trinity in the creation of the physical world.

The contrast between Thomas's and developmental psychology's interpretation of the human person and the way these two can be interrelated give us an illustration of how Thomas's philosophy and a contemporary scientific cosmology can interrelate.

In Thomas Aquinas's philosophy of the human person there is both a phenomenological and a metaphysical dimension. He says, for example, that there is a special word, 'person', used for the individual human being, because such individuals, as distinct from lower animals, "have mastery over their own acts; they are not only acted upon, like others, but they act of themselves."[32] They do not have an automatic response when presented with a stimulus but can through freedom and reason initiate their own response. This represents a call upon experience, and thus a kind of phenomenology.

Then in his philosophy Thomas seeks to know the structure of being that enables humans to act in this way. He relates such action to the roots in the person, namely the person's nature as a rational animal and existence itself. The person's intellectual capacity emerges as a property from the substantial form, the soul. The existence (*esse*), a metaphysical principle of the person along with the human nature, is associated by Thomas with the good. As he writes: "the good is that which all things desire . . . but all things desire to be in act (*esse actu*) according to their measure, which is clear from the fact that everything of its nature shrinks from corruption. To be in act therefore (*esse igitur actu*) is the essential notion of the good."[33] What evokes love and desire (*eros*)—and so action—is the good, the perfection or actualization of the person and that to which this actualization is related, like that of other human beings and God himself. Thomas examines in depth the activity of the intellect in knowing and the human will in loving and acting, but the first intrinsic source of these capacities is the substance (form or soul and matter) and the existence or *esse* of the being. The agency of the human person has as its metaphysical root this dynamic structure and as its intrinsic horizon his or her actualization as a person.

Erik Erikson also analyzes the roots of the characteristic activity of the human person, specifically what enables the adult human person to be a mature person. For him this maturity involves the concern to foster, even at some significant personal cost, the next generation, an attitude he calls "generativity." He accounts for it as an attitude that emerges in men and women only through a sequence of stages from infancy. He interprets this emergence through relating it to certain psychic structures that he borrowed and adapted from Freud—social processes (superego), somatic processes (id), and ego processes (ego). The individual goes through stages of infancy, childhood, adolescence, and adulthood in which there are interactions between an enlarging social environment and the individual's maturing human potential that are marked by successive critical stages calling for the individual's restructuring of the self. In this process there is necessary at each stage a response that promotes certain ego-strengths. These strengths have a cumulative effect in the genesis of that generativity that characterizes the mature human being. But at each stage there is also the possibility for degrees of failure on the part of the social environment or the individual that present obstacles to such growth and that can call for therapeutic intervention. The basic reason for the individual's growth here is the meaning such interactions have for the individual and for his or her social environment.

One can see that Erikson's analysis of the roots of the activity character-istic of the human person is largely phenomenological rather than meta-physical. In fact, the psychoanalytic tradition has been criticized for not get-ting beyond the ego, superego, and id, for it presumes "that there is no such entity as a human person aside from the sum of these subdivisions of the psy-chic apparatus."[34] Particularly in his later writings, however, Erikson seeks to get beyond this apparatus to some sense of a metaphysical 'I', though he does not achieve clarity.[35]

It is clear that Thomas's and Erikson's analyses of the human person are very different. But, I propose, they can correct and complement one another. As fruitful as Erikson's study of the emergence of a mature human disposition through stages is, it leaves questions unanswered that call for another form of analysis, one we can call metaphysical. Thomas's analysis of the person does get beyond the "psychic apparatus" to the one who acts. And it can explicate (by *esse*), on another level than the "id" (or modifications of the id proposed by Erikson or others), the motivation and energy that moves the growing person. This can give a basis for what Erikson seems to assert at times, namely, that there is a constitutive human good that is normative for human growth; the *esse* that motivates human desire and love is the good of a specif-ically *human* being. The child cannot be formed by any blueprint people may choose to impose upon it. But Thomas's interpretation of the human person is brought up to date and corrected by a contemporary phenomenology of hu-man experience and its interpretation by Erikson and others. For example, Erikson's study shows that the capacities for mature human action emerge through a succession of intermediate agencies that are evoked by the inter-action between the social environment and the maturing human potential at critical junctures. This implies a correction of Thomas's philosophy of the person. It means that the human nature and existence are in principle the metaphysical origin not simply of "faculties" but of a whole succession of sub-ordinate agencies that emerge largely as Erikson and others analyze this. The metaphysical principles of the person are the internal root of the epigenesis of adult personality structures; their influence is explicated temporally. This modern phenomenology also shows that the person is essentially a *cultural* being, because the social environment is an essential principle of such emer-gence. I suggest that this interrelationship between classical philosophy and contemporary human science is fruitful for both.[36]

Following this model, how could Thomas's theology/philosophy of the physical universe and a modern cosmology based on the physical sciences interrelate to show something about how the Trinity is reflected in our world? We have seen that Thomas, in continuity with Scripture, relates the physical world to the triune God acting through his Word and his Spirit. Through the Word God has an exemplar of what he makes the world to be in its different kinds and its overriding unity; through the Spirit the eros of the world participates in some way in the love that is the Spirit. God is efficient cause of the physical world, and he does so act because of the divine goodness which all things in their desire to be seek. The unity of the world is neither accidental to God's creative work, nor it is simply externally imposed, for it results from the interrelation of the different kinds of created beings God makes and their action seeking their good, the good of the larger universe, and ultimately God. In the design present in God's mind and in the physical world we see what is called at times a downward causal influence. In the search for being present in all creatures (e.g., active matter) we see what is called at times a "bottom-up" causal influence. Many physicists and biologists recognize these two causal influences in their contemporary view of the world.

1. A Current Cosmology

How do many current cosmologists interpret the structure of the physical world and the activity of matter within it? We use particularly fragments of the work of the physicist Paul Davies, who has sought to write in a way that is accessible to the lay reader, and specifically his book *The Cosmic Blueprint: New Discoveries in Nature's Creative Ability to Order the Universe.*[37] We use this book to ask how the structure of the physical world reflects God's trinitarian continuing causal influence. We refer the reader to this book and restrict ourselves to two key aspects of his and other scientists' interpretation of the physical world that are particularly relevant to our question.

Before beginning our use of this book, we should note that though they recognize the existence of design in the world, many physicists and biologists deny the purpose or teleology in nature that Davies and many others assert. This rejection can be simply a methodological rejection, meaning that the discernment of such purpose is beyond the questions and methodology of physics. The rejection in many cases, however, goes further, because some physicists and biologists try to erect a materialistic metaphysics that holds that "the mechanisms of natural selection and random mutations" are "capable of providing the driving force responsible for macro-evolution"; they hold that there is *no* purpose in nature or macro-evolution.[38] We can agree that it may well be that physics and biology cannot by their method discern teleology in nature and that Davies and many others who acknowledge such teleology are relying on evidence available to a larger human knowledge of the physical world than physics for their assertion of it. Davies, together with many others, points to evidence of such teleology, and thus evidence against a naturalistic or materialistic metaphysics. In our view, Davies's evidence shows a widespread and solidly based contemporary interpretation of the physical world that reflects the presence of trinitarian creation differently than an earlier theology did. We can discern a kind of consonance between a contemporary cosmology that is not scientism and our belief that God as triune is acting in the physical world.

We need not recall that the world appears differently to many physicists today than it did in the Newtonian universe, because the world now is viewed within an evolutionary framework, in which there is a more holistic and less deterministic approach than earlier, and there is a recognition that the universe cannot be adequately interpreted according to the second law of thermodynamics as dying.

For contemporary science "the universe began in featureless simplicity, and grows ever more elaborate with time [in] . . . complexity" (21). Complex systems (e.g., cells) appear abruptly, are rarely closed systems, and have characteristics as wholes that cannot be adequately understood by the action of the simple parts. This gave rise to *chaos* theory. Many systems of nature are not linear systems. One cannot know their initial conditions completely, and there is a randomness that is part of movement to successive states. For example, in a weather system a very small disturbance in the initial condition can with time have an effect totally out of proportion to its size (in weather patterns this is at times called the "butterfly effect"). Thus, "the entropy of automaton states can decrease, and order can spontaneously appear out of disorder" (67). *Self-organization* then occurs in matter counter to what one might conclude from the second law of thermodynamics: "A crucial property of far-from-equilibrium systems that give rise to process structures is that they are open to their environment . . . a universe apparently dying under the influence of the second law nevertheless continually increases its level of complexity and organization . . . the universe . . . increase[s] both organization and entropy at the same time" (84–85). Ilya Prigogine has called this characteristic *active matter*, because of its potential to spontaneously and unpredictably develop new structures. It seems to have "a will of its own." Disequilibrium, claims Prigonine, "is the source of order" in the universe; it brings "order out of chaos" (87).[39] A system in disequilibrium can move for a while and then abruptly either randomly decompose or form a new pattern.

We find something similar in life or living organisms. Organisms are open to their environment yet distinct from it, receive input from it and are in a state of disequilibrium with respect to it. There seems to be an *arrow of time* in the evolutionary process from less-complex organisms to the human, from what most people would call "lower" to "higher," though this process has many byways and is thus not orthogenesis. An organism shows teleology; that is, "As noted by Aristotle, organisms develop and behave in an ordered and purposive way, as though guided toward a final goal in accordance with a preordained plan or blueprint" (95). This is noted by many biologists, without their being able to explain this adequately. Mechanism is particularly incapable of explaining the development of the embryo from a single cell that according to some blueprint gives rise to a complex organism with many diverse organs, each very different (e.g., eye, ear, skeleton) and spatially related to one another according to a pattern. The embryo operates as a whole. This is somewhat similar to nonlinear, nonorganic systems in disequilibrium; but, as distinct from these, embryos are predictable in their development and robust in the process.

The problem with a mechanistic analysis of the organism reappears with a vengeance when it is applied in the form of random mutation and natural selection to explain the evolutionary process as a whole or the emergence of living organisms from nonliving as a matter of pure chance (chapter 8). "How can chance alone be responsible for the emergence of *completely new and successful* structures, such as nervous system, brain, eye, etc. in response to environmental challenge?"(108). Random shuffling, for instance, of a deck of cards, tends to produce simply a drift with no coherent directionality, but there is an arrow of time in evolution. And in the calculation of the probability of the emergence even of a small virus from a pre-living "soup," "the odds work out at over $10^{2,000,000}$ to one against" (118). Davies gives some varied answers to this problem, before he opts for one that accords with what he has earlier shown of the nonequilibrium context of matter at every level. He writes:

> We have seen how the concept of random shuffling belongs to equilibrium thermodynamics. The sort of conditions under which life is believed to have emerged were far from equilibrium, however, and under these circumstances highly non-random behavior is expected. Quite generally, matter and energy in far-from-equilibrium open systems have a propensity to seek out higher and higher levels of organization and complexity. . . .
>
> Prigonine's work . . . and Eigen's . . . both indicate that the primeval soup could have undergone successive leaps of self-organization along a pathway of chemical development. (119)

When we apply this to the unfolding universe (chapter 9), we see enormous structures such as galaxies and clusters of galaxies. There is evidence for something like a "big bang" some ten to fifteen billion years ago, because the universe is expanding and there is still discernable a kind of background heat radiation that comes from that initial event. This big bang that is the physical beginning of the universe as we know it appears to have been at an infinitesimal moment after the event one of maximal heat and expansion. With the big bang's expansion and gradual loss of extreme temperature, the initial symmetry is broken, and in the subsequent 'inflationary universe' helium is the first element formed, then hydrogen, then "The pulling together of the primeval gases . . . the formation of galaxies and stars . . . the production of the heavy elements, the planets, the vast range of chemical substances" (135). The gravitational force was the trigger for this "cascade of self-organizing processes" (135).

Our solar system is one of these organizations or systems, and it and the planet Earth show an "unreasonable degree of self-regulation" (131). This fact led James Lovelock to introduce the idea of Gaia, though many physicists resist this combination of myth and science: "Named after the Greek Earth goddess, Gaia is a way of thinking about our planet as a holistic self-regulating system in which the activities of the biosphere cannot be untangled from the complex processes of geology, climatology and atmospheric physics" (121). All of this development is against the odds and the influence of the second law of thermodynamics. As nature undergoes spontaneous transitions to "new states of higher organizational complexity" (142), new laws of nature emerge: "the organizing principles . . . harness the existing interparticle forces, rather than supplement them, and in so doing alter the collective behaviour in a holistic fashion" (143). Specifically, in living organisms there is a hierarchical organization in virtue of which the smaller units are integrated and constrained to comply with the collective behavior of the whole. This is at times called "*downward causation*" (149, my emphasis).

There is a search for cosmological principles that account for the uniformly orderly nature of the universe over incredible distances. Much effort is expended to find sources of this on the microscopic level, as disequilibrium gives rise to order. For example, Prigogine concludes from his studies that "At all levels, be it the level of macroscopic physics, the level of fluctuations, or the microscopic level, nonequilibrium is the source of order. Nonequilibrium brings 'order out of chaos'" (156).[40] One aspect of universal uniformity is the constants of nature, that is, of certain definite numbers operative in very different physical laws.

The constants of nature have, it appears, assumed precisely the values needed in order that complex self-organization can occur to the level of conscious individuals. Some scientists . . . subscribe to something called the *strong anthropic principle*, which states that the laws of nature must be such as to admit the existence of consciousness in the universe at some stage . . . a sort of organizing meta-principle, because it arranges the *laws themselves* so as to permit complex organization to arise.(163)

The quantum theory holds that on the submicroscopic level there is an indeterminism radically different from classical physics. Description on this level, for example, of the electron as a wave function or state vector, is more abstract than at the macroscopic level. On this level *probabilities* are found (166). Such predictions are *statistical*. This indeterminism, found particularly when the velocity or position of bombarded subatomic particles are measured, has given rise to paradoxes. Some clarity emerges, Davies suggests, if we recognize that there is in this measurement a "downward causality" because we use a macro-world measuring device (e.g., Geiger counter) on a micro-world reality (e.g., electron): "Here we find not only the whole being greater than the sum of its parts, but also the existence of the parts being defined by the whole in a gigantic hardware [measuring device]—software [electron wave]" (176). Davies concludes that the elementary particles are secondary: "Rather than providing the concrete 'stuff' from which the world is made, these 'elementary' particles are actually essentially *abstract* constructions based upon the solid ground of irreversible 'observation events' or measurement records" (175). Thus too, though there is a quantum dimension in molecular biology, "downward causation in biology would seem to be unavoidable" (178); the whole affects the parts toward its own needs. There is thus teleology here as well: "it is a gross error to envisage biological organisms as classical machines, operating solely by the rearrangement of molecular units subject only to local forces" (182).

2. How Does This Reflect a Trinitarian Creation?
While we recognize that parts of this analysis can be contested and perhaps will be revised, we propose that the overall picture is broadly held today. In an article more recent than his book, Davies compares God the creator to one who creates a game like chess, with its own laws such as the diverse pieces and their specific kinds of moves—a game that because of these initial laws proceeds in both an orderly and creative way, leaving room for chance. Davies writes:

[F]rom the uniformitarianist perspective taken in this paper, I am proposing that God "initially" selects the laws, which then take care of the universe, both its coming-into-being at the big bang and its subsequent creative evolution, without the need for direct supernatural intervention. By selecting judiciously, God is able to bestow a rich creativity on the cosmos, because the actual laws of the universe have a remarkable ability to canalize, encourage, and facilitate the evolution of matter and energy along pathways leading to greater organizational complexity. . . .

[T]he concept I am discussing is "teleology without teleology." God selects very special laws that guarantee a trend toward greater richness, diversity, and complexity through spontaneous self-organization, but the final outcome in all its details is open and left to chance. . . .

[This view] is in favor of a modified uniformitarian view of God who not only presides over a universe of subtle ingenuity and creativity, but of a universe in which the emergence of life and consciousness were part of God's blueprint at the most fundamental level.[41]

What Davies writes here already shows us some major ways in which a contemporary scientific understanding of the creative process can be related to the triune creator. We briefly add a few comments on this theme from the background of our acceptance of Scripture and of a modified Thomistic metaphysics.

What takes first place in our understanding of God is Scripture's and tradition's witness to the personal triune creator. As we have seen, Scripture and Thomas both say that God creates through his Word and his Spirit. With the contemporary scientific understanding of the universe as evolutionary, creation reflects the work of the triune God very differently than the authors of Scripture and Thomas understood. God created the species we see today through an initial creation of a single unbelievably dense and simple material reality that by a process of continuing creation through billions of years' duration led to the complexity of physical reality we now see in our universe. Thus by his Word as exemplar God envisaged and caused this series of physical realities or beings in their temporal and interconnected sequence leading up to the greatest natural expression of the capacity of material reality that we know, the human person and human community. (This does not preclude the existence of intelligent life elsewhere in the universe.) We cannot think that this effect of creation, the human person and community, was outside God's initial intention in creation. But God adopted means to effect this that are very different from the way classical theology understood this, and these means express the unity of material creation differently from the classical understanding. The Word is an exemplar of creation not so much as an architectural sketch but more like a plan in the mind of the creator of a drama, or like a goal in the sense of a form to be achieved through process, but in a way that includes the process itself. However, it respects the internal demands of the system and leaves more room for chance than this analogy implies, and actually uses chance constructively.

The Word is not only an external exemplar of the creative process. Somehow God's Word is an intrinsic organizing principle in physical creation and its evolutionary process. The anthropic principle, namely that the emergence of consciousness is written somehow into the evolutionary process from its beginning, shows that there is a "downward" causal influence operative in the evolutionary process. Arthur Koestler writes:

> The purposiveness of all vital processes, the strategy of the genes and the power of the exploratory drive in animal and man, all seem to indicate that the pull of the future is as real as the pressure of the past. Causality and finality are complementary principles in the science of life; if you take out finality and purpose you will have taken the life out of biology as well as psychology.[42]

This 'pull of the future' is, in a way, the Word immanent in physical creation. Its existence or causal influence does not deny the reality of chance, because it is operating on physical systems that are themselves searching within the limits of certain structures and environments and so capable of many false starts, dead ends, parasitic developments, but which, as we see, are also capable of breakthroughs toward fuller realizations of the potentiality of the physical universe. The form or shape of the world desired by God was not totally given initially, but given in the character of natural laws and this "pull of the future" to be built up over time. The emergence of this future is, in a way, a participation in the procession of the Word within the Trinity, a mystery we will examine in the following chapter. The process that is the evolution of an anthropic universe shows us some pale image or vestige of the procession of the Word within the Trinity. In our final chapter we shall examine more explicitly how the universe and history are by God oriented to the Word become flesh, Jesus Christ, who through his death, resurrection, and exaltation was given the kingdom of God and governs history toward its fulfillment and liberation.

This "word present in created reality" was understood by classical philosophy largely by means of the notion of substantial form that gives the being its nature, its goal, and the direction of its proper behavior. Modern science was based on the rejection of substantial forms, but much contemporary science recognizes the "pull of the future," as in morphogenesis, and this calls for some principle such as substantial form. As Terence Nichols writes:

> [T]his emerging concept (or concepts) of holistic causality is in essential respects similar to traditional Thomistic notions of substantial form. Holistic

causes, like substantial forms, are organizing causes: they make wholes more than the sum of their parts and endow them with new characteristrics, properties and behaviors which cannot be found in the isolated parts. . . . Modern holism recognises that holistic systems evince a unity of operation and characteristics, a fact long recognized by Thomism but rejected by reductionism and mechanism.[43]

Modern science, however, calls for a modification of the Thomistic understanding of substantial forms in at least two ways. One of these we recalled earlier, namely, that kinds of being are relational to their environment. The other is that there seem to be subsidiary forms within an organism that retain their own identity and which, however, the organism as a whole pulls toward the needs and purposes of the whole organism. For example, in animal life, water that carries the blood seems to retain its own characteristics and yet is shifted to the needs of the whole. Nichols calls these subsidiary forms and an intermediary between the views of those classical philosophers, like Thomas, who recognized only one substantial form in an organism, and those who held for a plurality of them. I suggest that our example given above of the interrelation between the understanding of the human person in developmental psychology and in Thomas, as well as what we have seen on holistic causal influences in Davies, support such a modification of Thomas's philosophy.

The process of creation leading to the human is also through the mediation of the Spirit of God. The Spirit proceeds as love of the first good, and this love as known, as we shall clarify in a later chapter. All creation is an *eros*, as a participation in the Spirit—a dynamic movement toward that first good; the good that physical things seek as their completion is itself a participation in the divine good. We understand this dynamic movement very differently than classical theology did, because through the help of modern science we see that the movement emerges in the big bang and "proceeds" through many intermediate organizations of matter to more interior expressions of this *eros* (as Teilhard de Chardin would say) and eventually even to one who can love freely and rationally.

This dynamism is expressed, for example, in lower living organisms as they seek their own good, the good of their species, and, indeed, all sorts of possibilities of physical life offered by the environment, including those greater than the possibilities of their own species—because we see that organizations far from equilibrium erupt into new patterns of material organization as through a dynamic search. This *eros* is a teleological movement, though to see this dimension of matter is beyond the questions and methodology of physics and biology. It is not conscious in the vegetative world and not self-conscious and free in the animal world. God is acting through this *eros*, though Western theology has not articulated this to the degree that it has articulated God's action through his Word. This is what classical philosophy has spoken of as God's 'concurrence' with created activity. In an earlier treatment of this I wrote:

> God effects an action of a created agent with it, not only as first efficient cause or ultimate final cause, but as concurring cause, with the creature responding to the good and to the agency of God operating through the good and environment. Thus God acts not only in what evokes the creature's action, but in and with the creature's response. The creature's spontaneity, creativity, and dynamism are participations in God's spontaneity, creativity, and dynamism. Creatures, and particularly human beings, can be called co-creators with God.[44]

Similarly, classical theology has not acknowledged sufficiently some forms of human agency that share in this creative action of God, for instance, a mother's sharing her life with her children in all of their life stages, and so evoking their growth, as much as it has acknowledged human agency more directly reflective of the Word.[45]

Perhaps the understanding of physical creation made available to us by contemporary science, at least that which is not restrictedly mechanistic or statistical, shows us that creation reflects the "process" that is present in what are traditionally called the divine processions of Word and Spirit far better than the classical understanding of physical creation. The unity of the divine love is shown by creation better when the *eros* of creation is not as disparate as it would be if everything was initially created in its own species, but is rather interrelated through emergence from one big bang. Through seeing the incredible sweep of time and stages in the expression of this dynamism in the physical world we may have some deeper sense of the infinite immensity of the love present in the Trinity. And through seeing the immeasurable diversity and increasing complexity of the forms of material organization that the evolutionary cosmos manifests we may have some deeper sense of the mystery of the procession of the Word within the Trinity.

We should raise the question of how one would envisage the influence of the biblical symbol *Wisdom* in this process. We have seen something of how the process reflects Word and Spirit, though, of course, we are not saying that in the process the Word and Spirit are present as in the Incarnation and the trinitarian indwelling of the sons and daughters of God by grace. The question of Wisdom is a difficult question, and we should not expect clarity as we compare distinct modes of discourse.

Perhaps we can see two aspects of Wisdom. One is the craftsman who is active with God in his creative work (Prv 8:30), and here one is closer to the Word. Another is that artificer in whom "is a spirit intelligent, holy, unique, manifold, subtle, agile, . . . pervading all spirits . . . mobile beyond all creation, and she penetrates and pervades all things by reason of her purity" (Ws 7:22–24). In this influence Wisdom seems closer to Spirit. We can see a distinction in the Wisdom books of the Old Testament between that wisdom that was an *experience* of the sage whereby he comes to a new and affective knowledge of God's ways, and that wisdom which was the *illumination from above* that comes to him through this experience.[46] The former is the movement of the human—through grace, we would say—toward the divine, and the latter is the descent of illumination from the divine to the human mind. In the very movement of the human toward the divine there is present spirit and wisdom associated with spirit. We can see wisdom in a sense analogous to this operative throughout the whole evolutionary creative process; physical creation has a direction from within, a within that manifests the immanence within it of divine Spirit and Wisdom. The Wisdom that comes from above as from the craftsman and thus from God the Father through his craftsman reminds us more of the Word through whom God created and directed creation's movement toward his purposes. In our final chapter we will refer to the Spirit more specifically as sent by the Father and the exalted Christ from the future kingdom to give the world and history the dynamism toward the kingdom of God that is the fulfillment and liberation of history.

One question we should raise even in this telescoped treatment of evolution in relation to the trinitarian God is the emergence of the human from lower animals. Many Catholic theologians who accept evolution continue to ascribe this emergence to a special creation on the part of God. Classical philosophy speaks of man's soul as spiritual and thus a form that cannot be educed from the potentiality of matter. Scripture speaks of the coming to be of the human by a twofold principle, the dust of the earth and God's breathing into it (Gn 2:7). This has been a constant part of the Christian tradition, and affirmed again and again by the church, perhaps most recently in a statement by the Sacred Congregation for the Doctrine of the Faith concerning the future life: "The church affirms that a spiritual element survives and subsists after death, an element endowed with consciousness and will, so that the 'human self' subsists. To designate this element, the church uses the word 'soul,' the accepted term in the usage of scripture and tradition."[47] We do not justify this statement here; we accept it and just note that many philosophers, theologians, and even scientists still resist a reduction of the human self to matter.[48] It may seem on this view that there must be a supplement to the process of evolution in the way of a special intervention by God to account for the emergence of the human.

Karl Rahner is a theologian who has treated this question at length; he has argued that the distinctiveness of the human can be preserved without our asserting a special intervention by God in the creation of a soul for each human being, if we understand matter philosophically as active transcendence under God.[49] Partially in agreement with him, we can say that we are here considering the evolutionary process not restrictedly as it is studied by the physical sciences but as one in which God is operating throughout by a kind of continuing creation or concurrence. The evolutionary process is a participation in the process immanent in God himself, and indeed in the trinitarian God. There is indeed a creative self-organization of material reality with spontaneity and newness as contemporary science shows, and science can teach us the physical antecedents and constituents operative in this process. But it cannot as science tell us that nothing else is operative in this process. With the dynamism or *eros* or spirit operative in the transcendence of matter, as Rahner calls it, God is operating through his continuing creative, concurring, and conserving power. Thomas's metaphysics would explain how physical beings seek their own fulfillment within an environment by the fact that they are energized and motivated to do so by the *esse* as the first intrinsic principle of their being. This intrinsic principle induces them as agents to some extent to seek their own being and through that the being of their species and indeed the being possible to the whole physical order; and thus they are drawn to act by the final causality of these grades of good. God is acting through this *esse* as final cause and with their active self-organization as concurring cause in the actions of these physical agents.

Transitions or leaps such as that from nonliving to living and then, even more so, from animal to human, are possible metaphysically only because these agents are operating under the agency of God. Perhaps we can say that the human principle of life emerges from the potentialities of matter—not exclusively, but through matter's participation in the Spirit of God. God can perhaps use the interiority of the instrument that active matter is to effect a consequence higher than its innate capacity, as an artist can convey beauty through physical lines and pigments. I present this as a possibility to be evaluated; the more important point is to continue to affirm the distinctiveness of the human. Even if God does create each human soul in the traditional sense, this is not outside God's design for the world and not outside the evolutionary direction and purpose of the physical world.

To acknowledge an "arrow of time" directed toward the emergence of humanity is not to opt for an orthogenesis or to deny the reality of contingency and chance in evolution. At a large number of levels of evolution, it seems that a multitude of possible interactions with the environment were tried, some parasitic, some advances but dead ends, some regressions, some advances that were open to still further developments to an environment more broadly conceived. If we look at this in relation to God, we can say that God wished a vast multiplicity of expressions of his being and goodness and used the evolutionary process for this purpose, but with the intent of this process leading to the human. We note that even for Thomas, chance on one level need not be chance on a higher level. He writes:

> It happens at times that some event as related to lower causes is fortuitous or accidental, but as related to a higher cause is found to be essentially intended. For example, if two servants of the same master are sent by him to the same place, the one ignorant of the other, the meeting of the two servants, as referred to them is accidental, because it happens beyond the intention of either. If, however, it is referred to the master who prearranged it, it is not accidental but intended.[50]

We are not saying that God positively intended each biological organism that resulted from an interaction between an organism and its environment. We say he intended levels of biological organisms, pluralism at these levels, and humanity through this intrinsic dynamism of material reality. He allows some things to happen that are incidental to a larger purpose lest a greater evil result from preventing them.

In conclusion, we have in this chapter addressed only partially an enormously important contemporary problem concerning the Trinity, namely, the presence of the Trinity in the economies of salvation and creation. Failure to treat this question contributed to the marginalization of the Trinity in modern classical theology and in Christian consciousness. And failure to see some divine order in the physical world leads many people to fail to see it as a norm in their human lives. We will return to this issue from the perspective of a trinitarian spirituality in our final chapter.

Notes

1. DS, 3016.

2. I treated this question in my *Faith in God through Jesus Christ* (Collegeville, Minn.: Liturgical Press, 1997), 227–229, 272–274. See M.-D. Chenu, "La Somme Théologique," *Introduction à l'étude de Saint Thomas d'Aquin*, 2d ed (Paris: Vrin, 1954), 255–276. Michel Corbin contests this interpretation in his *Le chemin de la théologie chez Thomas d'Aquin* (Paris: Beauchesne, 1974). See the rich review of this

issue by Jean-Marc LaPorte, S.J., "Christ in Aquinas's *Summa Theologiae*: Peripheral or Pervasive?" *Thomist* 67 (2003): 221–248, especially 247: "In this (LaPorte's) approach, Christ continues to be a culmination, as Corbin claims, but within an *exitus-reditus* context, as Chenu reminds us."

3. See Gilles Emery, *La Trinité Créatrice* (Paris: Vrin, 1995), and G. Emery, "Trinité et Création," *Rev. Sc. Phil. et Théol.* 79 (1995): 405–430.

4. Emery, "Trinité," 423.

5. See N. Max Wildiers, *The Theologian and His Universe: Theology and Cosmology from the Middle Ages to the Present* (New York: Seabury Press, 1982), especially 57–58. Also see also Thomas Litt, *Les corps célestes dans l'univers de Saint Thomas d'Aquin* (Louvain, 1963). These books give the documentation for their claims.

6. See Wildiers, *Theologian*, 73.

7. Depending on Litt and others I argued in *God's Work in a Changing World* (Washington, D.C.: University Press of America, 1985; now available from Washington, D.C.: Council for Research in Values and Philosophy), 242–247, that Thomas's philosophy is not essentially connected with his cosmology.

8. See chapter 1, 16–17. Also see Robert Jenson, "Jesus in the Trinity: Wolfhart Pannenberg's Christology and Doctrine of the Trinity," in Carl Braaten and Philip Clayton, eds., *The Theology of Wolfhart Pannenberg* (Minneapolis: Augsburg, 1988), 188–206. See also Pannenberg's response to Jenson, also in *The Theology of Wolfhart Pannenberg*, 326–327, for Pannenberg's later expression of this. Also see an exchange between George Hunsinger and Robert Jenson in *Scottish Jounral of Theology* 55 (2002): George Hunsinger, "Robert Jenson's *Systematic Theology*: A Review Essay," 161–200, and Jenson's response, 225–232.

9. See chapter 2, 41–44.

10. See chapter 2, 45–46.

11. Karl Rahner, *The Trinity* (New York: Herder and Herder, 1970), 22. On Rahner's thesis, see Walter Kasper, *The God of Jesus Christ* (New York: Crossroad, 1984), 273–277.

12. See J. Farrelly, *Belief in God in Our Time* (Collegeville, Minn.: Liturgical Press, 1992), 312–321, 329–331. For a survey of recent theological studies on this theme, see John Thompson, *Modern Trinitarian Perspectives* (New York: Oxford University Press, 1994), 53–63; and a collection of articles on "God and Change" in *New Blackfriars* 68 (1987): 210–263. In this collection Michael Dodd, O.P., in "St. Thomas Aquinas and the Motion of the Motionless God," 233–242, interestingly relates the procession of the Word and the Spirit to Thomas's teaching on the acts of knowledge and love as 'actus perfecti', that is, dynamic actions which do not of their nature imply potentiality. And he holds that Thomas acknowledges 'change' in God in that his wisdom imprints itself on creation, and in the missions of the Son and Spirit. This whole issue also involves that of God and temporality. See, for example, Gregory Ganssle, ed., *God and Time: Four Views* (Downers Grove, Ill.: InterVarsity Press, 2001).

13. See Earl Muller, S.J., "Real Relations and the Divine: Issues in Thomas's Understanding of God's Relation to the World," *TS* 56 (1995): 673–695.

14. See Norris Clarke, S.J., *Person and Being* (Milwaukee: Marquette University Press, 1993), and his response to an objector in *Thomist* 61 (1997): 617–624.

15. See *ST* I, 21, 3.

16. Karl Rahner, "On the Theology of the Incarnation," *Theological Investigations*, vol. 4 (Baltimore: Helicon, 1966), 113–114. We will return to the question of real relations in chapter 8.

17. Muller, "Real Relations," 691, argues that: "The only real relation that God can have to the world must be understood in terms of a Person-to-person relationality rooted in the eternal relations. It should be possible, however, to understand all of God's covenantal relations with humanity in such a fashion."

18. See Hans Urs von Balthasar, *Mysterium Paschale: The Mystery of Easter* (Grand Rapids, Mich.: Wm. B. Eerdmans, 1993; originally published in 1970), 11. Also see Gerry O'Hanlon, S.J., "Does God Change?—H. U. von Balthasar on the Immutability of God," *Irish Theological Quarterly* 53 (1987): 161–183.

19. Balthasar, *Mysterium*, 24.

20. This is found in Walter Kasper in his own way. See *God of Jesus Christ*, 195: "Only if God is in himself love can he reveal himself as such in an eschatological and definitive way. From eternity, therefore, God must be self-communicating love. This in turn means that God possesses his identity only in a distinction within himself between lover and beloved who are both one in love."

21. *Belief in God*, 190–191, fn.; also see 195–198. For surveys of and judgments on kenotic theologies, see Balthasar, *Myterium*, 27–41; Kasper, *God of Jesus Christ*, 190–194; P. Henry, "Kénose," *DBS* 5: 7–161.

22. Balthasar, *Mysterium*, 29–30.

23. See Jean Galot, *Dieu souffre-t-il?* (Paris: P. Le Thielleux, 1976); Galot, "La réalité de la souffrance de Dieu," *Nouvelle revue théologique* 101 (1979): 224–245; "Le Dieu trinitaire et la Passion du Christ," *Nouvelle revue théologique* 104 (1982): 70–87; and Kasper, *God of Jesus Christ*, 194–197; Warren McWilliams, "Divine Suffering in Contemporary Theology," *Scottish Journal of Theology* 33 (1980): 35–53. I treated the question of God's suffering briefly in *Belief in God*, 328–331. I think that Thomas Weinandy treats this question too defensively in his *Does God Suffer?* (Notre Dame: University of Notre Dame Press, 2000).

24. Abraham Heschel, *The Prophets*, vol. 2 (New York: Harper and Row, 1975 reprint), 56. This is quoted in McWilliams, "Divine Suffering," 54.

25. Galot, "Le Dieu trinitaire," 71; he is quoting from Origen's *Rom.* 7.9; *Selecta in Ezech.*, 16; *Homilia VI in Ezech.* Also see J. Chéné, "Unus de Trinitate Passus est," *Recherches de science religieuse* 53 (1965): 545–588, on the patristic period.

26. O'Hanlon, "Does God Change?" 176.

27. See chapter 2, 34–37.

28. See above, 127–129; and Thomas, *ST* I, 45, 6 and 7.

29. See *ST* I, 46, 1–3.

30. For the continuing dominance of science in American academic and intellectual life, see David Hollinger, *Science, Jews, and Secular Culture: Studies in Mid–Twentieth*

Century American Intellectual History (Princeton: Princeton University Press, 1997); Daedalus (1997, Winter); and Michael Lacey, "The Backwardness of American Catholicism," Proceedings of the Catholic Theological Society of America 46 (1991): 1–15.

31. I have discussed this question with the help of such guides as Ernan McMullin and John Deely in "Human Transcendence and Thomistic Resources" in Farrelly, God's Work in a Changing World, especially 231–247.

32. ST I, 29, 1.

33. CG, I, 37. See Farrelly, "Existence, the Intellect, and the Will," New Scholasticism 29 (1955): 145–174.

34. D. Yankelovich and W. Barrett, Ego and Instinct: The Psychoanalytic View of Human Nature—Revised (New York: Random House, 1970), 323.

35. See Erik Erikson, The Life Cycle Completed: A Review (New York: Norton, 1982), 85f.

36. I treat this more extensively in Belief in God, 179–204.

37. Paul Davies, The Cosmic Blueprint: New Discoveries in Nature's Creative Ability to Order the Universe (New York: Simon and Schuster, 1988). Also see John Polkinghorne, The Faith of a Physicist (Princeton: Princeton University Press, 1994); John Haught, Science and Religion (New York: Paulist, 1995); Robert J. Russell, Nancey Murphy, and C. J. Isham, eds., Quantum Cosmology and the Limits of Nature: Scientific Perspectives on Divine Action (Vatican: Vatican Observatory Publications, 1993); Christopher Mooney, S.J., Theology and Scientific Knowledge: Changing Models of God's Presence in the World (Notre Dame: University of Notre Dame Press, 1996); Robert J. Russell, William R. Stoeger, and Francisco Ayala, eds., Evolutionary and Molecular Biology: Scientific Perspectives on Divine Action (Berkeley, Calif.: Center for Theology and the Natural Sciences, 1998); William Stoeger, S.J., "Theology and the Contemporary Challenge of the Natural Sciences," Proceedings of the Catholic Theological Society of America 46 (1991): 21–43; and articles on God and the physical sciences in the October issue of Theology Today 55 (1998). Paul Davies also has later books, and articles in the Russell, Murphy, and Isham volume, "The Intelligibility of Nature," 145–161, and the Russell, Stoeger, and Ayala volume, "Teleology Without Teleology: Purpose through Emergent Complexity," 151–162. Page citations in the text in this section are to Davies's book.

38. William Craig, book review of The Anthropic Cosmological Principle by John Barrow and Frank Tipler (Oxford: Clarendon, 1986), in International Philosophical Quarterly 27 (1987): 437–447, on 444. The whole review makes the distinction just made in the text. Craig also comments on Stephen Hawking's proposal in A Brief History of Time (London: Bantam, 1988), as does George Coyne, S.J., in "The Universe: Scientific Understanding and Its Theological Implications," Origins 26 (January 9, 1997): 478–481. A larger human knowledge and philosophy do discern purpose in the physical world, and for biologists to state that this is not knowledge is a philosophical and not a scientific statement. I treat some relevant epistemological questions with the help of J. Piaget and others in Belief in God, 243–259, and "Developmental Psychology and Knowledge of Being," God's Work, 287–314. Also see Anne

Clifford, "Creation," in Francis Schüssler Fiorenza and John Galvin, eds., *Systematic Theology: Roman Catholic Perspectives*, vol. 1 (Minneapolis: Fortress, 1991), 197–248.

39. Davies is citing Ilya Prigogine, *From Being to Becoming: Time and Complexity in the Physical Sciences* (San Francisco: Freeman, 1980).

40. Davies is citing Ilya Prigogine and Isabelle Stengers, *Order Out of Chaos* (London: Heinemann, 1984).

41. Davies, "Teleology Without Teleology," 158, 159–60, 162. In an article in Russell, *Molecular and Evolutionary Biology*, entitled "The Immanent Directionality of the Evolutionary Process, and Its Relationship to Teleology," William Stoeger, S.J., largely agrees with Davies on the directionality coded into physical reality, and says of chance: "What we refer to as chance, or contingent, events do not disrupt the directionality of evolution. They contribute strongly to it"(173). However, he does not think that the regularities presently discovered "provide the overarching holistic laws of nature, or the long-range teleological embodiment of purpose and goal in natural process for which some people yearn . . . such laws are not needed, even from a theological point of view, and will not be discovered at the level of the sciences" (181–182).

In a conference on cosmology at Harvard in October 2001, Paul Davies responded to the multiple-universe theory, saying that this theory was developed when science showed that the universe seemed precisely designed to produce human life. Because of this, scientists must choose between a view that the universe is the result of intelligent design or is the outcome of a gigantic cosmic lottery. This view cannot show that multiple universes exist or even explain the origin of natural law itself (see *Washington Times*, October 28, 2001).

42. Arthur Koestler, *Janus: A Summing Up* (New York: Random House, 1978), 226. Koestler distinguishes finality from causality, but perhaps this is because he takes physics' notion of causality as normative; in a larger sense finality has always been recognized as a causal influence, and he treats it as such. He speaks of this "pull of the future" when he writes of the evolutionary process as reflecting "the active striving of living matter towards the optimal realization of the planet's evolutionary potential" (213).

43. Terence Nichols, "Aquinas's Concept of Substantial Form and Modern Science," *International Philosophical Quarterly* 36 (1996): 311.

44. *Belief in God*, 298. As God's preservation in existence of creation is called conservation, we can call his causal influence on which the coming to be evident in evolution properly depends concurrence. Thomas writes (ST I, 104, 1) that "the coming to be of a thing cannot remain on the cessation of the action of the agent which is the cause of the effect according to its coming to be (*fieri*). In the same way neither can the existence (*esse*) of a thing remain on the cessation of the action of the agent which is the cause of the effect not only according to its coming to be but also of its existence (*esse*)."

45. See *Belief in God*, 298–299.

46. See above, chapter 2, 36–37; and Roland Murphy, *The Tree of Life: An Exploration of Biblical Wisdom Literature* (New York: Doubleday, 1990); Bernard Lee, *Jesus and the Metaphors of God* (New York: Paulist, 1993).

47. "Letter on Certain Questions Concerning Eschatology," *Origins*, August 2, 1979, 133. Also see Rainer Koltermann, "Evolution, Creation, and Church Documents," *Theology Digest* 48 (Summer 2001): 124–132.

48. See Charles Taylor, *Sources of the Self: The Making of the Modern Identity* (Cambridge: Harvard University Press, 1989); and John Cooper, *Body, Soul, and Life Everlasting: Biblical Anthroplogy and the Monism-Dualism Debate*, 2d ed. (Grand Rapids, Mich.: Wm. Eerdmans, 2000); Niels H. Gregersen, et al., eds., *The Human Person in Science and Theology* (Grand Rapids, Mich.: Wm. Eerdmans, 2000); Vance Morgan, "The Metaphysics of Naturalism," *American Catholic Philosophical Quarterly* 75 (2001): 409–432.

49. See K. Rahner, *Hominisation* (New York: Herder and Herder, 1965); "Christology within an Evolutionary View of the World," *Theological Investigations* 5 (New York: Seabury, 1975); Denis Edwards, "A Theological Reading of the Story of the Universe," chapter 3 of *Jesus and the Cosmos* (New York: Paulist, 1991); Michael Barnes, "The Evolution of the Soul from Matter and the Role of Science in Karl Rahner's Theology," *Horizons* 21 (1994): 85–104; and C. Mooney, *Theology and Science*, 158–161.

50. *ST* I, 116, 1. See Mooney, *Theology and Science*, 161–164; Timothy McDermott, "Design vs. Chance: Eavesdropping on Aquinas and Darwin," *Theology Digest* 43 (1996): 313–322; Elizabeth Johnson, "Does God Play Dice? Divine Providence and Chance," *TS* 57 (1996): 3–18; Joseph Bracken, "Response to Elizabeth Johnson's 'Does God Play Dice?'" *TS* 57 (1996): 720–730; a report of a seminar on the dispute between Johnson and Bracken in *Proceedings of the Catholic Theological Society of America* 53 (1998): 130–131, 135–136; and M. J. Farrelly, "Providence," in Michael Glazier and Monika Hellwig, eds., *The Modern Catholic Encyclopedia* (Collegeville: Liturgical Press, 1994), 699–701.

CHAPTER SIX

The Father's Generation of the Son

We now turn to a theological reflection on the meaning of our belief in the Trinity of Father, Son, and Holy Spirit within the Godhead itself. What do we mean or signify when we profess that the Father generates the Son, or that the Father, Son, and Holy Spirit are three persons in one God? Our reflection here is wholly dependent upon what the Father has revealed through the missions of his Son and Spirit, but treats directly what this makes known to us of the Father, Son, and Holy Spirit in their mutual relations within the Trinity rather than restrictedly their relations with us or one another in the order of salvation and creation. We are following both Scripture and tradition in recognizing that the missions of the Son and Spirit show us something of the relations they have to the Father and one another antecedent to and not ontologically dependent on their missions.

This is a matter of *constructive* theology, as we explained at the beginning of chapter 5. To *inculturate* our understanding of the Trinity demands that we relate this understanding to preunderstandings of our own time, as Nicea did for its time and Thomas did for his. We are doing this specifically in the context of the North Atlantic countries deeply influenced by science and modern historical consciousness. We shall later show that what we propose is relevant to and enriched by an awareness of world religions. We must in part critique current preunderstandings but also use elements of them as a resource for elucidating the mystery, under the control, of course, of Scripture and tradition.

Thomas, in dependence on Augustine, used spiritual activities of human beings, their knowledge and love, to help us understand the generation of the

Son by the Father and the procession of the Holy Spirit from Father and Son. Human beings are made in the image of God, and so tradition has held that under revelation we can use our understanding of the human to get some analogical understanding of God and specifically God as triune. This approach is rejected from several contemporary standpoints. In our first chapter, we spoke of one major division among Christian theologians' interpretation of the Trinity as that between dialogical theologians and dialectical theologians.[1] Some theologians in each of these camps reject Thomas's approach.

Among dialogical theologians there are some English and American theologians who contest the traditional Christian doctrine of the Trinity as intellectually incoherent, not demanded by Scripture, and/or counter to a contemporary philosophical interpretation of the man–God relationship. Traditional Christian trinitarian theology, they hold, does not cohere with a contemporary understanding of God, humanity, or the physical world. In answer to this we acknowledge that a classical interpretation of human knowledge, of the human orientation to God through time, and of God's relationship with time has to be modified to incorporate valid modern human experience. In part, we tried to do this in the preceding chapter. Here, we are seeking to show that our trinitarian belief does cohere with reason correctly understood and, indeed, that reason can help to illuminate the mystery. We may quote an encyclical of Pope John Paul II on this issue:

> Christian faith immerses human beings in the order of grace, which enables them to share in the mystery of Christ, which in turn offers them a true and coherent knowledge of the Triune God. . . . This truth, which God reveals to us in Jesus Christ, is not opposed to the truths which philosophy perceives. On the contrary, the two modes of knowledge lead to truth in all its fullness.[2]

This trinitarian mystery is not an abdication of reason. Indeed, the deliveries of human knowledge can illuminate Christian belief. Our study of the Trinity must answer those who hold that this mystery involves intrinsic contradictions.

Some dialectical theologians hold, in dependence on Karl Barth and in the words of Robert Jenson, that "traditional metaphysical doctrines, as the theology of another religion, have no inherent authority" in Christian theology.[3] Thomas Torrance, for example, holds that "the Word of God made flesh . . . embodies in himself not only the *exclusive* language of God to mankind but the faithful response in knowledge and obedience of humanity to God."[4] Torrance acknowledges that "the Old Testament Scriptures . . . provide the framework of divine meaning within which the New Testament

Scriptures are to be interpreted" (69), though in the New Testament we have "a radically new revelation of his [God's] divine Being and Nature as the God and Father of Jesus Christ" (67). He holds that nothing outside the Old Testament can offer part of this framework for interpreting the New Testament revelation of God. He concludes that we "may not understand what the Fatherhood of God means by analogical projection even *via eminentiae* out of human fatherhood" (160), and the same is true of what is meant by 'person' in the doctrine of the Trinity. Rather, human fatherhood and personhood are to be understood in terms of what is revealed of God as triune.

What can we say to this view? Following Barth, Torrance supposes that there is no revelation of God given outside of the Old and New Testament, or that what is given by God in this way has been necessarily distorted by human sin (see 19). Counter to this view, Paul supposes that God has revealed to the Gentiles something of his will and of himself (Rom 1:19–20), and that not all Gentiles reject this (Rom 2:15). These statements of Paul are in accord with the missionary method of the early Church (see Acts 17:22–31). Thus Torrance's view is, in fact, opposed to Scripture. It is similarly opposed to the wisdom writers who acknowledged that creation comes from God, and that God speaks or reveals, at times in the guise of Lady Wisdom, through creation to human beings.[5] It is true that what is controlling is the New Testament revelation. But we are not using God's full revelation if in seeking to understand the triune mystery we reject any of God's earlier revelations. As Jesus said to Nicodemus, "If I tell you about earthly things and you do not believe, how will you believe if I tell you about heavenly things?" (Jn 3:12).

Torrance makes significant use of the Greek Fathers in his elucidation of the trinitarian mystery, but he elides the fact that these men lived in a metaphysical age. So, though they modified words like *ousia* or *hypostasis* from their meaning in Greek culture when they used them to interpret the Trinity, still the Greek Fathers accepted them as legitimately signifying realities in the world and thus implicitly as metaphysically valid and as offering a partial context for the interpretation of the mystery of the Trinity. This is simply an instance of analogy. Thus, God's earlier revelation in both the Old Testament and through creation, particularly the image of God that human beings constitute, is intrinsically caught up into God's complete self-revelation of who God is in the triune mystery. To deny this hampers Torrance's ability, for example, to answer how God can have a Son (see 159). He does not use, in his reflection on the Father's generation of a Son, the analogy between human generation of a child and the intellectual act that results in a concept, and so cannot answer philosophical problems posed against God's revelation.

Another objection presented against the psychology analogy of Augustine is that *Logos* in John's prologue is, like *dabar*, *ruach*, and *sophia*, a metaphor. A metaphor is multivalent. But, the objection continues, the influence on Christianity by the Greek mind in the fourth century turned metaphor into metaphysics. This metaphysical transmutation was not justified by the poetics of Scripture and in fact distorted the meaning of Scripture in its use of *Logos*, since metaphysics gives it too specific a meaning and leaves out Spirit.

In answer, we acknowledge that Jesus is a *real* symbol of God, and in this sense a metaphor of the Father, who communicates both to our mind and our heart. Jesus is the Father's Word to us. But this is a metaphor that includes as well as transcends a metaphysical affirmation. Jesus is affirmed in John's gospel, and not only there, to be equal to God, since as his Son he has the same nature as God. As James Dunn writes of the prologue: "[B]y affixing the expanded poem to his . . . Gospel he [John] conflates its Logos christology with his own Son of God christology, whereby it becomes clear that for John the pre-existent Logos was indeed a divine personal being."[6] As we saw in an earlier chapter, the Fathers at Nicea used 'metaphysics' in a broad sense, because they used Greek words such as *ousia* (substance), but they modified such words significantly so that they would be able to express an aspect of the Christian mystery, for example saying that the Son is *homoousios* (the same substance) as the Father.[7] This word is not polyvalent, but the council's decision was to put its expression of belief in the form of a creed; and other words present in this creed (e.g., "Light from Light") preserved further dimensions of the Christian mystery and language. Scripture's language continues to be primary, and the creed's language was necessary to preserve the meaning of Scripture.

In principle, we will argue the legitimacy of Thomas's and Augustine's use of human acts of intellect and of love to elucidate the triune mystery. Augustine's and later Thomas's psychological analogy were not without antecedents, and were genuine efforts—and indeed advances—in dealing with a problem that earlier theologians had not sufficiently dealt with, namely how can God have a Son? We agree with Walter Kasper when he writes: "It is impossible to deny the spaciousness, depth and coherence of the classical Word-theology. It has a very satisfactory basis in scripture and tradition, and is a help that cannot be overvalued for a deeper understanding of revelation and of the latter's internal coherence and its correspondence to human knowledge."[8] An abandonment of these analogies has led in some instances to interpretations of the trinitarian relations in some generalized notion of love that left unanswered questions such as how the Father can share his own nature with his Son in a way that involves no subordination. There is indeed mystery here that we cannot plumb. A use of all the means God gives us to understand the mystery leaves it a mystery, but one that is more spiritually fruitful as well as intellectually and morally responsible. We shall then in this chapter seek to elucidate somewhat how the Father communicates his being to the Son, and in the next chapter how this being is communicated to the Holy Spirit. This is of itself not sufficient reflection on the three as three *persons*, so our chapter 8 will deal with the three as relational persons, and chapter 9 with some implications of this trinitarian mystery for Christian spirituality. In a way, our treatment of the generation of the Son by the Father before our study of the three specifically as persons follows the sequence of the crises on these issues in the church of the fourth century, as we showed in chapter 3.

Although we think that Thomas's analysis needs to be modified and supplemented in our age, we believe we should build on the past achievements of theologians rather than dismiss them and offer substitutes for what they have achieved. In what follows we shall (I) show Thomas's effort to use the analogy of an intellectual act to elucidate the Father's generating his Son, (II) propose a modification of this viewpoint needed today, and (III) dialogue with the objection that the classical articulation of the first procession is patriarchal.

I. Our Intellectual Knowledge as Analogue for the Father's Generation of the Son

We are asking who this man Jesus of Nazareth is. He claims to give a message or revelation that takes precedence even over the revelation given by God in his covenant with Israel, and his ministry for us is said to be God's greatest act of love for us. How is this possible? It is, as Scripture and tradition attest, because of who he is in himself—Son and Word of God. He is *the* Word of God, the Word through whom all things were made and the Word that enlightens all who come into the world. As Nicea said, he is "God from God, true God from true God, begotten not made, consubstantial with the Father, through whom all things were made." Thus he is one who has an existence antecedent not only to the Incarnation but to the whole of creation. He has an existence equal to and one with the Father though distinct from him as Son from Father. Our reflection here is not restrictedly on the eternal Word or Son of God, but on Jesus of Nazareth, the Incarnate Word or Son of God. In the light of our preceding chapter, we can add that by the Incarnation, the whole process of the universe's evolution terminates in what the eternal process of generation terminates in, namely the Word or Son of God.

The question is *how* can the Father have a Son? Our understanding of sonship is taken from what we know, and, among other things, it involves matter, the priority in time of parent to child, and potentiality because one is able to have an offspring before one does. These cannot be in God who is totally spiritual and infinite; nor can this kind of coming to be be predicated of the Son if he is equal to the Father. The Son's origin from God is totally distinct from that of creation, for it is through the Son that all things are created, and creation is an external product of God that comes from the free and contingent will of God. Generating an offspring is said properly of God according to the Council of Nicea; that is why the Son is equal to the Father. For God to have a Son is as essential to God as for him to be.

There is then *process* in God, but this must be one that is compatible with the divine being that is totally spiritual. Both the Eastern and Western Fathers have, in continuity with the prologue of John's gospel, identified God's having a Son with his having his Word. Thus Athanasius writes: "Since it has been said and shown that the Son is the offspring from the Father's substance, it would be doubtful to no one, but rather would be clear, that he is the Wisdom and Word of the Father, in whom and through whom he creates and makes all things" (*Oration Against the Arians*, Book I, 16). Thus, this generation is somehow a totally spiritual process. How can this be?

To gain some understanding of this mystery, we use an analogue from the created and indeed human order, as John used 'Son' and 'Word'. Because God is totally actual and spiritual, we take this analogue from the spiritual act of the human being—the intellectual order. To interpret this divine generation by the analogue of an intellectual act is not simply an esoteric philosophical move. It is initially and primarily a common language practice to associate an act of the intellect with generating or begetting. We call the product of a genuine act of knowledge an idea or a *concept*—what has been *conceived*. If we really understand something we conceive an idea about it or have a concept of it. And what we say externally and verbally of something that we understand comes from and expresses this concept or internal and intellectual word. Somehow people commonly draw a comparison between an intellectual act resulting in real knowledge and the human act of conceiving and bearing a child. Colloquially, they speak of a 'brain child'.

How can we articulate this philosophically? I present here, though in a severely abridged way and largely in my own words, Thomas's approach to this mystery. I accept Thomas's interpretation substantially. My later modification is to integrate will and the Holy Spirit more obviously into our understanding of this mystery. In spite of his defective biology, Thomas gives a basically valid definition of generation when he writes that it signifies "the origin of some living thing from a conjoined living principle . . . into the like-ness of the same specific nature (*originem alicujus viventis a principio vivente conjuncto . . . secundum rationem similitudinis in natura ejusdem speciei)*" (ST I, 27, 2). This kind of generating is found in mammals in a particularly striking way. But is it found analogically in an intellectual act?

Our intellectual activity is preeminently a form of life—action that comes from within the agent and remains within the agent, rather than a simple movement of something from outside (see Thomas, CG IV, 11). St. Thomas's analysis of the intellectual act of knowledge follows that of Aris-totle in large part.⁹ In human beings the act of knowing is preceded by the impact of the object known on the intellect. When this object is an aspect of the nature of a material thing (e.g., what is that walking in the distance down the road toward us?), the object first strikes the senses. Some charac-teristic of it (e.g., walking, human being) is abstracted through what Thomas calls the agent intellect from the sensible order (i.e., the object specifically as it impacts the senses by its external sensible characteristics) to make it proportionate to the intellectual level. In this condition which Thomas calls the "impressed species," the aspect of the sensible reality is presented to the knowing intellect. By this the intellect is activated, that is, moved from not knowing to knowing, and is in act or actively knowing. From this knowing comes a concept or idea or internal word (e.g., the judg-ment: it is a human being walking down the road) that we can express ex-ternally. This knowing is an act of the intellect, but the intellect acts in virtue of being activated or impregnated with an aspect of the reality known through the impressed species.

The act of knowing is what Thomas, following Aristotle, called an *actus perfecti*, that is, an act of a power already in act. This is distinct from an act like that of a body moving from one location to another. In this latter case we have an act of something in potency insofar as it is in potency. That is, the body moves insofar as it has not yet reached its destination, but once it has reached its destination it is no longer acting. Such an act essentially in-volves imperfection, but knowledge does not *essentially* involve imperfection. In us an act of knowing does, because we have to be activated before we know. But the act of knowledge itself is not this being activated, where the intellect is receptive and passive. In knowledge itself it is the knower who is acting. In fact, the more fully we are activated by or united with the object known the more fully we act or know. Also this act is *immanent* within the knower. This immanent act is distinct from a transitive act by which we move an object from one location to another. And the concept remains within the intellect.

The concept or idea or internal word is a natural resultant of the act of knowledge. And since it results from our intellect impregnated by the object, the act from which the idea results is appropriately called 'conceiving' (as "I conceive an idea") and the result itself is appropriately called 'concept'. The concept is like both the object known and the intellect itself; the more fully the object is known, the more like it the concept or idea is or the more the concept *is* the object intentionally (i.e., referentially). In such knowledge we directly express the object known, but we can reflexively concentrate our attention on the concept as concept as we are doing in this brief analysis of the intellectual act. Of course, this concept is not, as a child is, a distinct *being* from the intellectual act that generates it. Besides being the 'image' or 'likeness' to some degree of the object known, the concept has an existence as a modification of the intellect itself, as something that affects—and enriches—the intellect.

What we have been analyzing is the created analogue, and we now *apply* that analogically to the revealed mystery. We are not trying to prove that the Father in knowing himself says a word expressive of himself; we are trying to get some understanding of what has been revealed, namely, that the Father has a Son or he says a Word that is divine. What controls this application of the created analogue is divine revelation mediated by Scripture and tradition.

God the Father knows his own being, and in knowing himself expresses himself perfectly by a Word that is totally proportionate to his being. God expresses himself in creation too, but this effect or image is external to God, finite and the result of God's free act. But the Son or Word is "begotten not made (*genitum non factum*)." This process by which God the Father expresses himself perfectly is a process that remains within God. The intellectual generation of a word can show us to some extent both what it means to say that the Father has a Son and that it is not contradictory to the perfection of God to have a Son. As in us the concept results from a union of knower and object known, so in God there is a perfect and eternal union between God as knower and his being as known; God's being is infinitely actual, and his knowledge of this being is always infinitely actual. In God there is in fact no distinction between being and act, and so God's knowledge of his being and his being are one in a way that our knowledge and what we know are not, even when we know ourselves.

From revelation we know that there results from God the Father's knowledge of his being a Word totally expressive of the Father's being; this results eternally; it never began and never ends; it is an eternal process. The Son did not have a beginning, nor was there a time when the Father was not Father.

God's intellect is always one with the object known—the divine being; and this object known, as well as the divine intellect itself, is always totally actual, never potential. This process can properly be called generation, because there is found in the divine Word that results from this saying "an origin of a living being from a conjoined living being according to likeness of specific nature."

There are, as we have already indicated, many differences between our intellectual act resulting in a word and God's saying of his Word. As the Fourth Council of the Lateran (1215) said of analogy generally, "a likeness between creator and creature cannot be noted without a greater dissimilarity having to be noted between them."[10] One difference between our knowledge and God's is that we have innumerable concepts, while the Father says all he knows in his one Word or Son. Another difference is that our word is similar to the reality we know—or is the reality intentionally or referentially, but is not ontologically that reality. Our concept's existence (or *esse*) is as a modification of our intellect and not the existence of the object known. But in God the Word or Son *is* the same being as the Father. If the Son had another being than that of the Father, there would be two Gods. God perfectly understands his being, and its resulting Word is then totally proportionate to his being, and its existence not a modification of his intellect, but *is* his being; the Word is subsistent being. Otherwise it would not be a perfect expression of the Father's being; a simply conceptual rather than an ontological expression of his being would lack something. Thus the Son is *homoousios* or of the same being or substance as the Father. We shall show in chapter 8 that there is a real distinction of relationship in this divine generation, because the direction of the action and relationship the generator has to the generated (or the knower to the word said) is opposite to the reception and relationship that the generated has to the generator, or the word said has to the sayer and what he says.

This analogy then can give us *some* illumination of the revealed mystery that the Father has a Son. It is God specifically as Father who says a Word that is his Son. The Son and the Spirit perfectly know the divine being, but this knowledge does not result in a word. The Son is called a Word properly and not restrictedly metaphorically (see *ST* I, 34, 1).[11] God is as essentially trinitarian as he is God, and so the generating of a Son by the Father is a natural act as distinct from an act that proceeds from his will, as creation is. But it is an act of nature that is voluntary, as we are human beings voluntarily rather than by constraint (see *ST* I, 41, 2). Love accompanies the Father's generating of a Son rather than is the proper principle of this generation.

In saying himself, the Father says all that he knows, and thus the whole Trinity and indeed all of creation:

> As the knowledge of God is indeed only knowing of God, but both knowing and causing of creatures, so the Word of God is only expressive of that which is in God the Father, but both expressive and causative of creatures, and because of this it is said in Ps. 32, 'He spoke and they were made,' because there is found in the word a causative nature in reference to the things which God makes. (ST I, 34, 3)

The Father creates through his Son.

II. A Modification of Thomas's Theology of the Father's Saying of the Word

Since the mid–twentieth century a number of Catholic theologians have expressed dissatisfaction with Thomas's theology of the first procession within the Trinity. Much, but not all, of this dissatisfaction is reflected in varied forms of Spirit Christology, studies of which can be found elsewhere;[12] we will have occasion to return to this theme in our final chapter. Some of the suggestions for Spirit Christology come from efforts to answer difficulties raised by Orthodoxy to the Western Filioque. As one example, I will give Thomas Weinandy's proposal. He writes:

> I would argue that the Father begets the Son in or by the Holy Spirit, that is, that the Spirit proceeds (ekporeuetai) simultaneously from the Father as the one in whom the Son is begotten. . . .
> The image here is not that the Father sequentially breathes forth the Spirit through the Son . . . but rather that the Father speaks forth (begets) the Son by the breath of the Holy Spirit. The Father spirates (breathes forth) the Spirit, and it is in or by the breath of the Spirit that the Father speaks his Word. . . . The Son in turn breathes forth the Spirit as he cries out "Abba." Thus the Holy Spirit is the common breath (life) shared by the Father and the Son.[13]

This reconception modifies but does not reject the use of the psychological analogy, and, as we explain below, we acknowledge a legitimacy in the concern expressed in it.

Another reservation in reference to Thomas's view comes from reflection on the Trinity from the perspective of the cross of Christ, as shown in Walter Kasper: "The starting point of christological reflection must be the giving of the Son by the Father and the self-giving of the Son to the Father and for the many, rather than the generation of the Son by the Father as conceived according to the analogy of the production of the intellectual word."[14] It seems that a certain lack of emphasis on the Father's love in the psychological analogy is a central reason on the part of many theologians for dissatisfaction with Thomas's approach. The perspective of the cross emphasizes the self-giving or love in the relationship between the Father and the Son, and there is an antecedent for this in the trinitarian relations: "Love in him [the Father] is not . . . a losing of himself in giving himself, but a communicating of himself in giving himself."[15]

Also, as we saw in chapter 2, there is in Scripture's account of the order of salvation a certain precedence of the Spirit in Jesus Christ's mission, conception, and ministry, as well as a precedence of Jesus Christ in the Spirit's mission. Moreover, the Hebrew word for 'word' is *dabar*, which has a more dynamic meaning than the Greek *logos* or the English 'word'; it embraces the notion of effectiveness. In relation to this, the analogy of the word for the first procession within the Trinity as it was used by the Greek Fathers is largely a human being's external *saying* of a word, which shows the exercise of the will behind it and the accompanying of the word by breath or Spirit. These are some aspects of the procession of the Son from the Father that do not seem to be adequately reflected in Thomas's account. So, I agree that Thomas's theology here has to be modified. Granted the basic legitimacy of the psychological analogy, is there some modification of this analogy that may make it more adequate to the above data than Thomas's is? I propose that there is, and for this purpose will present a somewhat different model of human knowledge than that proposed by Thomas, but one that is rooted in his interpretation of human knowledge and love. Then, I will apply this to the divine procession of the Son or Word and answer some possible objections to this proposal.

1. A Model of Human Knowledge as Analogue
There are different forms of human knowledge. The form that Thomas used has continuity with that of Aristotle. It is the form found in human knowledge of the natures of things. However, is this the most appropriate model of knowledge to use here? It would seem that a more appropriate form is that knowledge found in our *act of faith* by which we respond to God's revelation and by which we are transformed into sons and daughters of God. In this knowledge, as distinct from that knowledge by which we know the natures of things around us, there is a holistic human response to God revealing.

Faith knowledge includes an act of the human will. Thomas says of this response of the will: "The one who believes has sufficient motive for believing.

For he is inclined to believe by the authority of the divine teaching confirmed by miracles and, what is greater, the interior appeal of God inviting him" (*interiori instinctu Dei invitantis*) (*ST* II-II, 2, 9, ad 3). The will of the one coming to belief is engaged, and through this willing the person is fitted, as it were, for true faith. Thomas writes of the *instinctus fidei:* "through the virtue of faith the human mind is inclined to assent to those things that agree with right faith and not to others" (*ST* II-II, 1, 4, ad 3).[16] Having the inclination proper to accept God's communication is intrinsic to the act of faith. Also, this knowledge of faith is *personal* knowledge, that is, a response to a person by a person, an insight into who the person is that is mediated not simply by objective knowledge but by one's subjectivity being engaged by the subjectivity of the other and one's acceptance of this engagement. This kind of knowledge is also found in our personal relation to other human beings, and it seems more proportioned than simply objective knowledge both to us as full persons and to the other as personal.

This type of knowledge also has affinities with aesthetic knowledge. As in faith we respond to the mystery of the person, so in aesthetic experience, as Louis Lavelle writes, we are interested not so much in the outside phenomenon as in "the within of the thing, that is to say, the interior movement which makes it be and of which it is the manifestation, and the within of ourselves by which precisely we try to seize the within of the thing."[17] For example, in acclaiming the beauty of nature, we mean that "in this nature the spirit finds once again a sort of accord with its own essential aspirations which nature anticipates and prefigures."[18] Here too then, as in faith, affectivity in part mediates knowledge. Of course, faith goes beyond aesthetic knowledge because it involves personal commitment.

Also, while the model of knowledge Thomas used as his analogue explaining the first trinitarian procession is that by which we know the forms of things, that is, what they are, our human knowledge by which we know 'being' would seem more appropriate as a model since this is a more complete knowledge of reality. Things are what they are by their natures or essences, but to know the forms of things is not necessarily to know their being, since the forms of things are not their 'to be'. Intellectual knowledge of the natures of things of itself does not account for the existential judgment which reflects knowledge of being.

For Thomas Aquinas, it seems that 'to be' is more immediately the object of our desire or acts of will than of the intellect. For he associates the good, which is the object of desire and love, in a special way with existence. He writes, "The good is that which all desire . . . but all things desire to be (*esse*) actually according to their manner, which is clear from the fact that each thing according to its nature resists corruption. To be actually then constitutes the nature of the good" (CG I, 37, 4).[19] This interpretation is supported even by our language. When we express an object of desire, it is frequently by an infinitive, such as "I want to eat," "I like to swim"; each of these desires is related to our orientation to our own 'be-ing', the infinitive, as it were, being a participation in the 'to be' of our person. Other objects, such as love of others, are mediated by this interior horizon of our desire, as we are asked to love others as we love ourselves.

As our intellectual knowledge of color depends in part on that power of knowledge that has color as its direct object, sight, so too our intellectual knowledge of 'be-ing' or 'to be' is mediated in part by our will. Knowledge of being, if it is more than simply habitual, is mediated by both direct intellectual knowledge and an intellectual knowledge participative in the movement of our will toward the good, a kind of knowledge by presence. St. Thomas writes at times about "judgments by inclination" or experiential knowledge, as we saw above in his words about faith—a knowledge we have through the participation in the inclination we have toward or away from some person, some act, or some thing. And this kind of knowledge is part of our knowledge of being. This existential knowledge seems to be a better model than the one Thomas uses to serve as an analogue in our interpretation of the first divine procession.

An exploration of how the good is present to the will and thus to the intellect that is a development faithful to Thomas's epistemology is illuminating here. The question of how the good is intentionally present to the will and thus able to solicit its response has usually been answered by saying that the good is presented to the will by the practical intellect. But this leads to the question of how *esse* or 'to be' is present to the will, since each thing wishes to be. The intellect's direct object is the natures of things, and so of itself it cannot present this good as such to the will.

Thomas's explanation of the function and nature of the agent intellect has something important to offer here. We can recall that Plato had thought that the intellect knows forms in a "world of ideas" and by a kind of remembrance, but that Aristotle had judged that we know forms (e.g., this is a human being) from their individual and concrete reality in the physical things about us. Since the forms are only potentially intelligible in physical nature, Aristotle had to infer in human beings a capacity to abstract these forms from individuating matter. By what he called the active intellect, what is potentially intelligible in sense knowledge of an object, as integrated by the interior sense of imagination or phantasy (called the "expressed sensible species"), is rendered actually intelligible.

Thomas compares the active intellect in its activity to light that makes colors actual: "In this way also light makes colors actual, not that it itself has the determinations of all colors in itself" (In III *De Anima*, 10, n. 739). The act proper to the active intellect is not a determining act. On the metaphysical level, there are both formal or determining acts and 'to be'. From the function of the agent intellect we see that its act must be of the order of the act of 'to be', since it actualizes rather than determines the form offered it in the phantasm so that the form is actually intelligible; the active intellect is determined by the form.

This act of the agent intellect emanates from the being of the human being, and thus must be a participation in the 'to be' of the person rather than properly a participation in the substantial form of the person, which is a determining act. As a participation in the 'to be' of the person, it is able to present the good intentionally to the will, as the form actualized by the agent intellect mediates the form of the external object to the knowing intellect. The good which draws the person and which he or she seeks is an enhancement of his or her own being. The act of the agent intellect presents this to the will, and also presents it in relation to some specific object known because it is the act of the intelligible form, and thus mediates the external object known. We would say then that the intellect presents the good to the will, but with the understanding that it is the agent intellect that presents the goodness of the proposed act or object to the will, and the knowing intellect that presents what is to be done or what is loved to the will.

In an earlier article,[20] I presented this diagramatically as follows:

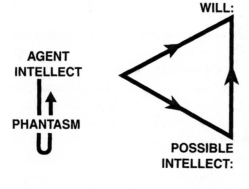

AGENT INTELLECT

↑

PHANTASM

U

WILL:
1. receives from A. I. an existential actuation.
2. receives from P. I. a formal actuation.

POSSIBLE INTELLECT:
1. receives from A. I.:
   a) existential actuation to reduce it to act
   b) formal actuation as object (species impressa)
2. receives from will the connatural or experimental knowledge of existence and goodness.

Thus, the will receives through the mediation of the agent intellect (A.I.) an *esse* or existential actuation that mediates the good to it. It receives from the knowing intellect (which Thomas calls the "possible intellect," P.I.) a form or formal actuation that mediates *what* it is that is loved or desired. The knowing or possible intellect receives through the agent intellect the actually intelligible form or the "impressed intelligible species" by which it is activated and understands its object. The knowing intellect is, as we explained earlier, reduced to act by the actually intelligible intentional object that impregnates it. I would not now say that the knowing intellect receives an existential actuation from the agent intellect, at least if by this is meant something further than the intelligible species itself. Also, there should be an arrow facing the knowing intellect from the will to accord with the fact it "receives from will the connatural or experimental [i.e., experiential] knowledge of existence and goodness."

2. Application of This Analogue, and Answer to Objections

From what we have seen earlier in Scripture and the Greek Fathers, and even in Augustine whose notion of knowledge was that which the person had of the self, and thus a more personal knowledge than that which Thomas's model envisages, it seems to us that it is appropriate to use the model we outlined above to give us some understanding of the first trinitarian procession. From the use of this analogue we are not trying to prove that the first procession is of this character, but rather trying to gain some understanding of the revealed mystery that the Father has a Son or says a Word from "analogy with those things we naturally know," as the First Vatican Council notes.

Though in God intellect and will are one, "the proper character of this or that procession . . . should be taken according to the order of one procession to the other. This order is found according to the nature of the will and intellect" (*ST* I, 27, 4, ad 1). So it is the character of the human acts of knowledge and of will that offers us an analogue for the divine action that is found in the processions of Son and Spirit. Just because in God knowledge and love are one does not mean that they do not have their distinctive characteristics, of which our acts of knowledge and love are participations.

The Father generates the Son as a personal act (see *ST* I, 40, 4), a theme we shall speak about further in chapter 8. Since the act of generating the Son or saying the Word is a personal act of the Father, it thus reflects his *personal* knowledge of his divine being. And the Son who is generated or the Word that is said reflects fully this personal being so known and the personal character of this knowledge. The Word *is* the divine being thus known, save that he is this being as Word or as received, and the Father is this being as Father or as saying or generating. There is order here, but not priority (see *ST* I, 42, 3).

From the human analogue we can see that the character of personal knowledge differs from simply intellectual knowledge of forms in that it is in part mediated by affectivity or will. Thus, the Father's knowledge of his divine being which is *said* in the Word or which generates the Son is more holistic than simply knowledge of the divine essence. The divine existence or 'to be' is more properly the object of the divine will than of the divine intellect, because of the distinctive character of the good as 'to be' and the will as oriented to the good, even though the divine essence and divine existence are one. Knowledge of the divine 'to be' is 'mediated' by the divine love of the infinite divine good. Specifically, it is by this holistic and personal knowledge that the Father generates the Son or says the Word.

Is this a claim that the Holy Spirit is involved in the generation of the Son? We are not only saying, as Thomas does, that the Father's will is involved in the generation of the Son as concomitant (*ST* I, 41, 2). We are suggesting that love is a principle of the Son from a perspective different from that of Thomas, namely, since the knowledge that results in the Son and that the Son expresses is fully personal. This is not to say that the Son proceeds as love proceeds, because the Son proceeds in the order of knowledge or generation. Thomas acknowledges, correlatively, that the Holy Spirit receives the divine nature from the Father, but that does not make her procession a generation since the nature is received in a procession of will or love: "that which proceeds by way of love both receives the divine nature and is not said to be born" (*ST* I, 27, 4, ad 1). In our explanation, the Son does not receive the divine nature from the love that is, in part, a principle of the saying of the Son, and so this love is not a principle specifically of the generation of the Son. Though dependent on the love that is the Holy Spirit, the Son proceeds properly as generated, not as love. There can be a sense, then, in which the Son in part comes from the Holy Spirit, without this origin being properly generation.

Our analogue, and indeed Thomas's own philosophy, show that there is a mutual priority between will and intellect. This is not contradictory since the will in part precedes the intellectual act of personal knowledge and the intellect in part precedes the act of love. The intellect's reception from the will is consistent with the intellect's act being one of knowledge rather than love, and its natural result being an internal word or "expressed species" as Thomas calls it at times. It is just that we are claiming that this word cannot be reduced to one that is merely expressive of objective knowledge of a form existing in the world. From the above it seems to us that there is as much reason to say that the Spirit has a part in the generation of the Son as to say that the Son has a part in the procession of the Spirit.

Even if one accepts the model for personal knowledge we presented, the argument could be made for the Father giving rise to the Son *without* the Spirit. But a similar argument could also be made for the Father giving rise to the Spirit *without* the Son. One could argue that the Spirit proceeds as love from the goodness that is the Father and from the *Father's* knowledge of that goodness, not the knowledge in the Son. We do not argue this way because of Scripture and tradition (particularly in the West) and because the human analogue shows that love proceeds from goodness and from the 'word'. Similarly, it seems that Scripture shows the Spirit to have a certain precedence to the Word in the economy of salvation, as we saw in chapter 2. And the analogue found in *personal* knowledge that we have of ourselves or others shows that in part this knowledge proceeds from our affectivity and the object of the will.

The Father's act of saying the Word or generating the Son is then an act of infinite and inexpressible love. It is out of love that he communicates his own whole being to the Son, and the Son is the full image or expression of the Father's personal being, equal to him in divine being because one with him in the divine being. The Father's self-gift and the Son's reception and mirroring of the Father are both personal acts. And in that sense they are free, not that they are contingent, but that they come from the fullest possible desire rather than from any, even minimal, constraint. The necessity of this self-gift is from the character of the Father's self-communication out of love because he is fully Father. To be God is to be this total self-giving and receiving who are the Father and the Son, as we know from revelation.

III. The Critique of the Father–Son Relationship as Patriarchal

Some theologians have recently claimed that the classical interpretation of the first procession is patriarchal and therefore damaging to women and, indeed, as Freud holds, to human adulthood more generally. For example, it has been said that this interpretation is based on metaphors, and these metaphors were developed in a patriarchal age. They are damaging to women because they interpret God too much through the lens of male experience and have not integrated women's experience into the symbolization of God. Moreover, this has been of a piece with a traditional view that man is the image of God and woman is the glory of man and only indirectly the image of God. But, some Christian feminists continue, this distortion can be corrected by Scripture itself. In the Old Testament, Wisdom (Sophia) is a feminine symbol of God, and Jesus can be seen as Wisdom incarnate or the daughter of Wisdom. The Synoptics speak of Jesus as Wisdom as does Paul, and there is much from the Wisdom tradition in the prologue to John's gospel.[21] And those influenced by Freud would say that the notion of God as Father keeps human beings in a state of childhood, validates a patriarchal culture, and is incompatible with adult human autonomy.

In dialogue with such positions, we note that this question deserves a more thorough investigation than we can offer here; this can be found elsewhere, as indicated by references we note below. Moreover, our total answer is not found here. In the next chapter, on the Holy Spirit, I will return to the thesis treated earlier in this book, namely that the major symbols of the Holy Spirit in Scripture are feminine.[22] Here we restrict ourselves to the question whether Scripture and tradition's teaching on the first procession demeans women or enhances their dignity, and some reflections on the gender of personal pronouns.

We first of all recall that the mystery of the Trinity is a *revealed* mystery, and its interpretation depends upon the relation of words to revelation. Here I presuppose that while the human authors of the books of Scripture did indeed use creative imagination to articulate God's revelatory interaction with human beings, their creative imagination was faithful to the creative imagination by which God initiated salvific actions and words through his intermediaries to make known something of himself and his plan of salvation for his people. And if we are to be faithful to this revelation we should search how the metaphors and symbols used in Scripture can be saving for us in our time.[23] In the Old Testament, God is not designated as Father for Israel in the way that gods of the surrounding peoples are spoken of at times as their fathers. Surrounding peoples considered themselves or their leaders as natural offspring of the gods, but for Israel it was only through God's loving, free choice that they were adopted as his children (see, e.g., Is 63:7–64:12), and only in this sense was he their father.[24] He is *not* their father in any natural sense, nor is God material or physical. His fatherhood is an expression of his loving *care* for his own people, for the king, for the just man, for those in need and for all he has created.

It is not that the designation of God as Father was adequate to God. Even the first chapter of Genesis shows that women are equal to men as image of God: "God created man in his image; in the divine image he created him; male and female he created them" (Gn 1:27). It was sin that distorted man's relation to God, men and women's relation to one another, and the earth's relation to human beings. Phyllis Trible examines the association between the terms for 'womb' and the idea of God (e.g., Ps. 103:13; Jer. 1:5, etc.) . . . concluding, "With persistence and power the root rhm journeys throughout the traditions of Israel to establish a major metaphor for biblical faith; semantic movement from the wombs of women to the compassion of God" (p. 56). [Also] she examines other associations of the God idea with female 'things'—breasts (Ps. 22:9–10); birth (Deut. 32:18); labour (Is 41:14b); mother (Is 66:12–14). . . . Her conclusion is just: "All these (are) partial metaphors—the basic metaphor (i.e. male and female) contrasts with the imbalance of these partial metaphors. It presents an equality in the image of God male and female, *although the Bible overwhelmingly favours male metaphors for deity*" (p. 22).[25]

Similarly, the symbol of Wisdom is used of God (see, e.g., Prv 8:22–26; Ws 7:25f; Sir 24: 3f), and this is a feminine symbol. Anne Gardner holds that "The development of *hokmah* or the figure of Wisdom is now understood as having grown out of the qualities of the goddess."[26]

In the New Testament, Jesus addressed God directly in prayer as Father, and specifically by the familiar word 'Abba'. He speaks of himself as Son, as we showed in chapter 2, and does so in a sense that suggests a certain equality between himself and his Father.[27] While it is true that Jesus used feminine symbols of himself at times (e.g., as a hen, Lk 13: 34), and this shows we must not make a total dichotomy between male and female images, still one can scarcely deny that maleness is constitutive of Jesus' humanity. We must acknowledge that God chose a male to symbolize the second person of the Holy Trinity in the economy of salvation, indeed one who in his resurrected life retains his masculine human identity. Is this of the same level as choosing a Jew to symbolize this divine person? Jesus did not constantly call himself a Jew and relate himself to God as Jew, but rather as Son to Father. Moreover, the evangelists constantly stress the importance of Jesus being Son of the Father, whereas they do not give that much importance in reference to salvation to the distinction between Jew and Gentile.

Through Christ's gift of the Spirit his Christian disciples share in his filial relation to the Father and can invoke him confidently as 'Abba': "For you did not receive a spirit of slavery to fall back into fear, but you received a spirit of adoption through which we cry *Abba*, 'Father!'" (Rom 8:15). This is the beginning of an unbroken tradition in Christian prayer and theology that Jesus is indeed Son of the Father. And, as distinct from the Old Testament, the word 'Father' becomes more than a metaphor. It is on the lips of Jesus and of his Christian disciples as a title or an invocative title or the name by which God is addressed.[28]

Some claim that since Jesus identified himself with Wisdom, a feminine symbol of God, it can be said that he is Wisdom incarnate or the daughter of Wisdom. In answer to this, we can acknowledge that Jesus, the evangelists, and Paul do speak of Jesus as Wisdom. But there seems to be a twofold way in which Wisdom was spoken about. In one way it is the *content* of the divine message or the mystery communicated by divine revelation, and in another way it is that experience by which the human person *discerns* and accepts the divine revelation. It is in the former sense that Jesus is spoken of as God's Wisdom, but it is in the latter sense that Wisdom is more closely associated with the Holy Spirit. This is particularly clear in 1 Corinthians where Paul speaks of Christ as "the power of God and the wisdom of God . . . Christ Jesus, who became for us wisdom from God" (1 Cor 1:24, 30). But later in the same passage, Paul speaks of how we discern God's revealed mystery, and here he associates Wisdom particularly with the Holy Spirit. Of this mystery he says,

> this God has revealed to us through the Spirit. For the Spirit scrutinizes everything, even the depths of God. Among human beings, who knows what pertains to a person except the spirit of the person that is within? Similarly, no one knows what pertains to God except the Spirit of God. We have . . . received . . . the Spirit that is from God, so that we may understand the things freely given us by God. (1 Cor 2:10–12)

James Davis agrees with the above assessment: "In 1 Co 2.6–9, Paul returns to the *content* of wisdom, and in 2.10–3.4 to the question of the *source* or *origin* of wisdom."[29] It is in the latter sense that Wisdom is a feminine symbol of God, whereas in the former sense it is more easily identified with Word that shapes the revealed message and, indeed, creation itself, through God's speaking. It is as enabling us to discern and accept what God reveals, for example through Christ, that the Spirit is associated with Wisdom and with the figure of Lady Wisdom in the Wisdom literature. There is both a Wisdom *experience* and that which is accepted through this experience; it is only through participating in the Holy Spirit who scrutinizes the depths of God that our own subjectivity can be enabled to accept what God reveals to us.[30]

The Christian understanding of God as Father was radically different from the relation of a human father to his sons and daughters. For example, Gregory of Nazianzus writes:

> It does not follow that because the Son is the Son in some higher relation (inasmuch as we could not in any other way than this point out that He is of God and Consubstantial), it would also be necessary to think that all the names of this lower world and of our kindred should be transferred to the Godhead. Or maybe you would consider our God to be male, according to the same

arguments, because he is called God and Father, and that Deity is feminine, from the gender of the word, and Spirit neuter, because It has nothing to do with generation.[31]

And the Eleventh Council of Toledo in 675 teaches, "It must be believed that the Son is generated or born not from nothing or from any other substance but from the womb of the Father (de Patris utero), that is, from his substance."[32] To speak of the womb of the Father shows how transcendent and paradoxical the Christian understanding of God as Father is and how nonunivocal our language about this mystery is. A number of medieval mystics had the experience of God as both Father and Mother. For example, Julian of Norwich (1342–1416) taught: "'God rejoices that he is our Father, and God rejoices that he is our Mother, and God rejoices that he is our true spouse, and that our soul is his beloved wife.' It is particularly Christ who is 'our Mother, brother and savior,' 'our kind Mother, our gracious Mother.'"[33] In continuity with this, Pope John Paul I said in 1978 that "God . . . is our Father, and even more our Mother."[34] We should add that lex orandi lex credendi, or "the way of prayer is the way of belief" for Christians. There is a primacy in the prayer that Jesus taught us, "Our Father who are in heaven," and in the baptismal formula in which the disciples of Jesus are told to baptize "in the name of the Father, of the Son, and of the Holy Spirit" (Mt 8:19). Also, liturgical prayer has been predominantly addressed to God or the Father through the Son in the Holy Spirit. While there should be pluralism in Christian prayer, it would be resistance to Jesus himself to resist prayer to the Father and baptism in the name of the Father.

Does this dominant Christian articulation of the first procession in prayer and theology demean women or rather enhance them and their dignity? Does it support a patriarchy against women's dignity or an inequality between women and men in practice or theory as image of God? There is no question that it has in the past been translated into actions and words that are adverse to women's full humanity.[35] But has this been through blindness or resistance to the implications of Scripture's designation as Father, Son, and Holy Spirit, or through fidelity to its implications? With many others we would argue that this designation is paternal but counter to patriarchy and that it supports the equality of men and women.

Paternity is counter to patriarchy because God addressed by Jesus as Father liberates men and women from an uncritical sense of obligation to their own parents or earthly authorities so that they can put first in their lives God and his kingdom (Mt 10:37). It makes them brothers and sisters of Jesus Christ and of one another, because it is an invitation into the relationship

Jesus himself had to his Father (Mt 12:48–50). It thus calls the disciples of Jesus to his trust in the Father's love, and enables them to pray "Abba! Father." Moreover, Jesus spoke of God as Father as one who cares deeply, who takes initiative to seek out the lost, and who forgives, as in the parable of the prodigal son (Lk 15:11–32). This is presented as a model of human fatherhood, because the primary meaning of fatherhood is found in God and flows from there as a norm to the human family. Paul writes: "I kneel before the Father, from whom every family in heaven and on earth is named" (Eph 3:14–15). Human fatherhood is a service that is a participation in God's paternity, and this is particularly true in the Christian church; its ministers have an authority, one of service, and their exercise of this will be judged by its accord with God's fatherhood. Paternity is supported here, but one that subverts patriarchy. It subverts the idolatry that some human fathers have encouraged through appropriating to themselves total control of their children, thus taking the place of God in their lives.

The great majority of Christian women do not find it difficult to address God as Father. In a survey on this issue, it was found that for most women God as Father is largely an idealization of the human father they have experienced, while for a significant minority, it is more a substitute for a parent who acted in a way radically opposed to God's care for his children. In either case it helps to free one from an overdetermination by a human father.[36] Moreover, we are all in fact dependent beings, and, "If speaking of God as father helps us not simply to face our transiency as something to overcome, but to affirm our dependency and to accept our finite and creaturely condition, then there is no reason why we should not do so."[37]

We should add that the First Person is called 'Father' through his relation to the Word, not through his relation to the spiration of the Spirit; paternity, even as analogically understood as it is, does not exhaust who the First Person is. The way that God was primarily revealed to the Jews was as Lord, Master, Savior, Creator, Spouse of Israel, and source of his Word. These are more masculine than feminine in the Old Testament, and thus there is truth to what Hans Fischer-Barnicol writes: "On the basis of nature one can hardly pray to 'our mother which art in heaven' or acknowledge 'our holy father the Church,' simply because this does not correspond to the basic experiences of father and mother."[38]

This understanding does not imply an inequality between men and women, even though this inequality seems to be implied by Paul at times (see 1 Cor 11:7–8, but also Gal 3:28). Although in honoring God we do honor a monarchy, it is not a patriarchy but a unique monarchy, as St. Gregory of Nazianzus writes:

The three most ancient opinions concerning God are Anarchia, Polyarchia, and Monarchia. . . . But Monarchy is that which we hold in honour. It is, however, a Monarchy that is not limited to one Person, . . . but one which is made of an equality of Nature and a Union of mind, and an identity of motion, and a convergence of its elements to unity. . . . This is what we mean by Father and Son and Holy Ghost.[39]

Both the Son and the Spirit are receptive from the First Person, but what they receive is the fullness of divinity, and so this implies an order but not a hierarchy. Moreover, as we showed in the preceding section, there is good reason to hold that the Son receives from the Spirit; it is not only the Spirit who receives from the Son. There is a kind of 'complementarity' between the Son and the Spirit, and the First Person creates and saves through both. Moreover, the First Person can be said to receive the imaging or reflection and the love that the Son and Spirit are. The distinctness of persons does not imply that one has a perfection that another does not.

It is not only women who have had difficulty with accepting God as Father. It is also men, as shown by Freud's experience and writings.[40] This difficulty is tied in with an experience of fathers as overcontrolling, and with an extension of this kind of patriarchy to notions of "fatherland" and even "Führer," with very destructive consequences. It is also tied in with the Enlightenment view that the individual adult, at least the man, should be autonomous, and thus with the rejection of any kind of authority.

Our primary response to this difficulty is to say that it is the relationship of Jesus to the Father that reveals the First Person to us. This is the relationship that Jesus shares with us, and it involves a relation that is explicitly opposed to slavery. Jesus says to his disciples: "You are my friends if you do what I command you. I no longer call you slaves, because a slave does not know what his master is doing. I have called you friends, because I have told you everything I have heard from my Father" (Jn 15:14–15). Jesus did indeed do what his Father commanded, but he did so freely because he knew the Father loved him and he wished above all to show the world that he loved the Father. Thus he acted freely and in total trust; obedience liberated him from what other agencies, and even his own fear of death, urged.

The Father he shares with us is both one whose care is beyond what we can fathom and one who calls us not to the nostalgia of a return to infancy but to an openness to and dedication to that eschatological kingdom that the Father seeks to bring about. In the Our Father we pray, "Thy kingdom come." There is no greater adulthood or creativity than that shown in Jesus in his relation to the Father and mediation of the kingdom for men and women. We should distinguish obedience from stereotypes we may have of it, and see it exemplified more by an event such as Vatican II than by an observance of a code already totally fixed. Also, as we will show more fully later, being a person means not primarily being autonomous in the sense of independent but being in relation as Jesus was and is.

Hans Urs von Balthasar's theology has helped us deepen our understanding of Christ's obedience to the Father. As Margaret Turek summarizes Balthasar's teaching:

> we can consider the modalities which are evidenced in the filial, obediential freedom of Jesus—namely, his *disponibilité*, self-abandonment, dependence and expectancy—as mirror-images of their paternal archetype: . . . To the incarnate Son, divine Being as primarily defined by the Father's mode of self-disposing . . . presents itself . . . as a free appeal that incites in him a total assenting correspondence. As for the freedom that Jesus, as the Child of God and of man, receives from his paternal Origin, it is always already given as the power to answer love with love; it is an autonomy proceeding from the paternal font of freedom in the form-quality of surrender of self to the other.[41]

A final question we should address here, at least in an introductory fashion, is the use of the third-person masculine pronoun of God. Language about God is of enormous importance, and that is why it has been such an issue in recent years. We are becoming more conscious of this. One powerful critique against the use of the third-person masculine pronoun of God is that given by Gail Ramshaw Schmidt. She writes: "If increasingly in American English 'he' denotes male sexuality, it becomes a simple matter of idolatry to refer to God as 'he' . . . [I]ncreasingly, gender equals sexuality. To the extent that this is true, expository prose cannot refer to God as he."[42] Schmidt gives varied alternatives that have been coined to substitute for the use of 'he' of God. But without examining these, we can briefly recall the use of grammatical and natural grammar, reasons for a continued use of 'he' of God, and—pointing to our defense elsewhere in this volume—a more general use of 'she' for the Holy Spirit—all in a way that, I hope, is sensitive to the legitimate concerns of many women and men in our time. I beg the forbearance of those who take a different approach to this contested question.

Many English speakers are not aware of gender classifications in other languages. Donald Hook and Alvin Kimel Jr. recall the variety of these classifications:

> In grammatical classification, gender refers to two or more subcategories within a grammatical form class (e.g., noun, pronoun, adjective) of a given language.

It is thus to be clearly distinguished from the sexual categories of male and female. . . . The number of gender classes varies from language to language: Hebrew, Spanish, and French, for example, have two (masculine and feminine); Greek, Latin and German have three (masculine, feminine, and neuter); Swahili six (not any of which correspond to the categories of male or female); Hungarian and Turkish none.[43]

Modern English has natural or notional gender. That is, its nouns and pronouns are classified according to meaning-related distinctions, particularly sexual. In the sentence, "The American athlete lost his shoe during the race," the context determines the gender of the pronominal adjective, which agrees with the sex of the noun it refers to. "The principal titles, names, and metaphors used to portray this God [at least in the Old Testament] are . . . masculine. God is Father, King, Shepherd, Judge, Husband, Master."[44] And so translators have used the third-person singular in translating personal pronouns that refer to God. The Old English word 'God' derives from the neuter proto-Germanic *guà*, but it appears that its transference into a masculine Old English noun was due to the Judaeo-Christian understanding of God.

This is in no way an indication that God was believed to be male, but is in accord with Scripture and Christian designations of God. "If the modern English *God* is masculine gender—and it is, when one considers there is a feminine counterpart, namely, *goddess* or *Goddess*—then the corresponding pronouns must also be masculine."[45] There is a default-masculinity in English by which masculine nouns (e.g., poet, actor, lion, priest) can refer to persons of either sex. And, "Linguist Aryey Faltz states, '[T]he default-masculinity of English usage makes it easier to apply a masculine word like Father to God *without* transferring male characteristics than it is to apply a feminine word like Mother without transferring feminine characteristics.'"[46] A linguistic pattern is inscribed in a child very early, and it is enormously difficult to change it for an individual or a culture. Thus it is unlikely that the dominant usage of the grammatically masculine pronoun for God will be changed.

However, it is clear that the Old Testament designations of God were in part due to Israel's conflicts with the deities of the surrounding peoples.[47] When some Christian mystics speak of God in a more feminine mode and use the corresponding personal pronouns, we need not fear pluralism. Moreover, while Hook and Kimel support the use of the masculine personal pronoun for the Holy Spirit, they acknowledge that they "cannot rule out by theolinguistic considerations alone" the emergence of "compelling theological argument for the unique symbolization or embodiment of a divine feminine principle in the hypostasis of the Holy Spirit."[48] As we have previously indicated, we think that such a compelling argument can be found in Scripture, and so it is appropriate to use the feminine personal pronoun generally of the Holy Spirit.

Notes

1. See chapter 1, 13–17.

2. John Paul II, *Fides et Ratio* (Washington, D.C.: United States Catholic Conference, 1998), paragraphs 33-34. See Thomas Guarino, "*Fides et Ratio:* Theology and Contemporary Pluralism," *TS* 62 (2001): 675–700.

3. Robert Jenson, "The Logic of the Doctrine of the Trinity," *Dialog* 26 (1987): 249.

4. Thomas Torrance, *The Christian Doctrine of God: One Being Three Persons* (Edinburgh: T & T Clark, 1996), 17, italics added. Page references in the text at this point are to Torrance's book.

5. *Fides et Ratio* touches on this at places, for instance, paragraphs 19–22, 24. See Angela Franks, "Trinitarian *Analogia Entis* in Hans Urs von Balthasar," *Thomist* 62 (1998): 533–559. Balthasar writes of analogy largely in the context of German theology influenced by Barth. As Franks writes, "the Trinity becomes the basis for the analogy between God and man" (542) in Balthasar's Christocentrism, but, "The appearance of revelation presupposes some similarity between created being and God's Being, or else revelation could not be seen or even occur at all. This relation of similarity is taken up in Christ" (542). Balthasar does affirm analogy based on being. In a partially de-Christianized Europe and United States, analogy has a critical importance in showing that the Christian message is not simply discontinuous with humanity and human knowledge. I have treated analogy in relation to Scripture in Farrelly, *Belief in God in Our Time* (Collegeville, Minn.: Liturgical Press, 1992), 101–113, 230–234, 360–371.

6. James Dunn, *Christology in the Making, A New Testament Inquiry into the Origins of the Doctrine of the Incarnation*, 2d ed. (Grand Rapids, Mich.: Eerdmans, 1996), 244. Also see R. Schnackenburg, *The Gospel According to St. John*, vol. 1, trans. Kevin Smith (New York: Herder and Herder, 1968), 234: "It is only the fullness of divine being . . . which guarantees his [Jesus'] absolute power as revealer and redeemer."

7. See our earlier treatment of Nicea in chapter 3, and William Alston, "Substance and the Trinity," in Stephen Davis, Daniel Kendall, and Gerald O'Collins, eds., *The Trinity: An Interdisciplinary Symposium on the Trinity* (Oxford: Oxford University Press, 1999), 179–202.

8. Walter Kasper, *The God of Jesus Christ* (Herder and Herder, 1985), 188.

9. See *ST* I, 84–88; *De veritate* 8, 6; *ST* I, 18, 3; 34, 1, ad 2; 56, 1. The translations of Thomas here are mine, unless otherwise noted.

10. DS 806.

11. Thomas tends to consider metaphor as of less philosophical significance than proper analogy. An example of metaphor in this sense is "God is my fortress." But

there are instances that we can call metaphor that, while involving proper analogy, add the dimension of an appeal to human affectivity to engage the whole person. The Son as Word incarnate may be called a real symbol or even metaphor in this sense.

12. See Ralph Del Colle, *Christ and the Spirit: Spirit-Christologies in Trinitarian Perspective* (New York: Oxford University Press, 1994); and Paul Newman, *A Spirit Christology: Recovering the Biblical Paradigm of Christian Faith* (Lanham, Md.: University Press of America, 1987); Roger Haight, "The Case for Spirit-Christology," *TS* 53 (1992): 257–287; John Wright, "Roger Haight's Spirit Christology," *TS* 53 (1992): 729–735.

13. Thomas Weinandy, O.F.M., Cap., in "Kairos. Clarifying the *filioque*: The Catholic-Orthodox dialogue," *Communio* 23 (1996): 364–365; see also Thomas B. Weinandy, *The Father's Spirit of Sonship: Reconceiving the Trinity* (Edinburgh: T & T Clark, 1995). In his *Communio* article, Weinandy critiques in part the document of the Pontifical Council for the Promotion of Christian Unity, "The Greek and Latin Traditions Regarding the Procession of the Holy Spirit," of September 1995 (published, for example, in *Eastern Churches Journal* 2 [1995]: 36–46), as being too sequential in its understanding of the Spirit as third in the Trinity. Paul McPartlin, in his answer to Weinandy in *Communio*, writes that Weinandy "is in danger, I suggest, of being just as unilateral as the *filioquists* are when they build the immanent Trinity around the other half" (369).

14. Kasper, *God of Jesus Christ*, 189. Also, for instance, see Anthony Kelly, *The Trinity of Love: A Theology of the Christian God* (Wilmington, Del.: Michael Glazier, 1989); and Jean Galot, S.J., "La génération éternelle du Fils," *Gregorianum* 71 (1990): 657–678.

15. G. Vandevelde-Daillière, "L'"inversion trinitaire' chez H. U. von Balthasar," *Nouvelle revue théologique* 102 (1998): 378.

16. I have examined the act of faith in *Faith in God through Jesus Christ* (Collegeville, Minn.: Liturgical Press, 1997), 314–321; and *Belief in God*, 216–220, 230–234.

17. Louis Lavelle, *Traité des Valeurs*. Vol. 2, *Le Système des différentes Valeurs* (Paris: Presses Universitaires de France, 1955), 301. Also see Donald Haggerty, "A Via Maritainia: Nonconceptual Knowledge by Virtuous Inclination," *Thomist* 62 (1998): 75–96.

18. Lavelle, *Système*, 310.

19. See also *De Veritate*, 27, 1, ad 4; 21; *De Potentia*, 3, 6.

20. See "Existence, the Intellect, and the Will," *New Scholasticism* 29 (1955): 145–174. Also see "Developmental Psychology and Knowledge of Being," in *God's Work in a Changing World* (Lanham, Md.: University Press of America, 1985), 287–314.

21. See chapter 2, 50–53.

22. See chapter 2, 59–60; and "Feminine Symbols and the Holy Spirit," in *God's Work*, 49–76.

23. I treat this question in *Faith in God*, especially 144–155 and 306–312.

24. See chapter 2, 58; and Robert Hammerton-Kelly, "God the Father in the Bible and in the Experience of Jesus: The State of the Question," in J.-B. Metz and

E. Schillebeeckx, eds., *God as Father? Concilium*, vol. 143 (New York: Seabury, 1981); Jean Galot, *Abba Father. We Long to See Your Face: Theological Insights into the First Person of the Trinity* (New York: Alba House, 1992); and Raymond Collins, "We Cry, 'Abba! Father!'" *Priests and People* 12 (1998): 444–449. This whole issue of *Priests and People* is dedicated to the question of God as Father, as is the summer issue of *Communio* 26 (1999).

25. Hammerton-Kelly, "God the Father," 97–98. He refers to and quotes from Phyllis Trible, *God and the Rhetoric of Sexuality* (Philadelphia: Fortress Press, 1978); emphasis added by Hammerton-Kelly. Also see Anne Carr, *Transforming Grace: Christian Tradition and Women's Experience* (San Francisco: Harper and Row, 1988); Anne Carr and Elizabeth Schüssler Fiorenza, eds., *Motherhood: Experience, Institution, Theology. Concilium*, vol. 206 (Edinburgh: T & T Clark, 1989); Catherine M. LaCugna, ed., *Freeing Theology: The Essentials of Theology in Feminist Perspective* (San Francisco: Harper, 1993); Ann O'Hara Graff, ed., *In the Embrace of God: Feminist Approaches to Theological Anthropology* (Maryknoll, N.Y.: Orbis, 1995).

26. Anne Gardner, "Genesis 2:4b–3: A Mythological Paradigm of Sexual Equality or of the Religious History of Pre-Exilic Israel?" *Scottish Journal of Theology* 43 (1990): 14.

27. See chapter 2, 42–43.

28. See Ted Peters, "The Battle over Trinitarian Language," *Dialog* 30 (1991): 44–49, at 49: "The titles 'Father, Son, and Holy Spirit' are primarily titles used in address. Titles can be distinguished from proper names. Titles are translated from language to language, whereas proper names are transliterated. . . . There is only one trinitarian formula: Father, Son, and Holy Spirit. This is because it is tied inextricably to the event of revelation and salvation itself. In conjunction with other New Testament symbols, it identifies the God in whom we put our faith as Christians. To bypass the biblical terms in favor of some substitutes is to identify with a God other than that of Jesus Christ."

29. James A. Davis, *Wisdom and Spirit: An Investigation of 1 Corinthinas 1.18–3.20 Against the background of Jewish Sapiential Traditions in the Greco-Roman Period* (Lanham, Md.: University Press of America, 1984), 87. My emphasis.

30. On the mediation of revelation by the Holy Spirit see, for instance, *Faith in God*, 312, 319, 327–328.

31. Gregory of Nazianzus, *Oration* 31, 7. *Nicene and Post-Nicene Fathers*. Second series, vol. 7, 320 (Grand Rapids, Mich: Eerdmans, 1978 reprint).

32. DS 526.

33. Ursula King, *Christian Mystics: The Spiritual Heart of the Christian Tradition* (New York: Simon and Schuster, 1998), 128; See also Julian, *Book of Showings*, Long Text, chapters 52, 54, 62; Paula Barker, "The Motherhood of God in Julian of Norwich's Theology," *Downside Review* 100 (1982): 290–305; and Caroline Walker Bynum, *Jesus as Mother: Studies in the Spirituality of the High Middle Ages* (Berkeley: University of California Press, 1982).

34. Angelo Amato, "Paternità-Maternità di Dio. Problemi e prospettive," in Angelo Amato, ed., *Trinità in Contesto* (Rome: Lib. Salesiano, 1994), 274–296, 277.

35. See a brief recall of this in Catherine Hilkert, "Cry Beloved Image. Rethinking the Image of God," in Graff, *In the Embrace of God*, 190–205.

36. See Yorick Spiegel, "God the Father in the Fatherless Society," in Metz and Schillebeeckx, *God as Father?*, 5–6.

37. Dorothy Sölle, "Paternalistic Religion as Experienced by Women," in Metz and Schillebeeckx, *God as Father?*, 74.

38. Hans Fischer-Barnicol, "*Pater Absconditus:* The Problem in the Light of the History of Religion," in Metz and Schillebeeckx, *God as Father?*, 24.

39. Gregory of Nazianzus, *Oration* 29, 2. *Nicene and Post Nicene Fathers*, Second Series, vol. 7: 301.

40. See Dominique Stein, "The Murder of the Father and God the Father in the Work of Freud," in Metz and Schillebeeckx, *God as Father?*, 11–18. Yorick Spiegel (also in Metz and Schillebeeckx, *God as Father?*, 3–10) argues that in today's Western society the father in a vast number of families appears powerless, and is himself subject to the powers of bureaucracy.

41. Margaret Turek, "'As the Father has Loved Me' (Jn 15:9): Balthasar's Theodramatic Approach to a Theology of God the Father," *Communio* 26 (1999): 301–302, 308–309.

42. Gail Ramshaw Schmidt, "De Divinis Nominibus: The Gender of God," *Worship* 56 (1982): 127, 131. In the same volume see Erik Routley, "The Gender of God: A Contribution to the Conversation," 231–239. In "The Necessary Failure of Inclusive-Language Translations: A Linguistic Elucidation," *Thomist* 62 (1998), Paul Mankowski, S.J., questions whether there is the degree of abandonment of grammatical gender that Schmidt asserts. He writes that (460), "English 'man' remains a preeminently productive morpheme. This is obvious from the fact that speakers are continually using it spontaneously and unreflectively in the creation of new compounds, not only in such terms as 'hit-man,' 'bag-man,' 'airman' and 'manned flight,' but even in words . . . such as 'point man' or 'pacman.'"

43. Donald Hook and Alvin Kimel Jr., "The Pronouns of Deity: A Theolinguistic Critique of Feminist Proposals," *Scottish Journal of Theology* 46 (1993): 299–300.

44. Hook and Kimel, "Pronouns of Deity," 306.

45. Hook and Kimel, "Pronouns of Deity," 307.

46. Hook and Kimel, "Pronouns of Deity," 309–310. The authors are quoting here from Aryeh Faltz, "Comments on the Supplementary Liturgical Texts" (Prayer Book Studies 20, 1990), 16.

47. See, for example, Jonathan Tubb, *Canaanites* (London: British Museum Press for the University of Oklahoma Press, 1998), 73–77.

48. Hook and Kimel, "Pronouns of Deity," 313.

CHAPTER SEVEN

~

The Procession of the
Holy Spirit within the Trinity

Reflection on the Holy Spirit is one of the most important theological tasks in the church in our time. The Christian churches proclaim belief in the Holy Spirit, for example, in their frequent use of the Nicene-Constantinopolitan Creed in the liturgy.[1] In calling the Second Vatican Council Pope John XXIII prayed for a new outpouring of the Holy Spirit, and after the council Pope Paul VI called for a renewed theology of the Holy Spirit. The council itself was an experience, on the part of a great number of participants, of such an outpouring. Twenty years after the end of the council, the Synod of Bishops (1985) called the council God's greatest grace to the church in the twentieth century—a striking expression of confidence that the Holy Spirit presided at that event. The council and other experiences of the Spirit, for example, in the Pentecostal churches and the charismatic renewal movement, have animated the faith of numberless Christians.

There are a number of reasons why these dramatic renewals of the Holy Spirit have been vitally necessary in our time. Walter Kasper writes: "The loss of the dimension and reality which Western thinking has described by the term 'spirit' is perhaps the most profound crisis of the present time."[2] The rationalism of the Enlightenment is still dominant in many of the cultural, political, and economic leaders of our developed world. Many such people seek control through technology and pragmatic manipulation within the context of a modern historical consciousness that is at least in practice frequently naturalistic. Their trust in the future is vested in such human control, and that fact affects our societies at large. Transcendence and other people are sacrificed to assure a present or future on a restrictedly humanistic level for those in control. This was evident earlier in the twentieth century in Nazism, Fascism, and Communism; it is also present in a way that is as damaging for vast numbers of people (e.g., in abortion and in neglect of those most in need) in American naturalism.

Largely as a reaction against an "institutionalism," that is, institutions perceived as sacrificing individuals to their own purposes rather than serving them, there has also been an enormous shift in the locus of trust to *human experience*, that is, to those insights and directions for human fulfillment attested to and supported by experiences of individuals and groups. This shift was seen, for example, in the strong countercultural movement in the United States and elsewhere in the 1960s and following. Some of these individuals and groups found support for their positions in the wisdom of Native American peoples or of Asian religions, such as Hinduism. And some of this phenomenon is found today in the New Age movement. Some of these people experiment with drugs to enhance their consciousness or give them access to experience beyond the normal, and are ensnared by a primitivism and romanticism. But many too turn to mystics of past history, Christian and non-Christian, for support in their own search for transcendence, and ascribe their experiences to the Holy Spirit. Much of the spirituality of this multifaceted movement, however, is disengaged from institutional forms of Christianity and has solidified an individualism and interiority that abdicates engagement with the larger society and its needs.

How should a theology of the Spirit be constructed in view of these movements in our time? Barth and traditional Catholic theology, insofar as they treated the Holy Spirit, were in accord in wanting to give total priority to the truth of the Christian revealed mystery and to associate the Holy Spirit with the Christ of revelation, indeed as the enabler who empowers us to accept this revelation. Much modern Christian liberalism, on the other hand, wanted to affirm that God's Spirit is operating much more broadly in human experience and to articulate the Christian mystery in a way that would acknowledge this. They find indices of the Spirit in human experience of transcendence and relate the Christian message to these indices, without always succeeding in distinguishing the Christian Spirit from other spirits.

In face of present tensions between a genuine Christianity and our secular culture as well as among the diverse Christian strategies adopted toward our surrounding culture, we will in this constructive theology of the Holy Spirit depend on all we have seen to this point, especially in Scripture and tradition, and we will reflect (I) on a theology of the Spirit in the economy of salvation and (II) on the Spirit within the Trinity. Although we have treated the Spirit in the economy of salvation and creation earlier, particularly in chapter 5, we return to this theme from a somewhat different perspective here, namely, its relation to human experience. Particularly in the second part of this chapter we will address some tensions between the Western Church and Orthodoxy.

I. A Theology of the Holy Spirit in the Economy of Salvation and Creation

As indicated in chapter 5, we know the Holy Spirit only through the revelation and action of Jesus Christ and the mission of the Holy Spirit whom he sent, and so we can recognize and acknowledge instances of the Holy Spirit's presence outside of Christianity only if we have some previous knowledge of the Holy Spirit in the Christian dispensation.[3] Thus, we depend here on what we have seen in our chapter on Scripture concerning the experience of and reflection on the Spirit present in the early church, and the recognition of the Spirit in the life and ministry of Jesus—themes that have some preparation in the Old Testament and intertestamental Jewish reflection.[4]

There is a great mystery about the presence of the Holy Spirit; as Jesus said to Nicodemus, "The wind blows where it wills, and you can hear the sound it makes, but you do not know where it comes from or where it goes; so it is with everyone who is born of the Spirit" (Jn 3:8). But one thing that stands out in the experience of the Spirit in the early church is that experience of the Spirit and actions inspired by the Spirit came to Christians before reflection upon the Spirit. There are actions that manifest the Spirit. The coming of the Spirit upon the disciples of Jesus gathered together at Pentecost gave them an ecstatic experience, a new conviction, and an impulse to proclaim the good news courageously. And each of the 'spiritual gifts' is a "manifestation (*phanerosis*) of the Spirit" (1 Cor 12:4, 7). Here, *praxis* precedes *theoria*.[5] And so it is in our time.

What kind of actions manifest the Spirit? Once more, we take our clue from the primitive church. It is the actions that build up the church, the body of Christ (1 Cor 12); those that build up the individual into the image of Christ (2 Cor 3:18); those that inspire the individual to cry with confidence to God as "Abba! Father!" (Rom 8:15); those that animate the missionary activity of the church (e.g., Acts 13:2); and those that guide the church in council (Acts 15:28). And finally, the Spirit in the economy of salvation leads to doxology—to praise of God the Father through the Son and in the Holy Spirit.

There are other actions, even present among Christians, that do not build up the individual Christian or the church but that can be confused with movements of the Spirit; they come from alien spirits. Paul warns the Corinthians that such influences are still among them, "You know how, when you were pagans, you were constantly attracted and led away to mute idols" (1 Cor 12:2; see Lk 11:24–26). The actions and attitudes that manifest the Spirit come from God's greatest gift, namely the Holy Spirit. Paul tells us that "the love of God has been poured out into our hearts through the Holy Spirit that has been given to us" (Rom 5:5; see 1 Cor 13; Lk 11:13).

By these actions and attitudes the Holy Spirit is expressed *symbolically*. This is quite different from the way a declarative sentence, such as "this is a pen," expresses what it manifests or makes clear. Actions and words show or manifest the Spirit as the actions and words of a person in love manifest the love that animates him or her. Such actions and words are an expression of the person's devotion to the loved one; they express an interior disposition; they come from that disposition; they contain it; they convey it to the loved one; they affect the other; and they evoke from the loved one a response in kind. These actions and words also express the goodness of the loved one in the estimation of the person whose love they express. This kind of expression is radically different from a literal expression, a simply objective univocal or analogical expression of something. A similar kind of expression is found in actions and attitudes that manifest "team spirit," "school spirit," or "family spirit." And it is reflected in phrases such as "a spirited horse" and "a person full of spirit." Thus the actions and attitudes of Christians ascribed to the Holy Spirit reflect or express not simply the Christian's attitude but the Holy Spirit acting within him or her or in the community. This action comes from the Christian spirit, but this Christian spirit is the Holy Spirit.

The Hebrew word for 'spirit', *ruach*, initially meant wind and then was used to express some dynamic impulse, empowerment, or ecstatic experience present in judge, prophet, or king that came from God. Thus the word 'spirit' in 'Holy Spirit' signifies differently than the word 'Son' in the 'Son of God'. The first is close to what Ricoeur says of a symbol that has an analogical structure:

> By analogical structure, we signify provisionally the structure of expressions with a double meaning in which a first meaning [in our case, the dynamism present in an experience, act or attitude] sends us back to a second meaning [in our case, the Holy Spirit] which is alone intended, without however it being able to be attained directly, that is, other than through the first meaning.[6]

The title 'Holy Spirit' is not a proper noun, nor is it ascribed to the Third Person of the Trinity in the same way that the words 'Son' or 'Word' are ascribed to the Second Person. 'Son' and 'Word' are ascribed objectively and analogically; 'Spirit' is ascribed symbolically and indirectly through reference to an experience or action that manifests and contains the Spirit. It is closer to metaphorical language, as when a young man says to a woman, "You are my sunshine," than it is to objective speech in a declarative sentence. The Holy Spirit is the one who is reflected in the life, joy, enablement, and so forth that we have and experience as Christians.

How is the Spirit *known*? There are great disputes in our time as in many past times on which experiences, actions, beliefs, and attitudes reflect the Holy Spirit and which do not. In the Catholic Church such disputes have become particularly prevalent since Vatican II. Apparently the Spirit is known only with great difficulty. We do not know the Spirit as we know what is visibly in front of us, or as the physical sciences know objects, or simply intellectually. We know the Spirit basically by a kind of *sympathy*, a kind of being in the movement of the Spirit or 'feeling with', though not a feeling that can be identified with romanticism. Paul tells us that "the Spirit itself bears witness with our spirit that we are children of God"; hence we cry, "*Abba*, Father!" (Rom 8:16, 15). And so we know or experience the Spirit by being susceptible or responsive to this internal witness. One author writes of revelation that "the subjectivity of the receiver of revelation is co-constituted by God himself."[7] The Spirit is experienced in a way similar to that by which one subjectivity is experienced by another. The Spirit freely engages the human subjectivity and enables it or catches it up into sharing the Spirit's own movement. Paul makes this analogy when he writes: "Among human beings, who knows what pertains to a person except the spirit of the person that is within? Similarly, no one knows what pertains to God except the Spirit of God" (1 Cor 2:11). This knowledge is similar to the knowledge by connaturality Thomas Aquinas speaks of when he writes about the *instinctus fidei:* "the light of faith makes us see the things believed in. As by other virtues one sees what is appropriate to him by that virtue, so through the virtue of faith the human mind is inclined to assent to those things that agree with right faith and not to others."[8] The Holy Spirit enables us to believe by the very inclination she instills in us. We know or experience, to some extent, our own subjectivity, and by ascribing our faith and trust and love given us by God to the Spirit, we know the Spirit. There is given by the Spirit to some people a special capacity that is called "discernment of spirits" (1 Cor 12:10), by which they are enabled to test the spirits reflected in the Christian community and to distinguish what comes from the Holy Spirit and what comes from other spirits.

There are also external criteria by which one can discern the Spirit. As Paul wrote, "I tell you that nobody speaking by the spirit of God says, 'Jesus be accursed.' And no one can say, 'Jesus is Lord,' except by the holy Spirit" (1 Cor 12:3). What contradicts the Christian message or is destructive of the Christian community cannot come from the Holy Spirit. It is of vital importance to be aligned with the Spirit and thus discern what comes from the Spirit. Those who ascribe what comes from the Holy Spirit to an alien spirit miss and, perhaps, resist God's loving and saving presence and revelation, with destructive consequences for themselves and others (see Mk 3:22–30).

How, we may ask, does the Spirit bring about action? It is not simply by command; it is not simply or primarily by an external law; it is not by force. Rather, the Spirit acts as from within, as one called to the human being's side. This is indicated by the title Paraclete (*para-kletos*, one called to the side of another), a supporter and an encourager of this other. Thus the Spirit completely respects the other's freedom and in love seeks to catch the church and the human being up into the Spirit's own movement (or dance) of love for God and God's love for the world. The way the Spirit brings about action seems to be correlated with what Paul quotes from a Greek author, "In him we live and move and have our being" (Acts 17:28). Perhaps the closest classical philosophical articulation of this was through the concept of *concurrence*. We will return to that below, but here we can say that the influence of the Spirit upon us has been compared at times to wind in the sails of a boat or, as Moltmann puts it, "God at our back as it were."[9]

We have said that in the economy of salvation the Holy Spirit is expressed primarily by actions and attitudes that are manifestations of the Spirit. Thus, theology is a secondary expression of the Spirit. However, that is our task here, and such a theology can be beneficial to the practice and understanding of the Christian life as well. So we ask how we can express the Holy Spirit in the economy of salvation *theologically*. This is to express it conceptually in relation to other things and actions we know. Here, we should first of all recognize that the Spirit is a *dynamism*, an empowering of persons within a kind of eros or thrust which they in turn share.

Through premodern science (e.g., in Aristotle) and then again in contemporary science we acknowledge the existence of dynamisms in physical things much better than an earlier modern mechanistic science did, as we recalled in chapter 5.[10] We see this dynamism in an individual animal, for example, in its initiative and spontaneity to seek the goods of sex, food, and defense from aggressors. We see it in the active development of an embryo toward the emergence of a complex organism with many diverse organs. However, we see this dynamism more broadly in an active self-emergence of matter at each level of evolution in organic and even nonorganic, nonlinear systems in disequilibrium that are open to and in interaction with their environment and "seek" a kind of structure that enables them to be or live and, indeed, be or live more fully. There is a certain "arrow of time" that, with many byways and unsuccessful adjustments, is present in the emergence of different levels of nonorganic matter and then organic and living matter that leads eventually to human life.

As humans we are aware of this *eros* or dynamism in things lower than ourselves largely because we experience it in ourselves and recognize something analogous in animals, in vegetative life, and even in lower material reality. This dynamism in human life is analyzed in our time somewhat differently than in the time of Thomas Aquinas. In chapter 5 we briefly compared Erikson's developmental psychology with Thomas's philosophical analysis of the human person.[11] We showed that Erikson's approach calls for a philosophical understanding of the person as a whole—one that Thomas's study in part provides, if it is enlarged to do justice to the epigenetic principle, that is, the evolutionary character of the emergence of the adult person in interaction with his or her enlarging environment, somewhat on the model of the way an embryo develops in interaction with the womb that carries it.

Thomas recognized the distinction between a rational appetite (the will) and sense appetite, and in the will even a distinction between it as a natural appetite and as a rational appetite, pointing thus to the distinction between it as, antecedent to its engagement in act, a dynamic orientation to the good, and then its free act. But we can extend this notion of "natural appetite" to the human being as a whole, as manifesting itself by *eros* (dynamism) present through the stages of life from the initial existence of the embryo to the adult stages of the human person. This dynamism is characterized by a transcendence that has God and union with God as its goal and source. For Thomas, the natural appetite present in human beings is in diverse ways present in all things. He writes: "all things desire to be in act (*esse actu*) according to their measure, which is clear from the fact that everything of its nature shrinks from corruption."[12]

Perhaps this dimension of the human person is not brought to the fore sufficiently by Thomas's understanding of the human being as rational animal composed of body and soul. Paul, with much anthropology of his time and place, distinguished in the person "spirit (*pneuma*), soul (*psyche*) and body (*soma*)" (1 Thes 5:23). For Thomas "rational animal" referred to the *nature* of the human being, but, as he recognized, there is more to the person than the nature. There is also existence (*esse*), and the natural appetite is a dynamism that flows in part from this *esse* as source and goal. 'Spirit', particularly in the human being, expresses this dynamism perhaps better than the usual meaning of 'soul'. Karl Rahner's choice of the title of his first book, *Spirit in the World*, reflects this perspective on the human person.

The modern study of evolution brings enormous illumination to this *eros* or "desire to be actually according to their measure" present in all material things, for it enables us to see this dynamism as somehow coursing through and unifying all material reality in an arrow of time from the big bang till the emergence of the human. Some preliterate peoples and world religions seem to have been particularly struck by the phenomemena of initiative, creativity, and fruitfulness in the material world as the presence of the divine, and have related to the divine largely through honoring divinity so present and through seeking to live in accord with this primordial dynamism.[13] And some modern cosmologists have turned to their insights (e.g., in the goddess Gaia) as a metaphor for the phenomena of active matter in the evolutionary process.

Paul himself seems to draw an analogy between the *eros* present in us through the Holy Spirit and that *eros* present in material creation, for he writes, "We know that all creation is groaning in labor pains even until now, and not only that, but we ourselves, who have the first fruits of the Spirit, we also groan within ourselves as we wait for adoption, the redemption of our bodies" (Rom 8:22–23). Paul did not interpret this *eros* individualistically, for he looked forward to the kingdom of God. And an adequate understanding of the human in our time is only possible if we appropriate ourselves sufficiently to acknowledge that to be fully human is to be engaged in cooperating with others in building human communities, and doing this through time.[14]

Thus, we can understand the Holy Spirit in the economy of salvation somewhat by understanding her on the analogy of the dynamism or *eros* coursing through the evolutionary physical world, the development of the individual human person to his or her full capacity, and the movement of people together toward the building of genuine communities and the larger human community that unites us all. Obviously, this process is not simply a positive one going from triumph to triumph. Even Paul recognized that the material world is in some sense in bondage and its "groaning" is not simply for fulfillment but for liberation. Similarly, the Spirit of God is present not simply in the process toward fulfillment but in the exorcising of alien spirits, destructive of the individual and of the community—an exorcism that we all need as individuals and communities.

Natural and human dynamisms then offer us some analogues for the Holy Spirit's action in the economy of salvation. Much of this is not properly the divine spirit but "spirit in the world," the dynamism inherent in and proper to the material and human world. How now can we more properly identify the Holy Spirit in the order of salvation and creation? I suggest that the Holy Spirit present in the world is that *Ultimate Dynamism* or *Eros* that brings humanity, the individual, and the community of human beings to its ultimate fulfillment and liberation, namely God. This Ultimate Dynamism is that which empowers us to orient ourselves not only toward a little bit of liberation or a little bit of fulfillment, but all the way to our ultimate and only lasting fulfillment and liberation, namely our union with God. This movement to God is given to us through the gift of the Holy Spirit—"the love of God has been poured out into our hearts through the holy Spirit that has been given to us" (Rom 5:5). This Spirit finds its point of contact with us particularly in our human spirit: "the Spirit itself bears witness with our spirit that we are children of God" (Rom 8:16; see also 8:5, 6, 9, 10). This indwelling Spirit empowers us as individuals and communities and orients us to put first God and his kingdom through instilling in us the love of God and love of our fellow men and women as the dominant disposition of our lives. Human beings cannot so orient themselves on their own power. And only by this self-orientation is the history of the human community and of the individual person saved or liberated from self-destruction and given fulfillment. This is fulfillment in both the ultimate sense of union with God in the kingdom, and in the penultimate sense of having that disposition here and now in history by which we seek those instantiations of the kingdom that are possible in our smaller and larger communities.

We do not have this charity if we are not seeking the transformation of our world here and now so that it gives more signs of God's justice and mercy. Those who put first in their lives some small bit of human fulfillment or liberation at the cost of subordinating the love of God and our neighbors to this are not animated by the Spirit of God but by some alien spirit. It is only the Holy Spirit who exorcises these alien spirits from the individual and the community.

Perhaps we can understand the influence of this dynamism upon created reality and on the human being if we compare it to classical philosophy's study of God's causal influence on creation. Thomas Aquinas distinguished God's efficient causality, final causality, exemplary causality, and *concurrence*. He compares concurrence to the influence of a heavenly body, for example, the sun upon the operations of a physical body: "It is necessary that the divine power be present to every created agent, as the power of a heavenly body must be present to every elementary corporal agent . . . by his [God's] power every other power acts."[15] Concurrence seems to express the Spirit's influence that is pointed to by metaphorical expressions such as "wind in our sails" or "field of energy." There is a *proper* sense of this concurrence that can be ascribed to the Spirit in the church's and the Christian's experience of God's love and their response through acts of love of God in all their different manifestations. The more general movement toward God's goal we see in dynamisms natural to created beings is traditionally ascribed to the Spirit by appropriation since this has a kinship with the *eros* that is the Spirit, but is not properly a participation in the Holy Spirit.

The proper gift of the Spirit, as we have said earlier in this book, is given *from the future*, namely from that future kingdom into which Christ ascended. This gift of the Spirit orients us to transcendence through orienting us to the fulfillment and liberation of history which Jesus Christ will effect when he comes again and which he is already from the future kingdom bringing about in part in history itself. The Spirit is given initially to the church and to individuals as they are incorporated into the church through faith and baptism. The Spirit is more present to the church as a whole than to an individual within the church. This is not to deny that the Spirit is present wherever God is put first in human life, and specifically in the lives of many adherents to world religions—a presence in part mediated by those religions. Vatican II acknowledged that the Spirit was frequently present in a geographical area before the Christian missionaries arrived and the Christian message was proclaimed.[16] But the Spirit was not known as the Holy Spirit in these circumstances, for these people had not yet received the fullness of God's revelation or means of grace he offers humanity through Jesus Christ and the Spirit. The Spirit received in world religions was usually associated with a kind of primordial revelation God had offered these people. Mixed as it was with superstition, this primordial revelation was to be fulfilled (as Israel's was to be) by God's fuller revelation through Jesus Christ.[17]

How can the Christian Spirit or the Spirit of Christ have this effect within human beings? How can this Spirit be the *ultimate* dynamism in the world and history? This is so because of who the Spirit is in herself. In herself she *is* God's—the Father's and Christ's—own Spirit; through the gift of the Spirit the dynamism intrinsic and proper to the triune God is given to us, and so enables us to have God's dispositions—to put first what God himself puts first. Through the Spirit we are given not simply a created gift, but an uncreated gift (a theme we will reflect on further below). It is because of who the Holy Spirit is in herself that she can have this effect among human beings. And this invites us to reflect on who the Spirit is within the Trinity, in relation to the Father and the Son.

II. The Holy Spirit within the Trinity

In reflecting on the Holy Spirit within the Trinity, we repeat that we can only know the Spirit through the mission of the Son and the Spirit as revealed to us within the order of salvation. We suggest that a main context today in which to discuss the different theologies of the Spirit within the Trinity is the difference between Western Christianity and Orthodoxy. One reason why we make this suggestion is because this difference accentuates the question of the relation of the Spirit to the Son or Word, and vice versa—a question central to theology in our time. And in our first chapter, we suggested that a main theological problem about the Holy Spirit continues to be the *Filioque* question. We presuppose here that both Western Christianity and Orthodoxy are called to live within modern historical consciousness better than they have at times managed to do, and so while seeking to mediate their differences we relate our proposal to the theme we have treated earlier in this book, namely the coming to us *now* of the Son and the Spirit from the future kingdom. After briefly recalling some of these differences, we will develop in steps a proposal to mediate them. Many such proposals have been made, particularly efforts to show the Eastern and Western views of the Spirit as complementary to one another. We have learned from a number of them, and our proposal will be seen as in continuity with them; but in this introductory study we will not analyze these proposals in detail. They are analyzed and evaluated elsewhere.[18] We write simply in the hope of contributing a little to the dialogue. I write this from my Western Christian tradition and specifically from the tradition of Thomas Aquinas whose theology in this regard, however, many agree must now be modified.

Earlier in this book we reflected on these differences, and so here we simply recall them. We have written of Augustine and the Cappadocians' views of the Holy Spirit earlier in this book.[19] In the second half of his book on the Trinity, Augustine seeks images of the Trinity within creation, primarily within the human mind—for instance, its remembrance of self, expression of self that comes from this knowledge, and love of the self. This love is the image of the Holy Spirit, who within the Trinity is the person who is Love and is the bond of union between the Father and the Son. Athanasius and the Cappadocians sought to distinguish the Spirit from the Son. The Son is generated as the only begotten Son, while the Spirit proceeds (Jn 15:26, *ekporeuetai*). The difference between the origin of the Son and the Spirit is pictured at times under the image of the difference between a word coming from a person's mouth and a breath coming from the same mouth. Thus the two 'comings' are different, simultaneous, and both from the one who speaks; the breath does not come from the word as it does from the speaker. Transferring this image to the Trinity, the Father generates the Son or Word, and the Spirit proceeds from the Father. Gregory of Nazianzus understood the proceeding of the Spirit to be within the Trinity and not simply in the order of salvation; and he gave images for this "proceeding" such as source, spring, river, or sun, beam, light, though he acknowledged that he did not know what "proceeding" meant within God. Against Eunomius who claimed to know God's essence, the Cappadocians taught that human beings could know God's effects (*energeia*) but not God's essence.

There were centuries during which this pluralism of theology of the Trinity between the West and the East existed without destroying ecclesial unity. Part of the difference was due to vocabulary. The West's vocabulary was seen by Maximus the Confessor as being less exact than that of the East, though he defended the West against accusations of heresy.[20] The West had one word that they applied as a general word to cover the origin both of the Son and of the Spirit, *processio*, and to differentiate the origin of the Spirit from that of the Son who is generated. The East used the word for procession, *ekporeuesthai*, only for the Spirit. Some in the East did acknowledge that there is a sense in which the Spirit comes from (*proïenai*) or, better, *through*, the Son from the Father—somewhat as a breath is accessible or known through the word that is spoken, or as the breath receives from the word or rests in the word. There was an acknowledgment that in the order of salvation there is a sense in which the Spirit proceeds in its mission from the Son, but this for the East does not reflect a relationship between Spirit and Son within the Trinity.

The later differences in the theology of the Holy Spirit between the West and Orthodoxy, exemplified for example in Palamism, are perhaps best approached by recognizing that the East's approach to this mystery was more closely related to a spirituality than the West's, or at least to a different spirituality. And this continues until our time.[21] In the twentieth century, Dimitru Staniloae wrote that Christ "is seen as he who acts now in us by the uncreated energies of the Holy Spirit leading us toward his resurrected state."[22] Thus the Spirit is 'known' by a kind of knowledge totally dependent on a spirituality. The Spirit is known in the very process of our being opened to knowledge of the Father through faith and being sustained, raised, or transformed in the process of Christian worship and life, for it is all of this that the Spirit effects within us. This is not so much a theology based on or using a philosophy as an attempt to articulate an experience, even metaphorically.

The spirituality of the West in the twelfth and thirteenth centuries was largely influenced by Augustine's view of the human person as *imago Dei*.[23] Perhaps we can say that this approach to the Trinity is by way of exemplarity and the influence of the Word incarnate in transforming those who respond in faith. Thomas Aquinas sought a theological knowledge of the Trinity in continuity with Augustine, and he depended upon the principle that the trinitarian relations in the economy of salvation manifest those within the Trinity. This principle is called by Duncan Reid the "identity principle." He finds it present also, somewhat differently expressed, in Karl Barth and Karl Rahner; and he contrasts it to Orthodoxy's principle, "energies of the Spirit."[24]

Some major differences central to the different theologies of the Holy Spirit in Western Christianity and Orthodoxy are shown here. We see different images of the Spirit in Augustine and the Cappadocians, differences in vocabulary, and differences in spirituality between one which we can almost call *epicletic*, meaning one centered on calling down the Holy Spirit to sustain, raise, and transform us toward a doxological attitude and mystical or quasi-mystical prayer, and one based on restored humanity as *imago Dei*. With Vatican II itself and many other theologians I think that these differences are largely complementary rather than contradictory to one another.[25]

How can we know *something* of the way in which the Holy Spirit proceeds within the Trinity as distinct from that proceeding that is the Spirit's mission in the order of salvation? As the Western tradition has held rather consistently, it is by the relations shown in the order of salvation among the Father, Son, and Spirit and by the effects in the order of salvation particularly ascribed to the Spirit. We showed in the preceding chapter that, though the West has tended simply to recognize the priority of the Son to the Spirit, the relations between the Son and the Spirit in the order of salvation seem to represent a mutual priority. For example, the Incarnation occurs through the overshadowing of Mary by the Holy Spirit; and the Father sends the Spirit in the name of the Son, and the Spirit is the Spirit of truth. The effects in the order of salvation that are ascribed particularly to the Holy Spirit are acts of Christians expressive of love and thus acts oriented to the Father, the Son, and those loved by the Father and Son. This relationship to love is suggested by the very name of the Holy Spirit—'spirit' or *ruah* designating impulse, and 'holy' an impulse in freedom and love directed to God above all.

It is particularly Augustine who associated the Spirit with love in both the Spirit's effects and in the Spirit's proceeding within the Trinity. The Eastern Fathers knew that the Spirit was not generated and that the Spirit "proceeds," but they did not seek intellectually to analyze this proceeding further. Agreeing on this issue with the Western tradition, we take it as appropriate then to

(1) examine the human analogue of love in a way that may offer us insight into the Spirit's proceeding, (2) apply this analogically to the procession of the Spirit, with particular attention to the question of the *Filioque*, (3) answer some possible objections that may be raised to this, and relate it to the Eastern doctrine of 'energies'. We simply seek to understand this revealed message a little more by the help of analogy with things we naturally know.

1. The Human Analogue of Love

We use the psychological analogy here because the revelation that comes to us through Scripture seems to call for it, not at all because we think that we can prove something concerning the Holy Spirit by this analogy. There is a relation between the revelation that God gives us through Jesus Christ and the revelation which precedes Christian revelation, even that revelation that comes to us through created reality and, specifically, human beings made in the image of God. By the use of this analogue we are not constricting the infinite Spirit to the very finite and limited scope of our own human interiority. We have shown above that the Holy Spirit is the source of that dynamism present in and coursing through the whole of history that directs it toward God above all else. We use our interior act of love as a weak image of and participation in that Infinite Eros coming from the Father and the Son and coursing through history. As Augustine tells us, we should seek some understanding of God particularly in the spiritual dimensions of his creation. In our treatment here of this analogue, we will present our understanding of the human act of love, an understanding that is based on a modification of St. Thomas's philosophy of love, while acknowledging that in analogy between creation and God the difference is always greater than the similarity.

We begin with recalling Thomas's basic statement on the procession of the Holy Spirit within the Trinity.[26] The Holy Spirit is both God and distinct from the Father and the Son. She proceeds, as the Son does. This "proceeding" cannot be a proceeding *ad extra* or outside the Godhead, because this would either imply that the Spirit is a creature or support a kind of tritheism. The proceeding must be interior to divinity, as that of the Son is. It then cannot be of the material order but must be based on an action of the spiritual order. There are only two basic acts proper to a spiritual or intellectual being: knowledge and love. Since the Son or Word is the term of the first proceeding and is the 'only begotten', the Holy Spirit cannot be a term of an intellectual generation. Rather, as Scripture itself implies, the Spirit proceeds in the order of love.

In examining this analogue, we are looking for something analogous to what we found in the first procession (the relation of the Word to the saying, or the Son to the Father)—namely a basis on which we can affirm both the *distinction of relations* between the Spirit on the one hand and the Father and the Son on the other, and the *full divinity* of the Spirit. In this effort, I depend on what I presented in chapter 6 concerning the relation of the will's act to the good *(esse)* through the agent intellect and to the good known through the 'possible' or knowing intellect.

When we love someone or something, we are first *moved* and given focus by the good of that someone or something, and then we respond in love. This first stage here occurs in humans because we are *potentially* loving rather than essentially loving, as God is. Thomas articulates this reality by saying that in an act that remains within us, such as knowing or loving, the agent is activated by the *object* known or loved.[27] This way of being activated is distinct from the way my pen receives movement from me writing; in this latter case, the activating principle is external to the actor. Another difference in the case of the pen is that the movement or action is "an act of a reality in potency insofar as it is in potency" *(actus entis in potentia prout in potentia)*. That is, the pen is moving insofar as it has not yet achieved its terminal point. Such action is essentially imperfect. An act of the intellect or will, on the other hand, while in human beings it is activated or moved from potency to act by its object (e.g., the good), is essentially an *actus perfecti*, that is, an act of an agent already in act rather than in potency. When I love, it is I who love or act or move, and the more I have been activated by the good, the more I act. An act like love does not essentially imply imperfection or movement from not loving to loving, though of course in human beings there is a first stage of this act in which we are indeed activated. This initial stage is not of itself love, since it is an act not of the lover but of the good moving the lover. Once activated, the agent (the lover) is in act. In us this is of course a limited act, because we are limited beings. But the act of love as such does not essentially involve limitation. God's love is infinite, a totally proportioned response to his infinite goodness. This love is essentially and eternally active because God's divine will is one with the divine good and is not moved from potency to act.

We should note that the energy or act present in our act of love comes from the good present intentionally to us. The movement or actuation present in the good as intentionally present to us is from that good toward us who are being moved in this process. The movement present in our act of love is from us as lover toward the good, because love is an impulse toward the good and union with the good. The energy present in the act of love, or by which we love, is the same as that in the good as intentionally present to us. The *terminus a quo*, or origin of the movement, in the good intentionally drawing

us is in this good, while the *terminus ad quem* is us as potentially and then actually lover. In our act of love, the *terminus a quo*, or origin of the act, is in
us as lover, and the *terminus ad quem* is the good we love or seek. The distinction between these two acts is not by the energy, which is the same, but
by opposed relations. And what we say about the energy we say also about
the form or direction or focus (*opus operati*) of the act of love. Love is directed
not only to the good in general but to a particular good (e.g., an act or a person or thing). Love receives this direction through knowledge of the good
mediated to the will by the intellect's knowledge of the good and by what
Thomas calls the last act of the practical intellect—that is, the final direction given to the will to act by the intellect.

The above articulation is largely an introductory phenomenology of love
from a particular perspective. The metaphysics of this we presented in the
preceding chapter.[28] There we showed, in dependence on Thomas's metaphysics and anthropology, that the good is particularly associated with 'to be'
or *esse*, since everything wants to be and flees destruction; it is being and an
enhancement of being that is 'appetible' or desirable. Of course, this is the
being of a particular kind of being. This *esse* is intentionally present to the
will through the agent intellect, and the *kind* of good involved in the attrac-
tion that comes from a particular good that solicits our love is mediated by
the knowing (or as Thomas calls it, the possible) intellect. The response of
love is an act of the agent or lover, but is energized and formed by this complex actuation that solicits his or her love.[29]

2. Application of This Analogue to the Procession of the Holy Spirit, and the Question of the *Filioque*

How does this analogue help us to understand something of the procession of
the Holy Spirit? As the Father says or expresses himself in the Word that is
totally proportioned to his being, there is another expression of himself that
proceeds from the First Person. Love is an expression of the goodness of the
one who is loved, particularly if it is totally proportioned to the goodness of
the one loved. We know from revelation that the Holy Spirit proceeds from
the Father and the Son, and there is much in Scripture and tradition that
supports the view that the Holy Spirit proceeds as an act of love. The Father
knows, the Son knows, and the Holy Spirit knows. Similarly, the Father
loves, the Son loves, and the Holy Spirit loves. But only the Father in knowing *says* a Word. He is constituted as Father by thus generating the Son or
saying the Word, and the Son is constituted as Son by his being generated or
said as a perfect Word of the Father. These acts of Father and Son are called
notional acts, that is, acts by which each person individually is known, or acts

distinctive of or proper to each as a divine person and not shared by another. Similarly, the Holy Spirit is constituted as love who is a response to the Father and Son spirating. As only the Father is constituted a person by saying a Word, so only the Holy Spirit is constituted a person by being an act of love. In this case alone love in the Godhead is not essential love shared by the three persons, but notional love, that is, a love that is distinctive of or proper to the Holy Spirit.

How does the human analogue help us understand the procession of the Holy Spirit? The act of love in human beings gives us some illumination as to how there can be a distinction of relation between the Father and Son on the one hand and the Holy Spirit on the other, while there is a sameness in being. Through revelation we are informed that the goodness of the Father ("No one is good but God alone" [Lk 18:19]) gives rise to a divine 'impulse' of love expressive of this goodness who is herself a divine person. The human analogue of love suggests that it is the goodness *as* in the Father and *as* known and expressed in the Son that provokes (spirates) the response of love that is the Holy Spirit; eternally there is a response to the divine goodness *as* in the Father that is itself a person, the Holy Spirit. The being or energy or act that is this act of love is the same being as the spirating goodness and knowledge of this goodness, and thus it is infinite. But there is a real distinction of relations. The opposition of relations is found between, on the one hand, the *terminus a quo* or initiating agents that constitute the spirating good and knowledge of the good, namely the Father and Son, and, on the other hand, the *terminus a quo* or agent that is constituted by the response of love, namely the Holy Spirit. It is only the Holy Spirit who is constituted a person by the very act of love; this act of love is notional love and is specifically a response to the divine good *as* this is the Father, known and expressed by the Son.

This reality of the Holy Spirit as love is supported by the adage, *Bonum diffusivum sui*—good essentially shares itself, or it is characteristic of the good to share itself. Since God is infinite goodness, it should not be surprising that this goodness is expressed by a response that is a person constituted as such as Infinite Love. Perhaps we can present the following image to illustrate this. Imagine a whole ocean, such as the Atlantic Ocean, heaving itself by a gigantic tidal wave into a river, say an enormously expanded Hudson River, and then the whole of this dynamic flow rushing back toward the ocean.[30] Thus the goodness of the Father, an infinite ocean of being or actuality, spirates a response of love wholly proportioned to himself, and does this through the Word who thus as it were spirates the character or form of this response, as the river banks constitute the form of the flow of a river toward the ocean.

Thus the Holy Spirit by inspiring our prayer lifts us up to share her dynamic impulse of love for the Father through the Son, when we pray "Abba! Father!" (Rom 8:15). Another image is suggested by Orthodoxy's notion of the Father's *breathing* forth the Holy Spirit; this recalls God's breathing into Adam with the result that there is a response of life toward God in Adam.

The Holy Spirit constitutes a bond between the Father and the Son, or their mutual love, in the sense that as the Father says everything he knows in the Word, so too the Father and the Son express their love for each other and for all they love in the Holy Spirit. The Father loves and the Son loves; and since God's act *is* his being, it is true to say that "God is love" (1 John 4:8). But love in them is not (as it is in the Spirit) a notional act, that is, constitutive of what is *distinctive* of them as divine persons. The very word 'spirit' (*ruach*) means wind or breath—a dynamic impulse; and 'holy' means such an impulse toward the Holiest, that is, God. The Father expresses his goodness by this act of love, as the Son expresses the Father's goodness by this act of love. Thus this act of love is the Father's expression of love for himself, his Son, and all that the Father loves. And similarly, it is the Son's expression of love for the Father, for himself, and for all that he loves.

What are some implications this interpretation has for the question of the *Filioque?* I suggest that this explanation answers some of Orthodoxy's objections to Augustine's and the West's pneumatology while being faithful to what is essential to this pneumatology. As we saw, a major image in the East of the proceeding of the Spirit from the Father is that of breath coming from one who speaks a word. Thus it comes simultaneously with the word, and it comes from the same source as that of the word, but it does not as breath come from the word. By the distinction we have made between the Father and the Son as origin or 'spirators' of the Spirit, we come close to what is suggested by this image. The Spirit as infinite dynamic response of love to the divine goodness in the First Person reflects the image of breath coming from the speaker. The shape of the breath depends on the word spoken, and this image suggests the spirating of the "Spirit of truth" (Jn 16:13) by the Word, because a word conveys shape and form. The Spirit's procession from the Son does not prove that the Son properly is the principle of the *impulse* that the Spirit is, as the one who speaks a word also breathes forth, and breath as breath does not proceed from the word. The Spirit receives *form* from the Word as the human breath is given shape by the human word, and thus is the "Spirit of Truth" (Jn 15:26). Thus, because the Spirit receives from the Son as the Spirit of Truth: "she will *guide* you to all truth. She will not speak on her own, but she will speak what she hears" (Jn 16:13; see also Jn 14:25; my use of feminine pronoun). As we suggested in the preceding chapter, the Son takes from the Spirit the inclination *esse* gives. And as the good and the word are one principle of our act of love, there is one spiration, though two spirators. Perhaps this interpretation responds to reservations, expressed at times by the Orthodox, in reference to a notion of the Spirit as the mutual love between the Father and the Son, namely that this notion as frequently articulated in the West understates the priority of the Father.

This interpretation we offer may also help to explain part of the reason why many of the Eastern Fathers used a different word to express the relation of the Spirit to the Son (*proïenai*) than they did to express the relation of the Spirit to the Father (*ekporeusthai*). St. John Damascene speaks of the Spirit coming *through* the Son, and this is interpreted by J. Grégoire as meaning that the Spirit's hypostatic property, the procession, is accessible or understandable "by reference to the Son, just as the breath can only be accessible by reference to the word."[31] A breath is shaped by the word spoken, and so the Spirit is related to the Son as the Spirit of truth, both the Son and the Spirit coming from the Father who speaks and breathes. Some think the Western interpretation of the *Filioque* runs the danger of relating the Spirit too closely to the Son.[32]

Similarly, some see a danger in the Western interpretation of the *Filioque* in that when the Spirit is spoken of as the bond of love between Father and Son, "The Spirit is then seen as little more than a power or a dynamism of the one God . . . with the Spirit as a less than fully personal bond of unity between them."[33] We will treat the three as persons more fully in the next chapter, so what we say here is not our full theological interpretation of the three as persons. The analysis we have given does show the distinctiveness of the Spirit in a way that does not reduce the Spirit to a somewhat impersonal bond of love between the Father and the Son.

Perhaps too our analysis supports the Orthodox spirituality that can be called 'epicletic', that is, one that is a mode of Christian life seen as within the Spirit's lifting the human and empowering the human community and person to a doxological attitude of worship of the Father. The Christian worshiping community is caught up in the dynamic movement to the Father—that praise of the Father for his love shown to us through Christ and for his Spirit and all his gifts. This grateful and worshiping attitude and act constitutes a participation in the movement of love or return to the Father that the Holy Spirit properly is. We suggested earlier that this influence of the Spirit upon us can appropriately be called concurrence.[34] We shall return to this question later in this chapter when we treat the question of the divine energies.

There is then, we suggest, a mutual priority of the Son and the Spirit within the Trinity. Perhaps the *way* in which the West has seen a priority of the Son reflects our culture, and the enlargement found in recognizing a mutual priority offers us an insight that is desperately needed today.

3. An Answer to Some Possible Objections, and the Question of Divine Energies

An objection to our interpretation can be made that though in John 15:26, it is said only that the Holy Spirit *proceeds (ekporeuetai)* from the Father, Revelation 22:1 speaks of the Holy Spirit under the symbol of a great river and specifically as a "river of life-giving water, sparkling like crystal flowing *(ekporeuomenon)* from the throne of God and of the Lamb." So here the Holy Spirit is said to proceed both from the Father and the Son. And in John 20:22 it is said that on Easter evening, Jesus appeared to his disciples, "*breathed* on them and said to them, 'receive the holy Spirit.'" So it seems that the Spirit proceeds in the strict sense of the word as signified by *ekporeuēsis* both from the Father and the Son. However, we note that these two indications of the Spirit flowing from the Lamb and being symbolically breathed upon the disciples by Christ are both in reference to the risen and exalted Christ who, as exalted to the right hand of the Father, had, as Luke tells us, "received the promise of the holy Spirit from the Father and poured it forth" (Acts 2:33). There is another title here that accounts for his *pouring forth*, or *breathing* forth the Spirit, not the eternal relation of the three persons but the paschal mystery (see too Jn 7:37–39).[35] This does not seem counter to our view proposed above that while in their eternal relations, the Spirit *receives* (Jn 16:14) from the Son, she does not proceed from the Son in the restricted sense of flowing forth as a spring from its source or breath from one who speaks.

An objector may claim that Thomas's teaching is that the Holy Spirit proceeds from the Father and Son as they mutually love one another. Thomas writes, "The Holy Spirit proceeds from the Father and the Son as they are several *(plures)*; he proceeds from them as the unitive love of the two."[36] It seems that Thomas seeks a parallel to the procession of the Son in that of the Spirit. There is a kind of 'term' that results from our knowledge, namely a concept—an 'expresssed species'. Similarly in the act of love: "As from the fact that someone understands something, there comes a certain intellectual concept of the thing understood in the knower, so also from the fact that someone loves something, there comes (so to speak) a certain impression of the thing loved in the affect of the lover, according to which the loved one is said to be in the lover, as the understood is in the knower."[37] Thomas holds that our language in reference to love is not as adequate as our language in reference to knowledge. We do not have terms that distinguish in the act of

love the reference of love to the object and the reference of love to what results in the lover. We do have terms in the intellectual act by which we distinguish *knowing* (the object) and saying or *conceiving* (the word). Thomas
uses the word 'dilectio' to signify the notional acts of the Father and Son's
love for one another as 'spirating', and the word 'amor' for the notional act
that is the 'impression of the thing loved in the affect of the lover', namely
the Holy Spirit who proceeds from the mutual love. Thus an objector is saying that the explanation of the procession of the Spirit that I gave is not that
of Thomas.

In answer, we would first ask where it is said in Scripture that it is primarily by their mutual love that the Father and Son spirate the Holy Spirit? The
fact that the Spirit is shown to be in the order of love because of the Spirit's
effects does not imply that it is specifically through mutual love that the Father and Son spirate the Spirit. Actually, it is said that in some special sense
the Father is *good* (see Lk 18:19; the word 'God' in the New Testament usually refers to the Father), and *holy* ("Holy Father," Jn 17:11). The name of the
Spirit, 'Holy Spirit', then might make us think first of all of a *ruah* or dynamic
impulse toward the Father as the All Holy and All Good. And calling the
Spirit the "Spirit of Truth" (Jn 15:26) might make us think first of all of this
divine impulse as totally true or faithful, as bearing the imprint of Truth itself (see Jn 14:6)—an impulse that is a return to the Father as love that is
fully true.

Also, does the notion of a 'term' in the will come from a too-close interpretation of loving by the act of knowing and conceiving a word? M. T.-L.
Penido seems to suggest this:

> The act of love can be envisaged either as a reaction of the will, and then it is
> a movement toward the loved one—*amans in amato*; or as following on the
> presentation of a good, and then it is the attraction (*solicitation*) of the loved
> one—*amatum in amante*. But still, it is one and the same process, regarded now
> under the passive aspect—*motus in amato*, now under the active aspect—
> *motus ad amatum*. The loved one is only present to the lover in the movement
> of the lover toward the loved one. We cannot discover and situate a 'term' ef-
> fected by love and detaching itself [from the will's act] as the fruit from a tree.
> In the will in the grip of love, there is a certain procession, but what proceeds
> is not a term; it is an act.[38]

The intellect is impregnated by the known object, and so it conceives and
says a word. Here there is first unity and then distinction—the being impregnated and thus in act, and then the word said. But in the will, there is
first distinction—the known good soliciting the will—and then desire or

union—love responding in the power of that good. In our human experience, of course, it is frequently the love another has for us that breathes new life in us and gains a response of love from us. But it is also our experience that simple openness to the goodness of another or the truth of a reality, even when it is not directed toward us, breathes new life in us or evokes our response of love and acceptance. What Scripture says of the procession of the Holy Spirit seems more akin to this second case than to the first.

There is a very real sense in which the Spirit is the bond of love between Father and Son. The goodness of the First Person reflected in the Word spirates and so is expressed by the love that is the Holy Spirit. Thus the Holy Spirit is both the Father's and the Son's expression of love for one another, for the Spirit, and for all that they love. It may be that it is this that Thomas means when he compares the Father and Son loving one another *by* the Holy Spirit to a tree flowering by its flowers:

> We say that a tree blooms by its flowers (*est florens floribus*), although the flowers are not the form of the tree but rather a certain effect proceeding from it. . . .
>
> When love [*diligere*, not *amore*] is taken as a notional act, it is nothing other than to spirate love; as to say is to produce a word, and to flower is to produce flowers. As a tree then is said to bloom by its flowers, so the Father is said to be saying himself and creatures by his Word or Son. And the Father and Son are said to be loving [*diligentes*] each other and us by the Holy Spirit, or the love [*amore*] that proceeds.[39]

Perhaps Thomas is saying here that whatever the word spiration itself designates, we will use the word *diligere* for it. But it is by the Holy Spirit as the effect of this spiration that they are said to love *one another*, as the expression of this love that is a notional act.

Duncan Reid compares Western Christianity's dominant view of God's relation to the world with that of Orthodoxy as follows:

> Western theism has tended to see God either as the absolute subject, the one who looks down from the detachment of heaven upon the creation, or else as the absolute object, the one whom the saints encounter in the mystical beatific vision or whose word the congregation hears in the preaching of the church. . . .
>
> The doctrine of energies views the world as lying within God (in the womb of the one who holds all together), and as "transfused" with the divine energies. This necessarily involves a tendency to view the world holistically (*katholou*) rather than analytically, or according to the parts (*kath' ekaston*). Human beings are understood as persons in relationship, and reality as being in relation to God.[40]

While the West does teach God's indwelling in the graced individual, which it ascribes in a special way to the Holy Spirit, "the imaginative picture here is much more of the Spirit indwelling the individual creature than of the creation as a whole being encompassed by the Spirit, or dwelling *en pneumati* (Acts . . . 17:28)."[41] In Palamism, Orthodox theologians consider the individual Christian to be endowed at times in prayer with a vision of the glory of God—of God's uncreated energies, though not a vision of God's essence. It is these energies, largely mediated by the Holy Spirit, that dwell in the Christian. For many theologians in the West, it is the Holy Spirit herself who dwells in the Christian, though the primary understanding of grace for scholasticism was created grace rather than uncreated grace.

Earlier in this chapter as well as in chapter 5 we acknowledged a kind of divine presence in all created reality that was recognized but not sufficiently developed by Thomas and the Western tradition, namely a *concurrence* by which God is present in the very initiative, spontaneity, creativity, and growth of all created things. By their activities created things are participating in God's concurrence. This participation is expressed in the Greek adage used by St. Paul, "In him we live and move and have our being" (Acts 17:28), and reflects a kind of divine presence by concurrence. It is different from God's presence as efficient cause, final cause, and exemplary cause. It is a presence that is basic to the religious experience of some religions of Native Americans and of Asia, such as Hinduism and Shintoism. And of itself it does not imply any confusion between the uncreated and the created. It is a sense of God's presence that is very necessary for us in our time in reference to our awareness both of the physical world around us and of our own spirits in their relation to the Sacred or God. A greater awareness of God's immanence in the physical world may help us to be more ecologically responsible. Also, a greater awareness of God's immanence within us can help us see God's direction for our lives as witnessed to and authenticated by our own spirit as well as by the word of God that comes to us from without.

Orthodoxy's continued incorporation of this sense of God's presence through the centuries has much to contribute to the West's reawakening to partially lost Christian treasures. As Reid writes:

What we have here is the vision of a sort of penumbra of glory, or a field of energy that surrounds the trinitarian Godhead. In this way the universe can be considered as lying within God's field of energy or "field of resonance" while at the same time remaining distinct from and contingent upon God's superessentiality. Within this penumbra or energy-field, there is a resonating and a quickening of the natural, material universe, so that the material order is drawn into the experience—however we may understand "experience"—of God.[42]

As distinct from many Orthodox theologians, however, I hold with most Catholic theologians that it is the Holy Spirit, and not only the divine energies, who dwells within us, and we in the Spirit. As Thomas writes:

> Since charity by which we love God is in us by the Holy Spirit, it is necessary that the Holy Spirit himself is within us, as long as charity remains in us . . . as this is the case, it must be that through the Holy Spirit the Father and the Son dwell in us. . . . [And] it is necessary that through the Holy Spirit not only is God in us, but we also are in God. So it is said (1 John 4:16), "The one who dwells in love dwells in God, and God in him."[43]

Orthodoxy understands that the divine energies are mediated to us particularly by the Holy Spirit. We can see from all we have written in this chapter that there is an affinity between 'energies' and the Holy Spirit. In fact, most Catholic theologians would now say that there is a proper presence, and not only an appropriated presence, both of the Holy Spirit to the graced person and of this human being to what is proper to the Holy Spirit as a divine person. Some very limited experience of this relationship is accessible to us, though this experience like the relationship itself is simply a gift, is not under our control, and is a genuine mystery. This knowledge is experiential rather than direct or conceptual. An understanding of grace as primarily created grace is totally insufficient to the Christian mystery.[44] We are related to the Spirit somewhat differently than to the Father and the Son, but we will return to this theme when we discuss a trinitarian spirituality in our final chapter.

Notes

1. See, for example, *Confessing One Faith: An Ecumenical Explication of the Apostolic Faith as It Is Confessed in the Nicene-Constantinopolitan Creed (381).* Faith and Order Paper, no. 153, revised. (Geneva: WCC Publication, 1991), 73–81.

2. Walter Kasper, *The God of Jesus Christ* (Herder and Herder, 1985), 198.

3. On experiences of the Spirit and Christian theology, see, for example, Pope John Paul II's encyclical letter, *Dominum et Vivificantem* (1986); F. Lambiasi, *Lo Spirito santo: mistero e presenza* (Bologna: Edizioni Dehoniane, 1987); L. Bermejo, *The Spirit of Life: The Holy Spirit in the Life of the Christian* (Chicago: Loyola University Press, 1989); J. Moltmann, *The Spirit of Life: A Universal Affirmation* (Minneapolis: Fortress, 1993); Michael Welker, *God the Spirit* (Minneapolis: Fortress, 1994); the *Proceedings of the Catholic Theological Society of America*, vol. 51 (1996), an issue

largely on the theme, "Toward a Spirit Theology: The Holy Spirit's Challenge to the Theological Disciplines."

4. See chapter 2, 35–46, 43–44, 54–60.

5. In "Pneumatology Overview," *Proceedings CTSA* 51 (1996): 195, Kilian McDonnell writes: "Eduard Schweizer says: 'Long before the Spirit was a theme of doctrine [the Spirit] was a fact in the experience of the community.' . . . Rudolf Schnackenburg . . .[observes] that 'the Spirit for the Johannine community was an experienced reality." He quotes here from Schweizer, "pneuma ktl.," *Theological Dictionary of the New Testament* 6: 396; and Schnackenburg, "Die johanneische Gemeinde und ihre Geisterfahrung," *Die Kirche des Anfangs*, 286.

6. Paul Ricoeur, "Poétique et symbolique," in B. Lauret and F. Refoulé, eds., *Initiation à la Pratique de la Théologie*, vol. 1 (Paris: Cerf, 1982), 44.

7. Josef Schmitz, *La rivelazione* (Brescia: Queriniana, 1991), 130. Perhaps this kind of knowing is what St. Ignatius called "consolation without reason."

8. ST II-II, 1, 4, ad 3. Translations from Thomas are mine unless otherwise noted.

9. Moltmann, *Spirit of Life*, 292.

10. We have treated this in part in chapter 5, for instance, 141–142, 144–145.

11. See chapter 5, 140–142; also see J. Farrelly, *Belief in God in Our Time* (Collegeville, Minn.: Liturgical Press, 1992), 179–205.

12. CG I, 37.

13. One may think of Hinduism, Taoism, and much Native American religion. I have reflected on this briefly in *Belief in God*, 290–297.

14. See, for example, Vatican II, *Gaudium et Spes*, 24–25, 30.

15. Thomas, *De potentia*, 3, 7. I suggest that *concurrence* articulates the Spirit's influence in us better than the term 'quasi-formal causality', and that this concurrence and our correlative participation in it express what David Coffey rightly sees as essential to the Spirit's action in the economy of salvation, namely the Spirit's operating in Jesus Christ himself in an 'ascending' Christology and her influence enabling the return of the human community and individual person to God. See David Coffey, "The Holy Spirit as the Mutual Love of the Father and the Son," *TS* 51 (1990): 193–229; and Ralph Del Colle, *Christ and the Spirit: Spirit-Christologies in Trinitarian Perspective* (New York: Oxford University Press, 1994), 103, 115–116.

16. See, for example, *Decree on the Church's Missionary Activity (Ad Gentes)* paragraph 4, "Without doubt, the Holy Spirit was at work before Christ was glorified"; and *Gaudium et Spes*, 22, "we must hold that the Holy Spirit offers to all the possibility of being made partners, in a way known to God, in the paschal mystery."

17. See J. Farrelly, *Faith in God through Jesus Christ* (Collegeville, Minn.: Liturgical Press, 1997), 338–340.

18. See, for instance, Yves Congar, *I Believe in the Holy Spirit*. Vol. 3, *The River of Life Flows in the East and in the West* (New York: Seabury, 1983), 174–214; L. Vischer, ed., *Spirit of God. Spirit of Christ: Ecumenical Reflections on the Filioque Controversy* (London: SPCK/ Geneva: WCC, 1981); Theodore Stylianopoulos, "An Ecumenical Solution to the Filioque Question?" *Journal of Ecumenical Studies* 28 (1991): 260–280;

Pontifical Council for Promoting Christian Unity, "Traditions Regarding the Procession of the Holy Spirit," *Eastern Churches Journal* 2 (1995): 35–46; Thomas Weinandy, *The Father's Spirit of Sonship: Reconceiving the Trinity* (Edinburgh: T & T Clark, 1995); T. Weinandy, et al., "Clarifying the *filioque*: The Catholic-Orthodox dialogue," *Communio* 23 (1996): 354–374; Duncan Reid, *Energies of the Spirit: Trinitarian Models in Eastern Orthodox and Western Theology* (Atlanta: Scholars Press, 1997); Gary Badcock, *Light of Truth and Fire of Love: A Theology of the Holy Spirit* (Grand Rapids, Mich.: Eerdmans, 1997), 212–256; Ralph Del Colle, "Reflections on the *Filioque*," *Journal of Ecumenical Studies* 34 (1997): 202–217.

19. On Augustine see chapter 4, 95–99; on fourth-century Eastern views, see chapter 3, 85–90, chapter 4, 100–103.

20. See chapter 4, 101.

21. See chapter 4, 106–109.

22. D. Staniloae, "Le saint Esprit dans la théologie Byzantine et dans la réflexion Orthodoxe contemporaine," *Credo in Spiritum Sanctum* (Vatican: Vatican Libreria Editrice, 1983), vol. 1, 669.

23. See chapter 4, 104–105.

24. See Reid, chapter 2, "The Two Positions in Twentieth-Century Theology," in *Energies of the Spirit*, 27–54.

25. See Vatican II, *Decree on Ecumenism*, 17: "In the study of revealed truth East and West have used different methods and approaches in understanding and confessing divine things. It is hardly surprising, then, if some times one tradition has come nearer to a full appreciation of some aspects of a mystery of revelation than the other, or has expressed them better. In such cases, these various theological formulations are often to be considered complementary rather than conflicting." The Pontifical Council for Promoting Christian Unity has taken this approach in reference to the question of the Holy Spirit in "Traditions Regarding the Procession of the Holy Spirit," cited in endnote 18 above.

26. See *ST* I, 27, 3 and 4; *CG* IV, 19.

27. See *ST* I, 54, 2; Aristotle, *Metaphysics*, bk. 9, c. 8, 1050 a 25. See Thomas's commentary on this passage (lect. 8, n. 1862) and *ST* I, 27, 5; *De Potentia*, 9, 9.

28. See chapter 6, 172–175.

29. What we have written here is relevant to a view of David Coffey that Del Colle analyzes in *Christ and the Spirit*, 104–105. One question is whether Thomas changed his mind concerning the procession involved in an act of love between *De Veritate* 4, 2, ad 7 and *ST* I, 37, 1. We will return to this question later. Coffey sees a change in Thomas from his earlier to his later writing (see "The Holy Spirit," 224).

From what we have said in our text, I see the act of love itself (which is in a way an 'operation') as comparable to the 'word' in the intellect, in that there is an opposition of relation between the act of love and the goodness of what is loved, as there is between the word and the intellectual saying of it. But, as we will see below, in the Trinity the origin of this love and the love that proceeds is 'notional' or distinctive of the persons only in reference to the spiration by the Father and the Son and the proceeding of the Holy Spirit. Love in Father and Son is said essentially; spiration is said 'notionally' of them in reference to the Spirit. I see this as consistent with what Thomas writes, and I do not (as Coffey seems to) see Thomas's later view as denying a distinction between the nature of the intellectual and the volitional act.

30. My source for this image, though I adjust it, is Joseph Donceel, "Rahner's Argument for God," *America*, October 31, 1970, 340. He states that according to Rahner, "Man knows God somewhat in the way in which the Hudson River would know the ocean, if the river were aware of its own flow, which carries it irresistibly toward the Atlantic." Rahner's epistemology here is dependent upon his understanding of the human person as spirit in the world. My use of the image is in continuity with this, but applied to the Holy Spirit's relation to the Father and Son.

31. See chapter 4, 101.

32. G. Hendry critiques Barth's pneumatology in this way. As Reid puts Hendry's critique: "Barth binds the Son and the Spirit so closely together through the *filioque* that the Spirit becomes effectively just another form of Christ. Barth's pneumatology becomes a part of his christology." See Reid, *Energies of the Spirit*, 74.

33. Reid, *Energies of the Spirit*, 74.

34. Coffey abandons the 'procession' model for the 'bestowal' model (the Father's and Son's mutual bestowal of love on one another) or 'return' model because he does not think that the procession model supports this epicletic spirituality (see Coffey, "Holy Spirit," 228; and Del Colle, *Christ and the Spirit*, 115, 124–127). Perhaps if we in the West used the term 'procession' more as Orthodoxy does, that is, to refer specifically to the Spirit's coming from the First Person, we would see that this notion does support an epicletic spirituality. Our use of the notion of concurrence to explain the influence of the Spirit on the church and individuals and their participation in the Spirit also supports an epicletic spirituality.

35. On this theme see also *Faith in God*, 188–192, 274–281.

36. *ST*, I, 36, 4, ad 1. There is a difference of opinion among the commentators of St.Thomas. Some think that when Thomas started writing theology he held that the Spirit proceeds from the mutual love of Father and Son, but by the time he wrote *Summa theologica*, he held that the Spirit proceeds as the love of the first good, the good of the divine essence or being, and he reduced the mutual love theory to a secondary position. For this view, see M. T.-L. Penido, "Glosses sur la procession d'amour dans la Trinité," *Ephem. Theol. Lovan.* 14 (1937): 33–68; A. Krapiec, O.P., "Inquisitio circa Divi Thomas doctrinam de Spiritu Sancto prout Amore," *Divus Thomas* 53 (1950): 474–495. For a view that Thomas's teaching at the end of his life as at the beginning was that the Holy Spirit proceeds from the mutual love of Father and Son, see A. Patfoort, O.P, *Bulletin Thomiste* 8 (1947–1953): #1663, 853–861.

37. *ST* I, 37, 1.

38. Penido, "Glosses sur la procession d'amour," 44–45.

39. *ST*, I, 37, 2.

40. Reid, *Energies of the Spirit*, 106, 132.

41. Reid, *Energies of the Spirit*, 106.

42. Reid, *Energies of the Spirit*, 133. This recalls the metaphor of a field of force used by W. Pannenberg in his *Systematic Theology*, vol. 2 (Grand Rapids, Mich.: Eerdmans, 1994), 76–84, to illustrate the Spirit's influence in creation.

43. CG, IV, 21. See CG, IV, 20–22 for the effects of the Holy Spirit within us. Badcock seeks to overcome the sixteenth-century Reformers' (primarily Lutheran) interpretation of justification by understanding "justification and sanctification as pointing to two sides of the same thing. Each enriches our understanding" (Badcock, *Light of Truth*, 108). And he recalls that "Paul's thought is of the human spirit *made alive* by being made righteous in Christ, that is, by being within the sphere of the Holy Spirit's presence and power in mediating the risen Christ to the believer" (126).

44. See Mark Ginter, "The Holy Spirit and Morality: A Dynamic Alliance," *Proceedings of the Catholic Theological Society of America* 51 (1996): 165–179, for an analysis of the Spirit's presence to us according to Yves Congar, with many illuminating and beautiful quotations from Congar on this theme.

~

CHAPTER EIGHT

Father, Son, and Holy Spirit as Three Relational Persons in One Being

The mystery we face in this chapter is what we as Christians mean by asserting we believe God the Father, Son, and Holy Spirit are three persons in one
Being. How is this statement faithful to what has been revealed? Also, is this
doctrine a coherent mystery, or is it intrinsically contradictory? Theology itself is *fides quaerens intellectum* and so does not prove that God is triune but
accepts this from God's revelation and only then seeks some modest understanding of it—specifically, an understanding that is spiritually fruitful. What
we have written so far is not a sufficient answer to this question, because
while our study of the proceeding of the Son from the Father and of the Holy
Spirit from the Father and the Son or through the Son shows how the divine
being is communicated, it does not of itself show sufficiently how the three
are three distinct persons.

We have seen in an earlier chapter how this Christian belief has been a
very serious problem for many people. In the modern age there has been for
many an erosion of this belief and thus the emergence in the West of a post-
Christian world.[1] This Christian belief is also a scandal to non-Christians
such as Jews and Moslems who consider it counter to who God is as he has
been revealed to them and as internally contradictory.[2]

Even Christian theologians who accept this mystery differ seriously among
themselves in explaining it. For example, as we saw in the first chapter, Karl
Barth and Karl Rahner both reject the use of the modern understanding of
person in interpreting the Trinity as three; they prefer to speak of three
"modes of being" or "distinct manners of subsisting."[3] Some other theologians

who do accept a modern sense of person either deny that Christianity is a monotheism (Moltmann) or consider the unity of the divine being to be the communion of persons, and not the *homoousios* of Nicea.

Thus a treatment of this theme is essential to our study. We will first (I) recall the patristic development of understanding of the three as three persons and show how this development is indeed faithful to Scripture and coherent. God is indeed three persons in one being in the classical understanding of person. We will then (II) show at greater length Thomas Aquinas's interpretation, which we largely accept as our own, supporting its fidelity and coherence. Third, (III) we will ask whether and how we can say that Father, Son, and Holy Spirit are three persons in view of a modern understanding of person. Here we are supposing that experiences in the modern world have called for a development of our understanding of 'person', as experiences of the physical world have similarly called for a developed understanding of 'cosmos'. With other theologians, we will argue that there is something valid in this modern understanding of person that contributes to our understanding of God as three persons in one being. It does not contradict the classical view such as Thomas's but helps us to integrate further developments.

We cannot identify a classical understanding of person with a modern one. Stanley Rudman turns to classical and Christian understandings of person to put modern understandings into a larger context. But he also writes that there is a danger, for example, in claiming to see in the Cappadocian Fathers' theology of three persons in God "an ontology of personhood which reflects modern discussions of personhood . . . [or in asserting] that only a Christian view can establish the importance of relationality in personhood."[4]

It is important to interrelate a classical and a modern notion of person in theology generally. In an earlier work I sought to overcome a dichotomy between modern and classical understandings of person. For this purpose I evaluated a classical metaphysical understanding of person by the use of a modern phenomenology that used developmental psychology, particularly the work of Erik Erikson. I wrote: "We should evaluate this [classical view] by an articulation of human experience that integrates cultural differentiation, process or history, and the constructive or creative dimension of the way we shape our lives, because these elements of modern experience are thought to undermine a classical view of the person."[5] In my view such an approach both validates and enlarges a classical view of the person, and this is relevant to a contemporary theology of Father, Son, and Holy Spirit as three persons.

I. The Patristic Development of Understanding of the Trinity as Three Persons

We have seen elements of the development of this theological understanding in chapters 3 and 4. Here, we recall the meaning of this development of Christian understanding God to be three *persons* in one *being* to support this interpretation as still essential for our time, faithful to Scripture, and internally coherent. This development of doctrine was due to successive contributions of some of Fathers of the church and medieval theologians. This study shows something of the depth of this mystery, too easily discounted by our frequently self-satisfied and superficial age. Both Eastern and Western Christianity have contributed to this development. The West built on contributions from Fathers of the East, and Eastern Fathers, as late as the period of Palamas, showed appreciation for Western Fathers, such as Augustine.[6]

This development does show that there is illumination that the human mind can bring, by God's grace, to the revealed mystery through knowledge of the human and created world that comes from philosophy and other human sources. Counter to some evangelical Protestants, there is no essential dichotomy between what comes from these two springs of knowledge. And counter to some nineteenth- and twentieth-century liberal Christians, the use of these human sources need not result in a reduction of the mystery to the level of these philosophical concepts. The mutual contributions faith and reason make to Christian understanding have been stressed once more in Pope John Paul II's encyclical, *Fides et Ratio*.[7] Of the word 'person' in the context of faith and reason, Balthasar wrote:

> Historically, the word has vacillated between two very different realms: that of common sense . . . and that of Christian theology, in which the concept of person acquires a completely new sense first in trinitarian doctrine and then in christology. Now in the Christian era, the general (or philosophical) concept must already exist if it is to receive its special theological content. Yet the unique trinitarian or christological content that the concept acquires in theology casts its light back upon the general (or philosophical) understanding without the latter having, therefore, to leave the realm of what is generally human. . . . Philosophy can in some way appropriate for the human person the dignity bestowed on person by trinitarian doctrine and christology.[8]

We will recall in succession some contributions (1) before the mid–fourthth century, (2) from the Cappadocians, and (3) then by Augustine and Boethius.

1. The Patristic Age before the Mid–Fourth Century

The Latin word *persona* comes from the Etruscan word *phersu*. In the festival of the goddess Persephone, the mask used was called a *phersu* after the goddess. Another stream leading to the word *persona* was the Latin word *personus* from the verb *personare* which meant resound. This word was transferred to the stage and hence took on "different meanings—theatre mask, character in a play or 'theatre role', perhaps also as early as this 'person' in the grammatical sense. . . . [B]y Cicero's time it revealed all its riches at once."[9] By the first century *persona* was used to designate a real person, a juridical person with legal rights, and even a human substance in its own distinctively human individuality. The Greek word *prosopon* in part derives from the word meaning to see or be seen (*ops* in *pro-ops-on*) and initially meant face or countenance. It was also related to the word for mask, *prosopeion*, and later came to mean person. For example *prosopon* is used as 'face' in 2 Cor 4:6, where Paul writes of the "knowledge of the glory of God on the face of Christ."

An interesting and important source of the use of *persona* and *prosopon* for the three who are distinct in God is a form of exegesis of Scripture (but previously too of Homer) that is called prosopological. This is an exegesis, for instance, of the Old Testament prophets, by way of designating who is speaking in a passage, to whom he is speaking, and of what he is speaking. Interpreters looked at some passages of the Old Testament as being said by one or other of the divine persons. These distinctions were in the order of the economy of salvation, not within the Trinity itself, and were a question of different roles or speakers. For example, Justin writes: "But when you listen to the words of the prophets spoken 'as from a person' (*hos apo prosopou*), do not suppose that they are said by the inspired people themselves, but by the divine Logos which is moving them . . . sometimes it speaks as from the person of God the Ruler and Father of all things, sometimes as from the person of Christ. . . ."[10] The experience of the early Christians through the liturgy and the gospels included a sense of interactions between Father, Son, and, though not as prominent, Holy Spirit.

As we mentioned in chapter 3, Tertullian pushed the distinction among Father, Son, and Spirit further than Justin.[11] Tertullian interpreted the Christian message as signifying that there was distinction in God before creation, namely between God and God's reason or silent planning. God's reason was brought forth as Word when God was to create. Tertullian designated what God and the Word had in common by the word *substantia*, taken from the background of Stoic philosophy; he designated their distinctness by calling them three persons. He took the popular notion of 'person' as one who speaks and acts, and shows that the Father and Son speak to one another, and so on.

He showed their unity in substance and distinction from the Stoic notion of the *ens concretum physicum*. Grillmeier writes:

> From this aspect we can understand why *substantia* and *persona* can have something in common and why they are finally opposed. . . . [T]he Stoic idea of the *ens concretum* is built up from the *hypokeimenon* [what lies under]. . . . This is . . . made concrete by . . . properties . . . also described as *species, eidos,* as *forma, morphe,* as *character,* by which the individuality is made complete. Now this individuality is described as *prosopon,* as *persona.*[12]

Without going into this further, it is agreed that Tertullian was using these terms in a philosophical sense and that what is stressed by 'person' is the individual. He stresses that Father and Son are *unum* but not *unus*.

In the East, there was also the problem of finding a word to distinguish the three in order to remain faithful to Scripture and Christian tradition and to resist Monarchianism, particularly Sabellianism, which distinguished the three simply as appearances of the one God in the economy of creation and salvation. With time, particular importance for purposes of distinction was given to the word *hypostasis*. Of this term, Basil Studer writes:

> As a technical term, h. [*hypostasis*] first appears in Greek natural science with the meaning of a sediment precipitated in a liquid. The double idea behind it, solidification and appearance, would always be important in every use of it. . . . Thus, in the Greek Bible, h. referred in particular to true reality (cf. Heb 1,3: 3,14; 11,1). Stoicism saw in h. the ultimate individualization of the primordial essence; so, though on a wholly spiritual level and with the nuance of graduality, did neoplatonism. . . . [It was] taken up by the Origenian tradition to give the three divine realities an anti-Sabellian emphasis (cf. Orig., *C. Cels.* 8,12; *Jo.* 2,10,75).[13]

However, while Origen distinguished the Father, Son, and Holy Spirit as three hypostases, there appears to be some subordationism among the persons.

Nicea taught against Arius that the Son was so equal to the Father that he was of the same substance as the Father—*homoousios*. This followed from the fact that the Son was "generated not created," since what is generated has the same nature as that which generates it. But, as we showed in chapter 3, the danger of the word was that it could seem to deny or elide the *distinction* of the Son from the Father, and a few defenders of Nicea seemed to interpret it in this way.[14] This was all the more a danger since Nicea did not really distinguish *ousia* and *hypostasis*. In fact, Nicea condemned those who said that the Son came from another *ousia* or *hypostasis*. Though Athanasius

clearly distinguished the Father, Son, and Holy Spirit, he had no word by
which to designate them as three.

2. The Cappadocians

It was the Cappadocian Fathers who were most important in resolving the
difficulty of affirming the distinction of the three while holding to their
common divinity, as we showed in chapter 3.[15] Basil, Gregory Nazianzen, and
Gregory of Nyssa came from the party of Basil of Ancyra and his associates
who were initially suspicious of Nicea's formulation; they (c. 358) spoke of
the Son as *homoiousios* (of a similar substance) with the Father and, in partial dependence on Origen, of the three as three *hypostaseis*. In a diplomatic
move at a council in Alexandria in 362, Athanasius and his associates said it
was permissible to speak of three *hypostaseis* if one continued to hold *homoousios*, thus for the first time accepting a possible distinction of meaning
between *hypostasis* and *ousia*.

Basil was a pioneer in distinguishing substance and *hypostasis*, at times on
the analogy of the Platonist distinction between the general nature (e.g., humanity) and those who participate it (e.g., Peter and Paul). But he insisted
too on other analogies that correct inadequacies of this comparison (e.g., the
analogy may suggest that Father and Son are distinct in being as Peter and
Paul are). He used *prosopon* at times as an alternative to *hypostasis* and also
hyparxis (subsistence) and *tropos hyparxis* (mode of subsistence), insisting that
the three are distinguished by their properties or peculiarities, not by their
ousia. There is an order among the persons but not subordination.

Like Basil, Gregory Nazianzen too battled with those who claimed to
know God's essence and identified it with ingenerateness.[16] There is a unity
of nature between the Son and the Father, but their distinction is shown by
the names; the distinction between them: "is outside the Essence . . . there is
One Essence of God, and One Nature, and One Name; although in accordance with a distinction in our thoughts we use distinct Names . . . the Father is not a name either of an essence [or] of an action . . . . But it is the name
of the Relation in which the Father stands to the Son, and the Son to the
Father."[17] Difference in origin and resulting relations are the basis for distinctions of the hypostases, Father, Son, and Holy Spirit, and these relations
are not the essence but the reference of one to the other based on the action
of the Father to the Son and to the Holy Spirit. Those at the time who denied the unity of nature among the three used the categories of Aristotle to
deny there could be distinction that would not be a distinction of nature in
the Godhead. Thus Gregory used categories from Aristotle and perhaps from
the Stoics to show that there could be a distinction on the basis of origin and

relation, without implying a distinction of nature. What Scripture and Christian belief designated by Father, Son, and Holy Spirit called for was a distinction by relations as well as unity in one name or essence.[18]

Gregory of Nyssa teaches in a similar fashion. For example, he writes:

> the differentiation of the subsistences (hypostaseon) makes the distinction of Persons (prosopon) clear and free from confusion, while the one Name standing in the forefront of the declaration of the Faith clearly expounds to us the unity of essence of the persons whom the Faith declares—I mean, of the Father, and of the Son and of the Holy Spirit. For by these appellations we are taught not a difference of nature, but only the special attributes that mark the subsistences.[19]

As the Orthodox theologian John Zizioulas has pointed out, the Cappadocians give a priority to the persons over the essence in the sense that they begin with the Father and then the Son and Holy Spirit, rather than with the unity of the divine essence.[20] It would be a mistake, however, to assert that for the Cappadocians the union of the three was in their *perichoresis* or mutual indwelling in a way that diminished Nicea's teaching that the Son was *homoousios* with the Father because he was generated by the Father.[21] We can conclude by agreeing with Basil Studer that the Cappadocians "prepared the way for the later teaching of the *relationes subsistentes*."[22]

3. Augustine and Boethius

Augustine's understanding of the Father, Son, and Holy Spirit as three persons in one being has been variously interpreted and evaluated. We discussed his teaching on the Trinity in chapter 4; we will not repeat that here, but will say a bit about his view of the three as distinct persons.[23] Augustine stressed the unity of action and essence in God so emphatically because of those Arians called Homoians who argued for the subordination of the Son to the Father. This is not the same as holding to a priority of the divine essence over the persons. As Studer writes, in "Augustine's main trinitarian texts . . . his line of thought progresses from Father, Son and Spirit to the one God. . . . Thus Augustine represents a mode of explaining the trinitarian faith which is closer to the eastern tradition than it at first sight appears."[24]

In arguing against the Homoians who said that the Son could be distinct from the Father only by distinction of substance, Augustine argued that the distinction was by relation, since the Father is a name signifying relationship, as is the Son. In this he was a debtor to Gregory Nazianzen. But when he came to ask what word we should use to answer the question of what there are three of in God, Augustine showed puzzlement. He acknowledged that the Greeks spoke of one *ousia* and three *hypostaseis*; but the Latins translated the latter term by 'substance', since etymologically both terms meant 'standing under' (*hypo-stasis*, and *sub-stantia*) and so could not say that the Father, Son, and Holy Spirit are three substances. The Latin practice was to say the three are one substance and three persons. He acknowledged that this was for the purpose of giving some answer to the question and to avoid saying either that there were three beings or that, like the Sabellians, there was not a real distinction between Father and Son.[25] The mystery of God is beyond our comprehension and beyond our language.

Perhaps Augustine's difficulty with using the word 'persons' in the plural, a difficulty he did not have with the use of 'relations', came partially from the fact that he interpreted the word 'person' to be ascribed to a human being in reference to himself, not in reference to another. Thus he writes, "as the substance of the Father is just the Father, not insofar as he is Father, but insofar as he just is; so too the person of the Father is nothing but just the Father. He is called person with reference to himself, not with reference to the Son or Holy Spirit; just as he is called God with reference to himself. . ." (*Trin.* VII, 11). We will see that Thomas Aquinas deals with the same difficulty; but later we will propose that a valid modern understanding of person will be an asset in reference to this problem or, rather, mystery.[26]

In the sixth century, the philosopher Boethius in reflecting on the unity of humanity and divinity in Jesus Christ wanted to make the point that the predicate person could not be applied to a universal nature or substance but only to an individual substance. Thus he defined 'person' as an "individual substance of a rational nature" (*Liber de persona et duabus naturis contra Eutychem et Nestorium*, III). The question of 'relation' did not enter this context for Boethius, but his definition was very influential in later Western theology of the Trinity.

II. Thomas Aquinas's Theology of the Three Divine Persons

In this section I will offer a systematic defense and elucidation of the mystery of there being three distinct persons or hypostases in the one divine being by using the relevant teaching of the Thomas Aquinas, which I basically accept. The mystery was revealed by the interrelation between Father, Son, and Holy Spirit witnessed to by Scripture and Christian prayer and interpreted through the development of the church's teaching that we have seen in this and earlier chapters. For example, the Eleventh Council of Toledo in 675 had written: "This holy Trinity which is the one true God is not without number but is not comprehended by number. For number is found in the relation among the persons; in the substance of the divine what is numbered is not found. Therefore in this alone is number implied, that they are related to one another; and in this they lack number, that they are absolute (*ad se*)."[27] It is important to note that the earlier tradition and medieval theology use 'relation' to defend *distinction* of persons. They are not understanding by 're-lation' all that we with our contemporary understanding of person understand, though we will argue later that with our modern understanding of person we can legitimately see elements implicit in their theologies that they did not articulate.

In my explanation I am following Thomas Aquinas, but with several differences from him and some of his commentators. One difference is that I begin not with the divine essence, but with belief in God as 'personal being' as the Old Testament presents it. In an earlier book I started from Scripture's account of such belief, largely in the Old Testament but also in the New.[28] God did reveal himself as one personal being before revealing himself as triune, and in the New Testament account Jesus calls this God the Jews believed in 'Father'. The approach I adopted is thus different from the way many interpret the relation between the two sections of Thomas's theology in the first part of his *Summa*, namely, on the one God (*ST* I, 2–26) and on God as triune (*ST* I, 27–43), because the first section is interpreted as *philosophical* and on the *unity of the divine essence*, while I started with Christian *belief* in God as divine *personal* being. (I am not judging here the adequacy of the commentators' interpretation of Thomas's method.) This approach, I suggest, makes the following analysis more concrete and closer to the Eastern tradition than many Western theologies of the three divine persons do. In my earlier book, I also sought to show that there are bases in modern experience that critically support Christian belief in God as transcendent personal divine being, and specifically as related to human beings in history. So I integrated philosophy with Scripture, but definitely as a junior partner.

In an order a bit different from Thomas's we will examine successively (1) how the ascription of the word 'person' to God and the significance of 'person' as distinct from 'substance' elucidates this mystery and how this helps us understand a bit the revealed message that there are three really distinct persons who are one divine being, and (2) some consequences for the relations among the divine persons, and how language is appropriate to this mystery.[29]

1. How the Perfection of Person Should Be Ascribed to God, and What This Signifies in God, Namely the Distinct Subsistent Relations
Thomas treats the question of relation in God in *ST* I, 28, and the question of person in God in *ST* I, 29. We are reversing parts of these questions, and

we schematically recall several of Thomas's reflections on God as personal which we make our own.

The word 'person' was coined to express the *individual* within the human species because of the special *dignity* of the individual human being, whereas there is not a comparable word to express the individual within an animal species. This dignity is shown in the fact that human beings "have control *(dominium)* over their own actions, and are not only acted upon as other [material beings], but act of themselves" (ST, I, 29, 1) by their will and intelligence. Animals are stimulated by some object (e.g., food, sex, danger) and react, whereas human beings can reflect and choose how they will act. Thus, Boethius's definition of person is vindicated: "an individual substance of a rational nature." 'Individual' here designates the concrete real being or what is called 'first substance', as distinct from the 'species' such as 'humanity' that is predicated of all human beings bcause of their common nature and is called 'second substance'. Thomas does not mean by 'person' the substance if this is taken as distinct from the whole human being; rather, he means by person an individual *subsisting* human being or "what subsists in a rational nature *(subsistens in rationali natura)*" (Q. 29, 3). He uses the word *subsistentia* concretely when he says, "As it exists of itself *(per se existit)* and not in another, it is called a subsistence" (Q. 29, 2). This understanding may be taken as a modification of Boethius's definition, because Thomas does not include the notion of person wholly in the order of substance; it includes the existence *(esse)*. His definition approximates that of Richard of St. Victor: "a divine person is an incommunicable existence of the divine nature" *(De Trinitate, IV, 22)*, though for Richard 'existence' in this context implied a coming forth *(ex-sistere)* from another.[30] Thomas does have a phenomenological dimension to his understanding of person (e.g., one who initiates action from intelligence and freedom) and a metaphysical dimension; the latter is dominant.

The word 'subsistence' was initially a concrete word, being a translation of the Greek *hypostasis* which did not cause the confusion for the Latins that the translation as 'substance' did. Later it came to be understood more abstractly, as that in virtue of which an individual thing subsists. But for our purposes here it is important to point out that it is the whole being—substance and existence—that constitutes the person. This name 'person' then should indeed be ascribed to God, though of course analogically, because what person signifies, that is, "what is most perfect in the whole of nature, namely the subsisting reality in a rational nature" (Q. 29, 3), should be ascribed to God who is supremely perfect. And Scripture indicates that what constitutes person is found in God, even if the word 'person' is not used in Scripture of God.

What does the word 'person' designate in God? It designates the *individual* subsisting divine being. As Scriptures' account of how Jesus spoke of his relation to the Father and then Gregory Nazianzen and later doctrinal development showed, it was by *relation* that the Father was distinguished from the Son, and vice versa. The Father and the Son are one in being (Jn 10:30), but, as their relational names indicate, distinct by relations. What can this mean?

This question sends us back to where we discover relation in our human experience and how we analyze it. In our human experience relation is a central reality. It is not surprising then that Aristotle numbered 'relation' as one of the basic categories of being.[31] For example, there is a relation between a cause and that which it causes, between things as they can be compared as to quality or quantity, between teacher and student, governors and those governed, and so forth. Closer to our use here, within the family, parents have a relation to one another as husband and wife, and a relation to their children as parents or father and mother, while the children are by that very word designated by their relation to their parents, whether as sons or daughters. And so too these children have relations with one another as brothers and sisters. Relations are found very broadly in society, and indeed in the physical world as a whole. For example, as members of a particular society men and women have a relation as citizens to the goal of that society and the constitutive principles and origin of that society. A planet has relations to other bodies in its galaxy and the universe (from *uni* + *versus*, the past participle of *vertere* [to turn]—turned into one) as a whole—relations to its sources and to bodies that it in turn affects. Relations are largely what hold us together or unite us and what distinguish us.

There are elements found in a relationship, particularly one that is based on causality or action. There is the basis or *foundation* of the relationship, for example, the act by which parents generate an offspring. There are the two *terms*, for example, parents and child. And there is the *reference* itself or relationship. While the foundation may be transient, the ensuing relationship is enduring. And there is a real distinction between the terms. The *terminus a quo* of the parents' relationship is within themselves, while the *terminus ad quem* of this relationship is the child; and for the child the relationship is in the opposite direction. This follows the fact that the action originates in the parents and is received in the child.

Many relationships are *real*; that is, they are there in reality to be discovered. But some are called *relations of reason* to indicate that it is an act of a human mind that establishes the relationship. For example, a piece of cloth with alternating red and white stripes and a section with white stars on a blue background is a flag symbolic of or referring to the United States of America. It did not have this relationship before it was put there by a human decision. The words we use in a particular language have similarly been given a relationship to a particular reality or idea.

What does this have to do with the trinitarian persons? The early Fathers knew that Father and Son were distinct by generation. The Father communicates the divine nature to the Son by generating him, and the Son thus receives the divine nature from the Father. But when in the later fourth century philosophers said that if the divine persons are distinct they have to have different substances, Gregory Nazianzen said they were distinct by *relations*. The reality of divine generation of a Son or saying of a Word preexists our human insight into it, and we know it only by virtue of God's revelation through Jesus Christ and the Spirit. But once it is revealed, the elements of a real relationship similarly are present in God, though of course only analogically.

First, we must note that counter to the other 'accidents' or modifications of being, such as quality or quantity, relation as to its *nature* does not designate something inhering in the being to which it ascribed but its reference to another. As to its *existence*, in created beings relationship, like the other accidents, has an existence that is an 'inexistence' *(inesse)*, as distinct from the existence of the substance; that is, it exists in and in virtue of the existence of the being; in this sense it inheres in the being. When ascribed to God nothing that is an 'accident' or modification of being in creatures is ascribed as an accident. For example, wisdom is not in God as a modification of the divine being but as the divine being. Similarly, relation is not ascribed to the divine being as an 'inexistence'; it *is* the divine being; its *esse* is the divine *esse*. 'Relation' of its nature says something different from 'the divine being' because it says reference to another, but in reality it is not distinct from the divine being itself; its reality is that of the divine being itself.

What is essential to a real relationship is then found in the relationships that are really in God. In the relationship between Father and Son there is a real foundation or basis, the communication and reception of the divine nature; there is a real reference of the Father to the Son (Paternity), and the Son to the Father (Filiation); and there is a real distinction between these references or relationships. Paternity's *terminus a quo*, like that of generating, is the Father, and the *terminus ad quem* is the Son. In Filiation the *terminus a quo*, beginning from the one who has received the divine nature, is the Son and the *terminus ad quem* is the Father. This explanation is in no way an attempt to prove that such distinction exists in God. It is rather faith seeking understanding and an effort to remove objections to what is revealed, namely that the Father and the Son are one being and are yet really distinct from one another.

Thomas faces the following objection to this position: "It seems that the relations which are in God are not really distinct from one another. Whatever are one and the same with a certain reality are identical with one another. But every relation existing in God is the same in its reality with the divine essence; therefore the relationships are not really distinguished from one another" (ST I, 28, 3, obj. 1). His answer is as follows:

> According to the Philosopher (in 3 Phy., tex 21) that argument holds, namely that whatever are identical with one and the same reality are identical with one another, in those things which are the same both in reality and in meaning (ratione), like 'tunic' and 'clothing', but not in those which differ in meaning. Hence in the same place he says that although action and being moved or passion are the same movement, it does not follow that action and receiving action (passio) are the same, because in action there is implied a relationship in the one from which the movement occurs in the moved, in being moved however as that which is from the other. Similarly, although paternity is the same according to reality with the divine essence, and likewise filiation, however these two in their proper meanings imply opposite references; hence they are distinguished from one another. (ST I, 28, 3, ad 1)

A mystery and indeed a paradoxical mystery, yes; a contradiction, no.

The word 'person' directly designates in God the relation as subsisting (see ST I, 29, 4). It does not designate the essence directly, since in the meaning of person the nature is designated only indirectly; it is the individual that is designated directly. And although it is by relations that one person is distinguished from the other, the word person does not designate directly the relation as relation, because the word 'person' designates "a distinct subsistent in a rational nature" (De Pot. 9,4). The relation Paternity subsists by virtue of the divine being; it is not distinct from this divine being save by a 'rational' distinction; that is, when we say relation we mean something different than what we mean by 'divine being'. But God is so far beyond our concepts that what is distinct among varied concepts we ascribe to him is not distinct in God. Distinction occurs in God only between subsistent relations.

Thomas faced the objection that 'person' signifies something absolute, and so it does not designate in God something relative. He acknowledges the strength of this objection, but he says that "this name 'person' [in God] is said of something in itself, not in its relationship (dicitur ad se, non ad alterum), because it signifies the relationship not in its modality as relation but in its modality as substance, which is the hypostasis" (ST I, 29, 4, ad 1). We should note that this response by Thomas and some other passages seem to indicate he sees the fact that person designates in God the relationship almost as a liability. This response shows that he really does not fully share the modern notion of person and that he is primarily trying to clarify the three as *distinct* from one another while all three are one divine being. What he has done remains an essential and, I think, indispensable contribution to trinitarian theology that is of continuing importance. But later, with many contemporary theologians, we will suggest that relationship is not a liability in this matter.[32]

In the first procession then there are two mutually opposed and thus distinct relationships in that the Father generates his Son or speaks his Word.[33] The second procession is called spiration and/or procession, and Augustine particularly analyzed it on the model of love. We examined the use of the analogy of love in chapter 7 to understand a bit how the Father and the Son (or through the Son) communicate the divine being totally to the Holy Spirit—not that there is a 'receiver' as it were preceding and distinct from this communication, but the receiver is constituted by this communication.[34] The act of love is a response to the good presented to the will and, moreover, the good as known. In love properly, we love and thus respond to the good known. The energy that attracts us in this act and the energy present in our loving, or the energy that love is, are the same. But the directions of this acting energy differ in that in the good attracting us the movement is from the good known to the lover, while in the act of love the movement is from the lover to the good known. Thus, there is an action that is the basis for the relationship, and there are mutually opposed relationships. Applying this to what is revealed, we speak of the divine good *as* in the Father and this divine good *as* known in the Son spirating the love that is the Holy Spirit. It is the same divine energy or being operative in the spirating and in the love (what Thomas calls procession) itself, but it takes distinct directions. Thus it bases mutually opposed subsistent relationships.

Some may say that the two processions constitute four real relationships; should this then, logically, constitute four divine persons if the analogy is consistently applied? Not at all, because person is a distinct subsistent relationship in God, but there is not a basis to distinguish 'spiration' from Father and/or Son. The Father's generating and spirating are bases for two relationships, but there is not a mutual opposition between these bases so that they would constitute two persons; and the same could be said of the Son's being generated and spirating. Neither could spirating belong to the Father while processing belongs to the Son, since the Son proceeds by an act of knowledge or generation, not one of will or love as such. Thus, the analogy supports and does not weaken the revealed message that there are three and only three really distinct persons in God, Father, Son, and Holy Spirit.

2. Some Consequences for the Relations among the Divine Persons, and How Language Is Appropriate to This Mystery

In this section we will be discussing, in only an introductory fashion, some questions Thomas treats in ST I, 30, art. 3 and 4; 31; and 39–42. First, some questions about plurality in the Godhead, then about the relation of the persons to the essence and one another, and then a comparison of our understanding with that of some other theologians. These questions are about both what we are ascribing to God in accord with the revealed mystery and the language appropriate to the mystery. They are not insignificant, since the issues they treat have been the occasion for a number of heresies in the course of Christian history. What Augustine wrote about theological reflection on the Trinity more generally is true too of these matters: "Nowhere else is a mistake more dangerous, or the search more laborious, or discovery more advantageous" (De Trinitate, I,1,5).

a. Plurality in God

In speaking about the mystery of God being three persons in one being, our language is stretched to its limit. For example, number is in our common use based on quantity, and yet there is no quantity in God. But one of the 'transcendentals', that is, perfections that are ascribed to all being (truth, goodness, beauty, thing) is unity. When we ascribe unity as a transcendental attribute of being, it adds to being only the denial of division, not the addition of quantity. "Therefore whenever [in this sense] we call anything 'one', we mean that it is an undivided reality. . . . Likewise when we speak of 'many things', the many here refers to the things in question with the implication than none of them is divided" (ST I, 30, 3; Blackfriars' trans.). So in God we assert one being and three persons. The word 'person' used in the plural means that all the three are what is signified by 'person', but this word does not mean that they are all the same. As the term 'a certain man' is somewhat intermediate between predicating humanity of an individual and calling him by his given name, for instance, Socrates, so when we say there are three persons in God we are thinking of "what is common to the divine persons . . . the concept that each of them subsists in the divine nature and is distinct from the others" (ST, I, 30, 4; Blackfriars' trans.). In fact, each divine person is radically distinct as a person from the others.

How do we speak of this plurality in unity or unity in plurality? Unity refers to the essence, while Trinity indicates directly the persons. To avoid the error of Arius, we cannot say that the Father is another 'it' (aliud) from the Son because this (neuter) word refers to divine being; similarly, we should avoid words that signify a different essence, as saying that the Father is different from the Son. But to avoid the error of Sabellius, we must say that the Father is another *(alius)* from the Son (*ST* I, 31, 2) because this (personal pronoun) word refers to person; and we do say he is *distinct* from the Son. Jesus said, "The Father and I are one" (Jn 10:30).

The use of abstract and concrete terms of the persons also calls for caution (*ST* I, 32, 3). In our usual discourse, an abstract term (e.g., whiteness or humanity) indicates something simple but not existing, while a concrete term (e.g., white or man) indicates something existing but also composed. These creaturely 'modes of signifying' must be removed when we use such terms of God. We speak of both 'divinity' and 'God' without implying a distinction between what is signified by these two words. Similarly, we use both abstract and concrete terms of the persons, without indicating any distinction between what is designated by these terms (e.g., Paternity and Father). The abstract term used for a person is both a *property*, that is, that by which one person is distinguished from another, and a 'notion' *(notio)*, that is, an idea by which one person becomes known to us *(innotescit)* as distinct from another. The property is the same in reality as the relationship. The 'notions' or, to use another word, characteristics, are ideas referring to the relations, and having the note of some dignity for the person. Thus, for the Father, there are the characteristics of Paternity and Active Spiration, but also that of 'Unoriginated' to designate that he does not come from another—a characteristic that implies a certain dignity. For the Son there are the characteristics of Filiation and of Active Spiration. And for the Holy Spirit there is the distinguishing mark of Passive Spiration or Procession.

b. Relations of the Persons to the Divine Being and to One Another

Thomas treats these questions in *ST* I, 39–42. We say that the three persons are of one essence, considering the essence as the *form* of the persons. If we use *nouns* signifying the divine essence, they are predicated of the three in the singular, because the three persons share one form (as distinct, e.g., from three men who do not have the same form). For example, we say Father, Son, and Holy Spirit are one God and one Being. "*Adjectives* signifying the divine essence, however, are predicated of the divine persons in the plural because of the plurality of supposits. . . . [e.g., there are] three who are existent, wise, eternal, uncreated, immeasurable" (*ST* I, 39, 4, Blackfriars).

If we compare the persons to the relations, we have to say that the relation is the same in reality and according to our understanding as the person, which is constituted by relation. In fact, the persons are constituted more by relation than by the process of origin, since the latter is considered as the *way* to the second and third persons, and the relation is that *by which* one person is distinguished from another. In the case of the Father, we must make a distinction. When Paternity is considered as constitutive of the person, then Paternity is in our minds intellectually prior to the relationship since the person precedes its action. When Paternity is considered as a relationship, it is in our minds subsequent to the act of generating that is its foundation or basis (see *ST* I, 40, 4).

In reference to a consideration of the persons in relation to the acts by which they originate another or are originated (*actus notionales*, i.e., acts by which a person is distinguished from another), we recall that in chapter 6 we discussed the question of the presence of love and freedom in the Father's generating of the Son.[35] We shall not repeat this here, but below we will compare our view concerning the relation of the persons to their acts with that of some other theologians.

In comparing the persons to one another, Thomas follows creeds, councils, and the Fathers in holding their equality. Equality here is a question, of course, not of quantity but of perfection. From our human experience, some had thought that the Father precedes the Son in eternity. But the Father would not be Father without the Son, and generation in God does not involve successive acts, so the priority is one of order not of time. And this priority does not imply a superior power or majesty, since each is the divine essence. Indeed, the Father is in the Son by virtue of the essence he shares with the Son, by the relation which involves the presence of its correlative, and by origin since the Father communicates his divine being to the Son. We can speak similarly of the Son with reference to the Father, and of the Holy Spirit in relation to the Father and the Son (see *ST* I, 42, 5). St. Thomas does not use the words *circumincessio* or *circuminsessio* or, as the Greeks call it, *perichoresis*, but that is what he means when he writes of the mutual indwelling. When we speak of the modern sense of person, we will return to this question from a more personal perspective, though we may say that the indwelling of one person in another is indeed personal for Thomas since it is through acts of love and knowledge. These issues have a continuing validity and relevance for our time. Thomas's view is counter to some theologians who argue that the order among the divine persons involves a subordinationism and is counter to the equality of the persons.

c. Is the Act of Consciousness One or Three in God?

William Hill writes as follows:

> Consciousness in God is a prerogative of the divine nature, but by definition it calls for a subject or subjects who exercise such consciousness. . . . All three

persons know the divine truth and love the divine goodness and thereby are themselves known and loved. This constitutes *essential* consciousness, knowledge and love. . . . In the single act of eternal knowing, then, it is necessary to understand that *God* (or the Father by appropriation) knows and that at the very heart of such knowing, the *Father*, in an act that is proper to him and not appropriated [*notional* consciousness], utters his Word or generates his Son.[36]

In my understanding, if we take consciousness as an act, we should say that there are three who in the Godhead are conscious, the Father, Son, and Holy Spirit, because there are only three subjects, and acts are of or by the subject. If we take consciousness as a power, or that *by which* the three act, then this consciousness is one because the three know in virtue of the same divine essence or being. Therefore, there is not 'a single act of eternal knowing', because it is the Father, the Son, and the Holy Spirit who know. So also, when we speak of the divine knowledge from which the Word emerges as its term it seems to me that it is the Father who knows, not God and the Father only by appropriation. This knowledge, as distinct from the *saying* of the word, is an 'essential act' in the sense that it has the divine being as its object, but not in a sense that there is some subject, such as the divine essence, other than the three who know. The act of the Father knowing the divine essence is distinct from the act of the Son knowing the divine essence; the Son's knowing is by the same divine being, but it is his *as* by that divine being received through generation. The knowing is not proper to the Father in the sense that it is that which properly distinguishes him as a person from the Son as the subsisting relationship does; but since he is distinct from the Son, his act is distinct too. If we can say there are three who *are*, though they are by the same being, we can say there are three who know even in that aspect of their knowledge that is theirs by virtue of the same divine being.[37]

The interpretation of Thomas's position by Hill and others is in part behind Walter Kasper's preference for Richard of St. Victor's position. He writes, for example:

The defect in the main strand of Western tradition is that it interprets the adjustment of trinity to unity as a matter of knowing and willing and therefore of essential actions of God. . . . This tendency . . . ultimately leads to modalism. . . . [Counter to this] the doctrine of the Trinity must start with the Father and understand him as origin, source and inner ground of unity in the Trinity. . . . If we thus take God's sovereign freedom in love as the starting point and focus of unity in the Trinity, we are moving, unlike the predominant Latin tradition, not from the nature of God but from the Father who originally possesses the being of God that consists in love.[38]

As I indicated previously, I agree that theology starts with the personal God whom the Old Testament proclaimed and whom Jesus called Father, not with the divine nature. In this way I agree with Kasper. But if we put Thomas's position within the context of beginning with the personal God rather than the divine nature, we can conclude that Thomas's view as such does not lead to modalism. Also, is it not important to agree with Thomas and the larger tradition, somewhat counter to Richard of St. Victor, that the first procession is indeed one of 'saying' the Word or generation, though one that is infinitely loving, and thus an act properly of 'nature' rather than of will? It is true that God is Love, but God is also Truth. And the unity of Truth and Love is radically questioned or misinterpreted today. Perhaps this question cannot be resolved, even to the extent that questions about such a mystery can be resolved, within the limits of classical theology. So we turn to the question of how we would use a modern sense of person in a trinitarian theology, and in that context we will return to the question of the one and three.

III. A Modern Sense of Person and the Mystery of the Trinity

In the first chapter, we saw that a central issue in trinitarian theology in our time is how we relate a modern sense of person to the church's belief that there are three persons in God.[39] In this section we will propose a tentative reply to whether and in what sense a modern sense of the person may be used in trinitarian theology. For this purpose we will recall several relevant passages of Scripture, show limits of the classical teaching on persons to do justice to Scripture, indicate some modern meanings of person and why they are inadequate for understanding either human or divine persons, suggest some elements of a valid contemporary philosophy of the human person and ask whether this can be used analogically of the three divine persons.

The concrete personal relationships among Father, Son, and Holy Spirit, and between them and us shown in Scripture seem to go beyond the classical trinitarian concepts (at least Thomistic) in two ways. They stress the distinction in consciousness among the three, and they emphasize the relationality of each toward the other in a way that suggests that a divine person is as much a relation to the Other as an 'in itself'. For example, in John, Jesus says, "The Father and I are one" (Jn 10:30), indicating a personal consciousness distinct from that of the Father, or an awareness of himself as a subject distinct from the Father. Also, he prays, "that they may all be one, as *you*, Father, are in *me* and I in *you*, that they also may be in *us*, that the world may believe that *you* sent *me*" (Jn 17:21). This reflects the Father's assertion at the baptism of Jesus: "*You* are *my* beloved Son" (Mk 1:11). And of the Holy

Spirit: "The Advocate, the holy Spirit that the Father will send in *my* name—*he* [better: she] will teach you everything and remind you of all that I told you" (Jn 14:26). These passages suggest that the Father and the Son are identified as distinct centers of consciousness and agency or distinct subjects within a unity of being, and as relations of personal knowledge and love for the other.

In the primitive church, we are shown initiatives of the Holy Spirit. For example, in a key event in Antioch, "the holy Spirit said, 'Set apart for *me* Barnabas and Saul for the work to which *I* have called them'" (Acts 13:2). And at the conclusion of the Council of Jerusalem, the church leaders wrote, "It is the decision of the holy Spirit and of us. . ." (Acts 15:28). Thus we have personal statements as it were from each of the divine persons that show each as a distinct center of consciousness and agency, as well as one with one another in being and mutual personal indwelling. Moreover, in Christian prayer at times we address in distinct prayers the Father, the Son, and the Holy Spirit. Thus, we show our Christian consciousness in that we are addressing distinct centers of divine consciousness, according to the adage *Lex orandi, lex credendi* (the rule of prayer is the norm of faith).[40]

It seems to many of us that the classical theological interpretation of Father, Son, and Holy Spirit does not do justice to what Scripture and Christian consciousness in prayer reflect. The language of Scripture and prayer has a primacy over that of theology.[41] Much of theology is rightly and necessarily objective language about God, and thus it inevitably falls short of the full Christian belief and experience of God.

But even within the limits of objective language about the three persons, is Thomas's theology adequate? Actually, he thought that the Our Father was addressed to the Trinity as a whole and not to the Father (see *ST* II-II, 83, 9), and this is now not accepted as an adequate interpretation of this prayer. Moreover, as we have said before, the problem for classical theology after Nicea was to show that there could be three distinct persons who were *homoousion*, of one being, and thus the question was focused on the persons as *distinct* from one another. It is open to question whether Thomas did justice to the way that Scripture seems to attest to the three persons as three centers of consciousness with a dynamic mutual personal indwelling. He did speak of the persons as subsistent relations, but this was to show them as distinct 'individuals'. The way he answered objections to this position showed that he considered 'relationality' as something of a liability, since for him person signifies something *in itself* (*ST* I, 29, 4, c., and ad 1). Also, while Thomas spoke of the indwelling of one person in the other, this was by reason of essence, relationship, and origin (*ST* I, 42, 5). This explanation is implicitly a personal form of indwelling because the actions by which one is related to the others are of knowledge and love, but perhaps the dynamic personal character of this mutual indwelling could be more explicitly affirmed. Though we suggest that the theology of the three as persons can still develop further than Thomas brought us, we consider his theology here essential to contemporary trinitarian theology and as having constructive implications beyond those he explicitly drew. More on this later.

Some characteristic modern developments in the understanding of what it means to be a person have been paradoxical. In part we have to admit that the medieval church and theologians found it consistent with their understanding of person to justify slavery, to kill persons who were heretics, and to use torture. Up into the twentieth century, popes could consider most Catholics as not having an active share in the guidance of the church. St. Pius X wrote: "In the hierarchy alone reside the power and the authority necessary to move and direct all the members of the Church to its end. As for the multitude, they have no other right than to allow themselves to be governed and to follow their pastors in docility."[42] Such a view still exists in parts of our world. But Western philosophical developments in the understanding of the person have significantly contributed at least to eradicating such practices in the North Atlantic countries and to challenging practices counter to human rights in other parts of the world. The church has learned from modern developments in the understanding of what it means to be a person.

However, modern philosophical views on what it means to be a person have also been used to justify abortion, a radical individualism, total human autonomy in moral decision making, and a postmodernism that holds that: "One experiences only what can be experienced within historical time and space: (1) not foundations beyond history; (2) not realities that can be known, without bias, as objective correlatives; and (3) not universal subjective characteristics, inherent in all persons."[43] There have been many studies and critiques of the Western contemporary understanding of the person, but we shall severely restrict ourselves here and direct the reader to these more adequate sources.[44] Balthasar summarizes a great deal when he states that in the modern development of the meaning of person,

the philosophical "independence" of the person sought first to define itself as subjective self-consciousness (Descartes [and, we could add, Locke]), and this independence then absolutized itself very soon (Spinoza, Hegel) so that the individuals had to give themselves up to this Absolute. . . . Thus there was nothing preserved of a fundamental interrelatedness of persons—as a meaningfully understood *imago Trinitatis* would have demanded.[45]

Theological uses of modern philosophical interpretations of the meaning of person have been made in ways that are distorting of Scripture's and tradition's message concerning the mystery of the Trinity. For example, in the nineteenth century Anton Günther understood the person as self-consciousness. Applying this human experience of the self to the Trinity, he is interpreted as holding that as there are three persons, there are three self-consciousnesses, and thus too three substances and absolute realities, distinct one from the other. The unity that remained was a moral unity that came from relations of origin.[46] A number of commentators on Rahner and Barth's resistance to the use of a modern meaning of person in a theology of the Trinity ascribe to them the German idealist sense of the person as an absolute autonomous center of consciousness and action. With this interpretation a theologian must deny that Father, Son, and Holy Spirit are three persons.

Some theologians have rejected the classical view of person as a "subsisting reality in a rational nature" because they reject philosophy as having any competence in this area (e.g., Jenson, Moltmann). Consequently, they have rejected the Nicene-Constantinopolitan *homoousion*. Rather, they identified the divine unity with the interrelation of the divine persons. Counter to their assertion, they do not have support for their position in the Cappadocian Fathers.[47] Moreover they seem to make the distinction of divine persons dependent on the history, death, and resurrection of Jesus Christ which have a retroactive efficacy on the constitution of the Trinity as such. Ironically, this modern viewpoint manifests an unexamined dependence on a philosophy, such as that of Hegel, as well as a rejection of Scripture's and tradition's normative teaching. This same dissociation between a phenomenological identification of the meaning of person (e.g., the person is self-consciousness, or relationship with another person) and a metaphysical analysis is behind many contemporary justifications of abortion and mercy killings. Also, at least some uses of Whitehead's process philosophy (e.g., Pittinger) similarly constitute a rejection of Scripture and tradition as normative.

Yet, there are elements of the modern philosophical meaning of person that enhance our understanding both of human persons and divine persons. For example, the sense of the interiority and subjectivity of the person is accentuated by the modern emphases on self-consciousness and moral agency as characteristic of persons. In part, this emphasis is not discontinuous with classical theologians such as Augustine and Thomas, but in part too it cuts off the person from the larger world. To give both some positive and some negative elements of this understanding, we may offer two quotations from philosophers. McLean writes:

Another approach [distinct from Locke's] was attempted by Kant whose identification of the salient characteristics of the person has become a standard component for modern sensitivity. . . . For Kant the person is above all free, both in oneself and in relation to others; in no sense is the person to be used by others as a means. . . . This "glorious ideal" has been perhaps the major contribution to the formation of our modern understanding of ourselves as persons.[48]

Schmitz writes:

[W]hat is distinctive about the modern principle of subjectivity is the process of *inward uniqueness outwardizing itself*. In contrast to this modern sense of privacy, the older theological *interiority* arises out of an open intimacy with God. . . . The term *subjectivity* is intellectual short-hand for the modern history of the unique inwardness of individual human beings insofar as they feel themselves threatened by an objectified—and largely material, quantified and reified—world.[49]

While interiority is a major basis for the modern sense of the unassailable dignity of the individual person, modern experience has also led to a new emphasis on relationality. Balthasar ascribes the source of this insight partially to Feuerbach for whom:

existence as a person comes about only in the relationship between the I and Thou. The atheist materialist was the one who reached beyond Augustine to the insight about what man is, in Christian terms, as the personal *imago Trinitatis*. Martin Buber also began with Feuerbach and then sketched the history of modern personalism. . . . First with Guardini, then more strongly with Mounier, Gabriel Marcel, and Denis de Rougemont does something of a true image of the Trinity appear—in any case, the connection of the I, which is open to the Thou and the We and which realizes itself only in self-giving, with the image of man in Scripture, and above all in the New Testament.[50]

I previously sought to reach beyond contemporary dissociations concerning what it means to be a person in our world through evaluating Thomas's understanding of person by a phenomenology that uses the insights of modern developmental psychology, particularly Erik Erikson, and of contemporary social experience.[51] A modern phenomenology sees the human person as searching for his or her way in a world that is changing and enlarging as the person's human capacities and environment grow. Also, maturity involves a commitment by a person to a human community larger than himself or herself and a faithfulness to that commitment. The person is both a center of agency and a relationality. Relationality is central to who this person is, because the person's whole life is intentional, that is, directed to the human good, to others, and, we hold, to God, and also because the person owes so much of his or her being, initiation into self-awareness as a person, and engagement with others to persons around him or her and, of course, ultimately to God.

Is an authentically modern sense of person fruitful for illuminating our understanding in faith of God as three persons? We may recall that Rahner wrote, "there are not three consciousnesses [in God]; rather, the one consciousness subsists in a threefold way."[52]

The dictionary defines 'conscious' as follows: "having an awareness of one's own existence, sensations, [and, we may add, acts] and thoughts, and of one's environment," and 'consciousness' as: "the state of being conscious."[53] We have to agree that the three divine persons are not three *autonomous* centers of action or three centers of consciousness as three human beings are. But we ascribe 'person' to God only analogically where the differences are greater than the similarities, and it is the view of many theologians today that the modern sense of person has something of value to illuminate the revealed mystery of the Trinity. In the words of Scripture quoted earlier, the Son's knowing or saying "I" is not the Father's knowing or saying "I." Of the Father, the Son says "He," as the Father says "He" of the Son. The Father is conscious that his act of consciousness is distinct from that of the Son. If consciousness is an *act* or state of action, as it is, there are three who act, because the acts are ascribed to the subject and not directly to the essence; it is the person who acts, not the nature or essence; there are distinct *exercises* of knowledge as there are of being in the Godhead. Only if consciousness is considered as a power, namely, that *by which* the divine persons are conscious, then there is one consciousness in God as there is only one divine being by which the three are. We have treated this issue earlier in this chapter, and need not repeat it here. The mystery of the unity of being and the distinction of persons in the Trinity is a spiritually rich mystery because it shows us the unity and yet continuing personal identity to which we are called. We will reflect further on this in the next chapter.

In us, being and the exercise of personal being in freedom and intelligence are distinguished because we are finite and the latter take time to develop. In God, being and act are one, and as personal being, God should be more identified with active intelligence and love which in us are the perfection of personal being than with being that is in us the beginning of a long process. So in a way, God would be better conceived by us as the fullness of personal knowledge and love than as he who is, since the latter for us is the beginning of development. What should be preeminent in our conception of God is total knowledge and love, and these are the acts of the three persons, rather than being which is the oneness of God. This seems to be closer to the New Testament revelation of God. This allows us also to do more justice to the real mutuality of love among the persons in the Trinity than Rahner's resistance to the modern notion of person permits.

This brings us to another aspect of a modern sense of person, namely *relationality.* Psychological studies have shown that the infant who first identifies with the mother or mother figure distinguishes himself or herself from the mother around the age of two and only then reidentifies with the mother but now as a distinct person. The child develops a sense of self only through interacting with a person and differentiating self as a center of agency from the other. Relationality is in a way the source of the human person since he or she is brought into existence by an act of love and develops through the continuance of such love. An experience of relationality is essential for the development of the child to genuine personal living. And mature personal living is possible only for those who make and are faithful to the costly commitments of love for others that engagement in life for the community and not only for self entails. An autistic child for some reason has not developed early relationships, and so knows himself or herself in only a primitive way.

This allows us to recognize relationality as constitutive of person in a way that earlier theologians perhaps did not. The Father, Son, and Holy Spirit are persons in virtue of their relations to one another. Considering them as infinitely active persons, this means that this relationship is one of knowledge and love. Thomas considered the divine persons to be in one another in virtue of the one essence, relations, and origin (ST I, 42, 5). This is true, but perhaps it is better to see them as in one another more directly in virtue of knowledge and love; this is implied in Thomas's teaching. So too we should understand them as persons *in virtue* of this personal interrelationship, rather than this mutual indwelling as a *consequence* of their being distinct persons. That is, their interrelation is constitutive of them as three persons; they are not three persons antecedent to our consideration of (or abstracting from) this mutual indwelling. This mutual knowledge and love is what is meant by *perichoresis,* from a Greek word, *perichorein,* meaning making room for one another about oneself.[54] It expresses a dynamic interrelationship better than the Latin *circuminsessio,* or being in one another. We may quote from F. Bourassa here, as he integrates a modern sense of personal relationality in his interpretation of the Trinity:

For the divine person, the lived actuality of his relationship to the others is not a perfection to which the person comes as though passing beyond himself; it is his entire being, his divine existence—personal, eternal, infinite. In the pure and unique act of divine consciousness and love each of the persons exercises totally and personally, in the fullness of divinity, this pure act of divine existence as a total engagement of himself toward the others. The divine I is, insofar as I, substantially an I for the other (a subsistent relation)—from its origin a gift of self.[55]

Kasper shows how this difference of emphasis relates to the Eastern and Western approaches to the Trinity:

> The Greeks start with the hypostases and understand the perichoresis as an active reciprocal penetration; the perichoresis is as it were the bond uniting the persons. The Latin theologians, on the contrary, usually start with the unity of the divine nature and understand the perichoresis more as reciprocal coinherence on the basis of the one nature. In the Latins the perichoresis represents not so much movement in God as repose in God. Here, too, Thomas Aquinas seeks a synthesis; he bases the perichoresis both on the one nature and on relations of origin.[56]

It is our conviction that the perspective we have presented also helps us with the questions of equality and mutuality among the divine persons. The Father, Son, and Holy Spirit are really distinct ways of being persons, and yet all share equally the same divine being. None alone is the Trinity, and each is in some sense interdependent. The Son is 'dependent' on the Father, but the Father is not Father without the Son. To receive is not a sign of being less; in fact, love is not love if it only gives, it must also be receptive.[57] It is not only the Son who receives; the Father receives from the Son that imaging and response of love that are essential for the Trinity. Similarly, the Holy Spirit receives from the Father and the Son by their spiration, but the Father and Son receive the Love that is the Holy Spirit, without which, once more, God would not be Trinity.

It is our hope that the above introductory and tentative interpretation of the Father, Son, and Holy Spirit as three persons will contribute to the convergence between the Latin and Greek trinitarian theologies and will help somewhat to overcome disunity among Christian theologians in the West on this issue. Some implications of this interpretation for Christian living will be discussed in the following chapter.

Notes

1. See chapter 4, 112–115; chapter 1, 13–15.
2. See, for example, Piergiorgio Gianazza, "Mistero trinitario e Islam," in Angelo Amato, ed., *Trinità in contesto* (Rome: Libreria Ateneo Salesiano, 1994), 225–271.

3. See chapter 1, 10–12, 17–19.

4. Stanley Rudman, *Concepts of Personhood and Christian Ethics* (New York: Cambridge University Press, 1997), 129; see also 143.

5. J. Farrelly, *Belief in God in Our Time* (Collegeville, Minn.: Liturgical Press, 1992), 182.

6. See Reinhard Flogaus, "Palamas and Barlaam Revisited: A Reassessment of East and West in the Hesychast Controversy of 14th Century Byzantium," *St. Vladimir's Theological Quarterly* 42 (1998): 1–32. Flogaus shows that both Barlaam and Palamas use Augustine, and that this controversy is an intra-Orthodox dispute.

7. See *Origins* 28, no. 19 (Oct. 22, 1998): 317–347.

8. Hans Urs von Balthasar, "On the Concept of Person," *Communio* 13 (1986): 19.

9. Aloys Grillmeier, S.J., *Christ in Christian Tradition.* Vol. 1, *From the Apostolic Age to Chalcedon (451)*, 2d ed. (Atlanta: John Knox Press, 1975), 125–126. See also Kenneth Schmitz, "The Geography of the Human Person," *Communio* 13 (1986): 27–48.

10. 1 *Apology* 36, 1–2, as cited in Michael Slusser, "The Exegetical Roots of Trinitarian Theology," *TS* 49 (1988): 464. As Slusser writes in reference to Tertullian's use of the same method, "In other words, the dialogue structure of Scripture enables us to identify Father, Son, and Spirit as the interlocutors, inside or outside of the text" (465).

11. See chapter 3, 76–77. Also see Grillmeier, *From the Apostolic Age*, 117–131.

12. Grillmeier, *From the Apostolic Age*, 128.

13. B. Studer, "Hypostasis," in *EEC* 1:401. On Origen's use of this word, see above, chapter 3, 77–79.

14. See chapter 3, 82.

15. See chapter 3, 86–88. Also see two articles in Stephen Davis, Daniel Kendall, S.J., and Gerald O'Collins, S.J., eds., *The Trinity: An Interdisciplinary Symposium on the Trinity* (Oxford: Oxford University Press, 1999): Joseph Lienhard, S.J., "*Ousia* and *Hypostasis*: The Cappadocian Settlement and the Theology of 'One *Hypostasis*,'" 99–122, and Sarah Coakley, "'Persons' and the 'Social' Doctrine of the Trinity: A Critique of Current Analytic Discussion," 123–144. Lienhard shows how strong the 'one *Hypostasis*' interpretation of the Trinity was in the fourth century and how the Cappadocians stressed even more the unity of action among the three than the unity of nature. Coakley shows how wrong some contemporary theologians are who use the Cappadocians to support a social doctrine of the Trinity.

16. See, for example, Gregory Nazianzen, "The Third Theological Oration," #2, in *NPNF*, vol. 7: 301.

17. Sections 13, 16, NPNF 7: 305, 307. Also see "Fifth Theological Oration," especially section 9 (320), where he distinguishes the three by "their mutual relations one to another"; "the very fact of being Unbegotten or Begotten, or Proceeding has given the name[s] . . . that the distinction of the Three Persons may be preserved in the one nature and dignity of the Godhead."

18. See, for example, Catherine LaCugna, "The Cappadocian Theology of Divine Relations," in *God for Us* (San Francisco: Harper, 1991), 53–79.

19. Gregory of Nyssa, *Against Eunomius*, book II, 2, *NPNF*, vol. 5, 103. In this section, Gregory underlines the name of Father as a name of a relation, not of nature. And see his "On Not Three Gods," to Ablabius: "while we confess the invariable character of the nature, we do not deny the difference in respect of cause, and that which is caused, by which alone we apprehend that one Person is distinguished from another" (*NPNF*, 5: 336).

20. See John Zizioulas, "On Being a Person: Towards an Ontology of Personhood," in Christoph Schwöbel and Colin Gunton, eds., *Persons, Divine and Human: King's College Essays in Theological Anthropology* (Edinburgh: T & T Clark, 1991), 33–46.

21. See Rudman in note 4 above. To clarify a controversy on this question we can quote from Yannis Spiteris, "La Dottrina Trinitaria nella Teologia Ortodossa: Autori e prospettive," in Amato, *Trinità*, 45–70. Zizioulas interprets Basil as follows (see Spiteris, 63): "Instead of speaking of the unity of God in terms of a *single nature*, he prefers to speak in terms of the *communion of persons*: the communion is for Basil an ontological category. The *nature* of God is communion. This does not signify that the person has an ontological priority over substance in God, but that the one substance of God coincides with the communion of three persons" (from Zizioulas, "Christologie, Pneumatologie et institutions ecclesiale—Un point de vue orthodoxe," in G. Alberigo, ed., *Les Eglises après Vatican II. Dynamime et perspective. Acts du colloque international de Bologne 1980* (Paris: 1981), 131–148. A. De Halleux in "Personnalisme ou esentialisme trinitaire chez les Pères cappadociens? Une mauvaise controverse," *Revue théologique de Louvain* 17 (1986): 129–155, 265–292, writes as follows: "Is it legitimate to oppose the 'personalism' of the hypostases to the consubstantiality of Nicea, holding that the Cappadocian Fathers had repudiated the language of essence to adopt a language of communion? A simple examination of the texts taken by him [Zizioulas] in this sense will show that this is not the case" (quoted by Spiteris, 64). Also see Lucian Turcescu, "The Concept of Divine Persons in Gregory of Nyssa's 'To His Brother Peter, on the Difference Between *Ousia* and *Hypostasis*,'" *Greek Orthodox Theological Review* 42 (1997): 63–82. For example, Turcescu shows that the word Gregory used for unity of nature (*koinotetos*) differed from the word he used for the communion among the persons (*koinonia*). Also see Sarah Coakley, "'Persons' and the 'Social' Doctrine of the Trinity."

22. Basil Studer, *Trinity and Incarnation: The Faith of the Early Church* (Collegeville, Minn.: Liturgical Press, 1993), 147. We should mention that Gregory Nazianzen was the first to use the word *perichoresis* (mutual indwelling), but he used it of the two natures in Christ; John Damascene was the first to apply this to the relation among the divine persons. See Walter Kasper, *The God of Jesus Christ* (Herder and Herder, 1985), 284 and references.

23. See chapter 4, 96–99.

24. Studer, *Trinity*, 174. He cites "Trin. I 4.7; VII 3.5f. See especially Solil. I 1.2-6; CatRud 24.47, and also the fact that Augustine uses in the *Confessions* the word *Deus* for Father, e.g., VIII 1.2; IXC 4.9; XI 9.11; XIII 4.5." Michal Barnes in "Rereading

Augustine's Theology of the Trinity," in Davis, *Trinity*, 145–176 commends Studer's interpretation of Augustine's doctrine of the Trinity (149).

25. See *Trin.*, V, 10; VII, 7–11.

26. Brian Horne argues in "Person as Confession: Augustine of Hippo," in Schwöbel and Gunton, , *Persons*, 65–73, that Augustine's autobiography shows him to be closer to the modern experience of 'person' as constituted by past experiences and decisions than the Cappadocians were, with their more cosmological understanding of hypostasis.

27. DS 530.

28. See my *Belief in God*, chapter 3.

29. See Thomas Aquinas, *ST* I, 27–43. Good translations of this are found in *Summa Theologiae*, Latin text and English translation, Introduction, Notes, Appendices and Glossaries by Blackfriars (New York: McGraw Hill, 1963), vols. 6 and 7.

30. See Edmund Fortman, *The Triune God: A Historical Study of the Doctrine of the Trinity* (Philadelphia: Westminster, 1972), 191–194.

31. See *Categories*, 7. Also see *Relations: From Having to Being*, the *Proceedings of the American Catholic Philosophical Association*, vol. 66 (Washington, D.C.: Catholic University of America, 1992); and A. Krempel, *La Doctrine de la Relation chez Saint Thomas. Exposé historique et doctrinal* (Paris: Vrin, 1952); Mark Henninger, *Relations: Medieval Theories, 1250–1325* (Oxford: Clarendon Press, 1989); Earl Muller, S.J., "Real Relations and the Divine," *TS* 56 (1995): 673–695.

32. For an excellent article on this theme, see François Bourassa, S.J., "Personne et conscience en théologie trinitaire," *Gregorianum* 55 (1974): 471–493, 677–720. Bernard Lonergan's writings are prominent among those which Bourassa cites. Also see W. Norris Clarke, S.J., *Person and Being* (Milwaukee: Marquette University Press, 1993).

33. See also chapter 6, 166f.

34. See chapter 7, 204f.

35. See chapter 6, 170–171.

36. William Hill, O.P., *The Three-Personed God: The Trinity as a Mystery of Salvation* (Washington, D.C.: Catholic University of America Press, 1982), 270.

37. This confusion may be related to the classic dispute whether there are three subsistences in God or one, or one absolute and three relative subsistences in God. See, for example, A. Michel, "Relations divines," *DTC* XIII. 2, 2153–2156; and Iosepho Dalmau, S.J., *De Deo Uno et Trino* in *Sacrae Theologiae Summa* (Madrid: Biblioteca de Autores Cristianos, 1952), vol. 2, 399–402. It is in part a question of words. Like the Council of the Lateran (649) (see DS 501), Thomas uses the word 'subsistence' as a concrete term; he writes (*ST* I, 29, 2, ad 2, Blackfriars): "Just as we speak in the plural of three 'persons' and three 'subsistences' in God, so the Greeks speak of three 'hypostases'."

Later the word 'subsistence' was used also as an abstract term, namely that by which things subsist. And, as Thomas asserted, abstract terms like divinity are predicated absolutely of God; and so we could say in this sense that there is one 'subsistence' in God in the sense that each person subsists, or exists as a substance, in virtue of the same divine being.

38. Kasper, *God of Jesus Christ*, 298–299.

39. See chapter 1, 10–12, 17–19.

40. See Geoffrey Wainwright, *Doxology: The Praise of God in Worship, Doctrine and Life. A Systematic Theology* (New York: Oxford University Press, 1980), 218ff.

41. See *Belief in God*, 265.

42. Pius X, *Vehementer nos*, February 11, 1906; as quoted in Mark Mealey, O.S.F.S., "The Parish Pastoral Council: An Expression of the Lay Christian Faithful's Mission in the Parish," in William Ruhl, O.S.F.S., ed., *Salesian Spirituality: Catalyst to Collaboration* (Washington D.C.: De Sales School of Theology, 1993), 61.

43. William Dean, *History Making History: The New Historicism in American Religious Thought* (Albany: State Univiversity of New York Press, 1988), 6.

44. See, for example, Charles Taylor, *Sources of the Self: The Making of the Modern Identity* (Cambridge: Harvard University Press, 1989); J. M. Zycinski, ed., *The Human Person and Philosophy in the Contemporary World*, 2 vols. (Krakow: Pontifical Faculty of Theology, 1980); George McLean, "The Person, Moral Growth, and Character Development," in George McLean, Frederick Ellrod, et al., eds., *Act and Agent: Philosophical Foundations for Moral Education and Character Development* (Washington, D.C.: Council for Research in Values and Philosophy, 1986), 361–394; Rudman, *Concepts of Personhood*; Schwöbel and Gunton, *Persons*; articles by Balthasar and Schmitz; and *Proceedings* of the A.C.P.A., vol. 66.

45. Balthasar, "On the Concept of Person," 23–24.

46. See chapter 4, 171, and P. Godet, "Günther, Antoine," *DTC*, 6.2 (1920): 1992–1993. In 1857 Pius IX condemned some views of Günther, among them departures from the Christian explanation of "the unity of the divine substance in three distinct and eternal Persons" (DS 2828).

47. See above, fn. 21.

48. Mclean, "Person," 374–375.

49. Schmitz, "Geography," 39; see also, for example, Taylor, *Sources*, on interiority in Augustine and Descartes, 127–158, and his chapter on "Inner Nature," 185–198; McLean, "Person," 374 ff.

50. Balthasar, "On the Concept of Person," 24–25.

51. See chapter 5, 140–142, and *Belief in God*, chapter 5, "Conversion and Human Transcendence," especially 179–214. This is in continuity with Cardinal Wojtyla's interrelating phenomenology and Thomistic metaphysics in his book, *The Acting Person*. See Rocco Buttiglione, *Karol Wojtyla: The Thought of the Man Who Became Pope John Paul II* (Grand Rapids, Mich.: Eerdmans, 1997), chapter 5, "The Acting Person," 117–176. Also see Robert A. Connor, "Relational *Esse* and the Person," *Proceedings of the American Catholic Philosophical Association* 65 (1991): 253–267, and Connor, "The Person as Resonating Existential," *American Catholic Philosophical Quarterly* 66 (1992): 39–56.

52. K. Rahner, *The Trinity* (New York: Herder and Herder, 1970), 107. Also see Kasper, *God of Jesus Christ*, 285–290, on Barth's and Rahner's resistance to the use of a modern notion of person in trinitarian theology.

53. *American Heritage Dictionary of the English Language* (Boston: Houghton Mifflin, 1971), 283.

54. See Michael Lawler, "Perichoresis: New Theological Wine in an Old Theological Wineskin," *Horizons* 22 (1995): 49–65.

55. Bourassa, "Personne et conscience," 702. What he says of the divine 'I' we take as referring to the Father's 'I,' the Son's 'I,' and the Holy Spirit's 'I.'

56. Kasper, *God of Jesus Christ*, 284.

57. See Clarke, *Person and Being*.

CHAPTER NINE

~

A Trinitarian Spirituality

In this final chapter we seek to explore in an introductory fashion a trinitarian spirituality. At times in the past, unfortunately, theologians have not integrated a spirituality into their treatises on the Trinity, and so have by default weakened Christian appreciation of the relevance of the mystery of the Trinity for our individual and communal lives. By spirituality we mean the reality of the Christian's conversion and lifelong response to God's self-gift and invitation to union with God and to a share in God's saving work in the world. Here we mean specifically the theological study of such an interaction between the triune God and the Christian. So this is a study of the Trinity as it evokes this human self-gift and qualifies this self-gift, and as it is presence to this self-gift and its intentional object. We study this interaction between the Trinity and the Christian community as well as between the Trinity and the individual Christian, since the individual's call is mediated by the community, and the individual's response is partly constitutive of the community.

Our study here builds on everything we have written in this book and, indeed, on our presupposition that we human beings are by the very fact of being human seeking union with God in the depth of our being, and union with others on that basis. To be human is to be religious in this sense. And yet we and humanity generally have fallen into the power of alien spirits; we have been diverted from the loving purpose God initially gave us by creating us. Thus, we are in desperate need of being liberated from false and misleading views of ourselves and our future and from being controlled by alien spirits. Our understanding of the human subject within the context of modern

251

historical consciousness, however, is significantly different from a consciousness prevalent, for example, in the time of Thomas Aquinas. Along with a modern understanding of the human subject, there is also an evolutionary understanding of the physical world. An individual or communal subject with a valid contemporary consciousness faces God somewhat differently than a premodern subject does; the sense of being a pilgrim in a quickly changing historical environment is more prevalent—and threatening—today than at many periods of the past.

God has in his love chosen the way to save us, and it is through his Son Jesus Christ and his Holy Spirit. God's way of saving us is through his two hands, namely Jesus Christ who has gone into the future kingdom from which he shares even now that salvation he will give when he comes again, and the Holy Spirit, the power of the age to come, whom the glorified Christ sends. We now simply seek to articulate some of the implications for Christian spirituality of this mystery in an ecumenical context and our common Christian responsibility for contributing to the salvation of our world, split in so many destructive ways, and with our current awareness of other world religions with their own spiritualities.

What we study here is in the strictest sense a divine mystery—one that remains largely hidden even now after 2,000 years of contemplation by saints and study by theologians. Many Christians remain divided in their interpretation of this mystery and its implications for our Christian and human lives, even though Christ revealed it to support and model our Christian unity. With no pretensions to being complete or definitive, we present our proposals for what we may call a future trinitarian spirituality in the following sections: (I) The Trinity's saving presence to us through the church, (II) the Trinity indwelling the graced person, and (III) a trinitarian spirituality for the twenty-first century.

I. The Trinity's Saving Presence to Us through the Church

We study the Trinity's saving presence to the church before its saving presence to the individual Christian, since by God's normal dispensation the individual shares the Trinity's presence through being incorporated into the church by belief and baptism (Acts 2:38). What are some implications for spirituality that come from acknowledging both that the saving trinitarian influence on us comes now from Christ's future kingdom and that the Father exercises this influence through his two 'hands' or ministers, as Irenaeus expressed it (see *Adv. Haer.*, IV, pref. 4; V,6,1; IV,7,4; IV,20,1; IV,38,3), the Son or exalted Christ and the Holy Spirit? In classical Western Catholic theology neither the future kingdom as influencing the present nor the equal influence of the Spirit with the Son were sufficiently emphasized. In this section then we shall consider (1) several contemporary trinitarian ecclesiologies that contribute to but perhaps fall short of an adequate expression of this mystery, and then (2) Vatican II's communion ecclesiology in relation to the interpretation of the saving trinitarian influence now coming from the future through the Father's 'two hands'.

1. Several Contemporary Trinitarian Ecclesiologies

Miroslav Volf has written a book, *After Our Likeness: The Church as the Image of the Trinity*, in which he compares three ecclesiologies in their relation to the Trinity, that of Joseph Cardinal Ratzinger, that of Metropolitan John Zizioulas, and his own.[1] Without attempting an ecclesiology here, it may be clarifying to recall a few central trinitarian elements of these ecclesiologies and evaluate them in the light of what we have proposed so far in this volume.

Ratzinger has tried to analyze the inner character of Catholic ecclesiology and to do so in opposition to what he finds in our Western world today, namely an erosion of a classical ecclesiology due largely to the influence of the 'free church' model. Against modern individualism he is concerned to show the "communal shape of the Christian faith" (29); he is convinced that "only the whole sustains" (20). It is the church that mediates faith; and in accepting Christian revelation of the triune God, one enters communion with other believers and, in a sense, becomes one subject with Christ as Paul writes in Galatians 2:20. This oneness with Christ is not a "'distinctionless identity,' but rather . . . [a] 'dynamic union,' as a 'pneumatic-actual act of matrimonial love'" (34 [R]). Faith is a gift of the church, though also a personal act: "The believing self is the self of the *anima ecclesiastica*, that is, 'the "I" of the human being in whom the entire community of the Church expresses itself, with which he lives, which lives in him, and from which he lives'" (37 [R]).

The Eucharist expresses what the church is, and the church is fully in the celebration of the Eucharist. The local church exists in communion with the entire church or does not exist. There is a precedence of the universal church over the local church, as all churches came from the church at Jerusalem (see 45–47). Office is subordinate to sacraments and the word, and its context is the "Church, living in the form of the apostolic succession with the Petrine office as its centre" (55 [R]). This is counter to *sola scriptura* or simply the individual's interpretation of tradition. "[T]he primary category of his ecclesiology is *Christus totus*" (59). The unity of the church is also based in the unitary substance of the divine persons (see 71–72), while the relation of the individual Christian to the collective subject of the church presupposes an understanding of person as relational, in virtue of which the individual can become a single subject with Christ (see 67–68).

Before proceeding to Zizioulas's viewpoint, we can ask whether Ratzinger's view of the church as *totus Christus* can be better incorporated into a trinitarian context. If, as we propose, the Father is now effecting the church through his two hands—the exalted Christ and the Holy Spirit—from the fullness of the kingdom, this shows that the church is definitely in process toward fullness or the 'whole' which it will not reach till Christ comes again. Ratzinger claims that only the whole sustains, but his approach may suggest that this whole already fully exists in the church on earth and thus what comes from the present whole of the church sustains. However, the whole of the pilgrim church always needs to be reformed. It is not simply the present whole that sustains, but the whole that Christ is calling it to be.

In stressing the church as *totus Christus* perhaps Ratzinger is not giving sufficient place to the Holy Spirit in constructing the church. The enormous growth of the Pentecostal churches in this century, the prevalence of base communities in Latin America and elsewhere, and Vatican II itself show us that an earlier Catholic ecclesiology was too Christocentric.[2] The Spirit was initially given at Pentecost to *all* the assembled disciples of the Lord, and not only to the apostles, though it was given to the latter to enable them to exercise the leadership committed to them.

Specifically, there has been a need for "consulting the faithful," because growth in insight into the revealed message comes about in different ways, in part "through the contemplation and study of believers who ponder these things in their hearts (cf. Lk. 2:19 and 51). It comes from the intimate sense of spiritual realities which they experience" (Vatican II, *DV* 8). It therefore comes from parts of the church, and not only from the whole. From his study of the Arian crisis in the fourth century, Newman concluded that: "The Nicene dogma was maintained during the greater part of the fourth century, 1. not by the unswerving firmness of the Holy See, Councils, or bishops, but 2. by the 'consensus fidelium.' He [Newman] repeats it in the later appendix to the third edition of *The Arians* (1871). . . . But such events he does not consider to be generally the case."[3] To give full weight to the Spirit's presence and action in the church, can we not say, as a number of theologians now propose:

> Christians are called to have more trust in the Spirit given to the Church as a whole than in the Spirit within them as individuals or as a particular cultural group. But since even Vatican I asserted that God gave to the successor of Pe-

ter *that* charism of infallibility that he wanted the whole Church to be endowed with, the belief of the faithful as a community has an infallibility that takes a certain precedence over that of the pope (also see *LG 25*). Once more, there may be tension, but there is not contradiction between charism and institution.[4]

We will now look at Metropolitan Zizioulas's trinitarian view of the church. The church is in the image of the Trinity, and so we begin with Zizioulas's interpretation of the Trinity. He writes:

There seems to be an exact correspondence between the trinitarian theology, as it was developed particularly by the Cappadocian Fathers—especially St. Basil—and Orthodox ecclesiology.
. . . Instead of speaking of the unity of God in terms of His one nature, he [Basil] prefers to speak of it in terms of the *communion of persons*. . . . The *nature* of God is communion. . . . [T]he one substance of God coincides with the communion of the three persons.
In ecclesiology all this can be applied to the relationship between local and universal Church. There is one Church, as there is one God. But the expression of this one Church is the communion of the many local Churches. Communion and oneness coincide in ecclesiology.[5]

Thus, in the Orthodox Church, in Zizioulas's opinion, there must be an institution "which expresses the *oneness* of the Church and not simply its multiplicity. But the multiplicity is not to be subjected to the oneness; it is constitutive of the oneness" (136). In the local church there are the one and the many, the bishop and the people, and in the larger church there are the many equal local churches with their bishops in communion with one another, represented, for example, by synods in which there is a *primus*, for example, metropolitan or patriarch who has very limited authority in local churches. This is against a pyramidal view of the church in which there are superior and subordinate churches.
Another element of this ecclesiology is that while the church is instituted by Christ, it is constituted by the Holy Spirit: "The 'con-stitution' is something that involves us in its very being, something we accept freely, because we take part in its very emergence . . . [here, authority] is something that springs from amongst us" (140). Because of Orthodoxy's emphasis on the Spirit's action in the church in its spirituality, it has experienced very little anticlericalism.
The church is a strictly eschatological reality particularly realized in the Eucharist. "In the eucharist . . . the Church found *the structure of the Kingdom,*

and it was this structure that she transferred to her own structure. In the eucharist the 'many' become 'one' (1 Cor 10:17). . ." (206). This eucharistic identification of the church and Christ occurs in the Holy Spirit. Thus, the church can be found in all its fullness wherever the Eucharist is celebrated in a geographical locality. But local churches must live in communion with all other churches. The universal church is the communion of the local churches that are identical with this universal church.

In reflecting on Zizioulas, we must first acknowledge that his Orthodox view of the church has much to contribute to our Western view; for example, his view of the church in more of an eschatological context than found in much of Western theology, his emphasis on the Holy Spirit as constituting the church, and his interpretation of the church as fully present in the local church. With other Orthodox theologians Zizioulas acknowledges that in practice there is not the unity that Christ wants in the Orthodox Church, so perhaps the principles of his ecclesiology need to be complemented by something from the West.

For example, we saw in our preceding chapter, counter to Zizioulas, that the principle of unity in the Trinity is both the one divine being and communion among the three persons; the unity of the divine being cannot be reduced to the communion of the divine persons. Also, as the distinction and the order among the divine persons do not constitute one superior to the other, so too distinction and order in ministries among local churches do not constitute one superior and the other inferior. Jean-Marie Tillard argues that primacy is needed for communion: "The role of the primacy, rightly understood, always in relation to the *affectus collegialis* (in the rich sense of the Latin *affectus*)—is to widen the outlook, to open up the horizon, always to recall the *common good* of the Church of God in its visible reality. . . . The primacy has the mission of being guardian for this *common good* that characterizes God's Church."[6]

If we look at Volf's Free Church interpretation of the church, the place to begin is his view of God's eschatological new creation, namely the coming of the kingdom that Jesus proclaimed. He sees the church as emerging from the resurrection of Jesus and the sending of the Holy Spirit (128), and thus as the anticipation of the eschatological gathering of the entire people of God. This future of the church will be a communion with the triune God and with one another (1 Jn 1:3), and thus the church is a present experience of that communion. The church is where Christ and the Spirit are. The word, sacraments, and the people are essential for the church. The traditional Free Church holds to Christ's "unmediated, direct presence in the entire local church as well as in every believer" (134).

While Volf does not follow the Free Church tradition completely, he does "join this long tradition by taking Matt. 18:20 as the foundation not only for determining what the church is, but also for how it manifests itself externally as a church. *Where two or three are gathered in Christ's name, not only is Christ present among them, but a Christian church is there as well, perhaps a bad church* . . . but a church nonetheless" (136). He views public confession of Christ (150) and the "openness of every church toward all other churches as an indispensable condition of ecclesiality" (156); unity with other churches is, however, not such a condition. This means that on this side of the *parousia* there can be only churches in the plural. Volf interprets the church's mediation of faith and salvation quite differently from the Catholic and Orthodox Churches. He writes that "one must insist that the church is not the subject of salvific activity with Christ; rather, Christ is the *only* subject of such salvific activity" (164).

Volf finds support in the Trinity for his basic acceptance of the Free Church tradition. In his interpretation of the Trinity he follows Moltmann and places the unity of the divine persons in their perichoretic unity while denying the unity of one divine nature (see 203, 210). The one deity existing as Father, Son, and Spirit distribute different gifts to all Christians, and they do so for the benefit of all: "Like the divine persons, they all stand in a relation of mutual giving and receiving" (219). The church is characterized as a "polycentric community" (224), not as a single subject. Moreover, "office does not belong to the *esse* of the Church" (248). Offices are provisional and corresponding to charisms given to varied people in the local congregation; otherwise, "the sovereignty of the Spirit would be endangered" (239). Churches are not "subjects that the Holy Spirit might indwell apart from the Spirit's indwelling the hearts of those of whom the church consists" (213). Similarly, "there is no such thing as an infallible interpretation of . . . [God's] revelation . . . 'For we know only in part' . . ." (244). The church must make its decisions in a provisional way, always subject to revision.

In commenting on this view, we agree with Volf that the church is constituted by the resurrection of Christ and the coming of the Spirit—thus by a kind of coming from the future eschatological reality of the kingdom, and a coming of both the exalted Christ and the Spirit. But, counter to Volf, this coming makes the future communion with the triune God and among Christ's disciples real here in time through the church as sacrament and instrument of salvation. Also, we have differed very significantly from Moltmann and Volf in our interpretation of the unity of the Trinity and of a certain order in the Trinity by which the Father is first. And we have interpreted the gift of the Holy Spirit as being given initially to the *whole* community of Christ's disciples or the church at Pentecost, and through that to individuals who enter the community through faith and baptism. The promise of the Spirit to lead the disciples of Christ into all truth (Jn 16:12) was given to the church, and not only or initially to discrete individuals. The charism of infallibility given to the church and definite ministers in given circumstances is guidance offered to God's people to be received in the freedom of the Spirit and is not counter to this freedom. The Spirit is "the Spirit of truth" (Jn 14:17).

The Free Church tradition has something important to contribute to the reform of the church. Part of the resistance even among Catholics in our time to the church's proclamation of the message of Christ and his way of salvation comes from the at times one-sided exercise of authority that does not consult the sense of the faithful. The place of the Spirit in the life of the laity should be acknowledged institutionally, at least as a consultative body, but in a way that does not deny office as part of the *esse* of the church or the reality of the apostolic office and its continued presence today. The Free Church tradition has shown that it is incapable of bringing unity among Christians. It has been frequently captive to the individualism in the North Atlantic countries, particularly the United States,[7] and captive to regional prejudices, as in the South of the United States.

2. The Trinity's Saving Presence in the Church as Coming from the Future through the Father's Two Hands

In the 1985 Synod of Bishops commemorating the twentieth year of the completion of Vatican II, the bishops recognized *communion* as basic to the council's understanding of the church and a key to future theology of the church.[8] The bishops and theologians of the church are still in the process of exploring the implications of this interpretation of the church. What we offer here is simply a brief recall of the council's teaching with some few scriptural roots and postconciliar theological reflections—a teaching we integrate with our finding in earlier chapters that the saving trinitarian presence in the church is a participation of the age to come, that is, the kingdom of God from which the exalted Christ and the Spirit come as the Father's two hands.[9] We will reflect (a) on the church as the presence equally of the exalted Christ and the Holy Spirit, (b) on the somewhat different presence of Christ and the Spirit to and in the church, and (c) on the church as on her pilgrim way.

a. The Church as Mediating Equally the Presence of Christ and the Holy Spirit

Vatican II taught that it is only within a trinitarian context that one can understand the church, since the origin, goal, and model of church unity is the Trinity. The Father planned to save fallen humanity, and he sent his Son who by his life, death, and resurrection fulfilled the will of the Father and restored all things (See LG 2–3, and AG 2–3). When Jesus had risen and ascended, he sent the Holy Spirit "in order that he might continually sanctify the Church, and that, consequently, those who believe might have access through Christ in one Spirit to the Father" (LG 4; see AG 4). This teaching was a significant improvement over the earlier modern theological teaching on the church that had interpreted it in a too-Christocentric context. But it still leaves something to be desired. In the first place, as Kilian McDonnell expresses it: "It [LG] builds up the Church in christological terms, and then when the christological moment is all over, then the Spirit is added in a second moment (par.4). That is too late. The Spirit belongs to the first constitutive moment. This has profound implications for the life of the Church, evangelization, preaching, liturgy, the Christian life."[10] Yves Congar, for one, recognized this. He acknowledged that some of his own earlier formulations of the action of the Spirit in the church had to be corrected. "I was not sufficiently conscious of the unity that exists between the activity of the Spirit and that of the glorified Christ. . . . This activity of the Lord with and through his Spirit cannot be reduced to a mere making present of the structures of the covenant proposed by Christ while he was on earth. . . . It is the source of a new element in history."[11] The constitutive origin of the church is found in both the appearances of the risen Christ and the gift by the glorified Christ of the Holy Spirit, as we saw in chapter 2.[12] The church is a community of the age to come already present now, that is, of the future kingdom already operative in part now in the present age.

This gives special meaning to Vatican II's teaching that "the Church, in Christ, is in the nature of a sacrament—a sign and instrument, that is, of communion with God and of unity among all men" (LG 1), and that "the universal Church is seen to be 'a people brought into unity from the unity of the Father, the Son and the Holy Spirit'" (LG 4). The church is a sign or sacrament and instrument of a communion with God that is offered us from the future kingdom into which Christ was exalted and from which he sends the Spirit. The unity to which we are called is not primarily that primordial unity of the Trinity, but that of the Trinity as the goal of history, for it is from this goal that Christ now saves us and sends his Spirit. The church is the prolepsis of the parousia of Christ, the sacrament bringing that salvation Christ will bring at the parousia. This future is not simply the goal of the church; this future comes to us through the advent in time of the exalted Christ and the Spirit.

God's *definitive* salvation is mediated through the church. This is a salvation that goes far beyond liberating men and women from physical slavery, a particular human injustice, tragedy, or weakness. It is a salvation from what stands in the way of communion with God and one another in God, so that neither sin, alien spirits, nor death itself can jeopardize or overcome it. It is the only fulfillment and lasting happiness of the individual and human community. This salvation is the purpose of God's whole providence with humankind—the fulfillment and liberation of the whole of evolution and history. There is no purpose in history beyond this communion, and the church is the prolepsis of this salvation even here in this age. This definitive communion of humanity with God and with one another is what is offered us by the Father through Christ and the Spirit from the future.

This unity between us and God and among one another is the goal of the redemption by Christ and of the church. As Vatican II expressed it: "This is the sacred mystery of the unity of the Church, in Christ and through Christ, with the Holy Spirit energizing its various functions. The highest exemplar and source of this mystery is the unity, in the Trinity of Persons, of one God, the Father and the Son in the Holy Spirit" (UR 2).

The communion that is the church is effected by God the Father through the exalted Jesus Christ and the Holy Spirit. In Ephesians (Eph 3:3–6) the author encourages the Christians of that city to a unity that has a trinitarian origin and model; he recalls they have one God and Father of all, are one body (which he goes on to identify as "the body of Christ" with Christ as the head [Eph 4: 12, 15–16]), and in one Spirit.

John makes it clear that this unity or communion which the disciples of Christ form comes causally from the trinitarian intercommunion. As J.-M. R. Tillard writes: "[C]ommunion of the Father and the Son is much more than the model of fraternal *communion*; it is the source, the origin, the locus of it. That gives the special commandment 'love one another as (*kathôs*) I have loved you' (13:34)—an exceptional seriousness and explains why it is called special (unique)."[13]

The whole Pauline doctrine of the body of Christ shows the basis for the communion that is the church. Tillard calls upon Romans 12:3–6 and 1 Corinthians 12:4–27 to show:

> The internal unity of the community comes from the fact that all—each one with his or her own uniqueness and singularity—are gathered into the one and indivisible Body of Christ the Lord. . . . The Body of the Lord . . . assumes their multitude in him, the Spirit of his Lordship unifying this multitude in *koinonia*. . . . The Body . . . exists only in the Body of the Crucified, glorified by the Spirit. They are inseparable.[14]

The Body of Christ that is the church is an extension of the risen and glorified Lord, because it is an incursion into this age of the age to come—the future kingdom. And the coming of the Spirit from the glorified Lord is as constitutive of the church as the glorified Lord himself.

b. The Differentiated Presence of Christ and the Spirit in the Church

It is helpful to show examples of how the trinitarian presence in and influence on the church through both the exalted Christ and the Holy Spirit
is somewhat differentiated and united. The Son who became incarnate revealed the Father and the Father's designs to us and won redemption for
us through his life, passion, death, and resurrection. And now, as the exalted Jesus Christ, he sends his ministers to proclaim his message and thus
to give people an opportunity to believe and be saved. Also, Christ, the
'Ur-sacrament', is the main celebrant of the sacraments; when Peter, Paul,
or Thomas baptize, it is the exalted Jesus who is baptizing. And in the Eucharist, Christ is the main host in the sense that from beyond the veil he
shares with us an anticipation of that messianic banquet to which we are
called; he reminds us of the great love he has shown us in his sacrifice for
us; and he communicates himself to us under the symbols of bread and
wine transformed into his flesh and blood. He is with the church until the
end of time (Mt 28:20). He comes also through the poor and needy:
"whatever you did for one of these least brothers of mine, you did for me"
(Mt 26:40).

The influence of the Holy Spirit seems to have a somewhat different character to it. The Holy Spirit, of course, did not become incarnate or teach, suffer, die, and rise for us as Jesus did. One description of the agency of the Holy
Spirit in the church given by Vatican II is as follows:

> It is the Holy Spirit dwelling in those who believe and pervading and ruling
> over the entire Church, who brings about that wonderful communion of the
> faithful and joins them together so intimately in Christ that he is the princi-
> ple of the Church's unity. By distributing various kinds of spiritual gifts and
> ministries, he enriches the Church of Jesus Christ with different functions "in
> order to equip the saints for the work of service, so as to build up the body of
> Christ." (UR 2; quotation from Eph 4:12)

The ecumenical movement is ascribed to the Holy Spirit: "Today, in many
parts of the world, under the influence of the grace of the Holy Spirit, many
efforts are being made in prayer, word and action to attain that fullness of
unity which Jesus Christ desires" (UR 4). By her presence in hearers of the
word and the disciples of Christ, the Holy Spirit gives them dispositions to

accept the saving word and to seek communion with God and one another—
and to witness to the larger world. The Holy Spirit seems to affect immediately the subjectivity of the church and individuals within it, giving all a
share in the love that constitutes the Spirit, as we showed in an earlier chapter. In accord with this, Congar writes: "The Church is . . . a communion, a
fraternity of persons. This is why a personal principle and a principle of unity
are united in the Church. These two principles are brought into harmony by
the Holy Spirit."[15] And: "[T]he Holy Spirit [is said to be united to the
Church as] . . . one indwelling and acting: *to be with* always (John xvi. 16),
. . . the texts which express the relation of the Holy Spirit to the Church in
terms of *habitation, being with,* imply an intersubjective ontology."[16] And finally, "Only God can lift us up to the life of God; only a 'dynamic' principle
genuinely divine [the Holy Spirit] can direct and move us towards the objects
of the divine life."[17]

Thus, some now call the church "the communion in the Holy Spirit," a title not contradictory to "the people of God" or "the Mystical Body," but one
that brings out a dimension of the church that was too often neglected in the
pre-Vatican modern church. We can call this an 'epicletic' view of the
church, in that it sees the church from the perspective of the Holy Spirit
given and called down upon it to lift it up from within by giving it a share in
God's own love and subjectivity.[18] All of this has helped us see that the
church is fully present in the local church.[19] The communion spoken of here
is not only among the bishops of the church under the pope, but among all
the faithful in a local church and then in the communion of churches.

c. The Church on Its Pilgrim Way

This gift of communion is present in the church now as a missionary church
on its pilgrim way. The church is a community that is open to the larger
world and communicates the gift God has given us to the whole world. The
church, "that messianic people, although it does not actually include all men,
and at times may appear as a small flock, is, however, a most sure seed of
unity, hope and salvation for the whole human race" (LG 9).

For this mission, "Christ summons the Church, as she goes her pilgrim way,
to that continual reformation of which she always has need, insofar as she is an
institution of men here on earth" (UR 6). This need of reformation for the deficiencies of the church was present in the past and continues to be present in
reference to such things as "moral conduct, discipline, or even in the way that
the Church teaching has been formulated" (UR 6), and in the very manner of
the exercise of papal primacy, without renouncing anything essential to the mission of the papacy.[20] That unity is a participation and anticipation of the unity

that will be ours when Christ comes again. It is a unity that has from the time of the New Testament itself involved diversity; and it always will, because there are kinds of diversity that enrich the church as there is diversity in the Trinity itself. Diversity of itself is not disunity, except for those who identify unity with uniformity, a weakness of the church at times.[21] That communion is what will be and is already in part. We shall be of one mind and one heart, and insofar as we accept the influence of Christ and the Spirit we are on the way to that through God's self-gift in the present.

It is the trinitarian persons who through their saving presence are bringing about historical change in the pilgrim church, as by a participation in the paschal mystery of Christ. The costs and losses present in the growth in the church are the church's participation in the paschal mystery of Christ; the church's growth to new life is at the cost of such a participation. In a sense, Christ is continuing his paschal mystery in the church, and so giving the ultimate sign of his love for the Father and for humanity that his death was. He is the Way, and the church's pilgrim way is a share in Christ's Way. And, as the Spirit was present in Jesus' ministry, was handed over by Jesus at the cost of the cross (Jn 19:30), and sent upon his disciples after his ascension, so too it is through the same Spirit that the church constantly gives new life.

There is an analogy between the way the Trinity brings about growth in the church and the way the Trinity is operative in the evolution of material creation and history, as we developed in chapter 5. The Word and Spirit operative in the church as the exalted Christ and the Spirit he sent come, however, from the future. The whole Christ (or the Omega), fully faithful to the historical Jesus Christ, gives direction to the church's engagement with changing historical environments. And the Spirit, as a creative dynamism within the faithful and the church, brings about those smaller and larger initiatives that promote the unity and growth of the whole Christ. In this process that promotes the unity for which Christ prayed and which the Spirit fosters, we see the exercise of the truest form of freedom, similar to that of Jesus Christ as he faced not only his ministry but his passion and death—and, beyond this, the resurrected life. Christ's freedom is self-giving in love and truth, and is not without fruit that remains. It is this that builds up the church (see Eph 4:15–16), not simply at a particular time and place, but through history.

II. The Trinity Indwelling the Graced Human Person

Spirituality or our response to God's love depends more on the access the Father in love gives us to himself through his Son and Holy Spirit than on our searching. For our searching to be honest and fruitful, it must seek to understand God's loving ways and trust in them. God's love for us is shown preeminently by the divine call to us to dwell in the Trinity or the divine desire to dwell within us. It is that which we seek to explore in an introductory way in this section. Much of what we have written in the first part of this chapter is applicable to the present issue, because through dwelling in the church the Spirit dwells in each baptized person, who is a member of Christ. We will treat this question from two perspectives, that of a theology of the divine indwelling in the graced human person and, in the next part, that of a trinitarian spirituality.

The Trinity does dwell in Christian persons both as the origin of their Christian identity and life, or divinization, and as the object of their faith, trust, and love. And, counter to a longstanding Western theological tradition, the Christian has somewhat distinct relations to each of the divine persons. This area has been disputed by Catholic theologians, but there is more unity now than in the pre–Vatican II period. And this growing unity tends to reduce the difference between the Western tradition represented by Thomas and the Eastern tradition represented by Gregory Palamas. We will (1) recall some texts of Scripture that affirm the trinitarian indwelling, (2) show some statements from patristic and theological tradition that both support and seem to fall short of what we find in Scripture, and (3) then suggest an answer that is both somewhat corrective of the Thomistic tradition and jn accord with Scripture and Christian experience.

1. Scripture on the Divine Indwelling

Scripture clearly teaches that the Trinity indwells the genuine disciple of Christ. John stresses the intimacy that this effects. For example, he writes, "Jesus . . . said . . . , 'Whoever loves me will keep my word, and my Father will love him, and we will come to him and make our dwelling with him'" (14:23). And, "I will ask the Father, and he will give you another Advocate to be with you always, the Spirit of truth, which the world cannot accept, because it neither sees nor knows it. But you know it, because it remains with you and will be in you" (14:16–17). We can, with others, call this self-gift of the Trinity the uncreated grace.

This trinitarian self-gift is the origin of our transformation from sinner to justified and then of our progressive transformation or sanctification; and it is the intentional object of our faith, hope, and love. The Father and the Son are the origin and causal influence of our being children of God, for the Father has begotten us through the Son. John writes, "See what love the Father has bestowed on us that we be called the children (*tekna*) of God. Yet so we are" (1 Jn 3:1). And John calls us "begotten by God" (1 Jn 5:18; see Jn 1:13). We are children of the Father "in his Son Jesus Christ" (1 Jn 5:20).[22] Our living belief in God and in his Son Jesus Christ mediates our rebirth, and our knowledge of God through faith is the eternal life that is God's gift (see Jn 17:3).

It seems that Paul and John suggest that we have a distinctive relationship to each of the divine persons—Father, Son, and Holy Spirit. Even for the Synoptics, we are invited to pray specifically to the Father in the Our Father (Mt 6:9–15; Lk 11:2–4). We saw in chapter 6 that when Paul speaks of the Spirit as wisdom, it is in the sense that by participating in the Spirit we can "understand the things freely given us by God" (1 Cor 2:11).[23] That is, the Spirit is wisdom not in the sense of what is proclaimed or what is known, but in the sense of an interior principle that catches us up into the Spirit's knowledge of God, "for the Spirit scrutinizes everything, even the depths of God" (1 Cor 2:10), "for who knows what pertains to a person except the spirit of the person that is within?" (1 Cor 2:11).

It seems, similarly, that while Paul speaks of Jesus Christ as the "glory of the Lord" on whom we gaze and the image into which we are being transformed, he speaks of the Spirit as the Lord *by whom* we are being transformed (2 Cor 3:18). Elsewhere he speaks of the Spirit as the dynamic principle within us enabling us to pray, to put to death the deeds of the flesh, to trust in God as Father (see Rom 8). All of this suggests we have a distinctive relation to the Father, the Son, and the Spirit. As Prat comments on St. Paul: "From the supernatural being received at baptism, special relations with each of the three divine Persons are derived: a relationship of sonship with the Father; a relation of consecration to the Holy Spirit [i.e., as sanctifier]; a relation of mystical identity with Jesus Christ."[24]

2. Patristic and Theological Tradition Concerning the Trinitarian Indwelling of the Graced Person

If we look at the Fathers of the church, particularly at the Greeks, there seems to be, counter to a later Western theology, support for the interpretation of Scripture we have given above.[25] They insist on the divine indwelling and that while the Son is a natural Son, we are sons only through participation in the Sonship of the Son. For example, Athanasius writes: "The Son is in the Father as his own Word and splendor. For ourselves . . . [I]f we are made participators (*metoke*) of the Spirit, we are conjoined with divinity. . . . Hence as we are made sons and deified because of the Word whom we have in us, so also we will be in the Son and in the Father. . ." (*Adv. Arianos*, IV, 3, 24 and 25; my translation). Many of the Greek Fathers suggest that our being children of God is specifically a participation in the Son and through the relation the Father has to the Son, and that we share sanctification from the Spirit.[26] There are those patristic scholars who have disputed this, but they are fewer today.

One further witness we can give to our distinctive relationship to each of the divine persons is the teaching of Cyril of Alexandria:

> Union with God is impossible of achievement for anyone save through participation (*metousias*) in the Holy Spirit, instilling in us his own proper sanctification (*agiasmon*) and refashioning to his own life the nature that fell subject to corruption, and thus restoring to God and to God's semblance (*morphosin*) what had been deprived of this glory. For the perfect image of the Father is the Son, and the natural likeness of the Son is his Spirit. The Spirit, therefore, refashioning as it were to himself the souls of men, engraves on them God's semblance (*morphosin*) and seals the representation (*eikonismon*) of the supreme essence.[27]

'Sanctification' for Cyril has both an ontological meaning, namely our participation in God's nature or likeness to the Son, and a dynamic meaning, namely a life lived in harmony with this sanctification. In some of the patristic texts, the distinctive effect of the Son on the graced soul is related to his being the Image of God, while the effect of the Spirit is related to her proceeding from the Father as a breath emanating from one who speaks. Gregory of Nyssa spoke of the functions and effects (*energeia*) of the Spirit,[28] in seeming anticipation of the notion of the uncreated 'energies' of the Trinity, particularly associated with or mediated by the Holy Spirit, which were central to Palamism in a later century.[29] These 'energies' seem more immediately related to the breathing forth of the Sprit and its effects than to the image of sons and daughters into which we are regenerated, but the energies are operative in the coming to be in us of the image of God and our further transformation into this image.

In the West, the understanding of God's grace took primarily a different thrust. The Latin Fathers and particularly Augustine attributed justification to faith and love, not distinguishing much between the act and the habit of charity. They considered grace more from the perspective of the actual movements it confers upon the powers of the soul than as a permanent elevation of the being. The early scholastics began to distinguish habitual charity and the act of charity. And then in the early thirteenth century, grace and the virtues were compared respectively with the nature and powers of the soul, a comparison which St. Thomas greatly developed.

Thus the use of Aristotelian philosophy and concepts led to a whole new development in the theology of grace. Thomas and his followers distinguished sanctifying grace from charity, considering the former to be an entitative habit or quality permanently inhering the soul and elevating our being to the supernatural order, because it is a participation of the divine nature.[30] So too the Latin Fathers tended to concentrate on created grace rather than on the uncreated grace, though they acknowledged the indwelling of the Trinity, more as an intentional object of faith and love than as source of grace. Thomas did not teach a trinitarian indwelling whereby each divine person offers us something proper to himself, a teaching we find in Scripture and some Eastern Fathers of the church. He used the principle that the external activity of the Trinity reflects the oneness of God, and thus grace is the effect of God as one. Thomas thought our adoption as sons and daughters is common to the whole Trinity, though appropriated to the Father (see ST III, 3, 5, ad 2).

Theologians had difficulty in doing justice to what we have found in Scripture and the Greek Fathers, perhaps because the Aristotelian division of causes could not articulate what the earlier Christian sources seemed to be asserting about the relation to us of Father, Son, and Holy Spirit. This problem continued into the twentieth century. In Mystici Corporis Pope Pius XII cautioned that the union of grace never destroys the radical distinction between creator and creature and that, "in these matters all things are to be held as common to the Most Holy Trinity insofar as they refer to God as the supreme *efficient cause*" (DS 3814; emphasis added). To acknowledge the distinctive causal influence of a divine person in the order of incarnation and grace, M. de la Taille and others used the phrase "created actuation by uncreated grace," and Karl Rahner and others the phrase "quasi-formal" causality.[31] It is in this line that we make the following proposal.

3. A Proposal Concerning the Trinitarian Indwelling

We are given a participation in the divine nature and life through grace (see 2 Pet 1:4). How is this so? In the natural order our being and all our perfections are participations in the divine being. Thomas writes:

> Every creature is related to God as the air to the illuminating sun. The sun is light by its nature, but the air becomes luminous by participating light from the sun, but not by participating the nature of the sun. So also only God is being by his essence, because his essence is his to be (esse). Every creature is being by participation, and not because its essence is its to be (esse) (ST I,104,1).

The creature has its own created act by which it participates in the divine being. Thus, "all things are good, insofar as they are. But all beings are not called being through the divine being (*esse*), but by their proper being (*esse*)" (*ST* I, 6,4). Through God's efficient causality the Trinity as one creates finite beings. More specifically, this efficient causality involves exemplary causality by which creatures have the natures they do, and God's free sharing his own goodness by way of their created 'to be' (*esse*)—the created acts by which they are. Creatures participate in God, but not in what is formal to God, that is, not in what is distinctive of God. They are the results of God's freely given creation, an 'analogical causality', not a univocal causality.

In the order of grace, by God's mercy we participate in what is distinctive of the divine being, though in a created and contingent fashion. Thus we will see God as he is (1 Jn 3:2), and we are given a power under God to elicit these acts that are totally beyond our human capacity, though we participate in this in a finite manner (see *CG* I, 32). We do not participate in God's nature by his formal causality, that is, by God entering into substantial union with us; that would destroy the distinction between God and creation. There is a created effect in us, sanctifying grace and actual grace, as Thomas and Trent teach, by which we share in the divine being and acts. By God's efficient causality this 'quality' or form and, we should add, a proportionate life or 'esse' modify our being on the 'accidental' level as distinct from the substantial level.

The divine being as it is in itself is triune. And Scripture and Eastern tradition seem to teach that we participate in what is proper to the Son and proper to the Holy Spirit. How can this be? I would agree very largely with Malachi Donnelly whose work on this issue I read in the late 1950s. He applies de la Taille's notion of created actuation by uncreated act to the question of grace. As well summarized by Ralph Del Colle, his position claims:

> "that each of the divine Persons [is] . . . present to, and united with, the soul by a manner of presence and union that will in some way be different from the proper manner and presence of the other two divine persons." . . .
>
> Donnelly does not deny that created grace is a product of efficient causality, but here the intra-trinitarian relations do not enter. They do enter by the reception of divine grace into humanity according to the Thomistic principle *per quemdam modum passionis*—through whatever manner of being acted upon. . . . Created or sanctifying grace proceeds from the inhabitation of the Holy Spirit, not vice versa. ". . . the conferring of created grace takes place by the impression on the soul of the divine seal of the Persons of the Blessed Trinity. Thus created grace becomes, so to speak, the concave impression of the convex divine seal." . . . it is a communication according to "created actuation by uncreated act" (or quasi-formal causality in its Rahnerian adaptation). On the side of the divine, the *actio* is one and undivided but differs relatively and yet

properly according to the hypostatic distinctions of the trinitarian persons. Conversely, on the human side, the reception or *passio* corresponds to the "active communication of the particular divine person." So too, the uncreated act that actuates does not inform the creature [i.e., by formal causality] . . . , but the reception by the creature is a *passio* by way of information through the created actuation—the human person is made instrinsically just through sanctifying grace, as Trent declared.[32]

As an extension of this interpretation, we offer the following proposal. There is within us a *gratia operans*, that is, a grace within us but antecedent to our action, and a *gratia cooperans*, that is, our cooperation with this grace. Considering grace as both sanctifying grace and the theological virtues, grace in us, whether actual or sanctifying, is initially *gratia operans;* and thus through its effects (e.g., our act of faith, which is a *gratia cooperans*) it reflects a causal influence of the Father. From one perspective through faith the Father begets us as sons and daughters, from another through faith we participate in what is proper to the Son, such as in his likeness to the Father and in his knowledge of the Father. Through trust and love we share a movement of love that is the Holy Spirit. The divine persons are distinguished by their subsistent relations, and so it seems that there is an imprint on us of what is specific to each through sanctifying grace and the theological virtues. It is the Father who begets us as his sons and daughters which make us share what is proper to the Son. There is begotten in us an image of the Father far beyond what our creaturely status gives us. And through the Father's and the Son's sending of the Spirit (a participation in their spiration of the Spirit within the Trinity) there is in us trust and love that is a participation in the Holy Spirit, who is love as a person. Thus the Father, Son, and Spirit share with us what is proper to each—this being the uncreated grace that is the divine indwelling and the source of the created grace of sanctifying grace and the theological virtues. Also they are intentional objects of our faith-knowledge and love as a result.

There is a kind of causal efficacy of the Trinity here, but not one that can be identified with efficient causality, formal causality, or mere appropriation. There is a genuine 'begetting' that gives rise to a genuine participation in what is proper to the Son—a likeness to him that is a participation in his filial relation to the Father. And there is a genuine breathing forth of new life on us that gives rise to a participation in the response of love that is proper to the Holy Spirit. The participation in the Son has a quasi-formal character, while that in the Spirit is more by way of concurrence (an influence closer to the Palamite notion of 'energies'). Perhaps we can see in the former something close to Rahner's "quasi-formal causality" and in the latter something close to M. de la Taille's "created actuation by uncreated act."[33]

These causal influences have their more limited counterparts in the natural order, as we saw in relating God's ongoing creative activity to the natural evolution of the world by his word and spirit (Ps 33:6; Gn 1). The creation by word represents God's loving design and purpose for us, and thus a "top-down" influence, while that by concurrence represents an influence evoking the creature's initiative, spontaneity, and creative search for fullness of being appropriate for it.

We can consider a possible objection to this proposal. The divine persons are distinguished by their 'notional' acts, the Father begetting and the Son begotten, the Father and Son spirating and the Spirit proceeding. For them each to have a distinctive relation to the graced human being, it seems that each would have to have a *real* relation to the human being and thus share with that human being something proper to the 'notional' act or property specific to the divine person. Thomas denied that God has a *real* relation to the creature, and so it is even more difficult to conceive how each person has a distinctive real relation to the human person.

In a previous chapter we treated the question of the Son's real relationship to his humanity in the Incarnation and thus change in some legitimate sense. Similarly, we suggested that in virtue of the economy of salvation there is a legitimate sense in asserting a history of the Father, Son, and Spirit with one another and with us human beings.[34] Here, we can quote from Pope Pius XII who acknowledged that in heaven "in a manner wholly ineffable we will be able to contemplate the Father, Son and Divine Spirit by the eyes of our mind raised through a supernatural light, to share (*adsistere*) intimately in the processions of the divine persons eternally, and to be beatified by that joy with which the most holy and undivided Trinity is made happy" (DS 3815). If we are to be present to the distinct processions in heaven, somehow these processions of the divine Persons are already distinctively present to us since by grace we are given a beginning of eternal life through faith. There is a continuity between the life of grace here below and the complete happiness of the next life. To express this life of grace theologically, our vocabulary must grow, as de la Taille, Rahner, and others have asserted.

III. A Trinitarian Spirituality for the Twenty-First Century

After reflecting on a theology of the indwelling of the Trinity in the graced human person, let us reflect briefly on a trinitarian spirituality. We will (1) first reflect on the Eucharist as a paradigm for this spirituality, and (2) then examine some implications of this spirituality for our engagement in society and our relations to world religions.

1. The Eucharist as Paradigm for a Trinitarian Spirituality

One might usefully turn to the mystics of the Christian tradition for insights into a trinitarian spirituality. And indeed in the foregoing pages we have written briefly of the teaching of theologians who were also mystics, such as Origen, Augustine, Palamas, and, in our time, Karl Rahner. Specifically, we have had occasion to speak of the experiential, elusive, ineffable, and graced character of knowledge of the Christian mystery given in prayer through the Spirit of God. The theme of a trinitarian mysticism and spirituality is treated in varied publications.[35] But here, we suggest that a trinitarian spirituality may be appropriately expressed by the eucharistic liturgy. Vatican II spoke of the liturgy as "the summit toward which the activity of the Church is directed; it is also the fount from which all her power flows . . . [and] the primary and indispensable source from which the faithful are to derive the true Christian spirit" (SC 10, 14). This context is available generally to Christians, and it avoids identification with the *exitus–reditus* theology present in some Christian mystics.[36]

Such a trinitarian spirituality has been present in the church since its beginnings. A most striking example of such a spirituality and a paradigm for later times is found in the Last Supper discourse in John's gospel. We can look at Jesus' discourse after the Last Supper as a paschal and eucharistic spirituality.

Here Jesus recognizes the distress his disciples will experience when he is taken from them, is judged, crucified, and killed. But he encourages them by interpreting this paschal experience and showing them the life that will result for them from it. This life is specifically trinitarian. It is good for his disciples that he, Jesus, goes from them, "For if I do not go, the Advocate will not come to you. But if I go, I will send him to you" (Jn 16:7; see 16:13–14). If his disciples love him they will keep his commandments, "And whoever loves me will be loved by my Father, and I will love him and reveal myself to him . . . and we will come to him and make our dwelling with him" (14:21, 23). His disciples are like branches of the vine who is Jesus, and the Father is the vinedresser who prunes the branches so that they bear more fruit: "Remain in me, as I remain in you. . . . Whoever remains in me and I in him will bear much fruit, because without me you can do nothing" (15:4, 5). Jesus sends his disciples into the world as the Father had sent him, but he prays that the Father may "keep them from the evil one" (17:15). He prays too that "that they may all be one, as you, Father, are in me and I in you, that they may also may be in us, that the world may believe that you sent me" (17:13, 21). This prayer will ultimately be fulfilled when Jesus comes back again and to take his disciples to himself (14:2–3). But Jesus' prayer is being fulfilled in part in time and history from the gift of the Spirit who is given by the glorified Christ (7:39; 20:21–23).

The Eucharist makes God's revelation and salvation present to us sacramentally, and this gift is a trinitarian reality. As *Dei Verbum* puts it: "It pleased God, in his goodness and wisdom, to reveal himself and to make known the mystery of his will (cf. Eph. 1:9). His will was that men should have access to the Father, through Christ, the Word made flesh in the Holy Spirit, and thus become sharers in the divine nature (cf. Eph. 2:18; 2 Pet. 1:4)" (*DV* 2). We will present the eucharistic liturgy as expressing a trinitarian spirituality under four headings.

a. Gathering and Proclamation of the Word
First, the community gathers, "called together by God in the Holy Spirit . . . for the express purpose of worship,"[37] and so this very gathering is a presence of Christ, as Vatican II teaches: "he [Christ] is present when the Church prays and sings, for he has promised 'where two or three are gathered together in my name there am I in the midst of them' (Mt 18:20)" (SC 7). It is also a presence of the Holy Spirit who animates the people to come together as this community.

After the introductory penitential rite, we have the liturgy of the word. The liturgy begins with God revealing and addressing us. In the general pattern here, there is a reading from the Old Testament and then one from the gospel. And since the gospels were initially accounts of the pasch of our Lord, with the rest an introduction to this, this order reflects the fact that God's revelation finds its fulfillment in the paschal mystery. This revelation through the Word made flesh brings to their culmination the Old Testament and all earlier revelations. The Father addresses us in love through his Son in the Spirit; this is where salvation begins.

This revelation through Christ and the Spirit fulfills not only the Old Testament but all of God's earlier or lesser revelations to us. We will recur to how these earlier revelations relate to our trinitarian spirituality below when we treat world religions. But we note that this whole divine revelation comes not only from the past acts and words of God through Jesus and his predecessors; it comes to us now from the future. Since Scripture and tradition are God's word, the proclamation of them in the liturgy: "make the voice of the Holy Spirit sound again and again in the words of the prophets and apostles. . . . In the sacred books the Father who is in heaven comes lovingly to meet his children, and talks with them. . . . 'The Word of God is living and active' (Heb. 4:12)" (*DV* 21; see also *DV* 8). Also, "He [Christ] is present in his word since it is he himself who speaks when the holy scriptures are read in the Church" (*SC* 7). The glorified Christ proclaims the word through his ministers in the Eucharist; he is addressing this community in love from the future kingdom.

b. The Offering of Gifts

The next three parts of the Eucharist are in response to this revelation by which the Father addresses us through the glorified Christ and the Spirit. In the first of these, the offering of gifts, we present, as a consequence of our belief, bread and wine as first fruits of the earth and of our activity that prepares them to symbolize both our acknowledgment that everything we have we have as God's gift, and our inner dispositions of thanksgiving and self-gift to God. We use ordinary things and acts in this self-offering. The liturgy presupposes our recognition in thanksgiving of God in the ordinary; that is the condition on which their symbolic meaning in the Eucharist is possible. This offering symbolizes the offering, on the part both of the individual and of the community, of whole of the cosmos and of human activity and history.

Our offering takes its origin from God the Holy Spirit, from whom alone these dispositions can come about in us individually and as a community. This Spirit is the gift Christ sends from his future kingdom. Our gift is small, because we are infinitesimally small compared to the infinite God. But it symbolizes the gift of everything that we are and have. And we bring this to the table. This giving of our gift is in part an expression of our trust that the earth, our activity, and history itself have meaning in spite of experiences that tend to undermine this trust. And this meaning is found only in a return of these to God in whom we will find fulfillment and who invites us to this action from the future. The Passover meal is a type of the Eucharist, and thus the Eucharist is celebrated in the form of a meal in which the glorified Christ is the host in the sense of the one who invites us, presides at the meal, and shares his fellowship with us from beyond the veil. We can see this in Vatican II's teaching that, "By his power he [Christ] is present in the sacraments so that when anybody baptizes it is really Christ himself who baptizes" (*SC* 7). When the priest presides, it is the glorified Christ who uses this humble sacramental symbol to preside at the meal.

c. The Eucharistic Prayer

The third step in the liturgy is the action of Christ from beyond the veil recalling through the words of institution of the Eucharist what he has done for us in dying for us and the meaning of his paschal mystery. "No one has greater love than this, to lay down one's life for one's friends" (Jn 15:13; see Jn 3:16; Rom 8:32). He does this sacramentally, so that this reminder reactualizes what he did for us; but while it reveals for those with faith it also conceals the mystery. Thus Vatican II teaches that, "He [Christ] is present in the Sacrifice of the Mass . . . 'the same now offering, through the ministry of priests, who formerly offered himself on the cross'" (SC 7, quotation from Trent, DS 1743). Jesus presents this to the Father in intercession for us.

Jesus takes what is the sign of our self-offering, and it is this he uses to transform into his own action, his own body and blood. Thus he gives our self-offering an enormous value, by uniting it with his own. In the process he transforms us into himself and liberates us. In our world, our self-gift to God does not happen save through a death to self. We are active participants in this, his offering, through the priesthood of all the baptized and through the Holy Spirit, invoked in the epiclesis to raise us: "Grant that we, who are nourished by his body and blood, may be filled with his Holy Spirit, and become one body, one Spirit in Christ" (Euch. Prayer III). Our self-gift in Christ is not only for ourselves individually, but for us as a community. And, indeed, our sharing in the eucharistic liturgy is for the whole world. We pray, "We offer you his body and blood, the acceptable sacrifice which brings salvation to the whole world" (Euch. Prayer IV), and "May this sacrifice which has made our peace with you advance the peace and salvation of all the world" (Euch. Prayer III). The epiclesis is also an invocation that the Spirit transform the bread and wine into the body and blood of Christ. The Holy Spirit sent to us from the future kingdom operates as it were from below to raise us up. And this is for the glory of the Father: "Through him, with him, in him, in the unity of the Holy Spirit, all glory and honor is yours, almighty Father, for ever and ever, Amen" (Euch. Prayer).

This is of enormous importance for people of our time, many of whom have so little trust in the meaning of their actions and lives that they seek an ersatz fulfillment in the present and block out the future.[38] The unity of future and past in the Eucharist is found particularly in its character as a sacramental meal in which the exalted Christ presides from the future kingdom, recalls to us what he has done for us, sends the Spirit from the future to lift us up, and gives us an anticipation of the messianic banquet we will enjoy when he comes again.

d. Communion and Dismissal

This leads us to the fourth part of the eucharistic liturgy, the communion. In the Roman liturgy the Our Father and the sign of peace occur here, the first our expression in prayer of the dispositions of Christ to whom we have united ourselves and the second a symbolic expression of that sharing with others of the love we ourselves have received from Christ. In communion Christ shares himself with us individually and as a community, and gives us that communion which is the purpose of all God's design in creation and history—a share in that communion with God and with one another that Christ will give us when he comes again and that he now gives us in this anticipation of the messianic banquet. What he gives us is both an anticipation of that future communion and food for the journey we still have before us. In this the Eucharist makes the church:

> The reception of communion is not merely the coincidental juxtaposition of so many individual believers, each of whom is sacramentally united with the Lord in his body and blood. It is all those individuals being constituted as one body and as one body—*only* as one body!—united with the body's head, Christ, and animated by the one Spirit who has raised this body, the Church, from the dead. In this oneness which is accomplished by the reception of communion by all and in the sign which is thus made, we can then see in the Church the sign, the image, of the Holy Trinity, that is, many who are one.[39]

Human beings cannot achieve the unity for which they are made and which alone can make sense out of our individual and communal histories; only the Holy Spirit can raise us to this.

The celebration of the Eucharist ends with the dismissal, but this is not simply a dismissal. It is a sending us out as Christ was sent out in the Spirit so that we may share with the world what we have received, and do so in the Spirit of Christ who by his own *kenosis* has brought us salvation.

2. Some Implications of a Trinitarian Spirituality for Our Engagement in Society and with World Religions

It is clear that our Christian trinitarian spirituality in the twenty-first century must express itself in our lives in society and in our relations with world religions. It is appropriate here to recall briefly a few implications for these issues.

a. A Trinitarian Spirituality and Social Justice

The implications here have at times been obscured in part because Christian spirituality has been associated too much with an *exitus–reditus* theology and an inadequate anthropology. In the ministry of Christ and in the early church the trinitarian missions included a transformation of the social world, and this is a renewed emphasis in the period of Vatican II.

The Synoptics present the ministry of Jesus as centered on the kingdom (Mk 1:14). His ministry was dedicated to a renewal of his people. Peace, which he came to bring, is a social goal and good, not simply an interior individual state of mind; it implies the harmony of justice and mercy among the people. Jesus' ministry was a trinitarian mission. The Father was seeking the salvation of his people through his Son and his Spirit—a salvation that was indeed communion with him, but also a communion among people that entailed a conversion not only of individuals but of socially structured relationships. His call to conversion was in part a call to a dedication to a society based on mutual respect and concern as sons and daughters of God; one could not be a genuine believer without a dedication to such a society.

In the church of the apostolic age, we see in the Acts of the Apostles and in Paul's missionary journeys that the communion with God and one another evoked by the sending of the Spirit at Pentecost and nourished by the Eucharist led to a communion (koinonia). This was a communion in which the ethnic, class, and sexual differences were respected, but in which foundations for fragmentations or fissions based on them were to be overcome (Gal 3:28). And it was a communion that was open to the larger world and essentially missionary. In this sharing with others within the community and outside the community, there was specifically a sharing of material goods with those in need (e.g., Acts 2:43–45; Gal 2:10). This missionary character of a trinitarian spirituality is shown in the whole history of the church, in its evangelization of the Mediterranean world, the Germanic tribes, the Normans, the Slavs, the Americas, Asia, and Africa—not without the mixed motives, methods, and results that characterize and stain a pilgrim church.

The church at the time of Vatican II has interpreted the church within the context of the trinitarian missions and has seen in this the source, model, and goal of the koinonia or communion that should characterize the Christian church, as we saw earlier in this chapter. The conversion this calls us to involves our conversion to extend genuine care to the economic, political, and social needs of men and women within and outside the church. The trinitarian root of this call to care for all is expressed, for example, by the 1997 Special Assembly for America of the Synod of Bishops in their proposition 97:

Faced with a divided world which is in search of unity, we must proclaim with joy and firm faith that God is communion, Father, Son and Holy Spirit, unity in distinction, and that he calls all people to share in that same Trinitarian communion. . . . We must proclaim that the church is the sign and instrument of the communion willed by God, begun in time and destined for completion in the fullness of the kingdom.[40]

This calls us to a sense of solidarity with all people. Pope John Paul shows the scriptural basis for the synod's teaching:

> "Truly, I say to you, as you did it to one of the least of these my brethren, you did it to me" (Mt. 25:40; cf. 25:45). "Solidarity is thus the fruit of the communion which is grounded in the mystery of the Triune God, and in the Son of God who took flesh and died for all. It is expressed in Christian love, which seeks the good of others, especially of those most in need."[41]

This call is counter to some contemporary understandings of what it means to be a human person and to the way individualistic anthropologies are translated into economic and political structures. But basing ourselves on our analysis of the human person in chapter 8, the call is fully in accord with who we are as human persons. To be a person is to be distinct from others but also, from our own center of heart and mind, to be engaged with and concerned for others. In fact, it is to be in relation with and concerned for and loving others, because we are made in the image of the triune God. And these others are also made in the image of God. As the synod fathers and pope teach:

> "God's masterpiece, man, is made in the divine image and likeness. . . . The human being's dignity as a child of God is the source of human rights and of corresponding duties."
>
> For this reason, "every offense against the dignity of man is an offense against God himself, in whose image man is made."
>
> . . . The church . . . " must live with the poor and share their distress. By her lifestyle, her priorities, her words and her actions, she must testify that she is in communion and solidarity with them."[42]

By the Father's design the redemptive mission of the exalted Christ and of the Holy Spirit is to have a transformative effect to bring about more of that justice and mercy in society that during his lifetime Christ sought to promote, and so it calls us as Christ's disciples to make dedication to this goal an essential part of our own lives.

b. Trinitarian Spirituality and World Religions

There are two points I wish to make here. The first is that Christian revelation includes what God manifests through world religions, and the second is that this challenges the church to listen to world religions and learn from them for the sake of more deeply understanding the transforming trinitarian mystery. These issues call for much longer discussions, but these discussions would lead us too far afield and can be found elsewhere.[43]

While Vatican II and a number of theologians since then have been hesitant to acknowledge divine revelations in world religions, this seems not wholly consistent with the council's acknowledgment that God "has never ceased to take care of the human race" (DV 2), its quotation from Irenaeus: "From the beginning, the Son, being present to his creation, reveals the Father to all whom the Father desires, at the time and in the manner desired by the Father" (AG 2, n.2, from Adv. Haer., IV, 6,7) and its recognition that world religions "often reflect a ray of that truth which enlightens all men" (NA 2).[44]

This hesitancy may be tied to two presuppositions. One is the kind of distinction scholasticism has usually made between natural knowledge of God from his effects and supernatural knowledge. Wisdom literature in the Old Testament does not make the same kind of distinction. This literature presents to us Lady Wisdom speaking to humans through some experiences of the physical world and of themselves, since God as creator does manifest himself through these effects and images of himself. As Roland Murphy writes:

> She [Lady Wisdom] cannot be viewed apart from the Lord from whom she originates. Her authority also suggests that she is the voice of the Lord, the revelation of God, not merely the self-revelation of creation. She is the divine summons issued in and through creation, who finds her delight among the humans God has created (Prv 8:31). Lady Wisdom, then, is a communication of God, through creation, to human beings.[45]

Thus God does through creation communicate something of his saving revelation to human beings out of his desire to save all. This revelation comes from God's free decision and is oriented to the salvation to which we are all summoned, one of communion with the triune God and with one another. For human beings to respond to this revelation in a saving manner takes an act of faith and is possible only through divine grace. This revelation is what we can call a *primordial* revelation, since it is based on the physical world and humanity as they come from God's creation. And recognition of this origin aligns such revelation with many myths of world religions that are based on the way the world appears from their culture's perspective—a perspective which is true in part.

The other presupposition is that to assert that God reveals himself through world religions may equate these religions with Christianity. This is not the case, as it is not the case with Judaism and Islam where the church acknowledges there is the gift of partial but real divine revelation. It is similarly not the case with such religions as Hinduism and Buddhism. The church already acknowledges clearly that Judaism and Islam have been graced with a real, though partial, divine revelation. We will briefly recall what many other theologians have developed at length, namely, that these 'pre-Christian' and continuing revelations should be affirmed as real by Christianity; this affirmation is the condition for a genuine and fruitful dialogue with these religions. There are also, we can suggest, reasons intrinsic to these religions that can help them to be open to God's trinitarian revelation.

Israel succeeded, through God's revelation, in seeing beyond the polytheisms and henotheisms of its time to the oneness of God. As Pinchas Lapide, an observant Jewish theologian, writes: "Only the small people of the Jews was able to break through to the recognition of the true Oneness of God—thanks to the revelations which were granted it."[46] Lapide is aware that Jesus made his own Israel's Shema (Dt 6:2) when he said, "The Lord our God is Lord alone! You shall love the Lord your God with all your heart. . ." (Mk 12:29–30). And Lapide acknowledges that the Jewish mystics found a mysterious threeness in God in the Jewish Scriptures, for example, in Genesis 1; in Isaiah 6:3, the threefold "Holy, holy, holy is the Lord of hosts"; in Genesis 18 where three visit Abraham and he addresses them as one; and in God's self, Spirit and Word. Lapide accepts Jesus "as a believing Jew who had a central role to play in God's plan of salvation [but not as Messiah or as Son of God]. . . . I believe that I as a Jew should follow the Jewish path."

Briefly, we would ask Lapide and other Jews whether God could reveal something new about himself beyond what is in the Jewish Scriptures—particularly since Scripture intimates an unfathomable inner richness of God in what it says of God's word, wisdom, and spirit, and the prophets predict more divine mercies to come to Israel. Further, if God is one, is it not in accord with his design to wish the whole creation of human beings to come to a kind of unity? Also, without denying that Israel remains God's chosen people (Rom 9:4–5; 11:1, 28–29), can Israel's faith provide a unity for all humankind, or is it likely that God would simply want disparate paths to himself to be the final expression of the human community?

If one turns to Islam, its affirmation of God's oneness was in part dependent on Muhammad's knowledge of Judaism and Christianity (or an Arian variant of Christianity). As Robert Caspar writes of Islam's strict monotheism:

The definition was used first against the polytheism of Arabia in the sixth to seventh centuries, . . . [these gods'] couplings engendering other gods or heroes.

> The brief *sûra*, No 112, "the *sûra* of the *tawhîd* (oneness of God)," which is constantly repeated, . . . is directed in the first place to these engenderings: "Say: God is one, he is indissociable, he does not beget and he is not begotten." It was only later that it was applied to the Christian ideas of divine fatherhood and sonship, understood in a carnal sense.[47]

For many centuries Islam interpreted Christian belief in the Trinity as an 'associationist' interpretation of God or a kind of polytheism; but there were Moslem scholars in the Middle Ages and then again recently who recognize it as a monotheism, though not their own monotheism.[48] There is very much to respect in Islam's great reverence for God and its sense of the nearness of God found primarily though not exclusively in its mystics, at times persecuted. Islam and Christianity have much common ground, for example in opposition to a contemporary naturalism. There seems to be now the possibility of dialogue between Christianity and Islam in some areas of the Moslem world and, after September 11, 2001, a much greater urgency. As with Judaism, we have to ask whether Islam can present an understanding of God that can foster a world community.

When we turn to the question of how we with our belief in the mystery of the Trinity should relate to Hinduism and Buddhism, I think that part of what the early Raimundo Panikkar wrote is very helpful. He found three major spiritualities in world religions, "apophatism, personalism and divine immanence," and thought that it is the Trinity that could affirm these spiritualities and interrelate them.[49] Initially the church turned toward the Mediterranean world, and the mystery of the Trinity was articulated in relation to Greek thought. Thus *logos* was given prominence, but *logos* is not prominent in Asian religions. To affirm what is true in these religions and to show them that a trinitarian belief is not opposed to what they hold most dear, one must have a more fully trinitarian spirituality than a Christocentric one. If we keep to a predominantly *logos* theology, we may miss what is positive in Hinduism and Buddhism and what they can offer to the West.

We propose, in continuity with comparative religion experts such as Panikkar and Zaehner, that Hinduism has some affinity with a spirituality of the Holy Spirit and Buddhism has some affinity with a spirituality reflective of the First Person as source of the Spirit. But we propose that the "ray of that truth which enlightens all men" (NA 2) that informs these spiritualities is a *primordial* revelation that will find its completion in that eschatological revelation mediated by Jesus Christ and the Holy Spirit, once the interpretation of the Christian mystery has been open to the riches of Asia as it was earlier to that of the Greeks. Of course in practice, the pre-Christian spiritualities centered both on Brahman and on the Buddhist way of deliverance were, in the course of history, combined with other devotional and personal religious expressions that enriched and complicated what may perhaps be seen as their basic religious insights.

We restrict ourselves here to supporting this thesis by a few words on Hinduism and Buddhism. Panikkar speaks of the basic direction of Hinduism as follows: "The whole *scruti*, the hindu revelation, leads to this point and to this alone: to bring about the realisation that *atman* is *brahman* . . . that only I is."[50] This form of unity is related to a religious consciousness of the cosmos expresssed in a hymn in the Rig-Veda, where the most primordial reality is sensed as follows:

> That One breathed, windless, by its own energy: Nought else existed then.
> . . . In the beginning this [One] evolved, Became desire, first seed of mind.
> . . . Beneath was energy, above was impulse. . . . Whence this emanation has arisen, Whether [God] disposed it, or whether he did not—Only he who is its overseer in highest heaven knows. [He only knows,] or perhaps he does not know.[51]

It is this energy, desire, emanation from which all comes and in which all participate, and which the *scruti* helps the individual to eventually experience.

Zaehner points out a certain analogy between the religious consciousness expressed in the Rig-Veda hymn and the spirit in the first chapter of Genesis:

> We are immediately reminded of the opening words of Genesis: "Now the earth was a formless void, there was darkness over the deep, and God's spirit hovered over the water." The symbolism is the same—water and darkness representing chaos, the spirit, the 'breathing' One representing emergent life. In Genesis the spirit is God's spirit; in the Rig-Vedic hymn God is the "overseer in highest heaven" who may be responsible for creation or not.[52]

We are suggesting that something of God was manifested through this experience of the self and the cosmos and that it is expressed in the sacred writings of India. This something seems based on the active character of matter we examined in chapter 5, a dynamism that courses through all creation and that is, in a way, a participation in the Spirit of God.

If we turn to Buddhism, we find its privileged experience to be that of Siddhartha Gautama who lived in the sixth century B.C. in northern India. From the traditions surrounding his life, it is evident that his experience centered on the transience of such individual goods as health, wealth, and life itself and on the deceptiveness of the desire for personal gain that centers our lives on these goods. Through enlightenment, Gautama realized that the cure of life's dislocations is found in the extirpation of desire and in the following of the Eightfold Path (right knowledge, aspiration, speech, behavior, livelihood, effort, mindfulness, and absorption). Nirvana is the bliss that is the fulfillment of this emergence from the boundary of the finite self.

The theology associated with this spirituality is largely apophatic or negative, analogous to that of some Christian mystics, such as Meister Eckhart. The Buddhist way of knowledge is not knowledge in the primary Western sense, that is, by sense knowledge of what is outside us and then intellectual insight into this reality. The knowledge comes, rather, by way of interiority through the human orientation by affectivity and will toward the good; it is associated with a turning from lesser goods toward that which is the center of the human person at the deepest level. It is an experience of emptiness insofar as it is not intellectual knowledge and is a turning away from lesser goods.

If we relate this to the Trinity, we see an affinity between it and the way that classically the First Person has been understood as the origin of the Spirit, that is, as the good evoking the response of love. Buddhism relates to the ultimate not so much as the origin of creation but as the ultimate good transcendent to all lesser goods and as the only worthy focus of human aspirations. Dominic Dubarle asks: "Why cannot *nirvanna* itself be a sort of peaceful and silent union with the energy of the divine goodness, nameless and formless, existing as a withdrawal from all things, but never rejecting anyone who comes to it?"[53]

From these very brief references to enormously complex religious traditions, we wish to suggest that it is primarily the trinitarian revelation that can bring human beings together and that can be a basis for a world community. World religions must grow today to integrate a changing human experience, but we too with our belief in God as triune must also grow, in part through recognizing and learning from these other early and continuing revelations with which God has graced our world.

A trinitarian spirituality is what we desperately need today. The ultimate is not remote from us. It touches us immediately and personally. It reassures us of God's love as the source both of all we are and of the communion with God that we are offered, and that we even now share through the Father's gift of the Son and the Spirit. The importance of all of this for our lives is impossible for us to grasp save through the power of the Holy Spirit, and still in this life we cannot experience its full significance. This gift and revelation of the mystery of the Trinity, as well its implications for our lives, is particularly important today, for it shows us the basis and direction for change. It gives us the presence, the motivation, the power, and the direction for change that is

truly human and Christian. One basis for our difficulty
quately the meaning for us of the Trinity is that there is n.
mate in terms of which we can express it. Everything else has
in terms of our relation to the Father through the Son in the S,
last word about its significance for us cannot be what we gain fr.
worth is it for us that another reveals himself or herself and gives ⸺f or
herself to us? We are only free if we are beyond utilitarianism; friendship is
only for free persons.

Conclusion

In conclusion, we wish simply to recall that the Trinity is a mystery, and to
end with the praise that this revealed mystery evokes in Christians.

The Trinity is a mystery of faith that, as the First Vatican Council taught,
once revealed we may, by God's gift, penetrate partially. However, "the divine mysteries by their very nature so exceed the created intellect that even
when communicated by revelation and received by faith, they remain cov-
ered by the veil of faith and as though shrouded in darkness, as long as in this
mortal life 'we are away from the Lord, for we walk by faith and not by sight'
(2 Cor 5:6f)."[54] The Trinity is a mystery of faith before being a mystery of
theology. We are given to know the Father's love by the Son incarnate and
in the Spirit, an experiential and dark knowledge dependent on our response
of trust and love.[55] What the Father's gift of love and presence can lead to we
can see particularly but not exclusively in Mary, the saints, and mystics.
Among all Christian mysteries there is a certain hierarchy of truths (UR 11),
and that of the Trinity is the most central.

Our theological reflection on God as triune began with God's revelation
through Jesus Christ and the Holy Spirit, with the faith this revelation
evokes and the worship to which this faith gives rise. And similarly this reflection should terminate in this praise of God as triune—the praise of the
Father for what he has done for us through the Son and in the Holy Spirit
and so too for who God is, a praise that acknowledges God's glory and a
praise by which we go beyond our self-boundedness to the deepest dispositions appropriate for us as human and Christian, dispositions that allow and
foster the community of the disciples of Christ and promote the community
of the larger world.[56] We conclude with the prayer of the author of the Letter to the Ephesians (3:14–21):

I kneel before the *Father*, from whom every family in heaven and on earth is
named, that he may grant you in accord with the riches of his glory to be

strengthened with power through his *Spirit* in the inner self, and that *Christ* may dwell in your hearts through faith; that you, rooted and grounded in love, may have strength to comprehend with all the holy ones what is the breadth and length and height and depth, and to know the love of *Christ* that surpasses knowledge, so that you may be filled with all the fullness of *God*.

Now to *him* [the Father] who is able to accomplish far more than all we ask or imagine, by the *power* [the Holy Spirit] at work within us, to him be glory in the church and in *Christ Jesus* to all generations, forever and ever. Amen.

Notes

1. Miroslav Volf, *After Our Likeness: The Church as the Image of the Trinity* (Grand Rapids, Mich.: Eerdmans, 1998). See also the review of this book by Jaroslav Skira in *TS* 60 (1999): 376–377. The page references in the text here and in our later section on the Free Church are to Volf's book; where "R" is added in brackets after the page number, Volf is quoting Ratzinger. References to Ratzinger's book and articles used can be found in Volf's book. But see also Joseph Cardinal Ratzinger, *Introduction to Christianity* (New York: Crossroad, 1969); *Church, Ecumenism, and Politics: New Essays in Ecclesiology* (New York: Crossroads, 1988); and "The Ecclesiology of the Second Vatican Council," *Communio* 13 (1986): 239–251. In this article, Ratzinger treats the Church as the body of Christ, the people of God, and collegiality; he mentions the Holy Spirit only once. Also see Vatican Congregation for the Doctrine of the Faith, "Letter to the Bishops of the Catholic Church on Some Aspects of the Church Understood as Communion," *Origins* 22 (June 25, 1992): 108–112. For interpretations of the Church as communion offered in the process of the ecumenical movement, see A. Birmelé, "Status quaestionis de la théologie de la communion à travers les dialogues oecumeniques et l'évolution des différentes théologies confessionelles," *Cristianesimo nella storia* 16 (1995): 254–284.

2. See Veli-Matti Kärkkäinen, "The Ecumenical Potential of Pneumatology," *Gregorianum* 80 (1999): 121–145.

3. Jan Walgrave, "Newman's 'On consulting the Faithful in Matters of Doctrine,'" in Johannes-Baptist Metz and Edward Schillebeeckx, eds., *The Teaching Authority of the Believers. Concilium*, vol. 180 (Edinburgh: T & T Clark, 1985), 26. See articles in this collection, particularly parts 1 and 3..

4. M. J. Farrelly, "Holy Spirit," in Michael Downey, ed., *The New Dictionary of Catholic Spirituality* (Collegeville, Minn.: Liturgical Press, 1993), 501.

5. John D. Zizioulas, *Being as Communion: Studies in Personhood and the Church* (Crestwood, N.Y.: St. Vladimir's Seminary Press, 1985), 134–135. Page numbers in the text at this section are to this book. See also Zizioulas, "The Mystery of the Church in Orthodox Tradition," *One in Christ* 24 (1988): 294–303; "Primacy in the Church: An Orthodox Approach," in James Puglisi, ed., *Petrine Ministry and the Unity of the Church* (Collegeville, Minn.: Liturgical Press, 1999), 115–125; and Volf, "Zizioulas: Communion, One, and Many," in his *After Our Likeness*, 73–123.

6. Tillard, "The Ecumenical Kairos and the Primacy," in Puglisi, *Petrine Ministry*, 194. On some varied Orthodox views on the Trinity and their ecclesial implictions, see Yannis Spiteris, "La dottrina trinitaria nella teologia orthodossa. Autori e prospettive," in Angelo Amato, ed., *Trinità in contesto* (Rome: Libreria Ateneo Salesiano, 1994), 45–70.

7. See, for example, Robert N. Bellah, "Is There a Common American Culture?" *JAAR* 66 (1998): 613–625. He identifies the common American culture behind a good deal of contemporary multiculturalism largely with individualism, and he finds an important source of this to be in the Free Church or Baptist tradition. This tradition, for example in Roger Williams, insisted so much on the sacredness of individual conscience that it was an important source of modern notions of human rights. But Williams, who split from the Puritans and finally had a church consisting of only three people, was a "sociological catastrophe" (622). And: "Just when we are moving to an ever greater validation of the sacredness of the individual person, our capacity to imagine a social fabric that would hold individuals together is vanishing" (622).

8. See Synod of Bishops, "The Final Report," section C, 1 *Origins* 15 (1985): 448, "The ecclesiology of communion is the central and fundamental idea of the council's documents."

9. It is particularly in *Faith in God Through Jesus Christ* (Collegeville, Minn.: Liturgical Press, 1997) that I have developed this theme. See Geoffrey Wainwright, *Eucharist and Eschatology* (New York: Oxford University Press, 1981) for the presence of this scheme in the Eucharist.

10. Killian McDonnell, "Pneumatology Overview," *Proceedings of the Catholic Theological Society of America* 51 (1996): 189.

11. Yves Congar, *I Believe in the Holy Spirit*, Vol. 2, *He is the Lord and Giver of Life* (New York: Seabury, 1983), 11–12.

12. See chapter 2, 44–45.

13. J.-M. R. Tillard, *Church of Churches: The Ecclesiology of Communion* (Collegeville, Minn.: Liturgical Press, 1992), 51.

14. Tillard, *Church of Churches*, 23–24.

15. Congar, *I Believe in the Holy Spirit*, vol. 2, 16.

16. Congar, "The Holy Spirit and the Apostolic Body, Continuators of the Work of Christ," in *The Mystery of the Church* (Baltimore: Helicon Press, 1960), 171, as quoted by Mark Ginter, "The Holy Spirit and Morality: A Dynamic Alliance," in *Proceedings of the Catholic Theological Society of America* 51 (1996): 173.

17. Congar, *Mystery*, 102, 103, as quoted by Ginter, "Holy Spirit and Morality," 174.

18. See Yves Congar, *I Believe*, vol. 3, 228–274, on "The Eucharistic Epiclesis," "The Holy Spirit in our Communion with the Body and Blood of Christ," and "The Life of the Church as One Long Epiclesis."

19. See Hervé Legrand, "La Réalisation de L'Église en un Lieu," in Bernard Lauret and François Refoulé, eds., *Initiation à la pratique de la théologie*, vol. 3 (Paris: Cerf, 1983), esp. 159–170; also Tillard, *Church of Churches*; George Tavard, *The Church, Community of Salvation: An Ecumenical Ecclesiology* (Collegeville, Minn.: Liturgical

Press, 1992); Dennis Doyle, *Communion Ecclesiology* (Maryknoll, N.Y.: Orbis, 2000); the exchanges on this issue by Cardinals Water Kasper and Joseph Ratzinger in *America*, April 23–30, 2001, and Nov. 19, 2001; and Susan Wood, "The Church as Communion," in Peter Phan, ed., *The Gift of the Church: A Textbook on Ecclesiology in Honor of Patrick Granfield, O.S.B.* (Collegeville, Minn.: Liturgical Press, 2000), 159–176. We may note that in the Phan book, Pedro Rodriguez in "Theological Method for Ecclesiology," 129–156, gives a certain priority to the notion of the Church as People of God over that of communion. He suggests (132–143) we "must retrieve the theme of "People of God" as the basic concept to understand the Church." Part of the reason he gives for this is that it helps us "understand the Church as the term of this trinitarian action, which is the Church itself considered as the People of God who are a pilgrim in history and will be consummated in glory, a people whose mystery consists in Easter (Church as body of Christ) and in Pentecost (Church as Temple of the Holy Spirit)." Perhaps Rodriguez's purpose would be better served if he gave more prominence to the Father initiating the Church through the exalted Christ sending the Spirit from the future kingdom to draw us toward that salvation and consummation.

20. See the encyclical of Pope John Paul II, *Ut Unum Sint*, May 25, 1995, and reflections on it in Puglisi, *Petrine Ministry*; and John Quinn, *The Reform of the Papacy: The Costly Call to Christian Unity* (New York: Crossroad, 1999).

21. See Yves Congar, *Diversity and Communion* (Mystic, Conn.: Twenty-Third Publications, 1985).

22. Similarly for St. Paul. For example, Fernand Prat, *The Theology of Saint Paul*, trans. from 10th French ed. (Westminster, Md.: Newman Press, 1952), vol. 2, 261, writes: "Baptized in Christ, you have put on Christ, you have the form of Christ, and consequently also the adoption of sons inherent in that form." And J. Lebreton, *Les Origines du dogme de la Trinité* 5th ed. (Paris: Gabrielle Beauchesne, 1928), 361: "Si d'autres peuvent être ses fils (de Dieu) ce n'est que parce qu'ils sont incorporé au Fils premier-né."

23. See chapter 6, 180.

24. Prat, *Theology*, vol. 2, 320. Catholics and Lutherans are agreed on justification as a work of the triune God. For example, in the Lutheran–Catholic "Joint Declaration on the Doctrine of Justification," *Origins* 28 (July 16, 1998), paragraph 15, they state: "In faith we together hold the conviction that justification is the work of the triune God. . . . Justification thus means that Christ himself is our righteousness, in which we share through the Holy Spirit in accord with the will of the Father."

25. There are a variety of interpretations of the Greek Fathers on this issue, and a consequent variety of modern theologies on the issue. On this whole question see, for example, R. Moretti, "Inhabitation," *Dictionnaire de Spiritualité* (Paris: Beauchesne, 1971) 7: 1735–1767; and A Michel, "Trinité (Missions et habitation des personnes de la)," *DTC* 15: 1830–1855.

26. See, for instance, E. Mersch, "Filii in Filio," *Nouvelle revue théologique* 65 (1938) who sums up the thought of the Greek Fathers by writing, "According to

them all, then, Christians are divinized and adopted by incorporation in the Son, in him who is the second person. And this adoption by that and that only, but by that truly, has a real and special relation to this second person, in Christ and through his unique incarnation" (575).

27. Cyril, *In Ioannem* 11,11 (Pusey, 2, 730–731), as in Walter Burghardt, *The Image of God in Man according to Cyril of Alexandria* (Woodstock, Md.: Woodstock College Press, 1957), 72. Burghardt shows that, "In Cyril's eyes, the sanctifying role of the Spirit is essential. There is no convincing evidence that Cyril considered it exclusive, that he attributed to the Spirit a personal function in sanctification which belongs only to the Spirit, to the exclusion of Father and Son" (73). He discusses the modern controversy among patristic scholars on this issue, but he seems to agree with J. Sagües that while Cyril teaches that God's external activity "is due equally to the three Persons as efficient cause, still he somehow conceives of distinct functions of the distinct Persons in man's sanctification" (74, fn.). He also compares Cyril's notion of sanctification with the previous tradition of the Greek Fathers (77–83).

28. On Athanasius's and the Cappadocians' teaching on the Spirit, see chapter 3, 88–90.

29. See chapter 4, 107–109.

30. See St. Thomas, *ST* I-II, 110; and Stephen Duffy, *The Dynamics of Grace: Perspectives in Theological Anthropology* (Collegeville, Minn.: Liturgical Press, 1993), chapter 4, "Friar Thomas D'Aquino: Grace Perfecting Nature," 121–170. In a later chapter (173–218), Duffy discusses Luther's theology of grace. Toward the end of this chapter, he notes the difference of style that separates Luther from Thomas. For example, he writes (211–212): "While Thomas thought in ontological categories, Luther thought in the categories of relationship . . . the two differed in the basic concern and interest that forms the infrastructure of their reflection. . . . Luther is concerned with human anxiety over salvation; Thomas, with God as creator. Luther seeks solace for bruised consciences; Thomas, a theoretical framework for theology. . . . As Otto Pesch has contended, Luther's theology is 'existential,' and Thomas' 'sapiential.'"

31. See Ralph Del Colle, *Christ and the Spirit: Spirit-Christology in Trinitarian Perspective* (New York: Oxford University Press, 1994) chapters 3 and 4. In the latter chapter, he analyses David Coffey's theological developments further in this line.

32. Del Colle, *Christ and the Spirit*, 73. The interior quotations are from M. Donnelly, "The Inhabitation of the Holy Spirit: A Solution according to de la Taille," *TS* 8 (1949): 445–470. Other articles relevant to this controversy are cited by Del Colle.

33. D. Coffey also notes the similarities between "divine energies" and "created actuation by uncreated grace" (see Del Colle, *Christ and the Spirit*, 96).

34. See chapter 5, 132–139.

35. See, for example, C. A. Benard, "L'esperienza spirituale della Trinita," in E. Ancilli and M. Paparozzi, eds., *La Mistica: Fenomenologia e riflessione teologica* (Rome: Città Nuova, 1984), 295–321; Louis Dupré and James Wiseman, O.S.B., eds., *Light from Light: An Anthology of Christian Mysticism* (New York: Paulist Press, 1988); James

Wiseman, "'I Have Experienced God': Religious Experience in the Theology of Karl Rahner," *American Benedictine Review* 44 (1993): 22–57; Philip Sheldrake, *Spirituality and Theology: Christian Living and the Doctrine of God* (Maryknoll, N.Y.: Orbis, 1998); John O'Donnell, "Trinité et vie spirituelle," *Dictionnaire de Spiritualité* 15 (1991): 1311–1323; John Farrelly, "Notes on Mysticism in Today's World," *Spirituality Today* 43 (1991): 104–118.

36. See particularly Jeremy Driscoll, "The Eucharist and Fundamental Theology," *Ecclesia Orans* 13 (1996): 407–434; "Anamnesis, Epiclesis, and Fundamental Theology," *Ecclesia Orans* 15 (1998): 211–238; and "Liturgy and Fundamental Theology. Frameworks for a Dialogue," *Ecclesia Orans* 11 (1994): 69–99. Driscoll notes that he himself has gained much in this area from H. U. von Balthasar, J. Zizioulas, G. LaFont, and others. Also see Cyprian Vagaggini, *Theological Dimensions of the Liturgy,* 4th Italian ed. (Collegeville, Minn.: Liturgical Press, 1976), 184–246, chapter 7, "From the Father, Through Christ, in the Holy Spirit, to the Father: the Liturgy and the Christological-Trinitarian Activity in the Divine Plan"; Achille M. Triacca, "Inculturazione liturgica e mistero trinitario," in Amato, *Trinità in Contesto*, 343–373; Michael Witczak, "The Manifold Presence of Christ in the Liturgy," *TS* 59 (1998): 680–702; and John McKenna, "Eucharistic Presence: An Invitation to Dialogue," *TS* 60 (1999): 294–317. Also, for the mystery of the Trinity as an integrating principle of Christian catechetics, see Peter Phan, "Now That I know How to Teach, What Do I Teach? In Search of the Unity of Faith in Religious Education," *Salesianum* 60 (1998): 125–145.

37. Witczak, "Manifold Presence," 701.

38. See Driscoll, "Anamnesis," 231, where he quotes Zizioulas, *Being as Communion*, 186, 187–188.

39. Driscoll, "The Eucharist and Fundamental Theology," 430–431.

40. John Paul II's Apostolic Exhortation, *Ecclesia in America*, paragraph 33 (*Origins* 28 [February 4, 1999]: 576).

41. John Paul II, *Ecclesia in America*, paragraph 52; the quotation is from the Synod's Proposition 67. We must acknowledge that the Church's sharper awareness of the social implications of the trinitarian missions owes something to Western liberal democracies, to the political theologies of Moltmann and Metz, to liberation theologies, and to recent studies of the ministry of Jesus.

42. John Paul II, *Ecclesia in America*, paragraph 57, 58. The first quotation is from Proposition 72; the second is from Puebla Conference of the Latin American Bishops (1979), "Message to the Peoples of Latin America," and the third is from Proposition 73. For a study of human beings as images of God, see Anthony O. Erhueh, *Vatican II: Image of God in Man* (Rome: Urbaniana University Press, 1987). For a study of many current forms of liberation theology, see Peter Phan, "Method in Liberation Theologies," *TS* 61 (2000): 40–63.

43. As examples of such treatises, we may mention Gavin D'Costa, *The Meeting of Religions and the Trinity* (Maryknoll, N.Y.: Orbis, 2000), who argues against the pluralists (e.g., Paul Knitter and John Hick), but shows that the world religions do in-

deed challenge the church to understand the Trinity more deeply; Jacques Dupuis, *Toward a Christian Theology of Religious Pluralism* (Maryknoll: Orbis, 1997) and "'The Truth Will Make You Free': The Theology of Religious Pluralism Revisited," *Louvain Studies* 24 (1999): 211–263, where Dupuis argues that world religions such as Hinduism and Buddhism represent a partial self-disclosure and self-gift of the trinitarian God, that they have for their peoples a place in God's design somewhat analogous to God's dispensation with Israel, and that this is in line with God's covenant with Noah (Gen 9:1–17) and his descendents. See also Dupuis, "Le Verbe de Dieu, Jésus Christ et les religions du monde," *Nouvelle revue théologique* 123 (2001): 529–546; B. Pottier, "Note sur la mission invisible du Verbe chez Saint Thomas d'Aquin," *Nouvelle revue théologique* 123 (2001): 547–557; Pinchas Lapide and Jürgen Moltmann, *Jewish Monotheism and Christian Trinitarian Doctrine: A Dialogue* (Philadelphia: Fortress, 1981); Claude Jeffré and Jean-Pierre Jossua, eds., *Monotheism. Concilium*, vol. 177 (Edinburgh: T & T Clark, 1985); and Amato, *Trinità*; Jung Young Lee, *The Trinity in Asian Perspective* (Nashville: Abingdon, 1996). The last four books mentioned show possible openings in world religions to the revelation of the Trinity, while fully acknowledging difficulties to this. I have written briefly on these questions in *Belief in God in Our Time* (Collegeville, Minn.: Liturgical Press, 1992), 277–299, and *Faith in God*, 293–298, 338–340.

44. This opening to the possibility of revelations in world religions found in Vatican II is continued in later church documents such as Pope John Paul II's *Redemptoris Missio* (1990), paragraph 28, and the International Theological Commission's, "Il cristianesimo e le religioni" (1997), 84, 86. Also see a statement on this issue by the Theological Advisory Commission of the Federation of Asian Bishops' Conference in 1987 cited in Dupuis, *Toward*, 220.

45. Roland Murphy, "Introduction to Wisdom Literature," *NJBC*, 450. Also see his book, *The Tree of Life* (New York: Doubleday, 1990), 121–126. This revelation is of a somewhat different character from that which comes through the prophets. Also see David Carpenter, "Revelation in Comparative Perspective: Lessons for Interreligious Dialogue," *Journal of Ecumenical Studies* 29 (1992): 175–188. He finds a similarity between revelation in the Hindu tradition and that which comes through Wisdom in Scripture.

46. Lapide and Moltmann, *Jewish Monotheism*, 38.

47. Robert Caspar, "The Permanent Significance of Islam's Monotheism," in Jeffré and Jossua, *Monotheism*, 68; see the whole article, 67–78.

48. See Piergiorgio Gianazza, "Mistero trinitario e islam," in Amato, *Trinità*, 225–274, esp. 261–262.

49. Raimundo Panikkar, *The Trinity and the Religious Experience of Man* (Maryknoll, N.Y.: Orbis, 1973), 55. Also see R. C. Zaehner, *Concordant Discord* (Oxford: Clarendon Press, 1970) who writes of three major forms of mysticism: personal love of God, cosmic consciousness, and "mysticism of isolation." He finds the last of these particularly in Buddhism, though differently in different forms of Buddhism (59–60, 106f.). Panikkar gradually moved in his writings toward being a pluralist. See Camilia

Gangasingh MacPherson, A Critical Reading of the Development of Raimon Panikkar's Thought on the Trinity (Lanham, Md.: University Press of America, 1996).

50. Panikkar, Trinity and Religious Experience, 38. Also see in Amato, Trinità, Dominic Veliath, "La Trinità nella indiana contemporanea. Autori e prospettive," 171–190, and Daniel Acharuparambil, "Mistero trinitario e induismo," 199–212.

51. Rig-Veda 10:129, cited by Zaehner, Concordant Discord, 68–69.

52. Zaehner, Concordant Discord, 69–70. See Panikkar, Trinity and Religious Experience, 63: "There is no doubt that hindu thought is especially well prepared to contribute to the elaboration of a deeper theology of the Spirit."

53. Dominique Dubarle, "Buddhist Spirituality and the Christian Understanding of God," in C. Geffré and M. Dhavamony, eds., Buddhism and Christianity. Concilium, vol. 116 (New York: Seabury, 1979), 70. We do not raise the question of the operation of grace in Buddhism. On this, see Dubarle's article. Also see Hans Waldenfels, Absolute Nothingness: Foundations for a Buddhist-Christian Dialogue (New York: Paulist, 1980).

54. DS 3016. It is important to acknowledge both that the mystery of the Trinity transcends our understanding, and that we are given some genuine knowledge of this mystery. We must acknowledge and interrelate the apophatic and the kataphatic in discussions on religious and theological language. Even with Christian revelation darkness remains, as Thomas asserted: "through the revelation of grace in this life we do not know of God what he is, and thus we are conjoined with him as with one unknown" (ST I, 12, 13, ad 1). But this acknowledgment has been used at times to promote a kind of agnosticism. See for an answer to this, Mark Johnson, "Apophatic Theology's Cataphatic Dependencies," Thomist 62 (1998): 519–531.

55. The degree of darkness that one may experience is shown graphically in the lives of many people who are subject either individually or as communities to catastrophes. It is in another way shown to us in the lives and writings of saints and mystics, such as Thérèse of Lisieux. See Mary Frolich, H.M., "Desolation and Doctrine in Thérèse of Lisieux," TS 61 (2000): 261–279.

56. See Xavier Léon-Dufour, ed., Dictionary of Biblical Theology, Rev. ed. (New York: Seabury, 1973), on "Glory," "Praise," and "Worship" in Scripture. Also see LaCugna, God for Us, "Trinity, Theology and Doxology," 319–376.

~

Bibliographical Essays

This is a selection of main references, listed by chapter, that may be of help to the reader, particularly the student, for further study of the themes of each chapter. I give these generally in the sequence in which I use them, and I add some references not available to me at the time of writing this book but which may be helpful to readers. The more advanced scholars know that they can find fuller references in such publications as the yearly bibliographical surveys in *Ephemerides theologicae lovanienses*.

Chapter 1: The Trinity: The Theological Problematic

References to classic Christian theologies of the Trinity may be found in the bibliographical essays on chapters 3 and 4. A survey and evaluation of many twentieth-century trinitarian theologies may be found in William Hill, *The Three-Personed God: The Trinity: The Trinity as a Mystery of Salvation* (Washington, D.C.: Catholic University of America Press, 1982); Angelo Amato, ed., *Trinità in Contesto* (Rome: Libreria Ateneo Salesiano, 1994); Anne Hunt, *What are They Saying About the Trinity?* (New York: Paulist, 1998); Gerald O'Collins, S.J., "The Holy Trinity: The State of the Question," 1–28, in *The Trinity: An Interdisciplinary Symposium on the Trinity*, edited by Stephen Davis, Daniel Kendall, S.J., and Gerald O'Collins, S.J.. (Oxford: Oxford University Press, 1999). A contrast between major Catholic and Protestant trinitarian theologies in the twentieth century is offered by Karl Rahner, *The Trinity* (New York: Herder and Herder, 1970); and Karl Barth, *Church Dogmatics*, vol. 1. *The Doctrine of the Word of God. Part One* (Edinburgh: T & T Clark, 1975).

Some major differences in post–Vatican II Christian theologies are seen in the following: English and Process theologies: John Hick, ed., *The Myth of God Incarnate* (London: SCM Press, 1977); answered by T. V. Morris, *The Logic of God Incarnate* (Ithaca, N.Y.: Cornell University Press, 1986); John Cobb Jr., and David Griffin, *Process Theology: An Introductory Exposition* (Philadelphia: Westminster Press, 1976); Joseph Bracken, *The Triune Symbol: Persons, Process, and Community* (Lanham, Md.: University Press of America, 1985). On varied disciples of Barth, see J. Moltmann, *The Crucified God: The Cross of Christ as the Foundation and Criticism of Christian Theology* (New York: Harper and Row, 1974); Ted Peters, "Trinity Talk," *Dialog* 26 (1987): 44–48, 133–138; W. Pannenberg, "The Triune God," 259–336 in his *Systematic Theology*, vol. 1 (Edinburgh: T & T Clark, 1991); and Robert Jenson, *Systematic Theology*, vol. 1. *The Triune Identity* (New York: Oxford, 1997). On a social model of the Trinity, see John O'Donnell, "The Trinity as Divine Community," *Gregorianum* 69 (1988): 5–34; and John Gresham Jr., "The Social Model of the Trinity and Its Critics," *Scottish Journal of Theology* 46 (1993): 325–343. On the Holy Spirit, see Lukas Vischer, ed., *Spirit of God, Spirit of Christ: Ecumenical Reflections on the Filioque Controversy*. Faith and Order Document #103 (London: SPCK, 1981); Bradford Hinze and D. Lyle Dabney, eds., *Advents of the Spirit: An Introduction to the Current Study of Pneumatology* (Milwaukee: Marquette University Press, 2001). On feminist theology of the Trinity, see Anne Carr, *Transforming Grace: Christian Tradition and Women's Experience* (San Francisco: Harper and Row, 1988); Elizabeth Johnson, *She Who Is: The Mystery of God in Feminist Discourse* (New York: Crossroad, 1992).

Chapter 2: Scripture and the Roots of Christian Belief in the Trinity

On words important for Scripture's teaching on the Trinity, see ABD and TDNT articles on "word of God," "*logos*," "Holy Spirit," "Spirit," "*pneuma*," "wisdom," and "*sophia*." On intertestamental Judaism and Philo, see ABD, "Judaism in the Greco-Roman Period," and EEC, "Judaeo-Hellenism."

On Christ in the New Testament, see James Dunn, *Jesus and the Spirit* (London: SPCK Press, 1975); Dunn, *Christology in the Making: A New Testament Inquiry into the Origins of the Doctrine of the Incarnation*, 2d ed. (Grand Rapids, Mich.: Eerdmans, 1996); Rudolf Schnackenburg, *Jesus in the Gospels: A Biblical Christology* (Louisville, Ky.: John Knox Press, Fortress Press, 1993); Joel Green and Max Turner, eds., *Jesus of Nazareth: Lord and Christ: Essays on the Historical Jesus and New Testament Christology* (Grand Rapids, Mich.: Eerdmans, 1994); Brendan Byrne, "Christ's Pre-Existence in Pauline Soteriology," *TS* 58 (1997): 308–330.

On the Holy Spirit, see Dunn, *Jesus and the Spirit*; Green and Turner, *Jesus of Nazareth*; John Farrelly, "Feminine Symbols and the Holy Spirit," 49–76 in *God's Work in a Changing World* (Lanham, Md.: University Press of America, 1985); Farrelly, "Holy Spirit," 492–503 in *New Dictionary of Catholic Spirituality* (Collegeville,

Minn.: Liturgical Press, 1993); Max-Alain Chevallier, *Souffle de Dieu. Le Saint-Esprit dans le Nouveau Testament*, 3 vols. (Paris: Beauchesne, 1989–1991).

Chapter 3: Soundings in the History of Christian Reflection on the Trinity: To Constantinople I (381)

See Jaroslav Pelikan, *Credo: Historical and Theological Guide to Creeds and Confessions of Faith in the Christian Tradition* (New Haven: Yale University Press, 2003); J. N. D. Kelly, *Early Christian Doctrines*, 5th ed. (London: Black, 1977); E. J. Fortman, *The Triune God* (Philadelphia: Westminster, 1972); Basil Studer, *Trinity and Incarnation: The Faith of the Early Church* (Collegeville, Minn.: Liturgical Press, 1993); Bernard Sesboué and Joseph Wolinski, *Le Dieu de Salut*, vol. 1 of *Histoire des Dogmes* (Tournai: Desclée, 1994); Robert Gregg and Dennis Groh, *Early Arianism: A View of Salvation* (Philadelphia, Fortress, 1981); R. P. C. Hanson, *The Search for the Christian Doctrine of God: The Arian Controversy, 318–381* (Edinburgh: T & T Clark, 1988); Rowan Williams, *Arius: Heresy and Tradition* (Grand Rapids, Mich.: Eerdmans, 2002); Frederick Norris, ed., *Faith Gives Fullness to Reasoning: The Five Theological Orations of St. Gregory of Nazianzen*, translated by Lionel Wickham and Frederick Williams (Leiden: E. J. Brill, 1991).

Chapter 4: Later Soundings: The Fifth to the Nineteenth Century

For selections and essays relevant to the doctrine of the Trinity from councils, Fathers, and theologians through the ages, see Fortman, *The Triune God*; William La Due, *The Trinity Guide to the Trinity* (Harrisburg, Penn.: Trinity Press International, 2003). For Augustine through Palamas, see Augustine, *The Trinity*, with introduction, translation, and notes by Edmund Hill, O.P. (Brooklyn: New City Press, 1991); Catherine LaCugna, *God for Us: The Trinity and Christian Life* (San Francisco: Harper, 1991), chapters 3–6; for Western and Eastern theologies of the Holy Spirit, see Congar, *I Believe in the Holy Spirit*, 3 vols. in one (New York: Crossroad, 1997). See also Richard of St. Victor, *The Twelve Patriarchs. The Mystical Ark. Book Three of the Trinity*, with translation and introduction by Grover Zinn (New York: Paulist, 1979); Thomas Aquinas, *Summa theologiae*, 7 vols. Latin text and English translation (New York: McGraw-Hill, 1964); Gregory Palamas, *The Triads*, translated by Nicholas Gendle (New York: Paulist, 1983).

Chapter 5: The Trinity's Relation to the Orders of Salvation and Creation

On this theme see the references in chapter 1, above, to process theologies and to R. Jenson, J. Moltmann, W. Pannenberg, and T. Peters; the reference in chapter 4 to

C. LaCugna; also G. Emery, O.P., "Trinité et Création," *Rev. Sc. Phil. et Théol.* 79 (1995): 405–430; G. Emery, *Trinity in Aquinas* (Ypsilanti, Mich.: Sapientia Press of Ave Maria College, 2003). Also see Walter Kasper, *The God of Jesus Christ* (Herder and Herder, 1985); John Thompson, *Modern Trinitarian Perspectives* (New York: Oxford University Press, 1994); Hans Urs von Balthasar, *Mysterium Paschale: The Mystery of Easter* (Grand Rapids, Mich.: Eerdmans, 1993); Balthasar, "Creation and Trinity," *Communio* 15 (1988): 285–293; Gerry O'Hanlon, S.J., "Does God Change—H. U. von Bathasar on the Immutability of God," *Irish Theological Quarterly* 53 (1987): 161–183; Earl Muller, S.J., "Real Relations and the Divine: Issues in Thomas's Understanding of God's Relation to the World,," *TS* 56 (1995): 673–695; Jean Galot, S.J., "Le Dieu trinitaire et la Passion du Christ," *Nouvelle revue théologique* 104 (1982): 224–245; Thomas Weinandy, *Does God Suffer?* (Notre Dame: University of Notre Dame Press, 2000).

Also see Paul Davies, *The Cosmic Blueprint: New Discoveries in Nature's Creative Ability to Order the Universe* (New York: Simon and Schuster, 1988); Christopher Mooney, S.J., *Theology and Scientific Knowledge: Changing Models of God's Presence in the World* (Notre Dame: University of Notre Dame Press, 1996); Robert J. Russell, William Stoeger, and Francisco Ayala, eds., *Evolutionary and Molecular Biology: Scientific Perspectives on Divine Action* (Berkeley, Calif.: Center for Theology and Natural Sciences, 1998); Michael Barnes, "The Evolution of the Soul from Matter and the Role of Science in Karl Rahner's Theology," *Horizons* 21 (1994): 85–104; and Barnes, "Intelligent Design: The New Creationism," *Horizons* 29 (2002): 344–362.

Chapter 6: The Father's Generation of the Son

See above, the classic theologians such as Augustine and Aquinas, and modern theologians such as Rahner, Barth, William Hill, HansUrs von Balthasar, Kasper, LaCugna, Thompson, and Davis, Kendall, and O'Collins, *Trinity*; Jean Galot, S.J., "La génération éternelle du Fils," *Gregorianum* 71 (1990): 657–678; Also see Thomas Torrance, *The Christian Doctrine of God: One Being Three Persons* (Edinburgh: T & T Clark, 1996); Ralph Del Colle, *Christ and the Spirit: Spirit-Christologies in Trinitarian Perspective* (New York: Oxford University Press, 1994); Thomas Weinandy, O.F.M., *The Father's Spirit of Sonship: Reconceiving the Trinity* (Edinburgh: T & T Clark, 1995); Pontifical Council for the Promotion of Christian Unity, "The Greek and Latin Traditions Regarding the Procession of the Holy Spirit," *Eastern Churches Journal* 2 (1995): 36–46; M. J. Farrelly, "Existence, the Intellect and the Will," *New Scholasticism* 29 (1955): 145–174; and Farrelly, "Developmental Psychology and Knowledge of Being," 287-314, in *God's Work*.

On vocabulary appropriate for Trinity-talk, see J.-B. Metz and E. Schillebeeckx, O.P., eds., *God as Father? Concilium*, vol. 143 (New York: Seabury, 1981); E. Johnson, *She Who Is*; Farrelly, "Feminine Symbols and the Holy Spirit"; Gail R. Schmidt, "De Divinis Nominibus: The Gender of God," *Worship* 56 (1982): 117–131; Ted Peters,

"The Battle over Trinitarian Language," *Dialog* 30 (1991): 44–49; Donald Hook and Alvin Kimel Jr., "The Pronouns of Deity: A Theolinguistic Critique of Feminist Proposals," *Scottish Journal of Theology* 46 (1993): 297–323; Catherine LaCugna, ed., *Freeing Theology: The Essentials of Theology in Feminist Perspective* (San Francisco: Harper, 1993).

Chapter 7: The Procession of the Holy Spirit within the Trinity

See the systematic theologies cited above in chapter 6. Also see M. T.-L. Penido, "Glosses sur la procession d'amour dans la Trinité," *Ephemerides theologicae lovanienses* 14 (1937): 33–68; A. Patfoort, O.P., in *Bulletin Thomiste* 8 (1947–1953): #1663, 853–861. Also see F. Lambiasi, *Lo Spirito santo: mistero e presenza* (Bologna: Edizioni Dehoniane, 1987); J. Moltmann, *The Spirit of Life: A Universal Affirmation* (Minneapolis: Fortress, 1993); Michael Welker, *God the Spirit* (Minneapolis: Fortress, 1994); David Coffey, "The Holy Spirit as the Mutual Love of the Father and the Son," *TS* 51 (1990): 193–229; David Coffey, *Deus Trinitas: The Doctrine of the Triune God* (New York: Oxford University Press, 1999). Duncan Reid, *Energies of the Spirit: Trinitarian Models in Eastern Orthodox and Western Theology* (Atlanta: Scholars Press, 1997); Gary Badcock, *Light of Truth and Fire of Love: A Theology of the Holy Spirit* (Grand Rapids, Mich.: Eerdmans, 1997); Ralph Del Colle, "Reflections on the *Filioque*," *Journal of Ecumenical Studies* 34 (1997): 202–217; Jean Galot, "L'origine éternelle de l'Esprit Saint," *Gregorianum* 78 (1997): 501–522; Gilles Emery, O.P., "Chronique de théologie trinitaire," *Revue thomiste* 98 (1998): 467–496.

Chapter 8: Father, Son, and Holy Spirit as Three Relational Persons in One Being

See authors mentioned above: William Hill; Kasper; Davis, Kendall and O'Collins; LaCugna; and Studer. On the meaning of 'person' see Hans Urs von Balthasar, "On the Concept of Person," *Communio* 13 (1986): 18–26; Mark Henninger, *Relations: Medieval Theories 1250–1325* (Oxford: Oxford University Press, 1989); Christopher Schwöbel and Colin Gunton, eds., *Persons, Divine and Human: King's College Essays in Theological Anthropology* (Edinburgh: T & T Clark, 1991); Stanley Rudman, *Concepts of Personhood and Christian Ethics* (New York: Cambridge University Press, 1997); W. Norris Clarke, S.J., *Person and Being* (Milwaukee: Marquette University Press, 1993).

On its application in the Trinity, see F. Bourassa, "Personne et conscience en théologie trinitaire," *Gregorianum* 55 (1974): 471–493; 677–720; Dumitru Staniloe, "Image, Likeness, and the Deification in the Human Person," *Communio* 13 (1986): 64–83; J. O'Donnell, S.J., "The Trinity as Divine Community: A Critical Reflection upon Recent Theological Developments," *Gregorianum* 69 (1988): 5–34; Lucian

Turcescu, "The Concept of Divine Persons in Gregory of Nyssa's 'To His Brother Peter, on the Difference between *Ousia* and *Hypostasis*,'" *Greek Orthodox Theological Review* 42 (1997): 63–82.

Chapter 9: A Trinitarian Spirituality

On the question of the Trinity and ecclesiology, see Miroslav Volf, *After Our Likeness: The Church as the Image of the Trinity* (Grand Rapids, Mich.: Eerdmans, 1998); Joseph Cardinal Ratzinger, *Church, Ecumenism, and Politics: New Essays in Ecclesiology* (New York: Crossroads, 1988); Congregation for the Doctrine of the Faith, "Letter to the Bishops of the Catholic Church on Some Aspects of the Church Understood as Communion," *Origins* 22 (June 25, 1992): 108–112; John Zizioulas, *Being as Communion: Studies in Personhood and the Church* (Crestwood, N.Y.: St. Vladimir's Seminary Press, 1985); James Puglisi, ed., *Petrine Ministry and the Unity of the Church* (Collegeville, Minn.: Liturgical Press, 1999); Y. Congar, *I Believe in the Holy Spirit*; J.-M. R. Tillard, *Church of Churches: The Ecclesiology of Communion* (Collegeville, Minn.: Liturgical Press, 1992).

On the presence of the Trinity to the individual Christian, see A. Michel, "Trinité (Missions et habitation des personnes de la)," *DTC* (Paris: Letouzey et Ané, 1950), 15: 1830–1855; Walter Burghardt, *The Image of God in Man According to Cyril of Alexandria* (Woodstock, Md.: Woodstock College Press, 1957); Stephen Duffy, *The Dynamics of Grace: Pespectives in Theological Anthropology* (Collegeville, Minn.: Liturgical Press, 1993); M Donnelly, S.J., "The Inhabitation of the Holy Spirit: A Solution according to de la Taille," *TS* 8 (1949): 445–470; Del Colle, *Christ and the Spirit*; Cyprian Vagaggini, *Theological Dimensions of the Liturgy*, 4th ed. (Collegeville, Minn.: Liturgical Press, 1976); Jeremy Driscoll, "Anamnesis, Epiclesis and Fundamental Theology," *Ecclesia Orans* 15 (1998): 211–238.

On the Trinity and world religions, see Amato, *Trinità in contesto*; Jung Young Lee, *The Trinity in Asian Perspective* (Nashville: Abingdon, 1996); Jacques Dupuis, S.J., *Toward a Christian Theology of Religious Pluralism* (Maryknoll, N.Y.: Orbis, 1997); and Gavin D'Costa, *The Meetings of Religions and the Trinity* (Maryknoll, N.Y.: Orbis, 2000).

Index

Dubarle, Dominic, 282
Dunn, James, 44–50, 164
dynamism, 130, 150, 153, 196–200, 204, 281

Eastern church, 6, 19, 58, 82–83, 204, 244, 264, 266; independence from Pope, 7; and Spirit, 95, 100; and Western church, 102–3
ecclesiology, xiv
Eckhart, Meister, 105, 282
ecumenical movement, 9, 261
Eleventh Council of the Toledo, 100, 181, 226
Emerson, Ralph Waldo, 113
Emery, Gilles, 127
empiricism, 11, 13, 113
Encyclopedism, 113
Enlightenment, 7, 112–14, 191
entropy, 144
Ephesians, 283–84
Erikson, Erik, 136, 141–42, 197, 220, 241
eros, 197–98, 200
eschatology, 16
Eucharist, xiii, 1, 73–74, 253, 255–56, 270; as paradigm of trinitarian spirituality, 271–75
Eudoxius, 85
Eunomius, 86–87, 202
Eurocentrism, 23
Eusebius, 79–83
Eustathius of Antioch, 82
evolution, 139–40, 152–54; as analogue of God, 270
exitus-reditus, 106, 127–28, 271, 275
exorcism, 43, 199
Ezekiel, 35

Fabian, 100
faith, 171–73, 258
Faith and Order Commission, 70
Fascism, 192
Father: as generator of Son, 161–62, 165–69, 176–77, 181, 230; as term, 32–33. *See also* Father–Son relationship, First Person, God
fatherhood, human, 182

Father–Son relationship, 164–65, 182, 208, 212, 229; patriarchal, 177
Feast of the Trinity, 104
Fee, Gordon, 46
femininity, 13, 19–20, 28n33, 34, 37, 55, 59–60
Fides et Ratio, 221
Fifth World Conference of Faith and Order, 70
filiation, 230
Filioque, 19, 59, 99–100, 102–3, 170, 201, 204, 208–9
First Council of Constantinople, xi–xiii, 5–6, 71, 79, 90–91
First Person, 282
First Vatican Council. *See* Vatican I
Fischer-Barnicol, Hans, 182
foundationalism, 23–24, 69
Fourth Council of the Lateran, 104, 169
Fourth Council of the Toledo, 100
Fourth World Conference of Faith and Order, 70
Fox, George, 112
Free Church, 256–58
Freud, Sigmund, 177–78, 183
Fulgentius of Ruspe, 99–100
fundamentalism. *See* foundationalism

Gabriel, 72
Gaia, 146, 198
Galot, J., 138
Gardner, Anne, 179
Genesis, 51–52, 59, 178, 281
George of Laodicea, 88
Georgetown University, xiv
gnosis, 77–78
Gnosticism, 21, 52–57, 75
God: divinity, 17; as Father, 3, 33–34, 37, 41, 43; as First Person, 183; history, 17; language about, 184–86, 226; nature of, 16, 79–80, 85–86; Old Testament, 34; as process, 135, 166; relation to humans, xii, 133–34, 137; relation to Jesus, 41–44, 47; relationship to the Holy Spirit, 47; three-personed, 161, 242; will of, 176, 205; and Wisdom, 77, 179–80
grace, 10, 213, 266–67, 269

~

About the Author

M. John Farrelly, O.S.B., was a professor of theology at De Sales School of Theology, Washington, D.C., for many years, and is now retired. He has written widely on theology, philosophy, and spirituality, and lectured in the United States, Europe, and East Asia. His publications include *Predestination, Grace, and Free Will; God's Work in a Changing World; Belief in God in Our Time: Foundational Theology, I; Faith in God through Jesus Christ: Foundational Theology, II; God's Word Calls and Nourishes;* and *Homilies: Advent through Paschaltide* as well as over 100 articles and book reviews.

6

CPSIA information can be obtained at www.ICGtesting.com
Printed in the USA
BVOW02s1630160615

404545BV00001BA/60/P